Lewis & Clark

FOR

DUMMIES®

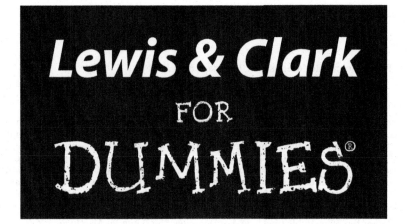

Lewis & Clark FOR DUMMIES®

by Sammye J. Meadows and
Jana Sawyer Prewitt

WILEY

John Wiley & Sons, Inc.

Lewis & Clark For Dummies®

Published by
John Wiley & Sons, Inc.
111 River St.
Hoboken, NJ 07030
www.wiley.com

About the Authors

Sammye Meadows comes from a family of storytellers and has written and published prize-winning short stories and contributions to Appalachian regional anthologies. Sammye has been executive director of the national Lewis and Clark Trail Heritage Foundation and communications director for the National Council of the Lewis and Clark Bicentennial. She currently works for the Circle of Tribal Advisors for the Lewis and Clark Bicentennial. Sammye has been a ski bum, a small-town bureaucrat, a national environmental advocate, a marathon runner, an arctic backpacker, and a high-country gardener.

Jana Sawyer Prewitt grew up Jana Sawyer near Camp Dubois on the Lewis and Clark Trail. She has been a writer, communications director, or press secretary for two cabinet secretaries, one deputy secretary, and two governors. As a Clinton administration appointee at the U.S. Department of the Interior, she led the interagency group working on the National Lewis and Clark Bicentennial. Today, Jana owns Seventh Generation Strategies, an Alexandria, Virginia, consulting firm, and is an associate of The Clark Group in Washington, D.C. Both companies help tribes and other clients achieve their economic, environmental, and energy goals. Jana has two grown children.

Dedication

Sammye Meadows

To the Circle of Tribal Advisors of the Lewis and Clark Bicentennial, a diverse, fascinating, smart, dedicated, and delightful bunch of Indians. I am honored to work for you. I hope we got things right — somewhat.

Jana Sawyer Prewitt

In memory of John E. Sawyer, beloved father and armchair historian.

Authors' Acknowledgments

Both authors want to especially thank editors Tere Drenth, Kathy Cox, and Susan Diane Smith, and technical reviewer Steve Witte.

Sammye Meadows

My deepest appreciation to Amy Mossett, Bobbie Conner, Jim and Dark Rain Thom, Allen Pinkham, Jeanne Eder, Chief Snider, Germaine White, the Circle of Tribal Advisors, Gerard Baker, the National Council of the Lewis and Clark Bicentennial, the National Park Service, the Lewis and Clark Trail Heritage Foundation, Tillie Walker, Mary Elk, Beatrice Miles, Ed Hall, Jana Prewitt, James Ronda, Gary Moulton, Paul Russell Cutright, Donald Jackson, Stephen Ambrose, Michelle Bussard, Clarice Hudson and so many more. Thank you all for the marvelous and unexpected journey.

Jana Sawyer Prewitt

A very special thank you to Michael Gauldin for more reasons than there is space to name them.

Heartfelt thanks to all the remarkable people who made studying Lewis and Clark a growth experience: Ed Hall III, Dark Rain and Jim Thom, Sammye Meadows, Gerard Baker, Suzy Hubbell, Michelle Dawson-Powell, Dayton Duncan, Dick Williams, Germaine White, Carla HighEagle, Bobbie Conner, Amy Mossett, Mark McDermott, Jane Henley, David Nicandri, Chief Cliff Snider, Ted Kaye, Jerry Garrett, Otis Halfmoon, Jeff Olsen, Clarice Hudson, Gale and Rosemary Baker, Tillie Walker, Tex Hall, Sam Penney, Birgil Killstraight, Lanny Jones, Sherman Fleek, Ken Smith, George Tabb, Michelle Bussard, David Borlaug, Allen Pinkham, Molly Buckey, Margaret Gorski, Steve Morehouse, Kim Prill, Jeanne Nauss, Kindra Reid and Thomasine Singleton.

Publisher's Acknowledgments

We're proud of this book; please send us your comments through our Dummies online registration form located at www.dummies.com/register/.

Some of the people who helped bring this book to market include the following:

Acquisitions, Editorial, and Media Development

Project Editor: Tere Drenth

Acquisitions Editor: Kathy Cox

Development Editor: Susan Diane Smith

Technical Reviewer: Steven Witte, Ph.D.

Permissions Coordinators: Holly Gastineau-Grimes, Mary Yeary

Editorial Manager: Michelle Hacker

Editorial Assistant: Elizabeth Rea

Cover Photos: ©Bettmann/CORBIS

Cartoons: Rich Tennant, www.the5thwave.com

Production

Project Coordinator: Maridee Ennis

Layout and Graphics: Seth Conley, LeAndra Hosier, Lynsey Osborn, Jacque Schneider, Mary Gillot Virgin, Shae Wilson

Illustrator: Lisa S. Reed

Proofreaders: John Tyler Connoley, Brian H. Walls; Aptara

Indexer: Aptara

Publishing and Editorial for Consumer Dummies

    Kathleen Nebenhaus, Vice President and Executive Publisher

    David Palmer, Associate Publisher

    Kristin Ferguson-Wagstaffe, Product Development Director

Publishing for Technology Dummies

    Andy Cummings, Vice President and Publisher

Composition Services

    Debbie Stailey, Director of Composition Services

Contents at a Glance

Introduction 1

Part I: Lewis and Clark's America 7
Chapter 1: Reflecting on the Legacy: Lewis and Clark, Then and Now 9
Chapter 2: Getting Acquainted with the Expedition's People and Places 23
Chapter 3: Compelling Lewis and Clark West 61

Part II: Into the Known: Monticello to Fort Mandan 71
Chapter 4: Gambling Big — the Jeffersonian Way 73
Chapter 5: Training an Explorer 89
Chapter 6: Wintering at Camp Dubois 107
Chapter 7: Traveling on the Big Muddy 119
Chapter 8: Pitching American Trade to the Western Tribes 127
Chapter 9: Enjoying a Cold Winter among Warm Mandans 149

Part III: Into the Unknown: Fort Mandan to the Pacific 165
Chapter 10: Journeying through Paradise and Purgatory
on the Northern Plains 167
Chapter 11: Searching for Snakes and Horses 185
Chapter 12: Making a Cold, Hungry, and Dangerous Trek
across the Mountains 199
Chapter 13: Recording "Ocian In View! O! The Joy" 221
Chapter 14: Coping on the Coast 239

Part IV: Bound for Home 257
Chapter 15: Stealing Away and Climbing Every Mountain (Twice) 259
Chapter 16: Exploring Far Horizons 277
Chapter 17: Heading Home 295
Chapter 18: Exploring the Fate and Lessons of the Corps of Discovery 309

Part V: The Part of Tens 335
Chapter 19: Twenty Places Lewis and Clark Saw: Ten Changed;
Ten Unchanged 337
Chapter 20: The Ten Best Places to Visit on the Lewis and Clark
National Historic Trail 343
Chapter 21: Ten Resources for Information about Lewis and Clark 349

Part VI: Appendixes 353
Appendix A: Tribal Homelands Visited by the Expedition 355
Appendix B: Glossary 359
Index 363

Table of Contents

Introduction *1*

About this Book 1
Conventions Used in This Book 1
How This Book Is Organized 2
Icons Used in This Book 6
Where to Go from Here 6

Part 1: Lewis and Clark's America *7*

**Chapter 1: Reflecting on the Legacy: Lewis and Clark,
Then and Now** **9**

Proving That Truth Is Stranger (and Better) Than Fiction 9
Meeting the Cast of the Saga 10
Accepting Mission Improbable 12
Placing Lewis and Clark in History 14
Retracing the Corps' Steps: The Lewis and Clark
    National Historic Trail 18
Joining the Journey: The National Bicentennial Commemoration 19

**Chapter 2: Getting Acquainted with the Expedition's
People and Places** **23**

Pursuing His Dream: Thomas Jefferson 23
Journeying to the Pacific: The Corps of Discovery 26
    Leading the expedition: Meriwether Lewis 27
    Co-commanding the Corps: William Clark 29
    Earning her fame: Sacagawea 30
    Becoming the youngest explorer: Jean Baptiste Charbonneau 31
    Behaving less than nobly: Toussaint Charbonneau 32
    Making history: York 32
    Having the right stuff: George Drouillard 33
    Fetching respect: Seaman, coast-to-coast canine 34
    Keeping the troops on track: The sergeants 34
    Carrying out the mission: The privates 36
Helping the Corps Survive and Succeed: The American Indians 41
    Attending the Council on the Bluff: Otoe and Missouria 41
    Welcoming the expedition: Yankton Sioux 42
    Challenging the Corps: Brule Band of Teton Sioux 42
    Offering hospitality: Mandan, Hidatsa, and Arikara 43

Providing the horses: Shoshone 45
Giving aid: Salish (Three Eagles) 46
Rescuing the Corps: Nez Perce 46
Showing the troops a different world:
    The Columbia River tribes 46
Teaching a lesson in trade: Chinooks and Clatsops 47
Encountering lethal force: Piegan Blackfeet 48
Offering Support: Tutors and Traders 48
Thinking big: Lewis's tutors 48
Supplying goods and info: Merchants and traders 49
Playing a Leading Role: The Land and the Rivers 50
Jefferson's backyard and the first stages of the journey 50
Expanding the country: The Louisiana Territory 53
Winding through the West: The expedition's water trail 53
Sprawling future farmland: The Great Plains 57
Presenting a vast barrier: The Rocky Mountains 58
Changing weather and cultures: The Pacific Northwest 59

Chapter 3: Compelling Lewis and Clark West . . . . **.61**
Don't Know Much about Geography 62
Looking for a new Eden 62
Dispelling myths about the West 63
Jefferson's Motto: If at First You Don't Succeed 64
Crossing swords with Catherine the Great 65
Hiring a spy 66
Copying a Scot 66
Jefferson's Euro Struggles 67
Jefferson finagles, Spain worries 67
The French kiss Louisiana good-bye 68

Part II: Into the Known: Monticello to Fort Mandan 71

Chapter 4: Gambling Big — the Jeffersonian Way **73**
Jefferson and Lewis: Almost Kinfolk 73
Kissing cousins 73
Losing a father 74
A doctoring mother 74
Becoming a rambling man 75
Getting a little schooling 75
Wanting out, signing up 75
White House Calling 77
Meriwether Lewis, presidential aide 78
Goading them on 79
Not perfect but close enough 79

Jefferson and Lewis Multi-Task 80
Taking Science 101 81
Requesting funds for a "literary pursuit" 81
Spending the cash 83
Considering the manpower 84
Clark for Co-Captain 85
William Clark, Kentucky frontiersman 86
At war with the British and then the Indians 86
Clark: The right man for the job 87

Chapter 5: Training an Explorer **89**
Traveling to the Wise Men 89
Taking a Rush course in medicine 90
Getting a crash course in natural history from Barton 92
Preparing for sloths and mammoths with Wistar 93
Surveying the earth with Ellicott 94
Navigating by the heavens with Patterson 94
Shopping for the Voyage 95
Buying scientific instruments and basic supplies 95
Choosing gifts for the tribes 96
Giving Lewis His Marching Orders 97
Serving God and green pastures 97
Getting it in writing 98
Recruiting Two Good Men (and a Great Dog) 100
Beginning the search for men 100
Drafting Seaman the sagacious 101
Getting the Boat to Float 101
Doubting the "drunkards" 102
Scraping down the river in a fog 102
Swimming squirrels, wandering men 103
Walking to a mammoth skeleton 104
Uniting with Clark and Shoving Off 104

Chapter 6: Wintering at Camp Dubois **107**
Rowing Against Time 108
Looking for a Few Good Men 109
Grading the recruits 109
Maintaining discipline (sort of) 110
Recruiting Drouillard, the cream of the crop 112
Forming the permanent party (don't forget the dog) 112
Stocking Up on Supplies 113
Collecting Bugs, Leaves, Stats, and Maps 114
Worrying about the American Indians 115
Just call me "dad" 115
Psyched out about the Teton Sioux 115

Keeping Rank Secrets 116
Braving the Storms: The Expedition Begins 117

Chapter 7: Traveling on the Big Muddy 119

Leaving "Civilization" Behind 119
Rowing, Poling, and Towing 120
Viewing the Vast, Bountiful Prairie 121
   Millions of "buffalows" 122
   What's for dinner? 122
Getting Sick, Lost, Scared, and Busted 123
   Illness afflicts the troops 123
   George Shannon gets lost 124
   The men face devil spirits 125

Chapter 8: Pitching American Trade to the Western Tribes 127

Poling Past the Platte 128
Peddling Peace and Prosperity to the Otoes and Missouris 129
   Eating "Water Millions" and preparing for
      the council on the bluff 129
   Trotting out the traveling military parade 130
   Welcoming the elusive Little Thief and Big Horse 131
Wooing the Sioux 134
   Hitting it off with the Yanktons 135
   Confronting the Tetons: at Bad River 137
Persuading the Arikaras 141
   Going ahead with the plan 142
   Cutting a rocky deal 144
   Sharing in Arikara culture 144

Chapter 9: Enjoying a Cold Winter among Warm Mandans 149

Promoting the American Trade Plan 150
   Visiting the villages 150
   Convening the council 153
Building Fort Mandan 154
Meeting Sacagawea 155
   Hiring a sneaky scoundrel and a man of no merit 156
   Sacagawea: An American icon 156
Trying to Manipulate Plains Politics 158
   Flawed diplomacy 158
   Dealing arms 159
   Neutralizing British fur interests 160
Living Life at 45° Below Zero 160
Making Maps and Feeling Optimistic about the Northwest Passage ...161
   Writing reports and recording languages 162
   Preparing the specimens (and that poor, pitiful prairie dog) 163
   Sharing ceremonies 163

Part III: Into the Unknown: Fort Mandan to the Pacific 165

Chapter 10: Journeying through Paradise and Purgatory on the Northern Plains 167

Closing Up the Fort and Sending the Keelboat Home 168
Never-Ending Enchantment on the Plains 169
   Encountering tame wildlife 170
   Exploring the land of milk and honey 170
   Exploring "seens of visionary inchantment" 171
   Eating, drinking, and breathing sand 172
   Dealing with "troublesom musquetors" 173
   Harassing grizzly bears 174
Appreciating Sacagawea 175
Deciding Which River Was the Missouri 177
   Standing at a fork in the river 177
   Trusting a hunch 177
Hearing the Roar of the Great Falls at Last 178
Sailing Boats over the Prairie 179
   Curing Sacagawea 180
   Surviving hail, heatstroke, and cactus 180
   Surviving a flash flood 181
Launching the Experimental Boat 182
   Pining for pine trees 182
   Getting that sinking feeling 183
   Harboring new canoes but no hard feelings 183
Savoring the Last Gill of Whiskey 183

Chapter 11: Searching for Snakes and Horses 185

Sailing through the Gates of the Mountains 185
Avoiding Assiniboines 188
Desperately Seeking Shoshones 189
   Throbbing feet and frayed nerves (but no Shoshones) 190
   Dealing with illness, note-eating beavers, and a lost man
     (but no Shoshones) 192
   Misunderstanding tab-ba-bone 193
Scaring Away a Shoshone 194
   Sending mixed signals 195
   Casting blame 195
Realizing the Awesome Truth about the West 196
   Celebrating the end of the Missouri 196
   Shattering a myth 197

Chapter 12: Making a Cold, Hungry, and Dangerous Trek across the Mountains 199

Needing the Shoshones (but the Shoshones Need to Leave) 200
   Depending on Shoshone guides and horses: The Corps 200
   Starving, afraid, and anxious to travel: The Shoshones 200

Hooking Up with the Shoshones 201
    Getting an overwhelming welcome 201
    Resorting to promises and insults 202
    Feeding the famished Shoshones 203
    Missing Clark 203
    Celebrating the reunions 205
Promising Guns in the Future for Horses Now 205
Returning from The River of No Return 206
    Clinging to hope for a river crossing 206
    Finding a guide (and understanding why Lewis's
      River was called the River of No Return) 207
Preparing for a Long Walk 208
    Caching goods and leaving Camp Fortunate 209
    Scaring Lewis 209
    Haggling for horses 210
Slipping, Sliding, and Hacking Their Way Up the Divide 210
Meeting "Welsh" Indians 211
Resting for the Next Climb 213
Freezing and Starving over the Bitterroot Mountains 215
    Getting a rough start 215
    Suffering terrain unfit for men or horses 217
    Dining on colt and candles 217
Descending Joyfully to Level Ground 218

Chapter 13: Recording "Ocian In View! O! The Joy" 221

Escaping the Mountains: Clark Reaches the Weippe Prairie 222
    Chowing down on Nez Perce food 222
    Dodging death, thanks to Watkuweis 223
    Bonding with Twisted Hair 223
Getting a Camas Bread Welcome: Lewis Joins
  Clark and the Nez Perce 224
    Throwing caution to the wind: Let 'em eat cake 224
    Nursing a collective bellyache 224
    Talking business and politics with the Nez Perce 225
Getting Back on the Water 226
    Making new canoes 226
    Saying goodbye to Old Toby 227
    Heading down the Snake River 227
Meeting the Salmon People: Wanapums, Yakamas,
  Walla Wallas, and Umatillas 228
    Holding a grand council 228
    Being astonished by salmon 228
    Taking a rain check with the Walla Wallas 230
    Scaring the Umatillas 231
Going to the Super Market 232

Running the Falls: Extreme Canoeing in the Columbia Gorge 233
   Drinking beer and shooting the rapids 233
   Saying goodbye to Twisted Hair and Tetoharsky 233
Loving to Hate the Chinookan Tribes 234
   Treasuring a Chinook canoe 235
   Misunderstanding Chinook customs 236
   Lunching with the Skilloots: A good day turns bad 236
Celebrating an Ocean View 238

Chapter 14: Coping on the Coast **239**
Holing Up at Cape Disappointment 240
   Waiting for the storms to clear 240
   Staring at the ocean 240
   Voting and making history 241
Building Fort Clatsop 242
   Picking a spot 243
   Getting to work 243
Getting to Know Cuscalar 244
Making Salt 245
Being Out-Maneuvered in Trade and Diplomacy 246
   Trading goods for food 246
   Trading Sacagawea's blue beads for pelts 246
   Failing to cross the cultural divide 247
   Abandoning diplomacy 248
Suffering through the Winter: Oh, How I Wanna Go Home 248
   Missing home and family during the holidays 249
   Writing again: Lewis revealing his thoughts 249
   Restricting the Indians 250
   Waiting for their ship to come in 251
   Going whale-watching 252
   Laughing at McNeal's folly 253
Mapping and Drawing 253

Part IV: Bound for Home **257**

**Chapter 15: Stealing Away and Climbing
Every Mountain (Twice)** **259**
Fleeing the Columbia River and Its Peoples 260
   Needing food but running out of trade goods 260
   Going from bad to worse: Corps-tribal relations sink
       to a new low 260
   Leaving Fort Clatsop and making the first portage 262
   Looking for horses and portaging The Dalles 265

Seeking Respite with the Walla Wallas 267
    Reuniting with Yelleppit 267
    Gift-giving: One good turn deserves another 268
Returning to the Nez Perce 269
    Breaking up a squabble 269
    Deliberating at council 270
Passing the Time at Camp Chopunnish 271
    Hard bargaining 272
    Doctoring 272
    Shooting, racing, and dancing 273
Facing the Bitterroots Again 273
    Disregarding Nez Perce advice 274
    Putting the mountains and snow behind them:
        Hello, hot tub! 275

Chapter 16: Exploring Far Horizons **277**
Splitting Up at Travelers' Rest 278
    Making Clark's to-do list 279
    Planning Lewis's agenda 279
Exploring the Yellowstone: Clark Leaves His Mark 280
    Making good time to the Three Forks 280
    Following Sacagawea 281
    Sewing horse moccasins 281
    Missing the heisted horses 281
    Christening Pompy's Tower (now Pompeys Pillar) 282
    Losing sleep because of bellowing buffaloes 284
    Improvising boats to replace the horses 284
Bringing Tragedy to Two Medicine 286
    Getting back on the plains where the buffalo roam 286
    Dealing with spoiled specimens and stolen horses 288
    Following the Marias to disappointment 289
    Running into Blackfeet 290
    Killing two Piegan youths 291
    Taking a bullet in the buttock from a nearsighted,
        one-eyed fiddle player 293
Reuniting the Corps 293

Chapter 17: Heading Home **295**
Trying Again to Impose the American Trade Plan on the Indians 296
    Giving up a cannon and getting lectured by the Hidatsas 296
    Failing with the Mandans 297
    Deceiving the Arikaras 298
    Coaxing the Cheyenne 299
    Reviling and riling the Teton Sioux 300
    Feeling relieved to see the Yankton Sioux 301
Parting with Sacagawea, Pomp, Charbonneau, and Colter 301

Returning to "Civilization" 302
        Opening the trader floodgates 303
        Coming back from the dead 303
        Cow-spotting 304
Reaching Cheering Crowds in St. Louis 304
Basking in Praise from the President, the Press, and the Public 304
        Briefing a joyful Jefferson 305
        Writing to Clark's brother and the newspaper 306
        Priming the press and lobbying for a reward 306
Disbanding the Corps 307

**Chapter 18: Exploring the Fate and Lessons
of the Corps of Discovery** **309**
Arriving in Washington 310
Dying Young: Meriwether Lewis 310
        Reaping rewards and lobbying for land 311
        Failing to publish the journals 311
        Drifting, drinking, and descending into madness 313
        Dying hard 315
Living Long: William Clark 316
        Serving as Indian agent 317
        Publishing the journals 318
        Policing the tribes 318
        Losing a race for governor 319
        Embracing the policy of removal 319
Expecting Freedom: York 320
        Refusing to take no for an answer 320
        Considering a happier fate for York 321
Becoming a Legend in Three Cultures: Sacagawea 321
Traveling Happy: Jean Baptiste (Pompy) 323
Surprising Outcomes: Men of the Corps 324
        Tracing the nine other young men from Kentucky 324
        Discovering more on the Corps 327
Breaking Promises to the American Indians 329
Altering the Land and Rivers 331
        Stripping the land and damming the rivers 331
        Threatening plant and animal life 332
Proceeding On 334

Part V: The Part of Tens *335*

**Chapter 19: Twenty Places Lewis and Clark Saw:
Ten Changed; Ten Unchanged** **337**
Ten Places Changed Completely 337
Ten Places Unchanged 339

**Chapter 20: The Ten Best Places to Visit on the
Lewis and Clark National Historic Trail** 343

Monticello 343
Falls of the Ohio State Park 344
Katy Trail State Park 344
Joslyn Art Museum 345
Native American Scenic Byway 345
Fort Mandan 346
Pompeys Pillar 346
Nez Perce National Historical Park 347
Columbia Gorge Discovery Center 347
Fort Clatsop National Memorial 348

**Chapter 21: Ten Resources for Information
about Lewis and Clark** 349

The Journals of the Lewis and Clark Expedition, Volumes 1–13 349
Lewis and Clark among the Indians 350
The Letters of the Lewis and Clark Expedition
    with Related Documents, 1783–1854 350
Lewis and Clark Pioneering Naturalists 350
Undaunted Courage: Meriwether Lewis, Thomas Jefferson,
    and the Opening of the American West 350
Lewis and Clark: The National Bicentennial Exhibition 351
In Search of York — The Slave Who Went to the Pacific with
    Lewis and Clark 351
Traveling the Lewis and Clark Trail 351
Lewis and Clark — The Journey of the Corps of Discovery 352
www.lewis-clark.org 352
We Proceeded On 352

Part VI: Appendixes **353**

Appendix A: Tribal Homelands Visited by the Expedition **355**

Appendix B: Glossary **359**

Index **363**

Introduction

● ●

*T*hanks for picking up *Lewis & Clark For Dummies.* We know you want to spend your reading time on actual Lewis and Clark stuff, so we'll keep this Introduction brief.

About This Book

The Lewis and Clark expedition was the greatest camping trip in history. It was one of those irresistible American adventures that many people dream of living. This book shares the delightful details of the journey that historians have gleaned from the group's journals and maps, and also discusses what's known of the Indian perspective of the expedition.

And while reading about the expedition is a lot of fun, you can also travel to the places the *Corps of Discovery* (the official term for the group) ventured and meet descendants of many of the same people. (You can even get bitten by descendants of the same mosquitoes!) So, this book gives you tips and ideas for traveling Lewis and Clark's route.

Conventions Used in This Book

In this book, you find the actual words of Lewis and Clark, quoted from their journals, which have been published in various forms since 1806. In this book, we use the most recent — and best: Meriwether Lewis and William Clark, *The Journals of the Lewis and Clark Expedition,* in 13 volumes, edited by Gary E. Moulton and published by the University of Nebraska Press (Lincoln, Nebraska), 1983–2001. (See Chapter 21 for additional details on these volumes.)

Please don't adjust your eyeglasses. The spelling and punctuation throughout the quotes from the expedition's journals, Moulton edition, are inventive. The captains were creative spellers (especially Clark), and we haven't cleaned it up for you. It's too much fun the way it is! In addition, we have used the spelling "Sacagawea" for the name of the young Shoshone mother who accompanied the expedition, because that is the spelling on which most historians agree. You may have seen her name spelled "Sacajawea" (the spelling the first editor of the Lewis and Clark journals changed it to in 1814 and the one still used by the Shoshones) or "Sakakawea" (the spelling used by the Mandans and Hidatsas). But we use "Sacagawea" because that's how Lewis and Clark phonetically spelled her name in their journals.

You may also notice some italicized words in the quotes from Lewis and Clark's journals and wonder how they got that way — you know that Lewis and Clark didn't take along a typewriter or computer! In the Moulton edition, italics are used for Lewis and Clark's corrections or alterations or for words they inserted between the lines.

In addition, throughout this book, we use certain terms associated with Lewis and Clark and the people who helped them on their journey. We also avoid other terms, including the following:

- ✔ **Native American:** When we discuss a tribe that Lewis and Clark met, we use that tribe's name — Mandan, Shoshone, Blackfeet, Sioux, Clatsop — or the term "Indian" to describe the members of several tribes, although we use that term sparingly to avert the notion that all Indians are alike.

  We avoid the term "Native American" for two reasons:

  - • To be as unconfusing as possible when discussing the culturally rich, fascinating, powerful, prosperous, and diverse pantheon of civilizations that Lewis and Clark paddled into.

  - • To honor our Indian colleagues who prefer "Indian" or "American Indian" over "Native American."

- ✔ **Chief:** This title doesn't appear at all in *Lewis & Clark For Dummies,* except when cited in a quote from the Lewis and Clark journals. Lewis and Clark (as did all American diplomatic and military emissaries of the day) bestowed the rank of 1st, 2nd, and 3rd "chief" on those Indian leaders they perceived to be most amenable to their American trade plan. The term, however, is not necessarily a traditional title for a tribal leader. To keep from perpetuating false assumptions, we simply use the terms "leader" or "headman."

- ✔ **Squaw:** This word doesn't appear in *Lewis & Clark For Dummies* either, except when cited in a quote. Tribal people consider it an extremely derogatory term for woman. And because we're both women, well . . . .

How This Book Is Organized

Throughout this book, you find out about Jefferson's western exploration, from his earliest efforts to see the Corps assembled through the aftermath for the explorers, the tribes, and the United States. But the focus of this book is on the period between Jefferson's confidential letter to Congress requesting dollars to mount a western exploration (January 18, 1803) and the expedition's triumphant (and improbable) return to St. Louis (September 23, 1806): forty-two months that changed the world.

Part 1: Lewis and Clark's America

This part tells you who the players were: Thomas Jefferson who dreamed the expedition for years, Lewis and Clark who led it, members of the expedition, the Indians, and the land. You find out why the expedition happened, what regions it explored, who saved it from disaster, and how history has judged it so far.

This part also explains erroneous 18th-century assumptions, like the existence of a Northwest Passage, of woolly mammoths, and of salt mountains.

Part 11: Into the Known: Monticello to Fort Mandan

This part follows the Lewis and Clark expedition from its conception at Monticello (Thomas Jefferson's west-facing mountain-top home in the Blue Ridge foothills of Virginia) to its winter garrison at Fort Mandan on the serene frozen prairies of today's North Dakota. You find out that Jefferson sent Meriwether Lewis to Philadelphia to study botany, zoology, climatology, archaeology, celestial navigation, paleontology, medicine, and everything else a first-rate explorer ought to know. And Jefferson also sent a confidential letter to Congress requesting money to pay for Lewis's upcoming trip.

Throughout this part, you live alongside Lewis as he studied; bought boats, supplies, and a dog; and asked William Clark — an old Army buddy — to share command of the expedition. You get to come along as the two young captains joined forces at the Falls of the Ohio and proceeded on to their first winter encampment at Camp Dubois (Camp Wood), where they recruited and trained the Corps of Discovery.

In May 1804, the entire wooly bunch set off up the Missouri River. Along the route, Lewis and Clark met with local Indians, trying to convince them to forsake old ways and join a trade alliance with their new Great White Father. You find out about friendly Otoes, Missouris, Yanktons, and Arikara, as well as less-cooperative Teton Sioux, that Lewis and Clark met before arriving at the Mandan Villages near today's Bismarck, North Dakota.

This part wraps up with the building of a second winter camp on the Missouri River (near the Knife River), where the Corps settled in for a warm and contented season among the Mandans. There, they met Sacagawea, who would become their interpreter, and included her and her new baby in their entourage.

Part III: Into the Unknown: Fort Mandan to the Pacific

This part details the expedition's journey from Fort Mandan to the Pacific Coast. First, the Corps paddled up the Missouri River through the bountiful Northern Plains, teeming with wildlife. They reached the Great Falls of the Missouri — a sight more wondrous than Lewis and Clark expected — and had to portage their boats around them.

You witness the Corps at the headwaters of the Missouri, where Lewis and Clark searched frantically for the Shoshones, Sacagawea's tribe, in order to procure horses for crossing the Continental Divide. They did succeed in meeting the Shoshones — led, by a stroke of great fortune for the Corps, by Sacagawea's brother Cameahwait — and began an arduous trek across the snow-covered Rocky Mountains.

You find out about the harrowing experience of the Corps and how they emerged, starving, on the western side of the Divide in Nez Perce country. An elderly Nez Perce woman convinced the tribe to spare their lives, and the men struggle to digest unfamiliar foods — camas (an onion-like root — see Chapter 12) and salmon. They then left their horses with the Nez Perce and built dugout canoes to travel on to the Columbia River.

In this part, you also get to ride along as Lewis and Clark zoomed down the mighty Columbia, and portaged around thunderous Celilo Falls, the ancient salmon fishery of the Columbia River tribes. On November 7, 1805, William Clark looked up from his seat in one of the canoes and recorded, "Ocian In View! O! The joy."

This part winds up as you witness Lewis and Clark taking an historic vote of the Corps of Discovery membership — including Sacagawea and York (Clark's slave) — to determine which side of the Columbia to winter on. The group selected the south side, so a third winter garrison of the expedition was built near today's Astoria, Oregon. The Corps of Discovery spent a wet, cold, hungry, and homesick winter in the middle of extraordinary natural and cultural wealth in the land of the Chinooks and Clatsops.

Part IV: Bound for Home

In this part, you watch as the homesick Corps started east for home on March 23, 1806. To their discredit, the group stole a canoe from their generous host, Coboway of the Clatsop Nation. To compensate, they bequeathed Fort Clatsop to Coboway and set out.

You also witness the group's trek over the mountains again and understand why the expedition split up, with Lewis and one crew going back to the Great Falls of the Missouri and exploring the Marias country, and Clark and his crew going back to the Three Forks of the Missouri and exploring Yellowstone country. Clark's journey was uneventful, but Lewis's resulted in misunderstanding and death for two Blackfeet youths, and one of Lewis's own men also shot him in the backside. Yet, the entire Corps survived to reunite on the Missouri River once more. At the Mandan Villages, Lewis and Clark said goodbye to Sacagawea and Pomp (Clark's nickname for Sacagawea's son) and proceeded down the Missouri River to St. Louis. There, they met a heroes' welcome.

Expect the story to end there? Not a chance: This part also describes what happened to the key players after the expedition.

Part V: The Part of Tens

In this fun part, we describe places on the Lewis and Clark National Historic Trail that are now completely changed (or completely unchanged) from how Lewis and Clark saw them. We also share our favorite and most recommended places to visit on the trail. Finally, we give you our favorite resources for additional information on the Corps of Discovery and on your own recreation of the expedition as you take the Trail yourself.

Part VI: Appendixes

This part includes reference material: a list of tribal homelands that Lewis and Clark visited and a glossary of 18th-century terms that Lewis and Clark used throughout their journey.

Icons Used in This Book

Icons — cool little images in the margins of this book — help you focus on significant events of the expedition, select parts of the Lewis and Clark Trail you may want to visit, ruminate over some amazingly creative spelling, and more. Here's a list of what the icons mean:

This icon points out significant Lewis and Clark facts that help you better understand the circumstances surrounding the Corps' journey. At the very least, you can use these tidbits of information to impress friends over dinner.

This icons brings to light any especially dangerous or foolish moment for the Corps of Discovery.

Next to this icon, you find quotes from the *Lewis and Clark Journals,* edited by Gary E. Moulton and published by the University of Nebraska Press. (See Chapter 21 for more on these journals.) These quotes present the exact words of Lewis and Clark as they wrote them — in non-standard English (according to today's standards, that is) with non-standard spelling. These aren't typos!

This icon marks valuable travel-planning information that you can use to recreate Lewis and Clark's journey.

This icon highlights information that you can skip if you want to: technical information like latitude and longitude, measurements, and other specifications.

Where to Go from Here

Unlike other histories of Lewis and Clark, this one is designed — like all *For Dummies* books — to be opened to any chapter or section within a chapter that interests you. You can start reading anywhere without getting lost. After all, you may want to know only what Lewis and Clark did 200 years ago when they were in your neck of the woods.

On the other hand, because this book relates the history of the greatest camping trip ever taken, you can also read it from cover to cover, following in the footsteps of the Corps.

Either way, go on and open the book wherever you like and start understanding who was in the Corps; visit the rivers, prairies, mountains, and the awesome Pacific Coast that Lewis and Clark saw; and meet the tribes who befriended and opposed the expedition.

Part I
Lewis and Clark's America

In this part . . .

You meet the cast of characters: Jefferson, Lewis, Clark, York, Sacagawea, Jean Baptiste, Charbonneau, Drouillard, Black Buffalo, Sheheke, Seaman, and the others. This part lets you peek in on the United States at the beginning of the 19th century and also opens your eyes to some of the consequences of the Lewis and Clark expedition. You also find out about the Louisiana Purchase and understand why Jefferson sent a scientific exploration out West to broker U.S. trade with the Indians. Finally, you get details about both the Lewis and Clark National Historic Trail and Lewis and Clark Bicentennial activities.

Chapter 1

Reflecting on the Legacy: Lewis and Clark, Then and Now

In This Chapter

▶ Getting acquainted with the Corps of Discovery and its fascinating story

▶ Figuring out what the Corps actually did

▶ Recognizing how the exploration changed America (for better and for worse)

▶ Commemorating the Lewis and Clark expedition

A s true stories go, you won't find a better one than the Lewis and Clark expedition. It includes a great multicultural cast of characters and a terrific action-adventure plot that's full of surprising twists and turns. And it's set in an inhabited paradise full of natural wonders that no American had seen before. This chapter gives you an overview of the story.

In the end, Lewis and Clark couldn't fulfill some of the expedition's goals, but they did increase America's knowledge of the West and opened the door for westward expansion. As you discover in this chapter, this was good news for U.S. growth and prosperity, but terrible news for American Indians and the natural environment.

Today, Americans are re-exploring the legacy of Lewis and Clark, as the National Bicentennial of the expedition is commemorated from 2003 to 2006. You, too, can get on the Lewis and Clark National Historic Trail to experience for yourself its scenes of "visionary inchantment," as Lewis so aptly described them. This chapter gets you started.

Proving That Truth Is Stranger (and Better) Than Fiction

It's an unlikely story: a melancholic presidential secretary and a genial frontier planter leading three dozen young Euro-American men, a handful of

French-Canadians, a black slave, an Indian girl, her infant child, and a large dog on a voyage to find an all-water route across a vast, uncharted continent to a faraway ocean.

With only their wits, frontier skills, and significant tribal assistance to guide them and keep them alive, this group trekked thousands of miles on foot, by canoe, and on horseback, carrying or dragging tons of supplies and trade goods from one Indian village to the next. See Figure 1-1.

After dozens of near-fatal mistakes and mishaps and 28 months of hardship and deprivation (long after they'd been given up for dead), they returned having lost only three men — one of their own to death by natural causes and two Blackfeet Indians killed in a gun and knife fight.

Lewis and Clark had remarkable skills and luck. They seemed to find whatever they needed at just the right time — tribes willing to guide them, transportation to get them to their next destination, the instincts and reflexes to overcome the next threat (heat stroke, grizzly bear attack, malaria, gunshot wound, and a flash flood). When their skill gave out, they relied on luck. And when their luck gave out, they mustered the will to "proceed on," which became their watchwords.

Meeting the Cast of the Saga

One of the reasons that the Lewis and Clark saga continues to fascinate people today is its large and colorful cast.

- The brilliant but troubled Meriwether Lewis
- Out-going and rock-steady William Clark
- The Indian child bride and mother Sacagawea
- Her un-heroic husband, Toussaint Charbonneau
- The "dancing" baby, Jean Baptiste
- York, the slave who became "Big Medison" (see Chapter 8)
- Generous Sheheke of the Mandan tribe
- Compassionate Cameahwait of the Shoshones
- The civilian jack-of-all-trades, George Drouillard
- The dog, Seaman
- The wise and proud Teton Sioux, Black Buffalo
- Cheerful, sincere Twisted Hair
- The one-eyed fiddler, Cruzatte

Chapter 2 shares many more details about this cast of characters.

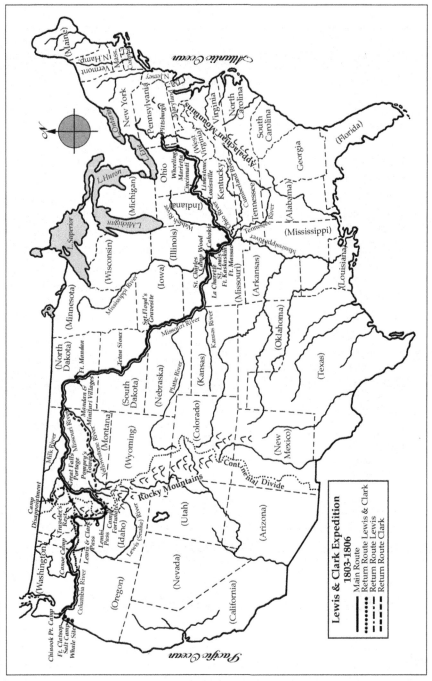

Figure 1-1:
Map of the
expedition.

Lisa S. Reed.

Supporting the Corps: American Indians to the rescue

Many tribes gave the expedition shelter, food, transportation, guides, maps, directions, and advice, including:

✔ The Mandan and Hidatsa of the Upper Missouri, who sheltered the Corps during its first winter

✔ The Shoshone, Salish, Nez Perce, and Walla Walla, who allowed the expedition to survive its march over the mountains

✔ The Chinooks and Clatsops of the Columbia River valley, who taught the Corps how to survive in the Pacific Northwest

Several individual Indians also stand out in their efforts to help the expedition:

✔ Early in the journey, Teton Sioux leader Black Buffalo saved the mission by diffusing tensions between his people and the Corps of Discovery at the mouth of the Bad River.

✔ Mandan leader Sheheke and his people took the Americans in for the winter, saying "If we eat, you shall eat; if we starve, you must starve also."

✔ Cameahwait, leader of a starving band of Shoshones, decided to delay a buffalo hunt (although his people needed the meat for survival) in order to help the first white men they had ever seen.

✔ Watkuweis, an elderly Nez Perce woman, saved the Corps by telling her tribe to "do them no hurt."

✔ Old Toby, a Shoshone, guided them west across the mountains.

✔ Unknown and unsung Shoshone women helped transport the expedition's bags.

The person who writes the words gets to tell the story. For this reason, most accounts of the Lewis and Clark expedition include some recognition of the role Indian people played in the explorers' survival, but don't include what Indians thought of Lewis and Clark. Comparing their impressions of the Corps of Discovery with Lewis's and Clark's recorded impressions of the tribes would give a truer, richer picture of those human encounters.

In this book, we try to present tribal perspectives but don't tell Indian stories about Lewis and Clark. They are not our stories to tell. We eagerly look forward to the time when we can read tribal accounts about Lewis and Clark in words written and published by Indian people. Until then, the saga of Lewis and Clark is only half written.

Accepting Mission Improbable

The primary mission of what Lewis called his "darling project" was to find the Northwest Passage, a mythical all-water or nearly all-water route from St. Louis to the Pacific Ocean (see Chapter 3). Thomas Jefferson directed Lewis and Clark to find "the most direct & practicable water communication across this continent, for the purposes of commerce."

Jefferson also instructed the Corps to carry out these secondary missions:

- ✔ Along the way, study Indian tribes, some felt to be hostile, and collect tribal vocabularies.

- ✔ Hold diplomatic meetings with the tribes in order to persuade them to enter into trade alliances with the United States and make peace with their enemies. These efforts were so that the United States could monopolize the burgeoning fur trade, squeezing the British out.

- ✔ Encourage the tribes to send delegations of important Indians east to meet Jefferson.

- ✔ Distribute enough (but not too many) gifts to the Indians to win their cooperation.

- ✔ Collect animal and plant specimens, as well as observe soils, minerals, and climate. Navigate by the stars.

- ✔ Keep journals and make accurate maps and drawings.

- ✔ Come back alive.

The explorers were to keep a sharp lookout for proof of woolly mammoths, Welsh Indians, a mountain of salt 180 miles across the prairie, and some shining mountains said to rise five miles above the plains in a single ridge, among other tantalizing fantasies that were part of 1803 Western lore. See Chapter 3 for details.

Exploring empty wilderness or inhabited, civilized homelands?

Members of the Corps of Discovery considered their journey a voyage of discovery. No one from the United States had traveled west of the Upper Missouri valley, so the Corps believed every bend in the river, sunset behind a mountain, tool made from bone, taste of fresh-pulled root, smell of bear fat, and notes of songs wailed in unfamiliar languages to be discoveries that expanded knowledge about the continent.

But Lewis and Clark didn't actually *discover* anything in the sense of being the first to find something out (as dictionaries define "discover"). The land and water that the expedition explored had been occupied, known, and actively used for millennia by native peoples. The 100-plus tribal nations in the expedition's path had their own languages, traditions, social and political hierarchies, health care, education, religions, and customs. The tribes operated far flung trade networks; established hunting, gathering, farming, and sacred boundaries; formed alliances; and made enemies as circumstances dictated. Lewis and Clark did not blaze their own trail — they traveled Indian roads, using Indian maps and advice.

Adding to scientific knowledge

On behalf of science, Lewis and Clark collected and recorded 178 plant species and 122 animal species. They were the first white people to create a nearly accurate map that showed the continent as it was. And they determined once and for all that no all-water Northwest Passage to the Pacific Ocean existed.

Everywhere Lewis went on the expedition, he observed and meticulously recorded plants and animals he believed to be new to science. Late in May of 1806, while the expedition stayed with the Nez Perce and waited for the snow to melt in the Bitterroot Mountains, the men brought Lewis a black woodpecker with a red throat and white and blood red breast. Lewis had seen the bird at a distance but not up close. Taking his time, he lavished a five-hundred-word description on it. We know the bird today as "Lewis's woodpecker." Its skin, the only zoological specimen that survives from the expedition, is at Harvard University. In addition, during his wait with the Nez Perce, Lewis had a very productive period as a botanist, collecting and preserving nearly 50 plants, including Lewis's syringa, purple trillium, ragged robin, and the green-banded mariposa lily.

While Lewis waxed poetic about animals and plants, Clark made detailed maps of the areas they traveled. Clark's famous map of the West (see Chapter 9) turned out to be off by only 40 miles out of the nearly 8,000 the expedition traveled. It has been useful to geographers and map makers ever since.

Lewis and Clark and the journal-keeping soldiers all recorded copious detail about the rivers and landscapes, weather conditions, and most of all, the people. Lewis's and Clark's *ethnological* (comparison of cultures) observations are revealing, both about the people recorded and about the ethnocentricity of the men doing the recording.

Placing Lewis and Clark in History

One of the ways that the Lewis and Clark journey stands out among all the other explorations of the Americas is the over one million words that Lewis and Clark wrote in their journals. Clark was the most faithful journalist, writing nearly every day, and he was also the most idiosyncratic speller. He spelled the word "mosquito," for example, over two dozen ways, without once spelling it the way Americans spell it today.

The journals are an unparalleled record of fact, opinion, bias, affection, anger, humor, sadness, and mortal danger. They make Lewis's and Clark's continental journey a human story, full of life and its triumphs and failures, joys and sorrows, and never-ending challenges.

Most of the intrepid explorers were dead just a few years after returning from the West, but because they kept journals that record every place they went and what they saw, heard, and did, the Lewis and Clark expedition lives on in American imaginations, hearts, and history classes.

The Lewis and Clark expedition, preserved in those journals, paved the way for rapid and radical change, and the country has made almost mind-boggling progress since the early 1800s. Yet that progress has come at a terrible cost to indigenous peoples and the environment.

Beginning Manifest Destiny

Manifest Destiny, the 19th-century doctrine that America's westward expansion was pre-determined and inevitable wasn't named until later in the century, but it was the obvious course of U.S. politics when Lewis and Clark set off on their voyage. The western half of the North American continent contained a million square miles in 1800, all unknown to United States citizens. This enormous uncharted land mass inspired visions of future U.S. power and prosperity in statesmen like President Jefferson, who conceived and planned the Lewis and Clark expedition. The West beckoned to men like Meriwether Lewis and William Clark, who were young, fit, courageous, confident, and willing to test their fortunes against it.

Jefferson believed that western tribes could be instrumental in the development of a fur-trade empire and would gradually be assimilated into white culture. If not, they would have to be removed to some other place. Jefferson worried that assimilation would not happen fast enough on the frontier — it had not happened with tribes in the East, who had moved or been run off from their lands or gone into hiding. And it was not happening in Indiana Territory at that moment, where settlers were deciding that the Indians needed to leave and were clamoring for government intervention.

Jefferson thought that the surviving Eastern and Midwestern tribes were best protected from whites and should be removed to somewhere west of the Mississippi River, somewhere whites didn't want to live. The logical extension to that thought was that eventually, some western tribes would also have to be removed, although Jefferson may or may not have thought that far in advance.

White Americans believed that it was their God-given right to settle the West, and the path had to be cleared. Nineteenth-century Americans perceived the presence of Indian tribes all over the continent as an obstacle to settlement of U.S. territory — wherever whites chose to live.

A century of conquest

As you look back 200 years to the Lewis and Clark expedition, the landscape has radically changed. The environment has been critically damaged, and the tribes were nearly decimated. The expedition may not have directly caused these changes, but it was the catalyst for change. The West was certainly never the same after Lewis and Clark's visit.

Disease brought by Euro-Americans was the first wholesale killer of American Indians. Then, conflict with white settlers resulted in the loss of traditional homelands and hunting territories and removal or confinement to reservations. White settlement depleted the game animals that the tribes depended on for food, clothing, and self-sufficiency. Federal policy built dams that buried tribal lands in water and stopped the great salmon runs. Poverty, starvation, and dependency plagued reservation tribes. Federal government policy took Indian children from their parents and placed them in faraway boarding schools, where they were forced to give up their languages and cultures. Solemn treaties with tribes were broken. Presidential executive orders and acts of Congress continually reduced tribal lands. Federal policy withdrew sovereignty status from tribes and rescinded support for struggling tribal governments, schools, and social services. Federal policy tried to eradicate Indians.

Today, the tribes are striving to preserve their languages — languages that Lewis and Clark heard and tried to phonetically record in their journals. Tribes are working successfully to revitalize their cultures, traditions, practices, arts and crafts, songs, and stories. American Indian tribes are beginning to recover.

Waging a century of war against the environment

The overwhelming bounty of the West that Lewis and Clark described over and over was gone by the end of the same century in which they described it. Many animal and plant species were driven to extinction and many remain endangered. The countless numbers of buffalo that covered the plains for

TRAIL TIPS
NORTH
SOUTH

Protecting the earth

The Sierra Club is participating in the Lewis and Clark Bicentennial commemoration with a five-year campaign to permanently protect the 56 million acres of remaining wildlands in Lewis and Clark country, preserve and restore key wildlife habitat, and protect threatened and endangered species (such as bison, wolves, grizzly bears, and salmon). Advocated solutions include wilderness designation, hands-on conservation, lands acquisition, smart growth, and an end to commercial logging on national forests and public lands.

The American Rivers organization has created a traveling exhibit called "Discover the Rivers of Lewis and Clark," to encourage citizen involvement in key decisions facing the Missouri, Snake, Yellowstone, and Columbia Rivers and to enhance public interest in river conservation. To find out more, visit www.sierraclub.org or www.americanrivers.org.

miles and held up Lewis's and Clark's canoes for hours while crossing rivers were decimated to near extinction by white hunters and settlers. Dams now constrict the natural flow of rivers. The huge salmon runs of the Columbia River and Pacific Northwest were stopped by dam after dam built to supply hydroelectric power, and some species of salmon recorded by Lewis and Clark are now extinct. These same dams buried the mighty Great Falls of the Missouri and the thundering Celilo Falls on the Columbia.

The beaver and otter were trapped out. Grizzly bears and wolves were forced to the brink of extinction. And the passenger pigeon that darkened the skies in Lewis's and Clark's day and provided supper for the explorers on occasion, perished completely from the face of the earth.

Today, many Americans are interested in conserving what bounty is left. National environmental organizations have focused their efforts on preserving and restoring the lands and waters traveled by Lewis and Clark. Federal, state, and tribal resource-management agencies enforce sustainable use regulations. And individual Americans are being more respectful, picking up their litter and contributing tax-deductible dollars to help protect and preserve America's natural treasures.

As a result, the rivers are slightly less polluted, although still dammed. Tribal consortiums are bringing back the salmon and buffalo bit by bit. Grizzly bears and wolves are multiplying again. Severe threats from resource extraction, growth, sprawl, drought, and general idiocy still exist, but for most Americans, what was once squandered is now valued.

Showing respect when visiting American Indian reservations

A good rule when planning to visit any American Indian reservation is to call the tribe or check the tribal Web site before your visit. Then go by the tribal headquarters as soon as you arrive to pick up any materials that may help you locate public events, attractions, and activities and to find out about any special rules to follow or permits you need. If the tribal headquarters are closed, locate a museum, visitor center, casino gift shop, motel, restaurant, or gas station and ask about what activities are encouraged and permitted on the reservation.

Tribal powwows, games, and rodeos are social events on reservations that usually welcome the public. Powwows are gatherings featuring generations-old drumming and dancing, along with traditional dress and food. Bring a lawn chair or blanket for an outdoor powwow, because seating is limited and generally reserved for the dancers and their families. The dance area is sacred, but guests may dance when invited by the emcee.

Most cultural and religious ceremonies require special permission to attend or, in some cases, may be closed to visitors.

Use established public roads, trails, and walkways. Never wander onto tribal or private property. Never disturb a sacred site or remove its artifacts. Instead, purchase mementos in wonderful shops and galleries that you find on reservations.

If in doubt, ask. Obey any posted rules and show the appropriate respect for cultural traditions, resources, and property. Flash and video photography are often not allowed at all on reservations without permission, or may not be allowed at specific events. Some tribes charge a fee for permission to photograph. If photography is allowed, always ask your subject's permission before snapping the camera.

Cultural and recreational activities, such as hunting, fishing, camping, hiking, and gambling, may be offered on the reservation. Tribes have rules that protect their land's environment and wildlife. Contact tribal offices or visit the tribal Web site for regulations concerning access, recreational opportunities, motels, restaurants, and casinos.

In other words, do unto others. Show respect and enjoy the vacation of a lifetime, while persevering the natural, cultural, and historical richness of the Lewis and Clark National Historic Trail and helping protect it for future generations.

Retracing the Corps' Steps: The Lewis and Clark National Historic Trail

Because William Clark made such an amazingly accurate map; because Lewis and Clark took and recorded so many navigational readings (longitude, latitude, distances, and courses of rivers); and because the captains and several of the men wrote clear, compelling descriptions of the lands that they were traveling through, today, you can visit the entire route that Lewis and traveled — from the birthplace of the expedition at Monticello (Jefferson's residence) to the awesome Pacific Coast. You can create your own personal exploration by car, boat, train, bus, canoe, kayak, bicycle, horseback, or hiking boots.

In 1978, Congress designated Lewis's and Clark's route as the Lewis and Clark National Historic Trail — part of the National Trails System. The 3,700-mile-long trail is administered by the National Park Service in partnership with other federal agencies, states, tribes, not-for-profit organizations, and private landowners. The trail officially begins at the Lewis and Clark Interpretive Center near Wood River, Illinois, and wanders up the Missouri River to the Rocky Mountains, down the Clearwater and Snake Rivers to the Columbia and on to the Pacific Ocean. From its beginning in Illinois, it then passes through the modern states of Missouri, Kansas, Nebraska, Iowa, South Dakota, North Dakota, Montana, Idaho, Washington, and Oregon. Some places, such as Monticello in Virginia and Lewis's Gravesite in Tennessee, are not on the official Lewis and Clark National Historic Trail but are integral to America's epic saga and, therefore, are designated as Lewis and Clark National Historic Sites.

All along the route, you find interpretive signs and centers, museums, state parks, marinas, big cities, small towns, Indian reservations, powwows, sweeping prairies, rolling grain fields, national forests, private lands, soaring vistas, sacred places, and great beauty. In a nutshell, you find the American West.

You can drive scenic byways and heritage corridors, take your boat up the Missouri, or ride Amtrak's *Empire Builder* train across the northern Plains. However you go, please take good care of this national treasure. For more information about Trail and related sites, log on to www.nps.gov/lecl or call 402-514-9311.

Joining the Journey: The National Bicentennial Commemoration

The bicentennial of the Lewis and Clark expedition is being observed by the United States from 2003 to 2006. The commemoration is a grassroots, cross-cultural, nationwide volunteer effort to help people explore one of the most significant turning points of America's collective past. It is actively supported by over a dozen federal agencies, 35 tribal nations, 19 state governments, countless not-for-profit organizations, hundreds of local communities, a bipartisan Congressional caucus, and the president of the United States. The first lady of the United States serves as honorary chairperson of the bicentennial commemoration.

Because Lewis and Clark were instrumental in the creation of a coast-to-coast nation, the 200th anniversary of their journey was originally conceived as a celebration of their achievements. But the Corps of Discovery also marked the path for the future conquest by one people over a number of others. The tribes who met Lewis and Clark wanted to participate in the bicentennial, but not in a celebration. They couldn't celebrate the loss of everything in life as they once knew it. Early organizers, eager for historical accuracy, changed the term from "celebration" to "commemoration" and linked arms with tribal leaders to honor all perspectives.

More than half of the tribes whose homelands Lewis and Clark traversed are participating in the bicentennial commemoration. They are telling their stories, revitalizing their languages, protecting sacred lands, building interpretive and cultural centers, developing cultural tourism opportunities, and inviting the public to visit Indian country and enjoy native hospitality. They are planning and hosting national signature events during the bicentennial and working shoulder to shoulder with their non-Indian neighbors to make your visit a memorable one.

Most of the tribes are members of the Circle of Tribal Advisors of the National Council of the Lewis and Clark Bicentennial — a historic coalition of 35 tribes working together to give national voice to Indian perspectives.

The National Lewis and Clark Bicentennial commemorates the pluck, luck, wit, and grit of Lewis and Clark in leading the Corps of Discovery across the continent. It applauds the cooperation between U.S. soldiers and American Indians. It honors the land and waters that the Corps of Discovery traveled. And it salutes the American Indians of this land who survived to tell their stories.

Participating in Corps of Discovery II

To commemorate the bicentennial, the National Park Service, with assistance from tribes and from other federal agencies, has created a touring exhibit and performance space called "Corps of Discovery II: 200 Years to the Future." On the road through fall 2006, it will visit dozens of communities and Indian reservations across 19 states, focusing on the nation's natural and cultural heritage and the stories of its people before, during, and after the expedition. Don't miss this exciting interactive traveling interpretive center when it comes to your town! For details, go to www.nps.gov.

Attending national signature events

Between January of 2003 and September of 2006, 15 national Lewis and Clark Bicentennial signature events are being hosted by communities along the trail:

- **Charlottesville, Virginia, January 14–19, 2003:** *Jefferson's West, Bicentennial Commencement at Monticello*

- **Clarksville, Indiana, and Louisville, Kentucky, October 14–26, 2003:** *Falls of the Ohio*

- **St. Louis, Missouri area**
  - **March 12–14, 2004:** *Three Flags Ceremony,* St. Louis, Missouri
  - **May 13–16, 2004:** *Expedition's Departure Camp Dubois,* Hartford and Wood River, Illinois
  - **May 14–23, 2004:** *St. Charles: Preparations Complete, the Expedition Faces West,* St. Charles, Missouri

- **Kansas City, Missouri area, July 3–4, 2004:** *Heart of America: A Journey Fourth,* Atchison and Leavenworth, Kansas and Kansas City, Missouri

- **Omaha, Nebraska area, July 31–August 3, 2004:** *First Tribal Council,* Fort Atchison State Historical Park, Fort Calhoun, Nebraska

- **South Dakota, August 27–September 30, 2004:** *Oceti Sakowin Experience: Remembering and Educating,* South Dakota Tribal lands and reservations

- **Bismarck, North Dakota: October 22–31, 2004:** *Circle of Cultures, Time of Renewal and Exchange*

- **Great Falls, Montana: June 1–July 4, 2005:** *Explore the Big Sky*

- **Fort Clatsop, Oregon: November 24–27, 2005:** *Destination 2005 - The Pacific,* Pacific County, Washington, and Clatsop County, Oregon

- **Lapwai, Idaho:** June 14–17, 2006: *Among the Nez Perce,* Nez Perce National Historical Park, Idaho

- **Billings, Montana: July 22–25, 2006:** *Clark on the Yellowstone,* Pompeys Pillar National Monument

- **Fort Berthold Indian Reservation, North Dakota: August 17–20, 2006:** *Reunion at the Home of Sakakawea,* New Town, North Dakota

- **St. Louis, Missouri: September 23, 2006:** *Confluence with Destiny: The Return of Lewis and Clark*

For more information about all of these national events, log on to www.lewisandclark200.org.

Getting more information

Hundreds of community and regional events are scheduled during the bicentennial. And along the Lewis and Clark Trail, you can find dozens of federal, tribal, and state parks; monuments; historic sites; wildlife refuges; and interpretative centers. To help you find out more about these places and events, here are some useful Web sites:

- National Council of the Lewis and Clark Bicentennial (calendar of events): www.lewisandclark200.org

- National Park Service/Fort Clatsop National Memorial: www.nps.gov/focl

- National Park Service/Lewis and Clark National Historic Trail: www.nps.gov/lecl

- U.S. Army Corps of Engineers (dams, lakes, parks): www.usace.army.mil

- U.S. Bureau of Land Management (National Monuments and federal lands): www.blm.gov

- U.S. Bureau of Reclamation (dams, lakes, parks): www.usbr.gov

- U.S. Fish and Wildlife Service (National Wildlife Refuges): www.fws.gov

- U.S. Forest Service (National Forests and Grasslands): www.fs.fed.us

- U.S. Geological Survey (maps): www.usgs.gov

To find specific state and tribal tourism sites, go to your favorite search engine and enter the name of the specific tribe or state.

Chapter 2

Getting Acquainted with the Expedition's People and Places

In This Chapter
- ▶ Revealing the mastermind of the expedition: Thomas Jefferson
- ▶ Acknowledging the members of the Corps of Discovery
- ▶ Recognizing the role of the American Indians
- ▶ Noting the tutors and traders who helped Lewis and Clark
- ▶ Honoring the land and rivers Lewis and Clark explored

Along with being intrepid Euro-American explorers, Lewis, Clark, and several other members of the Corps were some of America's first travel writers. Their diaries recount a journey thousands of miles up and down unforgiving rivers and across rugged landscapes inhabited by millions of native people living in distinct tribal nations and speaking hundreds of diverse languages.

To help you keep the who, when, where and why of the expedition straight, this chapter gives you a capsule of the cast of characters and the dramatic settings that made up the Lewis and Clark travelogue.

Pursuing His Dream: Thomas Jefferson

Why begin the list of characters in a book about Lewis and Clark with Thomas Jefferson? Because, like many other formative aspects of the United States, the Lewis and Clark expedition was born in the mind of the enigmatic genius who was America's third president (see Figure 2-1). For decades, Jefferson dreamed of exploring the West, and William Clark called him "the main spring" of the expedition. Lewis and Clark didn't just decide to go camping; they were following explicit directives from their Commander in Chief.

Figure 2-1:
Thomas
Jefferson.

*Thomas Jefferson, 1805, by Rembrandt Peale. Oil on canvas, 28 x 23.5 inches.
Collection of The New-York Historical Society, accession number
1867.306, negative number 6003.*

Thomas Jefferson was born in 1743 in Albemarle County, Virginia. He was an aloof observer, a man of radical political ideals, and a southern planter with extravagant tastes. His ideas were always ahead of public opinion. He stood over six feet, two inches tall, and he was lean, angular, and red-headed — a man of the Enlightenment who constantly sang to himself. Yet although his family was well-to-do, he grew up in a world that was still pretty rough around the perimeter, where life still included Indian encounters, hunting, trapping and trekking through rugged, untracked landscapes.

Jefferson wrote the Declaration of Independence and was a father of our country. But he was a man of extraordinary contradictions, for example

- He believed in equality and abolition of slavery, but owned 200 slaves.

- He distrusted federal power but used (and some say even abused) it to realize his vision of nation-building.

- He romanticized and stereotyped American Indians as "noble savages," but dreamed of acquiring their lands for an "Empire of Liberty" that would stretch "from sea to shining sea."

> ✔ He became known as the "father of American archaeology," but satisfied his bottomless curiosity at the expense of Monacan Indians (by excavating their ancestors' burial mounds near his home, Monticello, in Charlottesville, Virginia).

Elected in 1801, in April 1803, Jefferson made the greatest real estate deal in history when he engineered the United States' purchase of the Louisiana Territory from a cash-strapped Napoleon Bonaparte for $15 million (about 3¢ an acre). See Chapter 3 for the details of this deal.

Jefferson had previously made several unsuccessful attempts to send expeditions to explore the lands beyond the Mississippi River. On January 18, 1803, before the Louisiana Purchase was a reality, he sent a confidential letter to Congress requesting $2,500 for a "scientific" expedition. When Congress later ratified the Louisiana Purchase, he had greater latitude to direct his private secretary Meriwether Lewis "to explore the Missouri river, & such principal stream of it, as, by its course & communication with the water of the Pacific ocean may offer the most direct & practicable water communication across this continent, for the purposes of commerce." He hoped Lewis would not only find the mythical Northwest Passage (see Chapter 3), but also report back to him about the West's flora, fauna, geography, climate, and human inhabitants while he was at it.

Jefferson had many notions about the American West. But the West that he imagined was different from the West that Lewis and Clark explored and the American Indians knew as home.

Respecting the dead

From the beginning of the relationship with tribes in this country, Euro-Americans have felt free to dig up American Indian dead, scrounge around among the bodies for articles buried with them, loot the graves of their ancestors, and display this macabre booty in museums, galleries, and private collections. Although digging up bodies in a white cemetery in America and stealing objects buried with them has always been illegal, Indian burial mounds and sacred places have been desecrated freely, with little or no consequences.

Until the passage of the Native American Graves and Repatriation Act in 1990, no law prevented museums from archiving (or disposing of) hundreds or thousands of remains and sacred burial objects from looted graves. Now, on those rare occasions when enough federal grant money is provided to accomplish it, tribes can have their ancestors' remains and sacred objects repatriated to them.

If you follow the Lewis and Clark Trail, please protect the sacred sites of all people and immediately report anyone disturbing a site to local law enforcement.

Journeying to the Pacific: The Corps of Discovery

The Corps of Discovery, as the expeditionary force referred to itself, was a unit of the United States Army, co-commanded by Captain Meriwether Lewis and Lieutenant William Clark (his lower rank was kept a secret, and he was always addressed as Captain Clark by Lewis and the men). The permanent party — the group that traveled to the Pacific Ocean and back — consisted of 33 members shown in Figure 2-2: Lewis and Clark; 29 soldiers and civilians, including Clark's slave, York; one Shoshone Indian woman, Sacagawea; and Sacagawea's infant son, Jean Baptiste Charbonneau. (Each member is discussed in detail throughout this chapter.) Lewis's dog, Seaman, may be counted as the 34th member of the Corps of Discovery.

Clark recruited members of the Corps from Kentucky, while Clark was waiting for Lewis to join him at the Falls of the Ohio. These Corps members have become known as the *Nine Young Men from Kentucky*. The categorization reflects early racist attitudes about African Americans, however: York was also a young man from Kentucky but wasn't considered one of that group. Because York was as critical (and often more interesting) to the exploration as many of the others, we refer herein to *Ten Young Men from Kentucky*.

Figure 2-2:
Corps of
Discovery.

Lewis and Clark: The Departure from the Wood River Encampment, May 14, 1804,
by Gary R. Lucy. Courtesy of the Gary R. Lucy Gallery, Inc.

The original roster of recruits included others — not listed here — who accompanied the Corps as far as its 1804–1805 winter camp but who returned to St. Louis in the spring of 1805 when the permanent party proceeded on to the Pacific.

Leading the expedition: Meriwether Lewis

On August 18, 1774, in the same year as the Boston Tea Party, Meriwether Lewis was born at the Lewis family home, Locust Hill, in Albemarle County, Virginia — within sight of Jefferson's home, Monticello. Lewis, shown in Figure 2-3, was the second child and first son of William and Lucy Meriwether Lewis, cousins from two of Virginia's oldest and wealthiest families.

William Lewis died when Meriwether was five years old, and the boy's mother remarried within the year to Captain John Marks. The family matriarch, Lucy Meriwether Lewis Marks was a remarkable woman, widely acknowledged for her herbal medicinal knowledge and remedies, which she imparted to her son. Meriwether Lewis drew heavily on her teachings during the Corps of Discovery's journey west.

Figure 2-3: Meriwether Lewis.

Portrait of Meriwether Lewis. Artist: Charles Willson Peale ca. 1807–1808. Oil on paper on canvas 23 x 19 inches. Courtesy of Independence National Historic Park.

Confused about Army ranks?

In Lewis and Clark's day, Army officers began service at the rank of ensign and could be promoted to second lieutenant, then first lieutenant, then captain, then major, then colonel, then general. Lewis joined the Army at the rank of ensign and reached the rank of captain. Clark was serving as a captain when Ensign Lewis was assigned to his company of sharpshooters, but Clark resigned from the Army in 1796 to help out his brother George Rogers Clark.

When Clark re-joined the Army to accompany Lewis on the Voyage of Discovery, Lewis promised him the rank of captain, though the Army was not required to re-induct him at the same rank he held when he resigned. As it turned out, the Army re-inducted Clark at the rank of lieutenant instead of captain. In order to genuinely share command of the expedition, Lewis and Clark simply called each other "captain," and no one except the War Department knew the difference.

During Lewis's childhood, the family moved to the Georgia frontier, where Lewis learned the backwoods skills that served him and his men so well on the expedition. Around the age of 13, Lewis returned to Virginia to get a formal education.

In 1795, after some experience in the Virginia militia, Lewis joined the Army as an ensign and was stationed under General "Mad Anthony" Wayne in the Ohio country. Drinking and unruly behavior got him transferred to a company of elite sharpshooters, whose captain was named William Clark. The two respected one another and became friends. Lewis was promoted to lieutenant in 1799 and gained a reputation for honesty and thoroughness, but also for vanity, occasional melancholia, and heavy drinking.

On the eve of his first inauguration in 1801, Thomas Jefferson appointed Lewis to serve as his private secretary. Lewis moved to the President's House (now known as the White House) and took up quarters in the East Room — where Abigail Adams, the first First Lady to live in the house, had hung her laundry.

Immediately upon congressional approval of Jefferson's confidential request to fund a "scientific" exploration of the West, the president appointed Lewis to lead it and provided him with extensive instructions for the effort. He sent Lewis to Philadelphia to study under the top scientists of the day before embarking on the adventure. So Lewis spent the first six months of 1803 studying medicine, astronomy, mathematics, celestial navigation, botany, and fossils. He was also consumed with planning for the expedition. What armaments to take? What medicines? Books? Scientific and navigational instruments? How much whiskey? How much ink?

When he was chosen to command the expedition, Meriwether Lewis was 29 years old, six-feet tall, physically tough, smart, adventurous, ambitious, resourceful, organized, and determined. He knew how to lead men. But Lewis was not a perfect hero: He drank too much; he had a temper that he had trouble controlling; and he suffered from periodic bouts of severe depression.

In June, perhaps suspecting his own limitations, Lewis wrote to his old Army buddy and fellow Virginian William Clark, and asked him to share command of the expedition. Clark enthusiastically accepted, and thus began one of the greatest partnerships in American history.

Co-commanding the Corps: William Clark

Born on August 1, 1770, in Caroline County, Virginia (neighboring the Albemarle County homes of Jefferson and Lewis), William Clark was the much younger brother of General George Rogers Clark, hero of the American Revolution and the Northwest Indian wars. William Clark was four years older than Lewis.

The Clark family moved to Kentucky in 1785, settling at the Falls of the Ohio in an area that later became the city of Louisville. William never received a formal education like Lewis did, but was educated at home by his older brothers. The creative spelling in his expedition journals showed his lack of formal training. His education in wilderness skills, on the other hand, was supreme.

Clark was a six-foot-tall, red-headed, popular, tough, and commanding figure (see Figure 2-4) — a complementary contrast to the dark and moody Lewis. Clark also knew how to lead men. He was gregarious, level-headed, curious, dependable, good at mapmaking and drawing, and faithful in recording the day-to-day events in his journal. But he wasn't perfect, either. Like Lewis, Clark could lose his temper. He used his influence with the tribes against their interests, and he beat his slave York. Yet, in spite of their shortcomings, both Clark and Lewis were smart, observant, capable, and deeply respected by their men.

William Clark's military career began at the age of 19 when he volunteered to help fight the Wabash Indians. Shortly thereafter, he served under General "Mad Anthony" Wayne in the Ohio country, defeating the Indians at the Battle of Fallen Timbers. Clark served under Wayne as a captain in the 4th Sub-Legion and in that capacity, commanded Ensign Meriwether Lewis in the Northwest campaign.

Figure 2-4:
William
Clark.

*Portrait of William Clark. Artist: Charles Willson Peale ca. 1807.
Oil on board 23 x 18.75 inches. Courtesy of Independence
National Historic Park.*

After that war, Clark resigned from the Army because of family obligations. His brother George Rogers had gotten his financial affairs in a tangle, and William went home to help. Clark moved from the Kentucky side of the Ohio River to Clarksville on the Indiana side where his elder brother lived. There, on July 16, 1803, he received Lewis's letter inviting him to become co-commander of Jefferson's "scientific" exploration of the West.

Earning her fame: Sacagawea

Very possibly the most famous American woman in history, Sacagawea (sometimes spelled Sacajawea or Sakakawea) is also one of the most mythical. She was born around 1788 into the Agaideka'a band of Shoshone Indians in the vicinity of present day Tendoy, Idaho (just across the Continental Divide from Montana). At the time of Lewis and Clark, white traders referred to the Shoshones as the Snake Indians.

According to Lewis's journal, Sacagawea was about 12 years old when raiding Hidatsa Indians from present day North Dakota captured her near Three

Forks, Montana, where her band was encamped. They took her, along with other captives, to Metaharta, a Hidatsa village on the Knife River in present North Dakota, near the modern town of Stanton (see Chapter 9).

Later, the Hidatsas sold or gave Sacagawea and another captive Shoshone girl in marriage to Toussaint Charbonneau, a French-Canadian fur trader. Charbonneau was based in the Hidatsa villages, working for the Canadian North West Company.

When the Corps of Discovery arrived in the Mandan and Hidatsa villages to spend the winter of 1804–1805, Lewis and Clark learned of the Shoshones' reputation for having many horses. The explorers would need horses to cross the mountains from the Missouri River drainage to the Columbia River for the final leg of their voyage to the Pacific Ocean.

Charbonneau asked Lewis and Clark to hire him as an interpreter and informed them that his two wives were Shoshones, fluent in that language. Lewis and Clark hired him on the spot with the expectation that he would bring one of his wives to interpret when the Corps reached the Shoshones. Sixteen-year-old Sacagawea, who was pregnant at the time with her first child, spoke both Hidatsa and Shoshone, so the Americans selected her as the Charbonneau wife to accompany them to the Pacific.

Becoming the youngest explorer: Jean Baptiste Charbonneau

The baby who crossed a continent became William Clark's favorite, but the baby boy also convinced Indian tribes that the expedition wasn't a war party.

Jean Baptiste Charbonneau was born at Fort Mandan, the 1804–1805 winter camp of the Corps of Discovery, on February 11, 1805, to Sacagawea and Toussaint Charbonneau. Captain Lewis attended his difficult birth. Teenaged Sacagawea labored in severe pain until another French-Canadian fur trader at the fort, Rene Jessaume, suggested that Lewis administer the powder of a few rattlesnake rings. Lewis mixed the concoction and gave it to the girl. Within ten minutes, she delivered a healthy baby boy.

When the expedition got underway again in April 1805, Jean Baptiste was two months old and became the youngest explorer. It wasn't long before William Clark nicknamed him Pomp for his "little dancing boy" ways and started carrying the toddler on his shoulders as the expedition proceeded along.

Before his death (62 years after embarking with the Corps of Discovery), Jean Baptiste Charbonneau became an international celebrity, mountain man, Mormon expedition guide, Spanish *alcalde* (mayor), and Western gold seeker.

Behaving less than nobly: Toussaint Charbonneau

Historians know little of Jean Baptiste's father, Sacagawea's husband, Toussaint Charbonneau, before he came to live among the Mandans and Hidatsas. He was born somewhere near Montreal about 1759. Whatever his earlier life, he went to work for the North West Company as an engage (laborer) in the Knife River villages from 1793 to 1796. Eventually, he established himself as a free agent in the fur trade and lived in the village of Metaharta, near present day Stanton, North Dakota.

At Metaharta, Charbonneau purchased, or some say won in a gambling match, two captive Shoshone girls to be his wives. One of them was Sacagawea. During their winter at Fort Mandan in 1804–05, Lewis and Clark hired Charbonneau to go along on the expedition as an interpreter. His teenaged wife and infant son would accompany him.

Charbonneau's reputation on the expedition was less than noble. Lewis and Clark thought him to be of little merit, except as a cook. Lewis especially liked his *boudin blanc* (white pudding). He was not a good boatman, he panicked easily in a crisis, and Clark berated him once for striking Sacagawea.

Making history: York

William Clark didn't join the expedition alone. He brought his slave, York, who became the first African American to cross the continent. Born in Caroline County, Virginia, York was most likely the son of Old York and Rose, both owned by William's father, John Clark. York was about the same age as William Clark, maybe a few years younger, and had been Clark's personal body servant and companion since early childhood. He was a big man, and Lewis's and Clark's journals reveal him to be a fine marksman, a good cook, and a strong swimmer. He was a man of dignity, humor, and strong frontier capabilities. Clark calls him "fat" in the journals but he probably means large, not obese. This characterization is the only possibly derogatory comment Clark makes about York over the entire trip.

Born near the York River, York's early life was probably about the same as the other 200,000 slaves in Virginia at the time. A field slave had very few clothes and possessions, a poor diet heavy in starch, and housing that was tiny, cold, and windowless. He would have worked from sun up to sun down and been severely punished for small infractions of the slave owner's rules. His life would have improved on all counts when he became Clark's personal slave.

Clark and York were close, or at least knew the peculiar intimacy of a personal slave and his master. Although Clark called York "My boy," he also referred to himself and York as "two-self," each an extension of the other.

York went with the Clark family when they moved to Kentucky in the 1780s. Instead of becoming a plantation slave, York came into manhood in an environment where race relationships were less strict. On the frontier, some slaves handled guns, as York did on the expedition. Some slaves worked alongside whites and were able to buy goods on credit. York would have honed the same wilderness skills as Clark, the kind that would prove invaluable on the expedition.

During the Corps of Discovery's journey west, York carried a gun, and he hunted and functioned as an equal with the other men of the expedition. The Indians who encountered the expedition were in awe of his size, his nimbleness as a dancer, and especially his black skin. Suspecting that York had spiritual powers, the Arikaras called him "Big Medison" (see Chapter 8).

York's expedition experiences were wildly varied. The Indian tribes they encountered were completely fascinated and distracted by York. He discovered a new species of bird. He hunted and rowed, poled and portaged alongside the other men of the expedition. He tended the sick. He voted in an election. Although he received no pay for his labor, he received attention and congratulations along with the other men after the expedition successfully returned to St. Louis.

Having the right stuff: George Drouillard

The Corps of Discovery's best hunter, scout, woodsman, and interpreter of Indian sign language was a civilian. George Drouillard was born in French Canada, the son of Pierre Drouillard and a Shawnee mother. His father, Pierre, had reportedly served as an interpreter for George Rogers Clark (America in 1800 was a small community). In his youth, George moved with his mother's people to Cape Girardeau in Missouri.

Drouillard, whose name Lewis and Clark phonetically spelled "Drewyer" in their journals, brought great skill, endurance, and judgment to the expedition during dangerous times. Lewis recruited him at Fort Massac on the Ohio River, and Drouillard joined the Corps at Camp Dubois. He was with Lewis on the Marias River in 1806 when an encounter with a small party of Blackfeet resulted in the tragic deaths of two young Indians.

Fetching respect: Seaman, coast-to-coast canine

No list of the members of the Corps of Discovery could be complete without including Lewis's Newfoundland dog (see Figure 2-5), Seaman. Lewis paid $20 for him in Pittsburgh, and Seaman crossed the continent with his master.

Lisa S. Reed.

Figure 2-5: Newfound- land dog.

The Indians sometimes offered to buy him, and at one point, some Chinooks stole him, and in a rage Lewis stopped everything and threatened to burn villages in order to get him back. The big dog kept buffalo bulls and grizzly bears away from camp. He caught beaver, squirrels, and even an antelope, all of which the Corps eagerly cooked for supper. Even in the hungriest of times on the trail, Seaman seems to have eaten, and when the expedition was reduced to eating dogs that they bartered from the Indians, Seaman never became dinner.

Keeping the troops on track: The sergeants

The men of the Corps of Discovery were strong and talented, but they could also be rough and rowdy. Four men served as sergeants of the expedition, charged with making sure that the spirited men performed their duties and lived to tell about it.

TECHNICAL STUFF

The expedition journals — what would historians know without them?

The reason people know as much as they do about the Lewis and Clark expedition is because President Jefferson instructed Lewis to keep a record of every person met and place visited. Jefferson wanted it *all* recorded. Jefferson also said to make copies, in case one journal was lost or damaged. Both Lewis and Clark kept journals that are excellent but as different as their personalities. Clark wrote in his journal on a more consistent daily basis and included maps and sketches. Lewis's entries are more erratic but often more detailed and rich, with wonderful drawings of birds, animals, and plants.

The captains also ordered their sergeants to keep journals. A journal from Sergeant Pryor hasn't been found, but historians do have the journals of Sergeants Floyd, Ordway, and Gass (who replaced Floyd later in the journey — see Chapter 7). A surviving piece of a journal kept by Private Joseph Whitehouse also exists, but a journal believed to have been kept by Private Robert Frazer has never been found.

The journals offer a wealth of information from several perspectives, which is why the Lewis and Clark expedition is the best documented journey in early American exploration.

Sergeant John Ordway

Lewis and Clark weren't the only members of the Corps of Discovery to keep journals. Several of the men, including Sergeant John Ordway, also recorded their experiences, and Ordway's journal is illuminating with its keen observations of everyday Indian life and simple details of the voyage.

Born in Dumbarton, New Hampshire, in approximately 1775, Ordway was serving as a sergeant in the 1st Infantry Regiment at Kaskaskia, Illinois Territory, in early 1803. Lewis and Clark recruited him to join the Corps of Discovery at Camp Dubois, their first winter encampment, before launching the expedition up the Missouri River in the spring of 1804. Lewis and Clark put Ordway in charge of the camp, keeping orderly books along with his other sergeant duties. Ordway was educated and highly respected by Lewis and Clark and the men under his command. However, early in the expedition, the men were reluctant to follow orders given by anyone other than Lewis or Clark. Several of them defied Sergeant Ordway's orders, and during rebellious outbursts, two of the privates threatened his life.

Sergeant Nathaniel Pryor

One of the Ten Young Men from Kentucky, Nathaniel Pryor was born in 1772 in Virginia to John and Nancy Floyd Pryor. He was a first cousin to another sergeant, Charles Floyd — also one of the Kentucky Ten.

In 1782, the Pryor family moved to the Falls of the Ohio, where both parents died sometime before 1791, and their two orphan sons, Robert and Nathaniel, were placed in the custody of an overseer of the poor. Nathaniel married Peggy Patten in 1798 and was one of the expedition's few married men. Or perhaps he was a widower; history shows no record of Peggy in 1803 when Nathaniel left Louisville with the Corps of Discovery. Lewis and Clark described Sergeant Pryor as "a man of character and ability." He kept a journal, but it was lost before it could be published.

Sergeant Charles Floyd

Another of the Ten Young Men from Kentucky, Charles Floyd became famous as the only member of the expedition to die on the journey. He was first cousin to Nathaniel Pryor. Born around 1782 at Floyd's Station, a log fort near present day St. Matthews in Louisville, Floyd was one of the youngest members of the Corps of Discovery. In 1799, the Floyd family moved across the Ohio River to Indiana Territory, where they operated a ferry to Louisville. In 1801, at only 19 years of age, Charles Floyd became the first constable, or peace keeper, of the new settlement of Clarksville (named for George Rogers Clark, who had moved from Louisville to escape his debtors).

The Clark and Floyd families knew each other well. William Clark also moved to Clarksville in 1802 and was aware of Charles Floyd's abilities. He thought highly enough of the young man to recruit him for the Corps of Discovery. Like the other sergeants, Floyd kept a diary, which was published.

Sergeant Patrick Gass

Patrick Gass was promoted to the rank of sergeant after Charles Floyd's death. Gass was born at Falling Springs near Chambersburg, Pennsylvania, on July 12, 1771. He has been described as short, barrel-chested, and rough-talking; his language was unsuitable for polite society. Clark recruited him from the same 1st Infantry at Kaskaskia as John Ordway, and like Ordway, Gass signed on with the Corps of Discovery on January 1, 1804, at Camp Dubois.

Gass's Army career began in 1799 in Carlisle, Pennsylvania. He was a fine carpenter and woodsman. He also exhibited a strong sense of humor and quick wit while serving in the Corps. Like the other three sergeants, Patrick Gass kept a journal, and in 1807, it was the first account of the expedition to be published.

Carrying out the mission: The privates

History focuses a great deal of attention on Lewis and Clark, but the captains didn't make their way across the West alone. No one should forget that the privates of the Corps of Discovery demonstrated well-honed skills, brute strength, and indomitable spirits during the long struggle to fulfill their mission and reach the Pacific Ocean.

- **Private William Bratton:** A recruit from Kentucky, William Bratton was born in 1778 in Augusta County, Virginia, in what is now West Virginia; a descendant of Scots-Irish immigrants. His family moved to Kentucky around 1790, and William Clark enlisted him for the Corps of Discovery at the Falls of the Ohio. Chroniclers have described Bratton as over six feet tall, reserved, and with strict morals. He was one of the expedition's two highly skilled blacksmith and was also a gunsmith and a good hunter.

- **Private John Collins:** John Collins, born in Frederick County, Maryland, joined the Corps of Discovery, like most of the other men, on January 1, 1804, at Camp Dubois. He transferred from Fort Massac in Illinois Territory.

   Collins was a good hunter and eventually became an exemplary member of the expedition. However, his participation had a rocky beginning. While at Camp Dubois, he reportedly killed a farmer's pig and passed it off as bear meat. William Clark noted him in his journal as a *blackguard* (rude or unscrupulous person). After the expedition was underway, Collins was also court-martialed and punished for stealing whiskey while on duty to guard it.

- **Private John Colter:** One of the Ten Young Men from Kentucky, John Colter is often considered to be the first mountain man. He gained fame, and sometimes ridicule, after the Lewis and Clark expedition as the first non-Indian to see the geysers and thermal springs of what is now Yellowstone National Park.

   Colter was born around 1774 near Staunton, Virginia, the son of Joseph and Ellen Shields Colter. His family moved to Maysville, Kentucky, on the Ohio River when he was five years old, and he spent his boyhood there. Meriwether Lewis recruited John Colter at Maysville on his way down the Ohio from Pittsburgh to meet William Clark at the Falls of the Ohio. By all accounts, Colter was quick thinking, courageous, and skilled as a hunter.

- **Private Pierre Cruzatte:** The son of a French father and an Omaha mother, Cruzatte enlisted with the Corps of Discovery on May 16, 1804, in St. Charles, Missouri. He could speak the Omaha language and use Indian sign talk, making him valuable as an interpreter with the tribes on the lower Missouri.

   Cruzatte was a skilled boatman but is best known for his fiddle playing, entertaining members of the Corps as well as the Indians they met. He had only one eye and poor eyesight, which, on the return journey, caused him to mistake Lewis for an elk and shoot him in the derriere. Cruzatte never admitted the error.

- **Privates Joseph and Reuben Field:** The two brothers, Joseph and Reuben Field, were among the young men from Kentucky recruited by William Clark at the Falls of the Ohio. They were born in Culpepper

County, Virginia, the sons of Abraham Field. Joseph was born around 1774, and Reuben approximately two years earlier. The family moved to Kentucky in 1783.

Joseph's and Reuben's elder brother, Ezekial, had a salt-making business in Bullitt County, Kentucky, where he employed some of his brothers. That experience served Joseph well when the men set up a salt works at the Pacific coast to make salt from seawater for the expedition's return journey.

Reuben got into trouble at Camp Dubois for disobeying an order from Sergeant Ordway. But both brothers were excellent marksmen and hunters and became outstanding members of the Corps. They were also with Lewis on the Marias River when the explorers killed two young Blackfeet Indians.

✔ **Private Robert Frazer:** Born in August County, Virginia, Frazer was a member of the group that was to accompany the keelboat on its return to St. Louis from Fort Mandan in the spring of 1805. But when Private Moses Reed deserted the Corps in present day Nebraska, Lewis and Clark sent Reed back instead and appointed Frazer to take his place in the permanent party that was to travel on to the Pacific. Frazer kept a journal that was lost before he could publish it, although the map he made of the Northwest is preserved in the Library of Congress.

✔ **Private George Gibson:** Records tell little about this young man from Kentucky, recruited by Clark at the Falls of the Ohio. He was born in Mercer County, Pennsylvania, near Pittsburgh but raised in Kentucky. Gibson was a good hunter and rider, and he played the fiddle. Sergeant Ordway wrote that Gibson was also an Indian interpreter and shared a rivalry with George Drouillard in that capacity. However, some historians doubt that Gibson could have known any dialects of the western American Indians, although he may have known some sign language.

✔ **Private Silas Goodrich:** The primary characteristic known about Silas Goodrich is that he was a good fisherman, often supplying the men with a dietary change from the tons of meat that they consumed. He was born in Massachusetts and was in the Army when he transferred to the Corps of Discovery on January 1, 1804, at Camp Dubois.

✔ **Private Hugh Hall:** Born in approximately 1772 in Carlisle, Pennsylvania, Hall joined the Corps of Discovery from the 2nd Infantry Regiment in Tennessee. He had a drinking habit, according to Clark's notes, and was court-martialed with John Collins for stealing whiskey.

✔ **Private Thomas P. Howard:** Born in 1779, Howard was raised in Brimfield, Massachusetts. According to Clark, ". . . he never drank water." Lewis and Clark recruited him, like Hugh Hall, from the 2nd Infantry Regiment, and he reported to the Corps of Discovery on January 1, 1804, at Camp Dubois.

While wintering at Fort Mandan, Lewis and Clark punished Howard for climbing over the stockade walls into the garrison, an unthinking act that could have shown threatening outsiders how to penetrate the garrison.

✔ **Private Francois Labiche:** Like Cruzatte, Labiche was half French and half Omaha, and Lewis and Clark recruited him at Kaskaskia, although he didn't enlist until May 16, 1804, at St. Charles. He was an excellent boatman, tracker, and hunter, and he also served as an interpreter in French, English, and several tribal languages.

✔ **Private Jean Baptiste LePage:** LePage joined the Corps of Discovery on November 2, 1804 at Fort Mandan to replace John Newman in the permanent party. Lewis and Clark had Newman court-martialed for mutinous talk and expelled him from the permanent party. Little else is known about LePage.

✔ **Private Hugh McNeal:** Born and raised in Pennsylvania, Hugh McNeal served primarily as a hunter for the Corps of Discovery. McNeal is most likely best known for his narrow escape, with the help of his Clatsop girlfriend, at the Necanicum River, which Clark jokingly called McNeal's Folly. (See Chapter 14 for the details.)

✔ **Private John Potts:** Born in Dillenburg, Germany, about 1776, Potts was a miller. He joined the U.S. Army in 1800, transferring to the Corps of Discovery in November 1803 at Camp Dubois. Potts was one of Lewis and Clark's Tennessee recruits.

✔ **Private George Shannon:** One of the Ten Young Men from Kentucky, George Shannon was the youngest member of the Corps of Discovery. He was born in Pennsylvania in 1785 and joined Lewis at Maysville, Kentucky, en route from Pittsburgh to Louisville to meet Clark. During the Corps' journey west, Shannon twice became lost — once for over two weeks, nearly starving to death in a land burgeoning with game.

✔ **Private John Shields:** Another of the Ten Young Men from Kentucky, John Shields was the oldest member of the expedition, except for Toussaint Charbonneau (Sacagewea's husband). He was born in 1769, near Harrisonburg in Virginia's Shenandoah Valley, to Robert and Nancy Shields. In 1784 the family moved to Pigeon Forge, Tennessee, where John learned blacksmithing.

IN THEIR WORDS

Shields married in 1790 while living in Kentucky, so he was one of the few married men of the Corps. Shields was 34 when he enlisted in the Corps of Discovery as the head blacksmith and gunsmith. His skill also put corn on the table at Fort Mandan, when the Mandans and Hidatsas traded food for implement repair and the battle axes he made for them. Lewis and Clark profusely praised Shields's service and recommended him for a bonus. According to Lewis, "nothing was more peculiarly useful to us than the skill and ingenuity of this man."

- **Private John B. Thompson:** Journal entries tell little about John Thompson before or after the Corps of Discovery. He served as a surveyor and as a cook for the expedition, and Clark noted him as a "valuable member of our party."

- **Private William Werner:** Historians know little about William Werner. He was probably from Kentucky and in the Army when he joined the Corps of Discovery at Camp Dubois. He got into a fist fight with John Potts there, and then went AWOL (absent without leave) in St. Charles before the expedition's departure. Otherwise, he served the Corps well as a cook and one of the salt makers (the men who made salt for the return journey from the saltwater of the Pacific Ocean).

- **Private Alexander Hamilton Willard:** Alexander Willard was born in Charlestown, New Hampshire, in 1778 but was living in Kentucky when he enlisted in the Army. He served in the artillery as *an artificer,* or skilled workman, responsible for maintaining weapons and equipment, before transferring to the Corps of Discovery on January 1, 1804, at Camp Dubois. Willard served the expedition as a blacksmith and gunsmith. He fell asleep while on guard duty in July 1804 and received 100 lashes for it. He may have kept a journal, but if so, it has never been found.

- **Private Joseph Whitehouse:** Private Whitehouse, like most of the men of the Corps of Discovery, was born in Virginia, in Fairfax County, around 1775. As a boy of nine or ten, he migrated to Kentucky with his family, and they settled in Boyle and Mercer Counties. Although Whitehouse grew up in Kentucky, Lewis and Clark recruited him at Fort Massac, and he joined the expedition on January 1, 1804, at Camp Dubois.

Whitehouse made a reputation in Lewis's and Clark's journals as a tailor. He often sewed and repaired the men's clothes from buckskin. Unlike most of the other enlisted men, Whitehouse was literate and kept a journal, as did the sergeants and Lewis and Clark. His record of the journey has been published.

- **Private Richard Windsor:** Richard Windsor most likely transferred from Fort Massac and joined the Corps of Discovery on January 1, 1804, at Camp Dubois. He served the expedition as a hunter and went with Lewis to explore the Marias River on the return trip (see Chapter 16).

- **Private Peter Weiser:** Of German descent, Peter Weiser was born in 1781 in Pennsylvania. He transferred to the Corps of Discovery on January 1, 1804 from the 1st Infantry Regiment at Kaskaskia in Illinois Territory and filled the roles of quartermaster, cook, and hunter.

Helping the Corps Survive and Succeed: The American Indians

Lewis and Clark believed that they were exploring uncivilized, untamed wilderness. To the American Indians of the West, the land was none of that. It was home and was fully populated. Their languages didn't — and still don't — include words that mean or describe "wilderness."

Political relationships within and between tribes were intricate and complicated. Lewis and Clark often exacerbated, even created, rivalries by designating Indian leaders as first, second, and third "chiefs," bestowing artificial rank. But, despite Lewis and Clark's cultural arrogance and naiveté about these centuries-old civilizations, the Indians greeted the Americans with honor and hospitality. The only exceptions were the Teton Sioux and the Blackfeet, and those meetings may have gone differently if the Americans had understood political realities.

The Corps of Discovery wouldn't have accomplished their mission and probably wouldn't have survived without the help and guidance of the American Indians. (See the "Saving the Corps' bacon" sidebar.)

Attending the Council on the Bluff: Otoe and Missouria

After two months on the Missouri, Lewis and Clark still hadn't seen any Indians. They were disappointed. One of their foremost directives from Jefferson was to make contact, announce a new Great White Father, elicit peace, and negotiate trade agreements. They finally found the Otoes, who had been hunting, and met with them and the Missourias at Council Bluff. The Corps negotiated with the following tribal leaders:

- **Little Thief:** An important headman of the Otoe Nation and a shrewd trader, Little Thief met in council with Lewis and Clark in August 1804.

- **Big Horse:** The leader of the Missourias, Big Horse arrived naked to the meeting with Lewis and Clark to illustrate his poverty and need to trade for goods that the keelboat carried.

"Our mother's face"

The indigenous American world view was not understood by Lewis and Clark, or Jefferson, or other Euro-Americans.

"Our elders knew the curves of the hillsides and the lines of the trails as intimately as they knew the curves and lines of their mothers' faces.

Today our grandparents lament that children born on the reservations are like buffalo born behind a fence."

Germaine White, Confederated Salish and Kootenai Tribes

Welcoming the expedition: Yankton Sioux

At the mouth of the James River, the Yankton Sioux greeted the Corps of Discovery with warmth and honor, eager to cement their own role in the changing political climate of Missouri River trade. Like the Otoes and Missouris, they thought Lewis and Clark, with their merchandise-laden keelboat, were traders rather than promisers of trade to come. Lewis and Clark did, however, have beneficial meetings with the following men:

✔ **Weuche:** The Yankton leader Weuche offered to organize peace efforts among the Plains bands.

✔ **Half Man:** Another Yankton leader who met with Lewis and Clark with Weuche, Half Man warned the explorers about powerful tribes upriver who would be less friendly.

Challenging the Corps: Brule Band of Teton Sioux

In his journal, an angry William Clark described the Teton Sioux as "the vilest miscreants of the savage race. . . ." The powerful Brule band of the Teton Sioux controlled trade on the middle Missouri and intended to stop the Corps of Discovery from proceeding upriver. Their intra-tribal factionalism confused Lewis and Clark, and, to make matters worse, neither group could fully understand the other's words. The encounter was hostile and frustrating to both sides, but resulted in no violence.

Lewis and Clark encountered the following Brule leaders:

- ✔ **Untongarabar (Black Buffalo):** The leader of the largest band of Brule Sioux was the intense Untongarabar, whom Lewis and Clark called Black Buffalo and French traders described as being of "good character, although angry and fierce in his fits of passion." When Lewis and Clark met the Teton Sioux, Black Buffalo was vying for power with another Sioux leader, The Partisan.

- ✔ **Tortohongar (The Partisan):** Called The Partisan by white traders, Tortohongar was the leader of the next largest band of Brule. The French trader Tabeau considered him mercurial.

- ✔ **Buffalo Medicine:** Lewis and Clark considered Buffalo Medicine the third leader in the Teton power struggle. He accompanied Black Buffalo and The Partisan to the contentious and dangerous meeting between the Corps of Discovery and the Teton Sioux at Bad River, near present day Pierre, South Dakota.

Offering hospitality: Mandan, Hidatsa, and Arikara

At the time of the Lewis and Clark expedition, the agricultural Arikaras lived in earth lodges on the upper Missouri, south of the Mandan and Hidatsa earth lodge villages, but were allies of the Sioux. The Mandan and Hidatsa villages were the powerful and sophisticated center of trade on the northern Great Plains. Today, all three tribes live on the Fort Berthold reservation in North Dakota. Lewis, Clark, and their men enjoyed warm and friendly relations with the people of all three nations, including the following leaders:

- ✔ **Kakawissassa (Crow At Rest):** The civil leader of the Arikara village Sawa-haini on Ashley Island in the Missouri River, Kakawissassa was also known as Crow At Rest. At the time of Lewis's and Clark's visit, he was engaged in a competition for authority with another Arikara leader, Kakawita. Despite that, Lewis and Clark named Kakawissassa the "Grand Chief" of the Arikaras and gave him a peace medal, fueling the rivalry.

- ✔ **Kakawita (Man Crow):** Kakawita, or Man Crow, was the war leader of a small village called Narhkarica and a challenger to Kakawissassa's civil authority.

- ✔ **Pocasse (Hay):** Pocasse, also called Hay, was the leader of Rhtarahe, a village of 60 to 70 earth lodges upriver from Sawa-haini.

Saving the Corps' bacon

Every tribe that the Corps of Discovery encountered, except for the Teton Sioux and Piegan Blackfeet, saved Lewis's and Clark's bacon. Undoubtedly, the Corps of Discovery wouldn't have been successful — wouldn't even have survived — if not for the generosity, information, instruction, guidance, and friendship of the American Indians.

Specifically, we offer the following examples:

✔ The Yanktons provided valuable information about middle Missouri River tribes.

✔ The Mandans offered a place to winter in 1804–05 and provided maps and information, as well as food, for the Corps.

✔ Sacagawea, an adopted Hidatsa, turned out to be the Shoshone leader Cameahwait's sister, easing the Corps of Discovery's acquisition of Shoshone horses for the mountain crossing. She and her child also gave the traveling community a sense of family and signaled peace to other tribes they met.

✔ The Shoshones' Old Toby and a number of women guided the Corps and carried the Corps' baggage over the Bitterroots.

✔ The Salish provided more horses.

✔ The Nez Perce fed the starving crew when they emerged from the mountains, showed them how to build canoes, and guided them to the Columbia River.

✔ The Columbia River tribes traded with, fed, and informed the explorers.

✔ The Chinooks and Clatsops provided the final winter camp, and also traded, fed, and offered their women to the Americans.

All of these tribes shared music, dance, and merriment with the expedition.

Not long after Lewis's and Clark's departure from their lands, all these tribes saw their friendship, generosity, and hopes for trade with the United States repaid with an onslaught of American westward expansion and settlement that took their lands, assaulted their cultures, and changed their lives forever. But, despite 200 years of such expansion, all those tribes still thrive as a part of American life.

✔ **Piahito (Hawk's Feather** or **Eagle's Feather):** The leader of Waho-erha village — across Cottonwood Creek from Rhtarahe — was Piahito (Hawk's Feather or Eagle's Feather). The inhabitants of Waho-erha were ethnically more diverse and spoke a different dialect from the people of the other three villages, which Lewis and Clark referred to as the Arikara Proper.

✔ **Sheheke (Coyote, Big White):** The most prominent civil leader of the Mandan village of Mitutanka was Sheheke or Coyote. He was usually called Big White by Lewis and Clark. With an eye to the Corps of Discovery's boatload of trade goods, Sheheke invited Lewis and Clark to build their 1804–1805 winter garrison near his village.

- **Kagohhami (Little Raven):** Lewis and Clark appointed Little Raven, another civil leader of Mitutanka, as the "second chief" after Sheheke. On the expedition's return voyage, Little Raven, or Kagohhami, offered to go with Lewis and Clark to Washington, but then changed his mind.

- **Posecopsahe (Black Cat):** The second Mandan village, Rooptahee, was led by Posecopsahe or Black Cat. Black Cat became a welcome regular visitor and friend at Fort Mandan. He often supplied Clark with information about Mandan customs and culture, but amazingly, Clark felt it not worth recording.

- **Ompsehara (Black Moccasin):** The Hidatsa village of Metaharta, home of Toussaint Charbonneau and Sacagawea, sat on the Knife River about a mile above its junction with the Missouri. Ompsehara, or Black Moccasin, was the leader of Metaharta, and Lewis and Clark designated him the village's "first chief."

- **Le Borgne (One Eye):** The brilliant and powerful Hidatsa leader Le Borgne was headman of the largest Hidatsa village of Menetarra (a group of about 130 earth lodges). York fascinated Le Borgne, and at one point, the Hidatsa leader tried to rub off York's dark color, certain it was paint.

Providing the horses: Shoshone

The Agaideka'a Shoshone of present-day Idaho was the birth tribe of Sacagawea. When the Corps of Discovery reached Shoshone country, Lewis and Clark depended on the young Indian woman to translate for them in negotiations for horses to cross the Rocky Mountains. The Shoshones provided desperately needed help to the expedition:

- **Cameahwait:** In an absolutely extraordinary stroke of fate, the Shoshone leader, Cameahwait, turned out to be Sacagawea's brother! The expedition got its horses and enjoyed Cameahwait's hospitality, even though he was in a hurry to lead his hungry band across the mountains to go buffalo hunting on the plains.

- **Old Toby:** Cameahwait sent Old Toby, a member of his band, to lead the Corps of Discovery on the Nez Perce path over the mountains. The passage was unforgiving: It snowed heavily; Old Toby got lost once; some of the horses fell to their deaths; others were slaughtered and eaten by the starving party.

- **Unnamed Shoshone women:** The Corps of Discovery had horses to cross the jagged Bitterroot Mountains. But perhaps because no *Sherpas* (the acclaimed packers of the Himalaya) lived in North America, Shoshone women, unnamed and unheralded by Lewis and Clark in their journals, carried most of the explorers' baggage over the mountains.

Giving aid: Salish (Three Eagles)

Upon entering the Bitterroot Valley, before ascending the mountains, the Corps of Discovery met a large Salish — or Flathead as Lewis and Clark called them — Indian camp at Ross's Hole in present day Montana. The Salish leader, Three Eagles, concluded that the group was not a war party and welcomed, fed, and swapped horses with them.

Rescuing the Corps: Nez Perce

The starving, exhausted Corps of Discovery emerged from the mountains at Weippe Prairie in present day western Idaho, where they met the Nez Perce or Pierced Nose Indians. The Nez Perce, who had heard the explorers were coming, fed and sheltered the ragged group, taught them to make dugout canoes for the final river segment of their journey and looked after their horses until they returned the following spring. The following Nez Perce people provided valuable assistance to the Corps:

- ✔ **Walammottinin (Twisted Hair):** An elder leader of the Nez Perce, Walammottinin, or Twisted Hair, greeted Lewis and Clark warmly, drew them a map of the route to the Columbia River, and agreed to accompany the expedition and serve as intermediary with the tribes downriver.

- ✔ **Watkuweis:** An elder woman of Twisted Hair's camp, Watkuweis had once been a captive of the Blackfeet and later lived with white traders in Canada who treated her well. When the Nez Perce debated whether to kill the explorers for their guns and goods, she urged them to do the Americans "no hurt." Her people responded by welcoming the Corps with open hospitality.

- ✔ **Tetoharsky:** A younger Nez Perce leader, Tetoharsky traveled with Twisted Hair and the Corps of Discovery down the Columbia River as far as The Dalles (about 90 miles east of present-day Portland, Oregon) and translated for the Americans with the Wanapums and Yakamas.

Showing the troops a different world: The Columbia River tribes

After they proceeded as far at the Columbia River, Lewis and Clark met cultures and landscapes vastly different from any they had encountered before. These were salmon people, fishermen rather than hunters. On the upper river, they lived in reed mat houses, not tepees or earth lodges. Floating the upper Columbia, Lewis and Clark passed through Palouse, Wanapum, Yakama, Walla Walla, Cayuse, Umatilla, Wishram, Klickatat, and Wasco lands. The expedition was warmly received by these tribal leaders:

- ✔ **Cutssahnem:** The Wanapum leader Cutssahnem welcomed the Corps of Discovery with great pomp and circumstance and provided a map of the Columbia River tribes.

- ✔ **Yelleppit:** Hoping to keep the expedition's trade goods for his people, Yelleppit, the Walla Walla leader, welcomed the Corps of Discovery with warmth and tried to persuade them to stay longer in his territory.

Teaching a lesson in trade: Chinooks and Clatsops

On the lower Columbia, as it neared the Pacific, the tribes lived in plank houses and traveled in large, graceful, beautiful, seaworthy canoes. And they could out-bargain anybody. Clackamas, Skilloot, Multnomah, Cowlitz, Kathlamet, Wahkiakum, Chinook, Clatsop, Chilwitz, Clatskanie, and Tillamook people lived along the lower Columbia and Pacific coast. Lewis and Clark built their third winter encampment, Fort Clatsop, near present-day Astoria, Oregon, on the south side of the Columbia River. Relations with the neighbors were not as friendly as they had been with the Mandans the year before, primarily due to a failure to communicate (see Chapter 14).

Lewis and Clark encountered the following Chinook and Clatsop representatives:

- ✔ **Comcomly:** The most powerful political and trade leader at the mouth of the Columbia, Chinook headman Comcomly never visited Fort Clatsop.

- ✔ **Cuscalar:** The Clatsop Cuscalar visited Fort Clatsop and offered gifts and women. Lewis and Clark refused both, insulting Cuscalar and his family.

- ✔ **Coboway (Comowooll):** Coboway, also known as Comowooll to Lewis and Clark, was a friendly and honorable neighbor. But in a nasty breach of their own rules, Lewis and Clark stole a canoe from him for their return journey. In March 1806, despite Lewis's increasing paranoia and ranting about "treacherous savages," the Corps of Discovery gave Fort Clatsop to Coboway, and then headed home.

Encountering lethal force: Piegan Blackfeet

On the return journey, while Clark explored the Yellowstone country, Lewis took a small party, including Reuben Field, Joseph Field, and George Drouillard, to explore the Marias River drainage that ran deep into Blackfeet territory. The Blackfeet were the superpower of what is now Montana; they had guns and controlled the area's trade. In a fateful encounter between Lewis's party and a group of eight young Blackfeet men, the Americans killed two of the Indians. They were the only people other than Charles Floyd, who died of illness, to perish in the course of the exploration. The two following members of the Piegan Blackfeet nation died at the hands of the Corps:

- ✔ **Calf Looking:** In the dawn hours of July 21, 1806, 13-year-old Calf Looking was among the group of Blackfeet who took guns from the still-sleeping Americans. Reuben Field chased him and stabbed him to death.

- ✔ **Unnamed Piegan youth:** After Calf Looking's death, another Blackfeet youth tried to take Lewis's horses. Lewis, who was growing increasingly depressed and touchy, shot and killed him.

Offering Support: Tutors and Traders

Many people helped Lewis and Clark in their preparations for the expedition, and others provided service during the first months of the trek. This section gives an honorable mention of some of the people who played a brief but important role in the Voyage of Discovery.

Thinking big: Lewis's tutors

At Thomas Jefferson's suggestion, some of the finest minds of the time tutored Lewis in the sciences, providing him with information that was essential for the safety and success of the mission. He spent time studying with each of these men, who had made important historical contributions of their own:

- ✔ **Dr. Benjamin Smith Barton:** Barton was professor of botany at the University of Pennsylvania and Thomas Jefferson's long time friend and colleague at the American Philosophical Society. He had written the first botany textbook in the United States, which Lewis carried on the expedition. Jefferson sent Lewis to Barton to study botany and learn how to collect and preserve botanical specimens.

✔ **Andrew Ellicott:** Ellicott was America's foremost astronomer and mathematician. Jefferson sent Lewis to Lancaster, Pennsylvania, to study celestial navigation under Ellicott.

✔ **Robert Patterson:** Patterson was another Philadelphia mathematician who further instructed Lewis in the use of navigational instruments, such as the chronometer and sextant.

✔ **Dr. Benjamin Rush:** Thomas Jefferson's fellow member of the American Philosophical Society in Philadelphia, Dr. Benjamin Rush was the most revered physician of his time. Like Jefferson, Rush was a signer of the Declaration of Independence. He was the inventor of a particularly effective purgative pill that proved to be a godsend for the Corps of Discovery's occasional digestive disorders. Jefferson sent Lewis to Philadelphia in 1803 to study medicine with Rush before embarking on America's epic journey.

✔ **Dr. Caspar Wistar:** Another of the era's most prominent scientists, Caspar Wistar was another member of the American Philosophical Society, professor of anatomy at the University of Pennsylvania, and a paleontologist who believed, as did Jefferson, that woolly mammoths and mastodons may still exist in the West. He taught Lewis about fossils and how to look for them.

Supplying goods and info: Merchants and traders

A number of prominent merchants and not-so-illustrious traders provided Lewis and Clark with crucial goods and information, both before the expedition launched and in the first months of the journey. They include the following:

✔ **The Chouteaus:** Founders of the city of St. Louis, Pierre and Auguste Chouteau and their brother-in-law Charles Gratiot were the most prominent and powerful St. Louis citizens when Lewis and Clark arrived in 1803. They were wealthy merchants who sold Lewis flour, corn, salt, pork, candles, tools, and Indian gifts and trade goods (such as beads, cooking utensils, cloth, knives, and other items) for the journey.

✔ **Joseph Gravelines:** Gravelines was a trader who had lived among the Arikaras for 13 years when Lewis and Clark arrived in their territory. He spoke French, English, Sioux, and Arikara and provided valuable information to the Americans.

✔ **Manuel Lisa:** Another giant of the Missouri River fur trade, Manuel Lisa was a wealthy St. Louis merchant, a competitor of the Chouteaus, and an additional supplier of goods to the Corps of Discovery in 1803. Upon Lewis and Clark's return to St. Louis in 1806, Lisa mounted his own exploration of the upper reaches of the Missouri, subsequently establishing trading posts as far as the Yellowstone country.

✔ **James Mackay:** A Scottish immigrant, Mackay was manager of affairs for the Spanish Missouri Fur Company on the upper Missouri. In the 1790s, he had sent his own aborted expedition up the river, hoping to reach the Pacific. He was a Spanish official in St. Louis when Lewis and Clark arrived to make final preparations for their exploration. Mackay supplied them with valuable information and maps.

✔ **Pierre-Antoine Tabeau:** Like Gravelines, Tabeau was a fur trader living among the Arikaras. He provided a great deal of information about the political realities and jealousies of the Missouri River tribes.

Playing a Leading Role: The Land and the Rivers

No account of the Lewis and Clark expedition can be only about the people. The land and the rivers of the American West are what the Corps of Discovery explored, so in this section, we give you a brief look at the geography that the Corps of Discovery traveled. And the good news is: It's all still here for you to visit and enjoy! (The bad news is that some parts of the rivers that have been drowned by dams, cities that are now mostly paved, native vegetation that has been plowed under and planted in corn, and some wildlife that has become extinct.)

Jefferson's backyard and the first stages of the journey

When Jefferson instructed Meriwether Lewis to do the exploring, the preparations began in the president's backyard. The following are sites that were important in the birthing stage of the expedition:

✔ **Monticello:** Jefferson's home and architectural masterpiece in Charlottesville, Virginia, Monticello is where the Lewis and Clark expedition was conceived. Some historians have called it "Mission Control."

✔ **Washington, D.C.:** Then, as now, Washington was the seat of government and power for the United States. In 1800, however, right after Washington had became the nation's capitol, it had a smaller population than the Mandan and Hidatsa villages that Lewis and Clark would visit in 1804–1805. Meriwether Lewis served as President Jefferson's private secretary, living and working in the East Wing of the White House. There, the two men planned the greatest camping trip in history.

- **Harpers Ferry:** In March 1803, Lewis went to the U.S. Army Arsenal at Harpers Ferry in what was then Virginia, now West Virginia, to obtain armaments, ammunition, knives, tomahawks, and fishing gear for the expedition. He also supervised construction of his pet project there: an iron frame collapsible boat that he hoped to use on the shallow upper reaches of the Missouri River.

- **Philadelphia:** The City of Brotherly Love was *the* American city of 1800, home of the Liberty Bell and the Declaration of Independence. It was also home to most of America's most learned scholars. Jefferson sent Lewis to Philadelphia to study astronomy, botany, mathematics, celestial navigation, medicine, and other subjects he would need to gather scientific information about the West and to complete his journey safely and successfully.

- **Pittsburgh:** Lewis commissioned boat builders in the river city of Pittsburgh, Pennsylvania, to build the 55-foot keelboat that he and Jefferson had designed to be the flagship of the expedition. Lewis sent all the provisions and arms that he had purchased in Philadelphia and Harpers Ferry to Pittsburgh, where he put all the goods together. By August 31, Lewis and the keelboat were on the Ohio River headed for Louisville and co-captain William Clark.

- **Falls of the Ohio:** Lewis reached the Falls of the Ohio River between Louisville, Kentucky, and Clarksville, Indiana, in October 1803 to join Clark and his Kentucky recruits. The Falls are actually a series of long, wild, and beautiful rapids, cascading over shelves of fossil-laden limestone. The river made a 24-foot drop in little more than two miles — a navigational challenge at the time that was later tamed by locks and dams. An extraordinary interpretive center now overlooks the Falls at Clarksville.

- **Camp Dubois:** The Wood River, or River Dubois, flows into the Mississippi upstream from St. Louis on the Illinois side. Its mouth was directly across from the mouth of the Missouri River in 1803, although nature has since altered that layout. Lewis and Clark arrived there in November 1803. Fur trader Nicholas Jarrot allowed Lewis and Clark to use his 400 acres at the mouth of the Dubois to construct the Corps of Discovery's first winter camp. From there, Lewis and Clark recruited most of the rest of the party and departed for the Missouri River in May 1804.

- **St. Louis:** More than 40 years old when Lewis and Clark arrived, the city of St. Louis was the center of the fur trade for the Missouri River country. Its population was over 1,000, including many prosperous merchants and French traders, such as founders Auguste and Pierre Chouteau. St. Louis was already the gateway to the West. There, Lewis completed his purchases of supplies for the expedition. Also there, with great international ceremony, the transfer of the Louisiana Territory from Spain to France to the United States took place on March 9, 1803.

Pushing the boundaries: The U.S. in 1800

Although only 24 years old in 1800, the United States of America was already outgrowing its boundaries (see the following figure). According to the 1800 census, the population had grown 35 percent in a decade. The new western states of Kentucky and Tennessee were growing even faster — nearly 300 percent since 1790.

Lisa S. Reed.

America's great westward migration had begun. Several wars defeating the Shawnees, Mingos, and other tribes of what was then called the Northwest (present day Ohio, Indiana, Illinois, and Michigan) had opened up vast tracts of Indian country to American real estate speculation and settlement.

President Thomas Jefferson certainly was looking west. The agrarian Utopia he envisioned would require lots of land. While lamenting the tragic fate of America's "noble savages," he was planning the acquisition, exploration, settlement, and cultivation of their lands by white Americans.

✔ **St. Charles:** A charming village of about 450 mostly French Canadians, St. Charles was founded in 1769. Clark and the boats arrived there in May 16, 1804, from Camp Dubois and waited for Lewis to arrive overland from St. Louis. While waiting, the men occupied their time attending balls and generally being the toast of the town. On May 21, 1804, the Corps of Discovery put into the Missouri River and headed upstream, and the exploration began.

Expanding the country: The Louisiana Territory

Bounded by the Mississippi River on the east and the Oregon Territory and New Spain on the west, the Louisiana Territory comprised 828,000 square miles in the center of the North American continent. An overextended Napoleon Bonaparte and France sold it to the United States in 1803 for $15 million, or about 3¢ an acre. President Thomas Jefferson sent Meriwether Lewis and the Corps of Discovery to explore it via the Missouri River, open it to U.S. trade, and find the mythical Northwest Passage to the Pacific Ocean. (See Chapter 3.)

Winding through the West: The expedition's water trail

The most convenient mode of travel in 1800 was by river. Jefferson and Lewis surmised that the expedition could travel by river: up the Missouri to a short mountain crossing, then to the westward flowing Columbia River, and then to the Pacific Ocean.

The following lists the actual water trail that they traveled (see Figure 2-6):

✔ **Ohio River:** Lewis traveled the length of the Ohio River (through Delaware, Miami, Mingo, and Shawnee homelands) from Pittsburgh to Louisville (where he met Clark), to the mouth of the Ohio at the Mississippi River near Fort Massac. Then, as now, the Ohio was a major route of commerce.

✔ **Mississippi River:** Lewis and Clark traveled the mighty Mississippi from the mouth of the Ohio upriver to the mouths of the River Dubois (where they camped for the winter of 1803–1804) and of the Missouri River at St. Charles (where they embarked on the expedition). To an even greater extent than the Ohio, the Mississippi was, and still is, a great avenue of commerce.

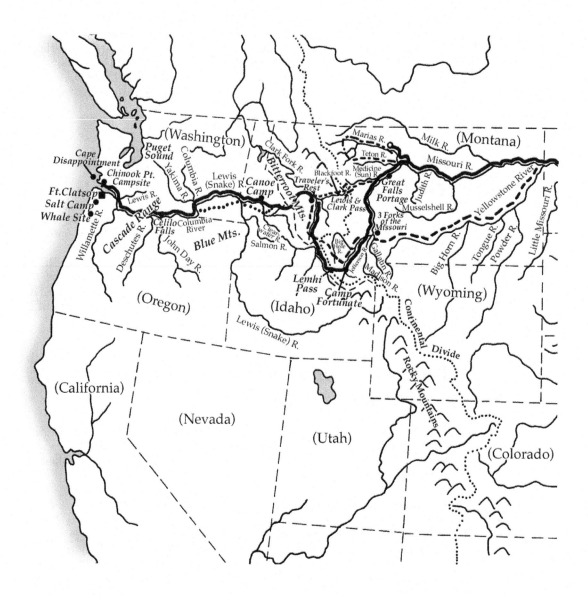

Figure 2-6: Rivers traveled by the Lewis and Clark expedition.

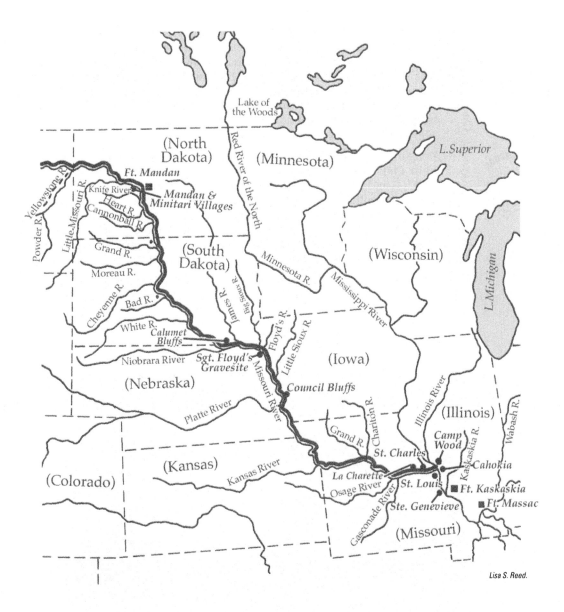

Lisa S. Reed.

- ✔ **Missouri River:** People described the Missouri River (see Figure 2-7) as the Big Muddy because it carried tons of mud that was dumped into it from prairie tributaries a mile wide and an inch deep. From its mouth near St. Charles to its headwaters in the mountains of present day Montana, the Missouri flowed through the homelands of Oto, Missouri, Osage, Ponca, Kansas, Pawnee, Omaha, Sioux, Arikara, Mandan, Hidatsa, Assiniboine and Blackfeet nations. It was the primary route of exploration for the Corps of Discovery.

  Along its length, Lewis and Clark recorded a paradise of flora, fauna, White Cliffs — which Lewis described as "seens of visionary inchantment" — and a series of Great Falls that also enchanted Lewis but caused a month's delay because the men had to *portage* (travel overland between bodies of water) their boats around them. The Missouri was rapid and shallow, clogged with sand bars, snags and crumbling banks. Progress upstream was challenging — full of mosquitoes and cultural misunderstanding — but beautiful, bountiful, and wild.

- ✔ **Columbia River:** The awesome Columbia marked the final approach to the Pacific for the Corps of Discovery. It was full of salmon and populous with Umatilla, Cayuse, Wanapum, Walla Walla, Cowlitz, Multnomah, Chinook, and other native people.

  By October 1805, the Corps of Discovery was passing through spectacular cliffs and having a wild ride down and around thundering rapids and cataracts extending 55 miles through the Columbia Gorge. The expedition passed the ancient aboriginal fishing area of enormous, thundering Celilo Falls — now completely inundated by the many dams on the Columbia.

Figure 2-7:
The Missouri River.

Courtesy of National Park Service, Lewis and Clark National Historic Trail.

- **Pacific Ocean:** "Ocian in View! O! the Joy" — William Clark's immortal words say it all. Upon the expedition's arrival at the western ocean, Clark estimated that the Corps had traveled 4,142 miles from the mouth of the Missouri.

- **Yellowstone River:** On the way West, the expedition passed the mouth of the Yellowstone River near the border between present-day North Dakota and Montana. On the return leg of the journey, while Lewis explored the Marias River, Clark and his party traveled down the Yellowstone to the Missouri, through Crow Indian country. There he left the only physical evidence that remains of the expedition along its entire route. He carved his signature into the soft sandstone wall of a massive rock formation he named Pompy's Tower for Sacagawea's son, the toddler Jean Baptiste Charbonneau (see the "Becoming the youngest explorer: Jean Baptiste Charbonneau" section earlier in this chapter).

Sprawling future farmland: The Great Plains

Most of the journey took place up the Missouri River, through the Great Plains (refer to Figure 2-7). Lewis and Clark recorded massive herds of game animals, many new to European science. Lewis also collected hundreds of botanical specimens for Jefferson, and the explorers pronounced the vast windswept prairies to be perfect for the expansion of American agriculture.

These are some of the important sites along the Corps' trail through the Great Plains:

- **Council Bluff:** After searching in vain for Indians to meet with to explain that the United States now owned their lands and that the Great White Father in Washington was their new leader, Lewis and Clark finally had their first meeting with Western tribes — Otoes and Missouris — at their Council Bluff camp, near, but not the same as, present-day Council Bluffs, Iowa.

- **Spirit Mound:** A bit farther upriver from Council Bluff, Lewis and Clark stopped to hike to the top of Spirit Mound near the White Stone or Vermillion River in present day South Dakota. The Omaha, Sioux, and Otoes, among others, believed that the mound was inhabited by fierce little devils who killed anyone who ventured there.

- **The Mandan and Hidatsa Villages:** The two Mandan and five Hidatsa villages that sat on the banks of the Missouri and Knife Rivers in present-day North Dakota, north of Bismarck, comprised the great agricultural and trading center of the northern plains. The Corps of Discovery arrived there in late October 1804 and built its second winter camp near the Mandan village of Mitutanka.

✔ **Fort Mandan:** Built of cottonwood logs on the east side of the Missouri, Fort Mandan housed the Corps of Discovery from November 1804 to April 1805, through the brutally cold northern plains winter. Although temperatures dropped to 45 degrees below zero, the men of the expedition developed warm relations with the Mandan hosts and hostesses.

Presenting a vast barrier: The Rocky Mountains

Lewis and Clark expected to have to cross mountains like Virginia's Blue Ridge — not too high, narrow in reach, and hospitable in climate — on their way to the Pacific. Instead, they encountered wave after wave of a sheer, high, snow covered, nearly impenetrable barrier, the Continental Divide (see Figure 2-8).

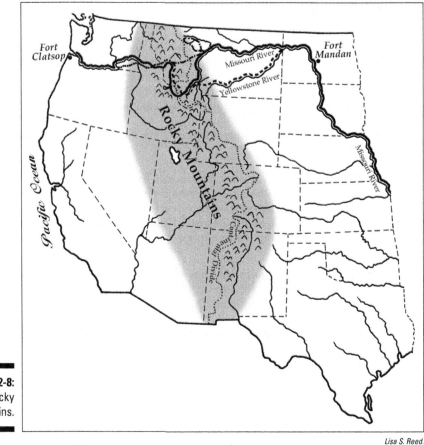

Figure 2-8:
The Rocky Mountains.

Lisa S. Reed.

The following were noteworthy sites on the path of the mountain crossing:

- ✔ **Gates of the Mountains:** In late July 1805, the Missouri River began to grow smaller and shallower as it got closer and closer to the mountains, near present-day Helena, Montana. It passed between steep cliffs that wore "a dark and gloomy aspect," according to the gloomy Lewis. He named the canyon Gates of the Mountains (see Chapter 11).

- ✔ **The Bitterroots:** In September and October 1805, with a Shoshone guide named Old Toby, the Corps of Discovery crossed the steep and rocky Bitterroot Range from present day Montana to Idaho. The crossing was dangerous, difficult, cold, and hungry, through deep snow and around steep drop-offs. With winter coming on, the party arrived safely in Nez Perce country that offered westward flowing rivers.

- ✔ **Two Medicine:** On the return journey, while exploring the Marias River area east of what is now Glacier National Park in Blackfeet territory, Lewis and his party encountered a small group of Blackfeet, or Piegan, Indians. The nervous meeting resulted in the deaths of two young Blackfeet — the only killings to result from the exploration.

Changing weather and cultures: The Pacific Northwest

After they were on the Columbia, the Corps of Discovery met different cultures, weather, and ecosystems than they had previously encountered — the great Northwest rain forests, savvy Chinook traders, and lots of rain. (See Figure 2-9.)

The expedition built its third winter encampment on the south side of the Columbia near present-day Astoria, Oregon, and settled in as guests of the Chinook and Clatsop Indians. It rained, rained, and rained some more. The group spent the winter in this wet and unfamiliar environment before packing the boats and beginning the long journey home.

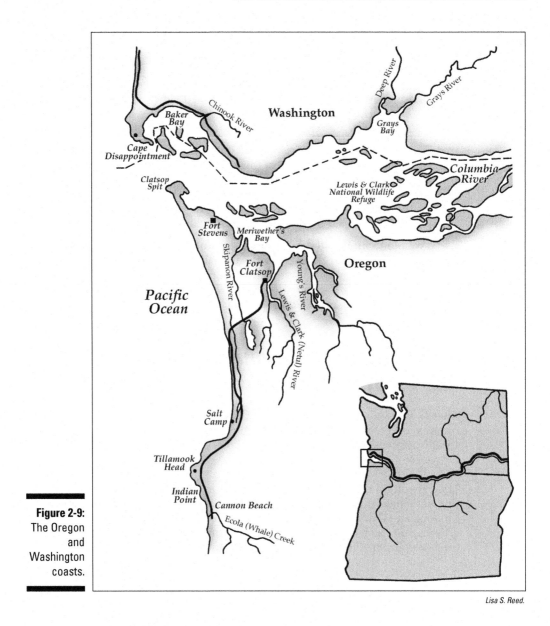

Figure 2-9:
The Oregon and Washington coasts.

Chapter 3

Compelling Lewis and Clark West

In This Chapter

▶ Speculating about mammoths, big salty mountains, and the western Eden

▶ Competing to find the mythical passage

▶ Understanding Jefferson's fascination with the West

▶ Buying Louisiana from Napoleon

*P*rior to the Lewis and Clark expedition, few Americans knew much about the American West. And most of the speculation was wrong (common theories involved woolly mammoths, big rock-salt mountains, and the lost tribes of Israel).

Several European countries vied for the discovery of a waterway across the West to the Pacific Ocean. The waterway, called the *Northwest Passage* or the *Passage to India,* was eventually proven by Lewis and Clark to be a figment of the Euro-American imagination.

Thomas Jefferson, who had many political, commercial, and scientific motives for sending explorers west, listed finding the passage at the top of his goals — even if the country his expedition would cross was inhabited by others. In fact, Jefferson was so intent on discovering the West that be began lobbying for such an expedition as early as 1783, although he wouldn't be successful until 1803. When Napoleon Bonaparte sold a big chunk of the American continent to the United States, Jefferson saw an easy opportunity to get the nation behind his dream.

This chapter describes how events unfolded that enabled Lewis and Clark to begin a journey that would dispel the myths and reveal the truth about the mysterious American West.

Don't Know Much about Geography

From the beginning of New World exploration, Europe's stubborn belief was that the world simply didn't have room for a continent between Europe and Asia. After they discovered that a continent did lie between them, Europe next believed that America was narrow from east to west and easily crossed by a waterway. The waterway across the continent was known as the Northwest Passage (also called the Passage to India) and was the one Christopher Columbus was looking for in 1492.

Looking for a new Eden

So convinced were the French of the Passage's existence that even the smallest scrap of evidence was enlisted in upholding the belief. If a discovery didn't absolutely prove otherwise, it became a confirmation of the existence of the Passage. So when explorers Marquette and Joliet found the mouth of the Missouri River in 1673, everyone involved believed that this river must be the Passage, or at least the key to discovering the Passage.

Keep in mind that no European country had actually explored the Missouri River to its source, and none had a clue whether another great river existed west of the Missouri. None of the European countries had explored the Rocky Mountains, so they didn't know whether the range was high or low, although some had guessed it marked a divide in the continent. Most of what was "known" by non-Indians about the American West boiled down to conjecture and wishful thinking.

Some people were convinced they knew what Lewis and Clark would see on their journey:

- About a thousand miles into the trip, they'd come to a mountain of rock salt that was 180 miles long and 45 miles wide.
- They'd see a number of volcanoes along the Missouri River.
- They'd encounter the woolly mammoth, long extinct elsewhere in the world. Jefferson himself believed they might find one.

In addition, the Indians of the West were believed to be different from those that the United States had already encountered and conquered. Some believed that western tribes were descended from pre-Columbian European explorers, such as the Norse or Welsh, or that they were remnants of the Lost Tribes of Israel. In some circles, it was assumed that Indian cultures became more advanced the further west they were located. Others believed that some tribes in the West would be white, and some would be black.

Mapping out the unknown

Among the most precious cargo on the Lewis and Clark expedition were maps that summarized the works of all the leading explorers and geographers of the day. They had a new map by Nicolas King, commissioned by Secretary of the Treasury, Albert Gallatin, for the expedition. Today, these maps are fascinating (as well as amusing) to look at because they bear almost no relation to the true geography of the West, especially the Missouri River, Rocky Mountains, and Pacific Northwest.

The flaws were not for lack of trying. Nicolas King had consulted two versions of the map of North America produced by Aaron Arrowsmith, the finest mapmaker of the time. The first version, from 1795, was made from data collected from the archives of the Hudson's Bay Company, the British fur trading company that had vast experience trekking around the West. It showed the Missouri River as a fragment unconnected to the "Stony Mountains" or the Mississippi River. A note said that the Stony Mountains were "3250 feet high above the level of their Base."

What you can ascertain from these primitive maps with their sketchy, mistaken information is that the Northwest was a deeply mysterious place to Euro-Americans of the time. The tendency was to fill in the parts that were least known with the most fanciful details.

The West represented new opportunity, new hope, so before it was explored by Lewis and Clark, the American West reached mythical proportions. It became the ideal, a garden, a new Eden — a place where the soils and climates were the best in the world, the natives were of ancient noble descent, the *portages* (traveling overland between bodies of water) were short, the mountains were small, and the barriers to a magnificent new existence were few.

Dispelling myths about the West

Even after Europeans found the continent to be rather substantial, faith in the existence of a waterway (or perhaps two waterways with a short overland trip in the middle) remained strong. Centuries passed, and many explorations were launched before minds were changed on this score. In fact, this was the main bubble that Lewis and Clark burst.

The history of the 130 years (1673–1803) that passed between the explorations of Marquette and Joliet and Lewis and Clark — although often disappointing in the details — didn't dim this belief. Explorations by the Frenchman Hennepin a short way up the Missouri in 1680 established the four central beliefs that Lewis and Clark would operate from when they began their journey from Wood River in 1804.

✔ The Missouri was a mighty river originating far to the west.

✔ Its source was in a range of mountains in the western interior.

✔ You could see the sea (or even ships) from those mountains.

✔ From those mountains, you could locate another great river that flowed to the Pacific.

The Missouri went through a "magnificent pass," one official wrote confidently in the early 1700s, "through a range of mountains not requiring a difficult portage." Pierre Charlevoix, a *Jesuit* (Roman Catholic religious order) sent by the French duke of Orleans to find out more about Louisiana, assured the duke that "after sailing up the Missouri as far as is navigable you come to a great river which runs westward and discharges into the Sea." France's search for the Passage to India ended in 1763, when Spain took control of Louisiana and Great Britain took over what was known then as "New France" (Canada).

But France's withdrawal didn't dampen enthusiasm for exploration. English, Spanish, and U.S. explorers took up the French gauntlet as the explorers of the Mississippi and Missouri river valleys in the last half of the 18th century. Little by little, improved scientific methods allowed for a more accurate view of the what the West was like. By the end of the century, longitudes and latitudes of key places could be determined and maps began to be accurate in a few of their details.

The sensational accounts of every journey that went a bit farther into the unknown were followed with fascination by the public and U.S. politicians. Thomas Jefferson avidly followed every report of every exploration on the continent, collecting and reading journals and pouring over maps. Jefferson was a rapt student during those intervening years of exploration before Lewis and Clark, and he would impart much of what he'd learned to Meriwether Lewis.

Jefferson's Motto: If at First You Don't Succeed . . .

President Jefferson was always thinking about the future of the United States and about the vast potential of the American continent. A century later, Henry David Thoreau would say that the United States had always been "realizing westward," and this fascination with the West was true of Jefferson more than any other early leader of the country. He believed that the West held the key to his country's future as a great republic.

Jefferson probably caught the Passage-to-India bug as a child at Shadwell, his father's estate in the Virginia piedmont. When Jefferson was a boy of 6, his father and some friends started the Loyal Land Company for the "discovery and sale of western lands" — meaning lands between Virginia and the Mississippi River. One of Jefferson's teachers wrote three years later that the Loyal Land Company was sending some people "in search of that river Missouri . . . in order to discover whether it had any communication with the Pacific Ocean."

Well-educated, a Francophile (lover of all things French), and fond of luxury, Jefferson's fascination with the American West as an adult seems contrary to his personality. In fact, he had made the long trip across the ocean to Europe but never traveled west past the Virginia border. Yet few people worked harder to discover the territory than Jefferson, and he understood that the future of the United States and the unexplored West were bound up together. Like leaders around the world, Jefferson believed that whichever country explored the continent to the Pacific Ocean could claim it for its own.

In 1783, twenty years before the Lewis and Clark expedition, Thomas Jefferson wrote to George Rogers Clark (William Clark's older brother) about leading an expedition to the West. Jefferson heard that the British were raising money for their own exploration from the Mississippi to California. Jefferson wondered: Would Clark lead an American party for the same purpose? Clark would not. He believed the trip, executed correctly, would take four to five years. Clark's debts had mounted during his Revolutionary War leadership, and he needed to spend those years repairing his financial affairs. But Jefferson didn't give up; his interest in exploration only continued and intensified.

Crossing swords with Catherine the Great

In 1786, when Jefferson was U.S. ambassador to France, he encouraged an English adventurer, John Ledyard, to make an expedition from Paris across Russia and Siberia. Ledyard, the plan went, would then pick up passage on a Russian ship across the Pacific Ocean to the Northwest and descend a river on the western side down to the Missouri River, working his way backward from what was to be Lewis and Clark's trip across the continent. Jefferson requested protection for Ledyard from Russia's Empress Catherine the Great, but she turned Jefferson down, calling the enterprise too "chimerical" for her taste. Not sure of his scheme but not liking it in any case, the Empress had Ledyard arrested in Siberia and deported to Poland.

Hiring a spy

In 1793, Jefferson led an effort by the American Philosophical Society to send Andre Michaux, a French botanist, from Philadelphia to the Pacific Ocean. The expedition was planned and underway when Jefferson found out that Michaux was a French spy and demanded that France recall him. (Perhaps Jefferson should have instead chosen Meriwether Lewis, who had applied for the job and been turned down as too young and inexperienced.)

After the Michaux mission failed, Jefferson lost interest, but only temporarily. For reasons other than the failed mission, he resigned from the office of Secretary of State under Washington and went into semi-retirement at Monticello for three years. Then he became vice-president to John Adams for four years. Expedition discussions did not resurface until 1801, when Jefferson became president. He was probably already thinking about who would lead the expedition when he asked his young friend Meriwether Lewis to be his secretary.

Copying a Scot

1802 saw the publishing of an account of the first successful transcontinental expedition by Alexander Mackenzie in 1792 and 1793. Mackenzie, a Scotsman employed by Britain's North West Company, had crossed Canada to the Pacific following the Peace River and its tributaries. Mackenzie had crossed the Continental Divide, and then tried to take the Fraser River to the coast. Finding the river too wild and its canyons too narrow for a boat, he went overland with some Indian guides to the coast, arriving at the ocean in what is now British Columbia.

Jefferson read Mackenzie's published account of the expedition in the summer of 1802, and it likely fanned the fire already burning in him to send an American expedition west. Alarmingly, Mackenzie recommended that the British government assume control of the Columbia River and West Coast. The British hadn't found the elusive Northwest Passage, but they had proved that a transcontinental expedition was feasible. Now was Jefferson's time to send an expedition across the Pacific Northwest to quash Britain's claims on the territory forever.

During the same decade, American Captain Robert Gray became the first white man to discover the Columbia River (which now divides the states of Washington and Oregon), so Jefferson knew that a mighty river on the other side of the Continental Divide matched the Missouri. If a short overland trek between them could be found, the elusive passage to the Orient would open a new economic frontier for the United States.

Jefferson's Euro Struggles

In the 1800s, the United States wasn't an isolated country. The U.S. had won a war for independence from Britain, but the Spanish and then the French owned and controlled a large portion of the North American continent. Then, as now, the destiny of the United States was bound up with the course of international events. Some foreign intrigue and a strange bit of kismet set the stage for the launching of the Lewis and Clark expedition.

Jefferson finagles, Spain worries

Late in 1802, Jefferson approached the Spanish minister, Carlos Martinez de Urujo, about sending a "small caravan" of Americans from the mouth of the Missouri to the Pacific Coast. Would Spain "take it badly" if he sent this purely scientific expedition across her territory? Of course, he told the Spanish, he'd have to tell Congress the expedition would be to advance commerce, but it *really* would be to advance knowledge. It would, in fact, be a completely noble and harmless venture.

"Ha," the Spanish must have thought. The Spanish minister replied that "an expedition of this nature could not fail to give umbrage [offense] to our Government." Jefferson appeared to drop the idea but Spain worried, as well she should have.

In January, 1803, just a month after hearing "no" from Spain, Jefferson sent a confidential message to Congress requesting funds for the Lewis and Clark expedition. It's only a matter of time, Jefferson told Congress, before Indians east of the Mississippi become farmers, and it was the government's duty to encourage this transition by establishing trading posts where they could buy their goods. British rivals working in Canada couldn't compete with a trade route along the Missouri, Jefferson predicted.

To cut down on objections from his political enemies, the Federalists, Jefferson cast the expedition as a "literary pursuit," an innocuous geographic and scientific exploration of the area. To get Congress to go along, however, he also had to play up the commercial advantages, the "great supplies of furs & peltry" that Indians on the Missouri River were sending to England. He requested the relatively paltry amount of $2,500 to supply the expedition.

The French kiss Louisiana good-bye

Napoleon Bonaparte, Emperor of France, was an unlikely booster of the Lewis and Clark expedition, but the timing of his political and military machinations in the New World set off a fortunate chain of events that changed the history of the expedition and of the United States.

A winding path to destiny

In the late 1700s, Napoleon became determined to restore a French colonial empire in North America. He began to realize his vision in 1800, when the Spanish government agreed in a secret treaty to "retrocede" — give back — to France all of the province of Louisiana, which encompassed 828,000 square miles west of the Mississippi River, along with the port of New Orleans (see Figure 3-1).

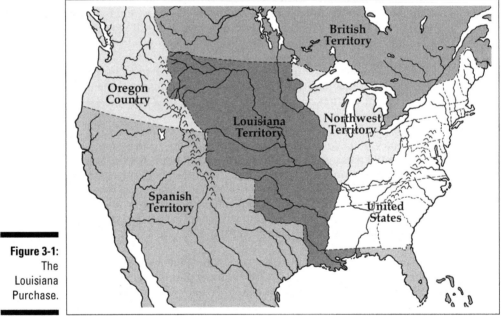

Figure 3-1:
The Louisiana Purchase.

Lisa S. Reed.

This news — greatly distressing to the United States — came from Europe in the spring of 1801. Instead of the weak and loose government of Spain on its western boundary, the United States would now have the aggressive militaristic France to worry about.

Jefferson anticipated the complaints that would mount about French control of the flow of goods on the Mississippi to the port of New Orleans. He urged U.S. Ambassador to France, Robert Livingston, to negotiate a sale from France of New Orleans and the colonies in Florida to the United States.

Although France had owned New Orleans since 1801, the French still had not shown up to take control of the port by the end of 1802. Late that year, the Spanish governor of New Orleans withdrew the U.S. right of deposit — the right to store goods waiting for shipment. The order shocked the country, infuriated the merchants, and annoyed the U.S. government.

Meanwhile, revolt rocked one of Napoleon's dependencies — the island of Santo Domingo in the West Indies, which was his staging ground to launch military forces, when they were needed, into Louisiana. Toussaint L'Ouverture, a brilliant former slave and now an army general, mounted an insurrection against Napoleon's 35,000 French troops and with the help of yellow fever, killed over 24,000 of them, including a French commander. Napoleon was understandably disconsolate. With this defeat, Napoleon became stretched too thin in men, arms, and money to carry out his plans for Louisiana. He was also desperate for funds to further his ambitions on his own continent. "I renounce Louisiana," he declared, knowing that he could no longer protect it militarily.

The real estate deal of the century

Sensing that Napoleon's troubles were just the opening required, Jefferson sent his friend and fellow statesman James Monroe to France to offer Napoleon $7 million for New Orleans and Florida. "The future destinies of this republic rest on the success of your mission," Jefferson told Monroe. It was at that moment in January of 1803 that Jefferson sent a confidential message to Congress, asking them to back what would become the Lewis and Clark expedition.

Monroe was on his way to France, but Napoleon was impatient. After months of having his foreign minister, Tallyrand, stall on the subject of a land sale of any size, Napoleon ordered Tallyrand not to wait for Monroe. Instead, he wanted to talk to Livingston and get this over with.

Tallyrand astonished Livingston at their next meeting with the question, "what would you give for the whole?", meaning all of Louisiana's 828,000 square miles. Monroe arrived the next day and was equally astonished (and frustrated), because neither he nor Livingston had authorization to buy more than New Orleans and Florida. The only way to communicate with Jefferson was by letter via a very slow transatlantic ship. What to do?

Monroe and Livingston decided to proceed with a deal for "the whole" on behalf of the U.S. government for $15 million, despite their lack of legal authority. At three cents an acre, it was the greatest real estate deal in the history of the United States, and they were overjoyed to make it.

A cracked Constitution and a sealed deal

Jefferson, receiving the news, called it "a transaction replete with blessings to unborn millions of men." He set about getting a treaty through the Senate affirming the deal and succeeded, signing it in October of 1803. He confessed privately that in order to complete the purchase, he had "stretched the Constitution until it cracked." The Constitution contained no provision for the federal government to buy new territory by treaty. In this case, Jefferson the nation builder overrode Jefferson the anti-Federalist and staunch believer in limited government power.

The upshot was that Jefferson could send Lewis and Clark through a territory now claimed by the United States, a distinct advantage when meeting with tribes. The Louisiana Purchase had changed the nature of the Lewis and Clark expedition from a semi-secret mission to gather intelligence to an open journey to scout out the best spots for trading posts, future settlements, and military defenses.

Lewis and Clark would go on to dispel some of the myths about the West and reinforce others. They would see animals, plants, rivers, and mountains unknown to any but native peoples. They would be awestruck by the majesty of the landscapes and the harshness of the conditions when traveling through them. The West they would encounter and describe in their journals would be in many ways more amazing than a young country's wildest imagining.

Part II
Into the Known: Monticello to Fort Mandan

The 5th Wave   By Rich Tennant

DURING THE WINTER OF 1804, LEWIS AND CLARK MEMBER PIERRE CRUZATTE ENTERTAINS THE MANDAN INDIANS AND BECOMES THE FIRST WILDERNESS STAND-UP COMIC

I love when he does this.

In this part . . .

You follow Meriwether Lewis as he studied the sciences and bought boats and provisions for a water exploration. You also keep an eye on William Clark as he shared command of the expedition and helped the first recruits of the Corps of Discovery settle into winter training at Camp Dubois.

You get front-row seats to the adventure as you read about how the expedition embarked on May 21, 1804, from St. Charles, Missouri, and made its way up the Missouri River to the Mandan villages in present-day North Dakota. There, they built their second winter encampment and got friendly with the Mandans while the temperature dipped to 45° below zero. And they delivered a baby boy who became the youngest explorer.

Chapter 4

Gambling Big — the Jeffersonian Way

In This Chapter

▶ Examining the pre-expedition life and times of Meriwether Lewis

▶ Seeking money, guns, and boats

▶ Signing up Clark as co-commander

The close relationship between explorer Meriwether Lewis and Thomas Jefferson began when Lewis was a child and their families were neighbors. While Lewis was serving in the Army, Jefferson became President, inviting Lewis to be his private secretary and two years later, to lead a "scientific" expedition through the newly acquired Louisiana Territory to the Pacific Ocean. Together, they raised funds and began to plot the expedition, buying guns and ordering boats built for the voyage. Lewis invited his former captain and friend, William Clark, to be his co-commander for the expedition.

In this chapter, we reveal how the personal histories of Lewis and Clark brought them together to share their historic adventure.

Jefferson and Lewis: Almost Kinfolk

Jefferson never appeared to waver in his decision to send Meriwether Lewis to lead the Corps of Discovery. Though he had turned Lewis down to lead a similar trip when Lewis was only 18 years old, he thought Lewis was ready the second time around. Jefferson had known Lewis nearly all of his life, and knew his roots. He wasn't just trusting a young man who was in his acquaintance.

Kissing cousins

Thomas Jefferson called the Lewis family one of the most distinguished in Virginia. Two of Jefferson's siblings had married into a line of the Lewis family, and Nicholas Lewis, Meriwether's uncle, became a close friend who managed Jefferson's affairs during the years that he was minister to France.

Meriwether Lewis's grandfather, Robert, was the first Lewis to come to America in 1635. A British Army colonel, he was given 33,033 acres of land in Albemarle County, Virginia, in a grant from the king. He became a successful planter. When the colonel died, his fifth son, William, Lewis's father, inherited a rustic plantation named Locust Hill near Jefferson's home of Monticello. William Lewis married his second cousin, Lucy Meriwether, in 1769. The Meriwether and Lewis families were extremely close, full of cousins who kept choosing each other for mates. The families intermarried 11 times in the 18th century. (Intermarriage between families was pretty common at the time.)

Losing a father

William and Lucy Lewis had three children: Jane, Meriwether (born August 18, 1774), and Reuben. For the first years of Meriwether's life, his father was away fighting in the Revolutionary War. Home in November on a brief leave from the Army, Lewis's father attempted to cross the icy, swollen Rivanna River at flood stage, drowning his horse and nearly himself. Soaked and freezing, he walked back to Locust Hill and went to bed. Two days later, he was dead from pneumonia. Meriwether was only five years old.

Meriwether's uncle Nicolas, Jefferson's friend, became Meriwether's *guardian* (a person, usually a relative, who looked after a minor's inherited property until the minor came of age). Six months after his father died, Meriwether's mother remarried a friend of the family, John Marks. Lucy and John Marks had two more children.

A doctoring mother

Lucy Lewis Marks lived to be almost 86 years old, an extremely old age in the 19th century. Meriwether's letters to her show how fond of her he was. A remarkable woman on several accounts, she was a country doctor without a diploma, riding horseback to treat her sick neighbors, as well as doctoring her family and slaves. Because there were no hospitals or clinics and few trained doctors in Virginia or anywhere else in the United States at the time, lay healers or field doctors were common — for the lay doctor to be a woman, however, was uncommon.

Lucy Marks understood the medicinal properties of plants and grew medicinal herbs. She taught Meriwether what she knew, which later was helpful to him both while he was in the Army and as he led the expedition. People who knew the family said that Meriwether inherited many character traits, including energy and courage, from his mother. He also inherited a tendency toward depression from his father.

Becoming a rambling man

When he was eight years old, Meriwether went with his stepfather and other Virginians on an expedition to colonize a piece of wilderness land in Georgia. Lewis stayed in Georgia three or four years and learned many of the skills necessary for survival on the frontier. There, he developed a love for rambling — walking alone for hours across the countryside, observing plants, animals, and the geography. It was a passion that would last his entire life.

Getting a little schooling

At 13, Lewis returned to Virginia to get more education and prepare to take over the operation of Locust Hill. Lewis was curious, adventurous, and a good student, learning to read and write without any formal schooling at all until he was 13. Because Albemarle County had no schools at that time, Lewis lived with various tutors in their homes, a common way to get a formal education in early America.

The tutoring, which lasted about four years, appears to have taught him basic math, botany, natural history, and geography, among other subjects. He improved his writing skill and probably read classic literature. He didn't receive a great education by the standards of the time but it wasn't a lousy one, either.

At age 18, Lewis took over Locust Hill, about 2,000 acres of tobacco plantation and food crops, 100 or so animals, and over 20 slaves. Management of a small plantation at the turn of the 18th century didn't mean backbreaking labor — that was done by the slaves — but he would have needed to master farming, distilling, breeding, slaughtering, blacksmithing, bookkeeping, and a host of other skills.

Wanting out, signing up

Lewis excelled at farming but had no passion for it. Instead, he wanted to see the continent, to explore, to continue the rambling that he loved — and he knew that his mother was fully capable of running the plantation, which Lewis had inherited because of Virginia's law of *primogeniture* (a father's property passes to the first born son). When the American Philosophical Society of Philadelphia began a subscription campaign at Thomas Jefferson's urging to send an expedition to the Pacific Ocean in 1792, Lewis "warmly solicited" Jefferson to let Lewis lead the expedition. Jefferson thought the world of Lewis and his family, but he thought Lewis was too young to lead a dangerous expedition and lacked the skills of the botanist chosen for the trip, Andre Michaux.

Not your modern Army

Lewis confessed to a love of the Army, but the U.S. Army in the early 1800s was not the "be all you can be" Army of today. There was one similarity, however: It was a giant ethnic melting pot, with men of many different backgrounds, social classes, and attitudes working side by side. Perks for officers like Lewis included taking one of the lower-class soldiers as a personal assistant or bringing one slave along to help out with the chores. Lewis would have been paid about $400 a year (the equivalent of $8,800 in 2003 dollars) and out of that, he would have had to pay for his own uniforms.

Rules for the officers could be strict but weren't always enforced: no swearing, no showing disrespect to a commanding officer or federal or state official, no leaving without permission, no keeping mistresses. Although drinking while on duty was forbidden, the chief pastime when not working was drinking heavily, as in, falling-down blotto. Consequently, the troops did a lot of arguing, brawling, and fist-fighting. Although, officially, it was prohibited, dueling was ignored (except when the result was death to one of the participants), because it was a common way of settling differences.

Flogging and other dire punishments were imposed on enlisted men who broke the rules. Many attempted to escape the regimen and the discipline and just disappear into frontier life. Frontier forts needed every soldier when Indians attacked, so desertion drew the harshest punishments, such as having to *run a gauntlet* several times (running between two rows of men who struck the deserter with clubs as he passed).

So, Lewis, restless and unhappy with a sedentary life at Locust Hill, volunteered at age 20 for the Virginia militia called out in 1794 by President Washington to put down the Whiskey Rebellion. (Scottish and Irish settlers in Pennsylvania running whiskey stills had taken up arms against the government in protest of a whiskey tax. They threatened to shoot the officials coming to collect taxes.)

Lewis was so eager to be in the 12,000-strong militia sent to quell the disturbance that he was one of the first men to enlist. He was a private until the fall of 1794, when he was commissioned an ensign (the lowest rung of commissioned officers, just below a junior grade lieutenant). "I am quite delighted with a soldier's life," he wrote to his mother after volunteering to stay in Pennsylvania when the rebellion petered out and the rest of the Virginia militia headed home.

He also wrote to his mother that when his enlistment in the militia was up, he was going to Kentucky to speculate in land and take care of some family business, but when the time came, he was commissioned as an ensign in the regular Army, instead. He was sent down the Ohio River to join General "Mad Anthony" Wayne's troops; he tried to explain his decision in a letter to his mother and signed it, "your ever sincere tho wandering Son."

Fighting a court martial

Lewis apparently did his share of heavy drinking, a regular event among officers in the Army of his day. He also argued a lot about politics: The Army was full of a political party known as the Federalists, yet Lewis was a Democratic-Republican (the anti-federalist party that Jefferson founded and led) and at odds with Federalist philosophy. Apparently he didn't get along, for political or other reasons, with his superior officer, and in November of 1795, when Lewis was 21 years old, he was brought before a court-martial on charges of getting drunk, insulting his superior officer, and disturbing the peace. He pled "not guilty" and after a full week of testimony, he was "acquitted with honor."

Meeting Clark for the first time

The commanding officer, General Wayne, knew about the conflict between Lewis and his superior officer and figured the problem wouldn't end with Lewis's acquittal on the court-martial charges. So he had Lewis transferred to a company of elite sharpshooters, commanded by Captain William Clark. For six months, Lewis and Clark got to know each other and became great friends. Clark left the Army in 1796 to go home to his family plantation near today's Louisville, Kentucky, to help his brother George Rogers Clark sort out some financial problems.

Finding an ideal job

In 1799, Lewis was promoted to lieutenant and posted to Charlottesville. A year later he was posted to Detroit and appointed regimental paymaster. That was a job Lewis really loved because he was able to travel by horseback to forts south of the Ohio River and travel up and down the river by *keelboat* (large, shallow freight boat) or *pirogue* (flat-bottomed boat like a canoe). In December 1800, Lewis was promoted to Captain.

White House Calling

Thomas Jefferson won the election of 1800 as the founder of the Democratic-Republican Party, a successor to the Anti-Federalists Party, that lasted until 1826. At the time, the Democratic-Republican Party was often referred to as the Republican Party, which is confusing, because the Republican Party we know today wasn't founded until 1854 as an anti-slavery political party.

When the contentious election of 1800 ended and Thomas Jefferson prepared to assume the office of president of the United States, he needed a private secretary to help him, and he knew exactly what man he wanted to fill the job. Eleven days before his inauguration, Jefferson posted a letter to Meriwether Lewis in care of General James Wilkinson, commander of the U.S. Army. Jefferson gave two reasons for wanting Lewis to be his aide de camp. First, for "his knowledge of the Western country and the Army" and second, because of a "personal acquaintance with him, owing from his being of my neighborhood."

"I most cordially acquiesce," Lewis replied to Jefferson's offer, "and with plea-sure accept the office." He accepted without having a clue about what his duties would be but believing Jefferson's promise that it would be an "easier office" than paymaster in the Army.

Meriwether Lewis, presidential aide

Jefferson wanted to cut the peacetime Army in half — in his view, it was too big, too expensive to keep up, and full of Federalists, the president's political enemies. But he needed someone to advise him about who the Army needed and who was expendable. So, in his first duties, Lewis devised a chart and a simple coding system for all commissioned officers. The system had 11 categories and corresponding symbols, including one for "first class men," second class, "second class but Republican (Democratic-Republican)," "opposed to the administration but respectable," "unworthy of their commis-sions," "unknown to us," and so on. Only those violently opposed to the administration were sure to be dropped. Otherwise, Lewis tried to make his selections based on merit.

Lewis took up residence in the White House with Jefferson, which sounds like an excellent perk but the house was a dismal place in 1801, sparsely fur-nished, cold and dank — and not even finished. Jefferson and Lewis were the only White House occupants besides the 11 servants Jefferson had brought with him from Monticello. (He even had to provide his own horse.) Jefferson and Lewis lived "like two mice in a church," the president wrote his daughter.

The house that each American president has called home has been at 1600 Pennsylvania Avenue since John Adams, the second U.S. president. The house was burned in the War of 1812 and then restored and painted a bright white, the reason people began calling it the White House. Even after it was renovated and furnished, most first families had difficulty enjoying the White House as a residence until central heating and air conditioning were installed. Lewis occupied what is now known as the East Room, an enormously beauti-ful space used today for White House entertaining or formal ceremonies, but a cavernous empty room in Lewis's day.

There, Lewis was exposed to "characters of influence in the affairs of our country," as Jefferson had promised, who would give him the advantage "of their wisdom." Contemporaries recorded Lewis's presence at important White House dinners. Social and official duties gave him many of the promised opportunities.

After a year of being private secretary, Lewis's role began to shift. He and Jefferson began to talk about another attempt to explore the continent to the Pacific Ocean. Lewis still had wanderlust, and Jefferson still had a burning ambition to expand the United States and ensure its prosperity (see Chapter 3).

Washington, D.C. and the White House Today

The nation's capital remains one of the most visited destinations in the world, despite a drop-off of travel after the September 11, 2001 terrorist attacks on the World Trade Center and the Pentagon.

Meriwether Lewis wouldn't recognize the White House or Capitol Hill, which have changed radically since 1803. The White House, whose tours are administered by the National Park Service, has had several facelifts and is a grand residence for the president and first family, as well as an office complex for the nation's highest ranking advisors.

Served by three airports — Dulles, Baltimore-Washington International (BWI), and Reagan National — Washington, D.C. is a monumental city, with memorials to presidents, veterans of war, and headquarters of Congress, the Supreme Court, the President, federal government agencies, foreign embassies, and thousands of national organizations. In addition to historical sites, Washington, D.C., boasts some of the nation's finest cultural attractions — the Smithsonian Museums, private museums, and the Kennedy Center for the Arts. It also has plenty of recreational opportunities, including boating and sailing on the Potomac and biking along the George Washington National Parkway or around the monuments. For Washington, D.C. visitor information, go to www.washington.org or call toll free, 800-422-8644.

Goading them on

In the summer of 1802, Lewis and Jefferson read an electrifying book about Alexander MacKenzie's successful expedition to the Pacific Coast across Canada. Having read it, Jefferson came to several conclusions.

- ✔ Although the journey to the Pacific Ocean across the continent via the Missouri River would be long and dangerous, it could and should be undertaken by the United States immediately.

- ✔ Based on MacKenzie's experience in the Canadian Rockies, the mountains to be crossed on the trip were relatively low-lying, probably like the Appalachians. So the route to the Pacific would be difficult but not *that* difficult.

- ✔ MacKenzie's call on the British to seize the day and claim the Northwest for themselves might actually happen, and time was wasting for the United States to make its claim.

Not perfect but close enough

In the summer and fall of 1802, Jefferson decided that Lewis would command the expedition — without even considering anyone else for the job. Jefferson explained that finding the perfect candidate, someone who was a botanist, natural historian, mineralogist, and astronomer and also had a rugged constitution, knowledge of the woods, and familiarity with Indians, was impossible. Without that perfect candidate, Jefferson decided that vigor and frontier experience trumped academics and that although he could teach Lewis enough science to suffice, he couldn't find anyone more trustworthy, fit, willing, and available.

Lewis was in great shape — over six feet tall with a lean frame. He was loyal and disciplined (when he wasn't moody and melancholic). He learned quickly what he needed to know, he was curious and observant, and he had a knack for writing and drawing.

Jefferson wasn't without trepidation about his choice. He admired Lewis greatly but also noted his tendency toward episodes of depression, or as Jefferson put it, his "melancholy" or "hypochondria."

And not everyone agreed that Lewis was the right choice to lead the Corps of Discovery. Jefferson's Attorney General Levi Lincoln thought Lewis was too impetuous and too much a risk-taker to lead an "enterprise of national consequence." "From my ideas of Capt. Lewis," Lincoln wrote to Jefferson, "he will be much more likely, in case of difficulty, to push too far, than to recede too soon."

One of the reasons that Jefferson chose Lewis was his "familiarity with Indians." But the fact is that Lewis didn't know a great deal more about Indians than Jefferson did, and knew little about Indians on the Missouri River. Hundreds of tribes and thousands of bands of Indians lived in the United States in 1803, and Lewis was acquainted with only a handful of them in the Ohio River Valley and from his boyhood in Virginia and Georgia. In addition, his experience with Indians as an Army officer had been adversarial.

Jefferson and Lewis Multi-Task

Thomas Jefferson's plan for the expedition called for Lewis to leave in the spring of 1803 and be in St. Louis by August 1, 1803, camping for winter midway up the Missouri River between St. Louis and the Mandan villages. But there was so much to do and so little time! He needed to go to Philadelphia to train in various disciplines the expedition required. Traveling in the winter was largely impossible, with no roads to speak of, unless you count dirt roads. A gravel road of sorts had just been built between Lancaster and Philadelphia, Pennsylvania, but that wasn't going to help him get to Philadelphia from Washington.

Lewis would have to wait until spring for passable roads that would allow him to travel to buy the things he needed and have them transported to Pittsburgh, where he would embark down the Ohio River.

What would the trip cost today?

One 1803 dollar is worth $12.24 today, so $2,500 in 1803 dollars is $30,600 in today's dollars. Of course, Lewis went seriously over budget, spending $38,722.35 on the expedition. That translates today into nearly half a million dollars. Still, it was a bargain then and would be now.

If you were budgeting for a caravan/boating/camping trip of 8,000 miles for 30 people over 28 months, you would spend about $756,000 if you figure that each person would cost you $30 dollars a day.

Some people have said that going to the Pacific Ocean in 1803 was like going to the moon in 1969. Making that comparison is difficult, however, because technology has advanced radically, and billions are spent on the space program. The analogy makes sense in terms of the enormity of the challenge but not in dollars and cents.

Jefferson set about drafting instructions for the expedition, setting out a clear mission and objectives. Meanwhile, Lewis had a thousand decisions to make. Who and what should he take? After St. Louis, there would be no place to stop and shop for supplies, nowhere to recruit more solders, nowhere to post a letter requesting aid. Whatever he decided about material and men, he needed to get it right early and often.

So Lewis and Jefferson planned and plotted the trip for two and a half months, with Jefferson teaching Lewis all he could.

Taking Science 101

To begin his preparations for the expedition, Jefferson took Lewis with him on one of his frequent retreats to Monticello, where Lewis not only had the mind of Jefferson to draw upon but the run of the Monticello library. He studied maps and books — everything written about previous travels and expeditions westward. Jefferson taught him the basics of botany by taking Lewis outdoors to observe plants first-hand at Monticello and in Washington, D.C. He introduced Lewis to the Linnaean system of giving plants two Latin names, and he explained how to use the system in his field observations.

Jefferson also taught Lewis what he knew about celestial navigation, specifically the use of a sextant and other astronomical instruments.

Requesting funds for a "literary pursuit"

One of the tasks that Lewis spent his time on in the fall and winter of 1802 was estimating what the expedition would cost. Jefferson would have to ask Congress for the money in the next budget cycle, so for the sake of budgeting,

Jefferson and Lewis agreed initially to man the expedition with one officer and 10 to 12 soldiers. They had an incentive to underestimate how many men would be needed — keeping the number as low as possible would reduce fears that a large party would arouse in the French, Spanish, and Indians and would keep Congressional resistance low. In light of these considerations, Lewis and Jefferson may have known that an estimate of $2,500 was unrealistic, but that's the number they gave to Congress.

Jefferson put his request for funds in a draft of his annual message to Congress in December, 1802, but Secretary of the Treasury Albert Gallatin suggested that it had better be a secret communication because it was proposing an expedition through foreign territory. So Jefferson sent his secret request to Congress on January 18, 1803.

Jefferson was a master of canny political spin. He tried to disguise the request as a commercial as well as "literary pursuit," a quest for knowledge that would add to the geographic and scientific understanding of that part of the country, by which he meant up to and including the Mandan villages. (And he succeeded.) He asked Congress for $2,500 "for the purpose of extending the external commerce of the U.S." He implied that through this expedition, the United States could steal trade with the tribes of "great supplies of furs and peltry" away from the British. Finally, like an afterthought, he said that because the expedition would be traveling the Missouri anyway, they might as well "explore the whole line, even to the Western ocean." He implied that the expedition would require very few men and was a sure thing; a terrific bargain.

Harpers Ferry, West Virginia

If you enjoy visiting places that haven't changed much in the last 200 years, you'll love Harpers Ferry, West Virginia. Home to Harpers Ferry National Historic Park, it's a great place to go for a vacation that combines rich history, great scenery, and lots of outdoor recreation. A bustling place in the 1800s at the confluence of the Potomac and Shenandoah Rivers and the junction of the states of West Virginia, Maryland, and Virginia, Jefferson called the river passage there "one of the most stupendous scenes in Nature."

Harpers Ferry is a historically preserved American treasure. The town witnessed the first successful American railroad, the first application of *interchangeable firearms manufacture*

(standardizing parts so they could be used in numerous rifle versions), the largest surrender of federal troops in the Civil War, and the education of former slaves in one of the earliest integrated schools in the United States. The abolitionist John Brown made his famous stand against slavery in Harpers Ferry. In addition to Thomas Jefferson and Meriwether Lewis, George Washington, "Stonewall" Jackson, and Frederick Douglass left a mark on this place.

The Harpers Ferry area offers first-class hiking, river rafting, biking, camping and other outdoor recreation. For more information, go to www.nps.gov/hafe/home or call 304-535-6298.

The comparative sum must have seemed paltry even to a Congress full of Jefferson's skeptics. They were still harrumphing about Jefferson's request the previous week for an appropriation of up to $9.375 million to buy New Orleans and Florida from the French. Anyway, the request to fund an expedition raised no eyebrows (which was the intent of the request's deft wording) and was approved.

Spending the cash

In the spring of 1803, Lewis visited Harpers Ferry (then in Virginia, now in West Virginia — people in the west of Virginia broke off to form West Virginia, a state loyal to the Union during the Civil War) to begin acquiring some of the essential goods that he would need for the expedition. First on the agenda were guns and then an iron boat he designed himself. From Pittsburgh, he ordered a keelboat built to his specifications. (Apparently, boat design was one of Lewis's many talents.)

Requisitioning guns

On March 16, Lewis rode to the U.S. Armory and Arsenal at Harpers Ferry. He arrived with a letter from Secretary of War Dearborn addressed to the Armory superintendent: "You will be pleased to make such arms and iron work, as requested by the Bearer Captain Meriwether Lewis and to have them completed with the least possible delay." In Harpers Ferry, Lewis requisitioned fifteen rifles, 15 powder horns, 30 bullet molds, 30 ball screws, extra rifle and musket locks, gunsmith's repair tools, several dozen tomahawks, and 24 large knives. The rifles were either prototypes of the U.S. Model 1803, a muzzle loading, flintlock rifle that could kill a deer at up to 200 yards, or they may have been *contract rifles,* rifles produced for the government by private contractors, short rifles in stock at Harpers Ferry when Lewis arrived. (The reason it's not known for sure what they carried is because all of the rifles were sold at auction immediately after the expedition.)

Framing the iron boat

In addition to requisitioning guns, Lewis went to Harpers Ferry to attend to the construction of a lightweight, collapsible iron boat frame of his own design. The strange water craft was made up of an iron frame that came apart in sections with a covering of animal hides. Lewis planned to use the boat, which resembled a canoe, to travel the shallower reaches of the Missouri and be more easily carried around portages because of its lightness.

The Armory smiths assigned to the project had trouble assembling the iron frame and forced Lewis to stick around a month, when he was planning to stay only a week. Finally, the frame for the unusual canoe was finished and a "full experiment" was conducted on two sections. In the end, Lewis was very satisfied with the iron ribbing he'd created. The two sections weighed only 99 pounds but could carry a load of 1,770 pounds. The complete iron boat, not counting the hides, weighed just 176 pounds and could carry a load of 8,000 pounds.

Unfortunately, when the expedition reached the point where Lewis hoped to use the iron boat, he was unable to find pine trees for pitch to seal the seams of the hides that stretched over the frame. A substitute tar of charcoal, beeswax, and buffalo tallow was used to seal the skins. When put into the water, "She leaked in such manner that he would not answer," Lewis wrote. It would be one of his greatest disappointments on the expedition.

Ordering the keelboat

From Pittsburgh, Lewis ordered a keelboat to be built to his specifications. He had designed the boat over the winter. It was like the one he'd used when he was an Army paymaster. Fifty-five feet long, it was eight feet wide and had a shallow draft (*draft* is the water depth that a ship displaces when loaded), 32-foot mast to support a large square sail, and a *foresail* (lowest sail on a square-rigged boat). It had two 10 foot decks, one in the front *(bow)* that formed a look-out platform (in nautical-speak, a *forecastle*) and one at the stern with a cabin underneath.

Up to 12 tons of goods would fit in the cargo area *(hold),* which was 31 feet long. Across the deck were 11 three-feet-wide benches, each accommodating two oarsmen.

Considering the manpower

Lewis had an overwhelming to-do list for the expedition, including designing boats and supervising their construction. But he had to turn his attention to the personnel who would man those boats and accompany him on the long journey.

Lewis didn't know how many men he would end up taking, but he probably knew it was more than the 10 or 12 Jefferson had asked Congress to pay for. Lewis wrote Army commanders in the Ohio River Valley and asked them to identify potential candidates for the expedition. For national security reasons, he told them that the expedition was going up the Mississippi River (which was within U.S. territory, while the Missouri River valley was still in foreign hands — see Chapter 3).

Lewis had one more critical task to add to his list. Jefferson was urging him to find and name his successor, someone who would take over if Lewis was killed or incapacitated to prevent "anarchy, dispersion, and the consequent danger to your party."

Clark for Co-Captain

Thomas Jefferson was leaning on Lewis to find a second in command for the expedition. Lewis went a step further than naming a second: He wrote to William Clark in June of 1803 and offered him co-command. In one of the most unusual moves by a commander in the history of the United States, perhaps in the history of the world, Lewis thought about a successor and decided not to find a subordinate but to offer to share his command. Sharing command is pretty much unheard of and thought to be foolhardy by the military — confusing and risky.

Historians have long speculated about why Lewis wrote William Clark and offered him co-command. Clark was four years older than Lewis and had previously been Lewis's superior officer. Or, perhaps, Clark's greater experience with Indians may have persuaded Lewis. Although Clark had fought tribes as an Army officer, he also knew a number of Indians as individuals and from his own perspective, and Lewis's, had an affinity with Indians.

Maybe Lewis badly wanted Clark on the trip and knew he wouldn't accept the role of junior officer. Lewis knew Clark had more experience than he did as a frontiersman and a frontline military leader. Lewis wrote Clark on June 19, 1803, to invite him to help find "some good hunters, stout, healthy, unmarried men, accustomed to the woods, and capable of bearing bodily fatigue in a pretty considerable degree." Also, and more critically, Lewis needed Clark to participate in the fatigues, dangers, and honors of co-leading the expedition.

The reason may have been that Lewis understood that he and Clark would complement each other, each making up what the other lacked, each taking up the other's slack. Maybe Lewis was an intuitive genius!

However, Lewis's wisdom and good intentions were overridden when Clark's commission came through the next year (after the expedition had launched). The War Department, in a fine show of red tape, made Clark a second lieutenant instead of captain. Clark had resigned from the Army at the rank of captain (to go home and help his older brother), but the Army didn't have to re-commission him at that same rank, and in fact did not. Lewis was furious and mortified, but helpless to change the official outcome. Instead of accepting it, however, he told Clark he would address him and treat him as Captain Clark, co-commander, and would keep the official lower rank secret from the men and anyone else they encountered on the expedition. The men of the expedition knew their commanders only as Captain Lewis and Captain Clark.

In any event, Lewis was correct that William Clark was the right man with the right experience for the job.

The Lewis and *Hooke* expedition?

There was a typically long delay (six weeks was average) in the mails between Lewis and Clark the summer of 1803. When Lewis hadn't received Clark's answer to his invitation by late July, he told the president that he was going to ask Lieutenant Moses Hooke, 26 years old, to be his second in command. If Clark said no, Lewis would take Hooke. For eight days, the likelihood grew that it would be the Lewis and Hooke expedition.

Hooke, Lewis wrote, was "industrious, prudent and persevering," with a good constitution and "a sensible well informed Mind." When Lewis got Clark's acceptance letter, though, Hooke was instantly forgotten and lost to history.

William Clark, Kentucky frontiersman

"Billy" Clark was the sixth son and ninth child from a family of ten children, born near the Rappahannock River on August 1, 1770. Attracted after the American Revolution by reports of rich land in the Northwest Territory, the Clark family, including 14-year-old Billy and a dozen or more slaves migrated across the Allegheny Mountains and down the Ohio River, settling above waterfalls near today's Louisville, Kentucky.

When the Clark family arrived, the Louisville area was a hot bed of conflict between Indians defending their territory and hunting grounds and settlers migrating from the East. One of Billy's older brothers was killed by Indians in a skirmish at the Little Wabash River.

At war with the British and then the Indians

All of Clark's brothers were Revolutionary War veterans, but it was George Rogers Clark, the family's second son and twenty-two years William's senior, who is best remembered for his Army exploits. As a general after the war, Rogers Clark gained a reputation as a cruel and pitiless Indian fighter, leading a series of raids into Shawnee country north of the Ohio River, burning and plundering anything and everything of value to the Shawnee.

William Clark grew up to be tall — about six feet — red-headed, strong, and muscular, with an easy-going manner. Following in his older brother's foot-steps, Clark joined the militia in 1789, becoming a supply officer and fighting in several Indian skirmishes, earning the reputation of a young man "brave as Caesar." On two occasions, he was sent to spy on the Spanish, who were building forts high up the east bank of the Mississippi. He then transferred over to the Army with a commission as a lieutenant in 1792, when he was 22 years old, and served under General "Mad Anthony" Wayne. He also led a military expedition to Chickasaw Bluffs near today's Memphis.

Fighting in the Battle of Fallen Timbers

During Clark's Army service, the United States and a confederation of Indian tribes — the Miami, Shawnee, Delaware, and their British allies — sought control of the Northwest Territory, a vast area north of the Ohio and east of the Mississippi rivers: modern-day Ohio, Indiana, Illinois, Michigan, Wisconsin, and Minnesota. The struggle culminated in the Battle of Fallen Timbers, where Clark commanded a rifle company and the Shawnee were killed or driven off the battlefield to a British fort, where they were turned away. Giving up their struggle for their homeland, the Shawnee signed the first treaty — the 1795 Treaty of Greenville — between the U.S. government and Indian tribes. It was the first time that the United States acknowledged the sovereignty of tribal nations.

By 1795, Clark had received successive promotions to leadership roles, attaining the rank of captain. Ensign Meriwether Lewis was among the men assigned to Clark, and the two struck up a lasting friendship.

Quitting the Army to help big brother

In 1796, Clark quit the Army and returned to his family and property in Indiana Territory, to Clarksville, a city named after his brother George Rogers, directly across the Ohio River from Louisville, Kentucky. He left the Army to help his brother recover from a financial jam: The elder Clark had pledged his own funds to support his earlier Army campaigns in the Illinois Country and was besieged by creditors.

Getting a boost from big brother

In December of 1802, George Rogers Clark wrote President Jefferson from the Falls of the Ohio to recommend his younger brother, William, for service in the government. "He is well-qualified almost for any business," Rogers Clark wrote. "If it should be in your power to confur on him any post of Honor and profit, in this Countrey in which we live, it will exceedingly gratify me." Jefferson surely remembered that letter when Lewis told him that he wanted Clark to be his co-captain.

Clark: The right man for the job

By 1803, William Clark was 33 years old and was an expert woodsman, waterman, and map maker. He had traveled extensively throughout the Northwest Territory, commanded military expeditions, built and supplied forts, and fought Indians. After seven years at home, with no wife or children of his own, he was probably bored numb with life above the falls and needed an adventure.

He certainly had the qualifications plus something else: Lewis liked and admired Clark, saying in his letter of invitation "no man on earth" is more qualified to be co-captain of an expedition to the Pacific.

Responding immediately, Clark sent a letter to Pittsburgh, where Lewis was readying boats and supplies for the journey, receiving the letter on July 29. Clark wrote: ". . . I will cheerfully join you. . . . This is an undertaking fraighted with many difeculties, but My friend I do assure you that no man lives whith whome I would prefur to undertake Such a Trip &c. as your self . . . ."

Chapter 5

Training an Explorer

. . . .

In This Chapter

▶ Studying with the best minds of the time

▶ Shopping between lessons

▶ Accepting expedition orders

▶ Hiring the crew and buying a dog

▶ Navigating the very low Ohio

▶ Joining Clark and heading for the Mississippi

. . . .

*B*efore Lewis could depart on the expedition, he had three major tasks to accomplish during the spring and summer of 1803: Prepare for the scientific mission by studying with Jefferson's appointed experts, shop for provisions for the long journey, and have the boats built to specifications. Lewis had to complete this monumental to-do list before the Ohio River got so low that he'd have to drag the boats down the Ohio River to pick up Clark.

In this chapter, we tell you about the whirlwind final preparations of Meriwether Lewis as he received his formal orders for the expedition and struggled down the Ohio to meet up with William Clark.

Traveling to the Wise Men

To give Lewis the training he needed to accomplish the goals of the expedition, President Jefferson asked five of his eminent academic friends, all leaders in their fields, to help tutor Lewis. The five scientists had a wide range of intellectual interests beyond their academic specialties:

✔ **Benjamin Rush:** Medicine, surgery, chemistry, and psychiatry

✔ **Benjamin Smith Barton:** Botany, zoology, and Indian history

✔ **Caspar Wistar:** Anatomy and paleontology

✔ **Andrew Ellicott:** Surveying and astronomy

✔ **Robert Patterson:** Navigation, surveying, and astronomy

They were great choices to prepare Lewis for success in meeting the scientific goals of the expedition.

Taking a Rush course in medicine

At the time of the Lewis and Clark expedition, there were few doctors on the frontier and no clinics or hospitals. People relied on amateur doctors, like Lewis and his mother before him, to treat injuries and illnesses. Diverse medical practices — such as setting a bone, treating malaria, digging out a bullet, delivering a baby, or putting someone peacefully beyond the reach of pain — were all just in a day's work.

Real doctors often did no better and sometimes worse than lay doctors when treating the ill. Deaths at birth, during childhood, or in early adulthood were common. Life wasn't so much cheap as it was hard to hold on to.

The most effective treatments sometimes came from herbalists, whose remedies were derived from plants that grew in the wild or were cultivated for their curative properties. A lot of herbal medicine was learned from contact with American Indians.

Jefferson knew that Lewis would be required to treat a wide variety of illnesses and injuries during the long journey. So the first eminent expert that he sent Lewis to study with was Dr. Benjamin Rush, 19th-century America's most respected physician.

Rush had been a signatory to the Declaration of Independence, was the vice-president of the American Philosophical Society, and was a professor of chemistry and medicine at the University of Pennsylvania. He was also a surgeon and the author of the first major work written in America on psychiatry.

Rush and Lewis talked about Rush's study of Indian medicine and health, conducted approximately 30 years earlier. Rush wrote a questionnaire for Lewis to take with him on the expedition that was similar to questionnaires Rush had used in gathering information on the Creek and Seneca nations in the early 1790s. The questionnaire asked detailed questions on health, medicine, morals, and religion. Topics ranged from menstruation, bathing, and childbearing to animal sacrifice during religious ceremonies. He also asked Lewis to check the pulses of children, adults, and the elderly at "morning, at noon & at night — before and after eating. . . ."

Purging, sweating, and bloodletting

Rush told Lewis how to treat various illnesses and calamities common on the frontier. The best medicine in 1803 is pretty scary by 21st-century standards. Take a look for yourself at some general techniques:

✔ **Purging:** Almost all patients were believed to be "improved" by a corrosive purging of the bowels and/or the contents of the stomach.

✔ **Sweating:** Patients were made to sweat as a recommended cure for various ailments.

✔ **Bloodletting:** *Heroic therapy* was a combination of heavy bloodletting — leeches were a favored technique — and purging. The respected Dr. Rush was a practitioner who believed in heroic therapy to treat yellow fever and other illnesses.

✔ **Quinine:** Malaria is a disease contracted by the bite of mosquitoes. It was treated with Peruvian bark, a bitter alkaloid concoction with a naturally occurring ingredient called quinine. Even today, quinine and its derivatives are the only treatments for malaria, which has no cure.

✔ **Mercurous chloride:** Intestinal worms were a major problem on the frontier. The treatment for intestinal worms was a white, tasteless powder of mercurous chloride to (of course!) purge the bowels.

✔ **Mercury:** Today, mercury is known to be a lethal poison (if you take enough of it), but it was once used in many drugs and ointments. Until penicillin was discovered, mercury was the only way to treat venereal disease. Mercurial ointment was used effectively to prevent infection.

✔ **Opium and laudanum:** To induce sleep or relieve pain from any source — toothache, headache, bone break, gunshot wound, appendicitis, or infection — opium or laudanum was prescribed. Opium is now known as a highly addictive drug that induces a temporary stupor. Its godchild, laudanum, is a combination of opium and alcohol.

Stocking up on thunderclappers and other cures

Dr. Rush gave Lewis a list of medicines and drugs to purchase for the trip, and Lewis bought the jaw-dropping quantity of the medicines that Dr. Rush recommended: 1,300 doses of laxative, 1,100 doses of emetic (for purging), and 3,500 doses of sweat inducers and drugs to increase urine and saliva production.

The doctor advised packing a large quantity of his namesake: Rush's Pills. A drug with the nickname *thunderclappers,* Rush's Pills were an over-the-top purgative guaranteed to rid the body of everything eaten and digested lately, whether it was causing distress or not. Lewis bought 50 dozen! Among other ingredients, the pill contained mercury, so it doubled as a treatment for syphilis, another common frontier illness.

Other drugs Rush recommended and Lewis purchased (but you won't find in *your* medicine cabinet) were Peruvian bark, julap (dried root of a Mexican vine), Glauber's salts (laxative), tarter emetic (poisonous, odorless, white salt that causes expectoration, vomiting, and perspiring), opium, laudanum, powdered rhubarb (for purging), sulfuric acid (also called acid of vitriol; a few drops were added to molasses or sugar and water with meals to aid digestion), and mercurial and blistering ointments.

Following Rush's rules

Dr. Rush also contributed a set of health instructions for Lewis's use on the expedition, and it reveals the state of the art of medicine at the time. The following list paraphrases the rules that Dr. Rush gave Lewis:

- ✔ **If you start to feel bad, lie down.** Don't eat, but do dilute what you drink. Drink something warm and take one, two, or three of the purging pills (Rush's pills).

- ✔ **Unusual constipation is often a sign of approaching illness.** Take one or more purging pills.

- ✔ **Not being hungry is a sign of approaching illness.** Take purging pills.

- ✔ **When you're marching or working very hard, eat lightly.**

- ✔ **Wear flannel underwear,** especially in wet weather.

- ✔ **Don't drink much alcohol.** If you're wet, tired, or out a long time in night air, drink a little alcohol straight. Three tablespoons undiluted are better than half a pint diluted.

- ✔ **Drink molasses or sugar and water** with a few drops of the acid of vitriol with meals.

- ✔ **If your feet get chilled, wash them in alcohol.**

- ✔ **Washing your feet in cold water every morning** will fortify them against the cold.

- ✔ **After long marches, lie down for two hours.** It will refresh you much more than resting longer periods in a different position.

- ✔ **If you wear shoes without heels,** your legs won't get as tired.

Getting a crash course in natural history from Barton

Jefferson asked Dr. Benjamin Smith Barton, America's leading botanist, to prepare Lewis in botany, zoology, and Indian history. A physician, naturalist, and lecturer at the University of Pennsylvania, he also wrote extensively on natural history and paleontology. Barton was the author of the first botany text written in the United States, which Lewis bought to take on the trip.

Lewis spent only about three weeks with Barton but learned a remarkable amount in that short time. From Barton, Lewis found out how to preserve the plant, bird, animal, and animal hide specimens he was expected to collect on the journey. Barton also taught him the accepted scientific method of labeling specimens (with the date, place, and name of the collection, if known). He reinforced lessons that Jefferson had taught him on the Linnaean system for classifying specimens by using Latin names.

TECHNICAL STUFF

Packing the books

Lewis received advice from the wise men — Jefferson, Ellicott, Patterson, Rush, Wistar, and Barton — about what books to take along on the journey. The main ones that he packed were

✔ Dictionary (four volumes)

✔ *Elements of Botany* by Benjamin Smith Barton

✔ *Elements of Mineralogy* by Richard Kirwan

✔ *History of Louisiana* by Antoine Simon Le Page du Pratz

✔ Linnaeus' two volumes of Latin classification of plants

✔ *The Nautical Almanac and Astronomical Ephermeris*

✔ *A Practical Introduction to Spherics and Nautical Astronomy*

Lewis was an especially good botany student, probably because of the herbal medicine his mother had taught him and his botany walks with Jefferson at Monticello. Lewis's journals display an advanced botanical vocabulary, a knack for apt description, and a talent for accurate botanical drawing.

His studying ultimately paid off. Lewis returned from the expedition with 226 plant specimens correctly collected, dried, and stored. They are preserved and displayed today at the Lewis and Clark Herbarium at the Academy of Natural Sciences, 19th Street and Benjamin Franklin Parkway, in Philadelphia.

Preparing for sloths and mammoths with Wistar

Lewis went for a tutorial to another well-known doctor in Philadelphia, Caspar Wistar, a colleague of Dr. Rush's, a professor of anatomy at the University of Pennsylvania, and author of the first anatomy textbook written in America. Wistar disagreed with Rush about bleeding people to cure them of yellow fever and was an early advocate of vaccination. His classes at the university were standing-room-only and had to be subdivided.

Lewis was sent to Wistar to talk about fossils as much as anatomy. Wistar and Jefferson had written a joint paper on the Megolonyx (giant sloth), a prehistoric beast whose bones he and Jefferson had helped discover in New York in 1801. He and Lewis probably talked about how to detect the presence of the giant sloth and the woolly mammoth, two extinct species that he and Jefferson were hoping could be found still living in the American West.

Philadelphia in 1803

Philadelphia was the largest and most sophisticated city in the United States in 1803. The first Capitol of the nation, it was home to the first hospital, as well and was the center of scientific learning in the country. A concentration of scholars and scientists lived there, and many belonged to formal organizations where intellectuals met and discussed the latest discoveries, theories, and studies. The most important of these was the American Philosophical Society, founded by Benjamin Franklin. Jefferson and the scientists Jefferson asked to teach Lewis were prominent members.

Today, Wistar is remembered for the innovative anatomical models he made out of wood to illustrate his classroom lessons. He is even more famous for illustrating his lectures with human cadaver limbs and organs injected with hot wax.

Surveying the earth with Ellicott

Lewis arrived in Lancaster, Pennsylvania, to study surveying and astronomy with the "extremely friendly and attentive" Andrew Ellicott in April, 1803. The son of a Quaker clockmaker, Ellicott knew how to manufacture precision scientific instruments and was famous as a surveyor of state and territorial boundaries, including the area that became Washington, D.C.

Under Ellicott's guidance, Lewis practiced using a *sextant* (used by navigators to measure the angular distance of the sun and stars from the horizon and calculate latitude), a *chronometer* (an extremely accurate watch used to calculate longitude), and other instruments.

Earlier in the year, Ellicott had answered Jefferson's letter about the expedition with a set of detailed instructions on calculating latitude and longitude. He also advised that the chronometer should be tied up in a sheep's bladder when not in use to "privent its being injured."

Navigating by the heavens with Patterson

After picking up some more rifles in Lancaster, Pennsylvania, Lewis went to Robert Patterson's home in Philadelphia. Patterson was a renowned astronomer and one of Philadelphia's leading scientists. He schooled Lewis in navigation, surveying, and astronomy. He also helped Lewis buy a chronometer (a precise watch that Andrew Ellicott had taught Lewis to use) to take on the trip. Lewis paid $250 (about $3,035 in today's dollars), making it the most expensive single object purchased for the trip. He sent the chronometer back to Lancaster for Ellicott to regulate before the expedition. (After all that expense and effort, his "highly accurate" watch would lose 14 seconds each day of the expedition.)

Although an instrument called the *theodolite* was the most accurate navigational tool of the time and Jefferson thought Lewis should try to take one, Patterson recommended that Lewis take his readings with a sextant, instead (see the preceding section) and forget about the sensitive, hard-to-transport theodolite.

Shopping for the Voyage

During the Pennsylvania spring of 1803, one man may have been as busy as Meriwether Lewis: Israel Whelan, purveyor (or buyer) of supplies for the federal government in Philadelphia. Whelan had received $1,000 to begin purchasing supplies from Lewis's lists, so Whelan was in shop-til-you-drop mode from early May to mid-June, calling on wholesalers and retailers throughout the city and shopping for hundreds of items. He and Lewis faced the enormous task of providing for all the demands of the expedition.

Figuring out how much of what stuff to take on the journey was a big job in itself. The list of necessary goods was endless: guns, clothing, food, gear, presents for Indians, tools, whiskey, and scientific instruments. When Lewis began shopping, he didn't know how many men he'd end up taking or how long they'd be traveling. With only so much room for supplies, Lewis knew they'd run out of many items (and they did run out of frontier essentials, such as salt, tobacco, whiskey, and blue beads, which were prized by the Indians). But they didn't run out of ink to write with nor guns, powder, and ammunition to keep them in food and clothing. Lewis's calculations were correct on that score. The Corps would survive and there would be a record of how they did it.

Buying scientific instruments and basic supplies

Lewis received more than scholarly instruction from the scientists with whom he had trained. He also heeded their advice about what supplies to take on the journey. Medical items Lewis bought on Dr. Rush's advice included tourniquets, syringes, *lancets* (surgical knives), and *forceps* (small tongs or pincers used in surgery). In addition to the sextant and chronometer recommended by his astronomy tutors, Lewis acquired a surveyor's compass, plotting instruments, and latitude and longitude tables.

To record information, observations, and drawings, Lewis ordered pencils, crayons, ink powder, journals, oilskin bags to store records in, and candles for writing at night.

Probably foremost in Lewis's mind were the supplies for camping, hunting, cooking, and defense. He requisitioned an air gun, chisels, a corn mill, fishing tackle, flintlock rifles, flints, gun powder, handsaws, hatchets, knives, Lancaster long rifles, lead (for bullets), mosquito curtains, oil-cloth tents and sheets, pliers, soap (12 pounds), steels (for striking sparks from the flints to make fire), tablespoons (two dozen), and *whetstones* (for sharpening knives).

Lewis also bought preserved foods, such as cornmeal, hominy, lard, portable soup, and salt pork, as well as three bushels of salt for preserving foods on the trail.

Choosing gifts for the tribes

From the earliest encounters with Indians in America, tribes displayed a sense of protocol about meeting and getting acquainted with strangers or visitors, and that protocol included the exchange of gifts. If Indians were invited to a meeting or a meal, they didn't arrive empty-handed and they didn't expect to leave empty-handed, either. Bringing presents was advisable for visitors to Indian villages and for anyone passing through their territories.

Lewis knew that glass beads were prized in all of Indian country, but he may not have realized how important blue glass beads were — so valuable that they were like money. But Lewis didn't buy enough of them, and it was a decision he would regret when the expedition ran out of them before they had reached the Nez Perce tribe. Next to blue beads, brass buttons were highly valued in Indian country. The expedition would run out of those, as well.

Whiskey was also prized among some, although not all, tribes. But the Corps knew that they would run out of whiskey before they were halfway through the trip and wanted to keep as much as possible for themselves. They also feared giving tribes whiskey would increase the likelihood of fights breaking out.

Tobacco was prized among the tribes, and the expedition took 50 pounds of it to give away as presents. Other items Lewis bought to give to tribes and tribal leaders were axes and tomahawks, brass kettles, brooches, calico shirts, fishhooks, ivory combs, knives, mirrors, moccasin awls, needles and thimbles, red flannel, rings, scissors, and textiles.

Lewis chose such a wide variety of tribal presents for a reason: He wanted to display a sample of the wares that the Indians could have on a regular basis if they kept the peace and established a trade relationship with the United States. When distributing goods and making speeches to tribes, Lewis repeated over and over that the United States wanted their trade, not their land.

The most highly sought-after gifts or trade goods in Indian country were guns and ammunition, but Lewis and Clark didn't distribute guns to the tribes in any quantity. The captains hinted and sometimes promised that guns would be available to tribes soon from American traders following behind Lewis and Clark, but the Indians weren't going to get them in time to shoot anyone in the Lewis and Clark party, accidentally or on purpose. The expedition did carry 50 pounds of gun powder, however, for tribes that already owned guns.

Giving Lewis His Marching Orders

The final version of President Jefferson's formal written instructions to Lewis in June of 1803 held no surprises. Besides showing drafts of the document to Lewis that spring, Jefferson had circulated a draft among his Cabinet officers and a select group of his intellectual friends in the United States and abroad. He incorporated some of their comments in the last version Lewis received before he left Washington, D.C., to start the expedition.

Serving God and green pastures

Attorney General Levi Lincoln's recommendation to give the expedition a religious task ended up in the final instructions. He had urged the adoption of a religious goal in order get the funds from Congress for the expedition: A religious theme kept the Federalists in Congress — dominated by conservative New England clergy — from attacking the trip. Jefferson instructed Lewis to inquire about Indian religions to help "those who may endeavor to civilize and instruct them." In other words, Lewis was to get information that would help future missionaries.

Lincoln also wanted Jefferson to be sterner with Lewis about how risky it was for Lewis and crew to become aggressive with the tribes. Lincoln suspected that Lewis was impetuous and might react violently to some provocation. Jefferson adopted Lincoln's recommended change in wording, warning Lewis not to fight a force larger than the Corps of Discovery or it would lead to "probable destruction."

Secretary of the Treasury Albert Gallatin offered no changes to the draft but wanted some instructions added. He wanted Lewis to collect information on the suitability of the Missouri River valley for farming. He flatly declared that the "great object" (the number-one goal) of the expedition was to find out how fertile the land was and whether it could accommodate a large number of settlers. Although Jefferson took most of Gallatin's suggestions, he continued to put commerce ahead of agriculture as the "great object" of the expedition.

Getting it in writing

On June 20, 1803, Jefferson gave Lewis his final orders for the expedition. Reading Jefferson's Instructions to Lewis is well worth your time, but the following bare bones version hits the highlights:

1. **You are appointed to execute the provisions of my confidential request to Congress to send an expedition west.**

2. **Your primary mission is to explore the Missouri River and other streams likely to lead directly to the Pacific Ocean.**

3. **Take observations of latitude and longitude at mouths of rivers, rapids, islands, and other natural landmarks.**

   Jefferson wanted accurate maps of the territory through which the expedition would pass. That's why he ordered Lewis to take key latitude and longitude readings and mentions these as the second-most-important of his instructions after the main mission. Everyone who would come after the expedition — explorers, traders, settlers, and the Army — would need good maps.

4. **Carefully record your observations and other notes, making copies and keeping them safe.**

   Jefferson stressed making copies of the records and protecting them from damage or destruction. He even specified the kind of paper to use, birch, which was tougher and harder to damage or destroy than paper made from other woods. The expedition would not be valuable, Jefferson implied, without a thorough written account.

5. **Get to know the Indians as well as time permits.**

   In expense of time and energy, Jefferson said that learning about the tribes came second only to finding the route to the Pacific. Jefferson gave Lewis a specific list of information to find out about the tribes:

   • Names of the tribal nations and their populations

   • Goods that each tribe owned

   • Languages

   • Traditions

   • Monuments

   • Jobs (farming, fishing, hunting, war, or art) and the tools the Indians used in these occupations

   • Food, clothing, housing, diseases and their remedies

- Differences among the tribes ("peculiarities" in their laws, customs, and attitudes)
- Trade goods that each tribe would have wanted to buy from or sell to the United States

6. **Observe and record minerals, the climate, and the seasons.**

7. **Explore the Missouri River valley, especially its southern side, and find out anything you can about the source of the Mississippi River.**

   Jefferson wanted the expedition to pay attention to the southern side of the Missouri in order to find out whether the land was suitable for agricultural settlement, as Gallatin had asked.

8. **Treat the Indians well: Tell them about the United States and encourage them to trade with us.**

   Jefferson instructed Lewis to arrange for "influential chiefs" to visit Washington, D.C. Lewis was told to assure the tribes that the U.S. government would bring up and educate any Indian young people who came to Washington.

9. **Distribute cowpox (vaccine against smallpox, which plagued the tribes) and "instruct and encourage them in the use of it."**

10. **If you come up against a superior force, retreat and come back. Don't risk lives. Bring the party back safely.**

11. **Write and send us letters and send a copy of your journal, notes, and observations.**

    Jefferson insisted that Lewis convert any sensitive text into cipher (or code).

12. **If you reach the Pacific Ocean, find out whether furs from that part of the country can be collected at the head of the Missouri River and transported via the Missouri, instead of circumnavigating the continent.**

    Jefferson wanted furs collected at the head of the Missouri River to beat the British in the Western fur trading business. The British would have a tough time competing with the United States if a Missouri River transportation system could be established.

13. **Try to find an ocean port and send two people back by sea around Cape Horn or the Cape of Good Hope.**

    Jefferson said to send some men by ship because he wanted news of the expedition's successful arrival at the Pacific Ocean, and he didn't want to have to wait for their overland return to hear about it.

14. **Return the way you came, correcting and confirming observations made on the way out.**

15. Upon re-entering the United States, pay and discharge the crew, assuring them that we will try to get them grants of land. Then come to Washington, D.C.

16. Name your successor in case you die.

With these instructions, President Jefferson gave Lewis the absolute authority to carry out his mission and to spend money without limit to accomplish it. Jefferson knew that the expedition would run out of money, so he supplied Lewis with an open-ended letter of credit from the federal government, assuring payment to anyone who helped the Corps.

Lewis said as much in his letter of invitation to Clark to join the expedition as co-commander: "To aid me in the enterprise I have the most ample and hearty support that the government can give in every possible shape."

Recruiting Two Good Men (and a Great Dog)

Meriwether Lewis and William Clark couldn't make the long journey alone. In the summer of 1803, Lewis had already begun recruiting potential candidates for the expedition (and one wasn't even human).

Beginning the search for men

The crew Lewis had assembled consisted of seven or eight Army recruits from Carlisle, Pennsylvania, to be released after the expedition descended the Ohio River.

Two other young men, George Shannon and John Colter, were being tested for inclusion in the permanent Corps. Shannon at 18-years-old would end up being the youngest member of the Corps, not counting Sacagawea and her infant son. John Colter would get as far the Mandan villages on the return trip in 1806 and be discharged at his own request to go back west. In late August, Clark wrote to Lewis that he had "engaged . . . the best woodsmen and Hunters . . . in this part of the Countery" for the expedition.

Lewis and Clark had each elected to seek the others' approval before officially accepting any man into the Corps. To be selected, the men had to be unmarried, good hunters, and physically fit. Presumably, an exception was made for John Shields, who was married with a daughter, because he was an ace blacksmith and hunter.

Lewis and Clark would collect and reject men for months before naming the official roster for the expedition.

However, Lewis did add one important non-human member to the crew: a dog.

Drafting Seaman the sagacious

Why Lewis decided he needed a dog for the trip is unclear, but while in Pittsburgh, attending to the construction of the keelboat (a large, shallow freight boat), Lewis paid $20 (about $250 in today's dollars) for a Newfoundland, a perfect breed for the journey. Originating in England and named Newfoundland for the island where they worked on fishing boats, the breed is large, gentle, and famous for its swimming ability.

Lewis named the dog Seaman. The big dog was black and would've been about 28 inches tall and weighed around 115 pounds. During the expedition, Lewis mentioned Seaman's "sagacity" more than once in his journal, although whether he meant "keenly observant" or the other definition, "having a keen sense of smell" isn't clear.

On the expedition, Seaman suffered many of the same trials as the men, especially mosquito swarms and bites. The mosquitoes were a trial for all parties, and Lewis noted, "my dog even howls with the torture he experiences." The heat also plagued Seaman, who had a thick, oily coat adapted for wet climates and cold temperatures. And just like the men, he suffered from cuts, bruises, and prickly pear cactus barbs.

Seaman performed valuable work — retrieving birds, running down squirrels and deer, rousting beavers from their lodges, catching an antelope and dragging it to shore, patrolling the campsite at night, and giving early warning to the men bunked down for the night about wandering buffalo and roving grizzly bears.

For his service, a stream in Montana that flows into the Blackfoot River was named Seaman Creek (today's Monture Creek).

Getting the Boat to Float

By July of 1803, it was past time for Lewis to depart. The flow of the Ohio River decreased with every hot summer day and if Lewis hadn't gotten started, he would have to have dragged the boat to Clarksville to pick up Clark: The river just wouldn't have been deep enough to carry the boat. With instructions from Jefferson in hand, knowledge from many of the wise men of the day in mind, and nearly two tons of supplies purchased, Lewis's last major task before setting off was getting the keelboat finished and into the water — preferably enough water to keep it afloat.

Doubting the "drunkards"

Lewis's contract with the boat builder called for the boat to be finished by the 20th of July. But when Lewis reached Pittsburgh the third week of July, the boat was nowhere near ready to float. All the other elements in Lewis's plan had been beautifully timed and had come together: All but one of a party of recruits had shown up by July 22nd, and the wagon with 3,500 pounds of provisions had arrived from Harpers Ferry. But the unbuilt boat was a huge wrench in the program.

The boat builder, who said he hadn't been able to get the timber he needed to complete the boat by July 20, told Lewis that the boat would be finished by the end of the month.

Lewis wrote Jefferson about the boat-builder's promise: "however in this I am by no means sanguine, nor do I believe from the progress he makes that she will be ready before the 5th of August: I visit him every day, and endeavor by every means in my power to hasten the completion of the work . . . ."

Lewis told the boat builder to put more men on the job. He did. Lewis showed up every day for a month to threaten, cajole, and beg. It did no good.

Lewis was beside himself. ". . . [I]t was not until the 31st of August," he wrote Clark, "that I was enabled to take my departure from that place owing to the unpardonable negligence and inattention of the boat-builders who, unfortunately for me, were a set of most incorrigible drunkards, and with whom, neither threats, intreaties nor any other mode of treatment which I could devise had any effect. . . ."

Adding insult to injury, the builders took 12 more days to make the poles and oars!

Scraping down the river in a fog

With the keelboat finally finished, Lewis left Pittsburgh on the last day of August, 1803, at 11a.m. with a party of 11 men and his dog. The water was at its lowest point of the year and the boats were fully loaded, the formula for a really tedious trip of dragging the boats for at least the first 100 miles.

For half of September, Lewis and the men struggled down the Ohio, a river reduced in many places to rapids and ripples too shallow to pass by boat. It was not smooth sailing. The men were often exhausted by their exertions. Lewis hired teams of oxen to pull the boat when he could find them; otherwise he and the men dragged the boats over the mud and rocks. On the first of September, they made 10 miles. On the third day out, Lewis complained about the people who lived on the Ohio River, who he says "live much by the distressed situation" of travelers, and are generally lazy, charge extravagantly and have no "filantrophy or continence." On the fourth day out, the expedition made only six miles.

By September 4th, the *pirogue* (canoe-shaped boat) was leaking. The canoe Lewis purchased to replace it also turned out to be so leaky that it had to be repaired before it could be used. Both boats continued to leak after they were repaired. Lewis ordered men to stay with them all night to bail out the water so they wouldn't sink by morning. A thick fog covered the water almost every morning, and they had to wait until 8 a.m. or later for it to lift before they could set out. You can almost hear Lewis's teeth grinding across the centuries.

Swimming squirrels, wandering men

On September 7th, the expedition passed Charlestown, a "handsome little Village, containing about forty houses" and reached Wheeling (in West Virginia today), with about 50 houses and a decaying fort. They stayed put for a while to rest, wash their clothes, eat some watermelons, and buy bread. Lewis met the son of Dr. Patterson, one of the scientists who trained him in Philadelphia. The younger Dr. Patterson said that he wanted to go on with Lewis as the expedition's physician. Lewis was willing, but at departure time, Dr. Patterson "could not get ready" and was left behind.

Shooting a woman in the head

On the very first day of the voyage, Lewis had a calamity — a near fatality not to himself, but to the expedition.

On September 1, the boats pulled up to rest for a few minutes at a river settlement called Bruno's Island. To amuse the assembled townsfolk, Lewis brought out the air gun that he'd recently purchased and fired it several times.

"Mr. Blaze Cenas" took a turn with the gun and fired it accidentally, shooting a woman in the head through her hat. She fell to the ground "instantly and the blood gusing from her temple we wer all in the greatest consternation suppose she was dead . . . ."

"Fortunately," Lewis wrote, "in a minute she revived to our enexpressable satisfaction. . . ."

The expedition passed several settlements along the Ohio. Mercifully, the river became a little deeper and the going was less tough. Lewis observed large numbers of fat, black squirrels swimming in the water from west to east. He sent his dog, Seaman, after bunches of them to fry up, a "plesent food," Lewis reported in his journal.

When they reached Marietta (now in Ohio), 100 miles from Wheeling, Lewis dismissed two crew members named Wilkinson and Montgomery, but he didn't mention the cause for dismissal in his journal. The next day, two other men got drunk and wandered off. When Lewis found them and brought them back, they were so drunk that they were useless.

The rapids were still creating difficulties as they passed a well-populated stretch of the Ohio on September 15th. Even so, they made 18 miles, a lot better than most days. The next day, they got a late start because of fog, and the men wore themselves out dragging the boats over rapids.

Walking to a mammoth skeleton

While taking a short rest in Cincinnati, Lewis talked with Dr. William Goforth, a local doctor who was excavating the ancient remains of a mastodon at the Big Bone Lick in Kentucky. Lewis left the boat on the river and walked overland to Big Bone Lick, arriving by October 4. The men traveled there by river. It was only 17 miles away by land, but it was 53 miles by water. The unusually named community of Big Bone Lick was called "Big Bone" for the large animal skeletons excavated there and "Lick" because of a nearby salt lick that had become a salt works. Big Bone Lick was the site of numerous finds of mammoth, mastodon, giant sloth, and other large prehistoric animal bones. (Jefferson would send Clark to Big Bone Lick in 1807 on the first organized vertebra paleontology expedition in the United States.)

Lewis picked up a few specimens, including a mammoth tusk and a couple "grinders" (teeth) and sent them to Jefferson, but the shipment never arrived. In a letter to Jefferson, Lewis compared bones of a mammoth he viewed at the Big Bone Lick site unfavorably with the famous mammoth skeleton that Jefferson and Caspar Wistar had excavated from Sawangunk, New York, in 1801.

Uniting with Clark and Shoving Off

On October 14, 1803, Meriwether Lewis and William Clark met in Clarksville near the Falls of the Ohio to make final preparations for the journey and assemble their crew. Seven men who had been recruited by Clark in Kentucky, plus the two that had made the trip with Lewis, were enlisted in the Army for the expedition: John Colter and George Shannon (who came with Lewis) and William Bratton, Joseph and Reuben Field, Charles Floyd, George Gibson, Nathaniel Pryor, and John Shields (who were recruited by Clark). See Chapter 2 for details on these men.

The other man who accompanied this crew was York, Clark's personal slave. See Chapter 2 for the background on this member of the Corps.

No one wrote journal entries while Lewis and Clark conferred in Clarksville for over a week, but they had loads to talk about. Lewis and Clark probably spent many hours planning the journey and getting advice from George Rogers Clark (William's older brother).

Falls of the Ohio

In 1803, the Falls of the Ohio were long rapids caused by a 24-foot drop of the Ohio River over a two-mile stretch of limestone ledges. This area became a natural stopping point for people traveling the Ohio River. The south side of the Falls became Louisville, Kentucky. On the north, the town of Clarksville, Indiana was founded.

William and George Rogers Clark both owned parcels of land at the Clarksville original town site, which is now part of the Falls of the Ohio State Park. Clarksville was the first American settlement in the Northwest Territory, established in 1783. George Roger's cabin and the surrounding area of the original town site on the riverbank were used as a base camp during Lewis's and Clark's preparations. George Rogers Clark operated a mill along nearby Mill Creek, 150 yards from where the creek entered the Ohio River.

Clarksville today is still a small town (population 22,000), a blend of old and new. The main attraction is Falls of the Ohio State Park, featuring the world's largest fossil beds, 368 million years old. The park features a spectacular interpretive center that overlooks the fossil beds. For information, go to www.town.clarksville.in.us or check out the Louisville site below.

Louisville, today, is famous for the Kentucky Derby, festivals, and a revived downtown.

Victorian mansions blend in with contemporary skyscrapers, paddle-wheel steamboats, cobblestone streets, sidewalk cafes, and boutiques. Horse-drawn carriages and motorized trolleys provide patrons two totally different views of the city. The Belle of Louisville, the oldest Mississippi-style sternwheeler in the country, still cruises the Ohio.

Downtown, you can enjoy theater, ballet, orchestra, opera, and a variety of other national and regional productions in three theaters. Nearby is the internationally acclaimed Actors Theatre of Louisville. Fully restored Civil War mansions, a great zoo, and Six Flags Kentucky Kingdom round out the attractions. For information, go to www.gotolouisville.com or call 800-626-5646.

In nearby Jeffersonville, Indiana, a 10-foot bronze cast statue of Thomas Jefferson, sculpted by local artist, Guy Tedesco, is scheduled to be unveiled on the 200th anniversary of the departure of Lewis and Clark.

The Clarksville Riverfront Foundation hopes to commission a series of Lewis and Clark–related statues to sit on a patch of land outside Clarksville, where the two explorers are thought to have first met.

Surely, Lewis shared some of the scientific instruction he'd been given, because Clark would succeed Lewis if he died or had to leave the expedition. They must have pored over the maps and lists of provisions, Jefferson's instructions, and the books Lewis had brought along. They became re-acquainted and may have shared their anxieties about succeeding in such a huge undertaking. And they probably got drunk (or close to it) at least once, listened to some music, dined on the best Clarksville had to offer, and had a few laughs.

On October 26, the water was high and strong as the keelboat and two pirogues left Clarksville. In 14 uneventful days, they arrived at Fort Massac, 35 miles upstream from where the Ohio River joins the Mississippi. The Lewis and Clark partnership had begun.

Chapter 6

Wintering at Camp Dubois

. . . .

In This Chapter

▶ Struggling to meet Jefferson's timetable

▶ Enlisting (and controlling) the rowdy recruits

▶ Securing supplies

▶ Doing the science

▶ Preparing to meet the tribes

▶ Keeping Clark's secret

▶ Weathering the storms to launch the expedition

. . . .

*E*ven before the official beginning of their expedition, Lewis and Clark had serious problems. They were already lagging behind the timetable set by President Jefferson. Recruiting qualified men was a constant concern, and controlling the drunk, disorderly, and defiant recruits was an even bigger challenge. They worried about their upcoming encounters with the Indian tribes and spent time plotting strategy. They bargained and sometimes fought with merchants to secure all-important supplies for the journey. They also had to devote time to their scientific mission, collecting info about the people and places that they were encountering. And, like career men of other time and place, they had to deal with their own personal concerns about rank and status.

Of course, through it all, Mother Nature tormented them with snow, ice, hail, thunderstorms, and mosquitoes.

As they camped for the winter, Lewis and Clark probably could have used some antacids and a good book on stress management. This chapter gives you a close look at the obstacles faced by the Lewis and Clark expedition during the countdown to their departure.

Rowing Against Time

The original plan by President Jefferson and Meriwether Lewis called for the Corps of Discovery to be 700 to 800 miles upriver on the Missouri before settling into a camp for the winter of 1803–1804. But it was October of 1803 before Lewis and Clark left the falls of the Ohio River on the Kentucky and Indiana borders (see Chapter 5). They still had to descend the Ohio River and to ascend the Mississippi River after that, so they knew that the party would get no farther than their next major stop — St. Louis, Missouri — before having to find shelter for the winter.

In late November, they stopped at an Army post in Kaskaskia, Illinois, sixty miles below St. Louis, to recruit some volunteers for the expedition (Lewis found only two to his liking). Lewis rode out on horseback to meet with the Spanish Governor of Upper Louisiana to discuss their path through Spanish territory. Clark and the men, on the other hand, left in the boats and headed for the settlement near Wood River, on the Illinois side (already occupied by the United States), directly across from the mouth of the Missouri River, where they hoped to camp for the winter.

During his trip to see the Spanish official, Lewis met a fur trader named Jarrot, who owned 400 acres of land at the mouth of the Wood River. He told Lewis he was welcome to use the land for the winter camp. In a hail and snowstorm, Clark arrived at Wood River on December 12, and he and Lewis inspected the Jarrot property. It had timber for log shelters and fires, game animals to hunt for food, fresh water from the river, and a nearby settlement where they could purchase provisions.

In his journal, Sergeant John Ordway called it Camp River Dubois. (In this book, we refer to it as Camp Dubois.) Americans called it Wood River. Clark had the men start building log huts, and Lewis left the party and went back to St. Louis to research the upper Missouri lands and people.

Defying the Spanish

Lewis met with Colonel Delassus, the Spanish governor of Upper Louisiana, to discuss the intended path through Spanish territory. Lewis presented the expedition as harmless, but Delassus wasn't buying his claim. He told Lewis that the expeditionary force could not go upriver from St. Louis until after the ceremonial transfer of the Upper Louisiana territory from Spain to France to the United States. That ceremony would not take place in St. Louis until early spring.

Lewis had no intention of beginning the trip up the Missouri so late in the year, but he did have in mind to set up camp north of St. Louis on the Mississippi River, in defiance of the Spanish governor's instructions.

Looking for a Few Good Men

When the Lewis and Clark party set off upstream toward St. Louis in late November, they had steered their boats into the dangerous main stream of the Mississippi River, a muddy, roiling river of boils and undertows, switchbacks and sandbars. They were forced to dodge uprooted trees and other floating debris. All the men rowing and poling with all their might translated into only about one mile per hour's progress! Lewis and Clark quickly realized that if these were the conditions they had to look forward to on their travels up the Missouri, they would need more men — perhaps twice as many as they already had. Recruiting became a top priority.

By the time they established Camp Dubois, the expedition included over 40 men, about a third of them young backwoodsmen recruited in Kentucky by Clark or French or French and American Indian men from around St. Louis. Among the civilians invited to try out for the Corps were hunters, boatmen, blacksmiths, a gunsmith, a tailor, carpenters, laborers, and farmers. The rest were soldiers recruited from Army posts on the Lower Ohio River. Many men came from Virginia and Pennsylvania, but the group also included men from Massachusetts, New Hampshire, Maryland, Canada, and Germany.

Grading the recruits

Clark watched the men and noted how they reacted to their new environment. He kept up this vigilance so that he could report to Lewis his recommendations for the Corps of Discovery detachment, the men he and Lewis would take with them to the Pacific Ocean and back (and the men they'd pick to go as far as the Mandan villages and return to St. Louis with information and specimens for Jefferson). Scattered in Clark's journals during that winter were lists of the men's names with checkmarks, plus signs, and zeroes. Apparently, he was keeping score. The notes show shifting totals, as well, as the captains debated how many men they needed.

Although Clark's journal isn't clear about how the men were being judged, several questions were surely on his scorecard. Who were the best hunters? Trackers? Who followed orders and who worked hard without being ordered? Who got along with others and stayed cool under pressure? Who handled the boat well or could bring down a deer without wasting ammunition? Skills they needed to select for survival were blacksmithing, metalworking, and gun repair. They also needed men who had experience on the Missouri River and men who knew the languages of tribes they would encounter. Clark didn't have a helpful stack of resumes and a human resources department to aid in his evaluation. He had to be keenly alert to each man's skills and weaknesses.

Maintaining discipline (sort of)

Clark did his best to keep the recruits busy. They finished building the huts and chopping piles of firewood. Groups went out regularly to hunt for game. He had some of the men help him modify the keelboat that Lewis had designed, adding a collapsible mast and storage lockers. Others helped him pack and repack and unpack and repack the supplies Lewis had brought from Philadelphia and the supplies he was acquiring in St. Louis. Clark had the men drill every day and take target practice.

Many of the men — especially the Ten Young Men from Kentucky (see Chapter 2) — were tasting Army discipline for the first time. During the three long winter months at Camp Dubois, the young men were waiting for spring and the voyage of discovery. They were cold, restless, and bored. Drilling in rain or snow or sleet and taking target practice of one shot per man per day didn't make them happy campers.

Clark's journal entries throughout the winter are sprinkled with references to discipline problems of one kind and another. Fights were common. Some of the men didn't want to follow orders unless they were directly commanded by one of the captains. Discipline was hard to maintain when Clark was present and nearly impossible when he left and put Sergeant Ordway (see Chapter 2) in charge. Lewis was "mortified and disappointed at the disorderly conduct," he wrote in the Orderly Book, where the captains' written orders were recorded. The following sections illuminate the captains' struggle with discipline.

Drunk, disorderly, and defiant

The recruits had signed up for a grand adventure, but at Camp Dubois they'd seen only the same 40 or so men in one hut village on one frozen riverbank. No single women were around except a few in the settlement and they were usually off-limits to the men. It was so cold that the men had to check their boots often to make sure that their toes weren't frostbitten. Each man got a ration of whiskey every night, four shots worth, a generous amount by today's standards. Dispensing a ration of whiskey to troops was standard practice of the time. But after enduring months of harsh conditions, the men considered the whiskey ration to be grossly inadequate.

In February, Lewis came back to the winter camp, and Clark went to St. Louis for a few meetings (one was to arrange for a group of Osage Indians to visit Washington, D.C., to meet with Jefferson). Lewis then also left Camp Dubois, putting Sergeant Ordway in charge. It was the first time that the men were expected to take instructions from anyone but Clark or Lewis.

So, naturally, some of the men snuck off to the nearby whisky shop. When Lewis returned to Camp Dubois in early March, seven men were on report, three for refusing to follow Ordway's orders. Four other men had conspired on a story that they were going hunting when they were really sneaking off to get drunk. The three men refusing orders were court-martialed and the four conspirators were confined to camp.

Temperatures rising

Unfortunately for Lewis and Clark, good weather didn't lead to good behavior among the men. Although frostbite was no longer a concern, the mosquitoes swarmed. Serious fighting broke out among the men in camp. After defying orders, Private John Shields threatened Sergeant Ordway's life and wanted to quit and go back to Kentucky. John Colter also loaded his rifle in defiance of Ordway, threatening to shoot him.

It was Private Shields's second major offense. He was the oldest man in the camp at 34 (except for Clark, who was also 34) and may have resented being ordered around by the younger Ordway. The offenders were put on trial for mutiny, with death as the outcome, if convicted. But the privates begged forgiveness and promised to shape up. The outcome of the trial wasn't recorded, but the punishment couldn't have been too stiff. A couple of days later Shields and Colter were accepted into the Corps of Discovery detachment.

No more Mr. Nice Guy

Clark had been tolerant of breaches of discipline in Camp Dubois. But when the Corps of Discovery began to get underway, he took a hard line. Too much was at stake on the trip to let order and discipline slide. He made sure that punishment for disobedience and other infractions was carried out, for example, in the case of Werner, Hall, and Collins.

On May 16, 1804, just a few days before the official launch of the expedition, the group pulled into St. Charles in present-day Missouri to wait for Lewis to come up from St. Louis. Clark found the folks of St. Charles, about 450 in all, "pore, polite and harmonious." Lewis's impression was harsher than Clark's. He pronounced them "miserable, pour, illiterate and when at home excessively lazy." Clark went to dinner with the family of the local grain mill owner, while the rest of the men had some fun. Three men had too much fun — William Werner, Hugh Hall, and John Collins. They went AWOL (absent without leave), and Clark wrote the next day that Collins acted in "an unbecoming manner at the Ball last night."

The unruly men were court-martialed on May 17. Ordway recorded that the jury sentenced Werner and Hall to 25 lashes with a whip (or ramrod or large stick), while urging leniency because of otherwise good behavior. Collins, who apparently was not a model soldier, was sentenced to 50 lashes, period. His was the only sentence carried out. Lashes may seem barbaric today, but this punishment was standard operating procedure in the Army at that time. Men were lashed for a wide range of infractions.

Two-day, three-flag, two-hankie ceremony

Lewis and Clark had to leave the men again in March, with Sergeant Ordway in charge, to attend the ceremonies in St. Louis marking the formal transfer of Upper Louisiana to the United States. The ceremony began as planned on March 9 with the Spanish flag being taken down. Then the French raised their flag, and the emotional crowd — nearly all of them of French descent — went wild. Crying, they talked the French agent into letting the French flag wave over the town for just one night.

The rest of the ceremony — the lowering the French flag, raising the U.S. flag, signing the papers, and giving a round of speeches — had to be postponed until the following day. After the second day of ceremonies, Lewis and Clark went with Amos Stoddard, a U.S. Army captain who stood in at the ceremonies as a deputized agent of France and temporarily assumed the post of military-civil governor of Upper Louisiana. They toured some of what Jefferson had bought from France — namely the Spanish military defenses. (See Chapter 3 for more on the Louisiana Purchase.)

Recruiting Drouillard, the cream of the crop

Despite the discipline problems among the enlisted men, Lewis and Clark enjoyed some recruiting successes. One was George Drouillard, who was half French Canadian and half Shawnee Indian.

Drouillard (whose name Lewis and Clark always spelled "Drewyer") was fluent in sign language and conversant in several American Indian languages. He was also an ace scout, hunter, and trapper. Lewis and Clark met him early on, while they were still traveling the Ohio River. His skills matched the needs of the expedition perfectly, and Lewis hired him immediately as a civilian interpreter (not an Army member) for the expedition.

Drouillard's name is listed directly under Lewis's and Clark's on the Detachment Order for the Corps of Discovery Roster of the permanent party.

Forming the permanent party (don't forget the dog)

During a ceremony, Lewis and Clark enlisted 27 other men (two of whom, York and Drouillard, weren't in the Army) into the permanent party "destined for the Expedition though the interior of the Continent of North America." The party included the two captains, three sergeants, 22 privates, Clark's slave York, Drouillard, and of course, Lewis's dog, Seaman. (See Chapter 2 for details.)

The men were divided into three squads, two led by newly minted sergeants Nathaniel Pryor and Charles Floyd, the third by Sergeant Ordway. Five soldiers led by Corporal Richard Warfington were chosen to travel with the detachment as far as the Mandan villages, and then return to St. Louis to send letters and specimens on to Jefferson.

Stocking Up on Supplies

When Lewis arrived in St. Louis in December of 1803, the city was 40 years old and had a population of between 1,000 and 1,400 (primarily French Canadians and French Canadian/Indians). It was a bustling trade center, with a heavy trade in furs that extended on the supply side to the far reaches of the frontier and on the demand side to most of the countries of Europe.

It was a good thing St. Louis was a bustling regional shopping center because Lewis and Clark had purchased supplies for only about 15 men and needed to supply a party of 45. Lewis had authorization from Jefferson to buy the goods he needed and charge them to the Army, so he spent many hours shopping until he dropped, and then having the goods shipped to Camp Dubois to be packed.

Clark's grocery list

The following is Clark's list for 40 days of provisions.

- 1,200 pounds of parchmeal
- 800 pounds of common parchmeal
- 1,600 pounds hulled corn (two listings, one of bags and one of barrels)
- 3,400 pounds of flour
- 560 pounds of "Biscuit"
- 750 pounds of salt
- 3,705 pounds of pork
- 8 pounds of candlewick
- 170 pounds of candles

- 50 pounds of soap
- 50 pounds of coffee
- 100 pounds of beans and peas
- 112 pounds of sugar
- 100 pounds of hogs lard
- 600 pounds of grease
- 50 bushels of meal
- 21 bales of Indian goods
- Tools of every description

He struck up an acquaintance with the town's leading businessmen, including the Chouteaus, who in years past had a monopoly on St. Louis imports and exports. (See Chapter 2 for more on local businessmen.) August and Pierre Chouteau, along with their trader brother-in-low, Charles Gratiot, were happy to sell Lewis as many supplies as he needed and throw in all the they knew about the upper Missouri country for free. Lewis also bought goods from a Spanish merchant, Manuel Lisa, but although the Chouteaus became friends of his and Clark's, Lewis would leave with no use at all for Lisa because Lisa whined to Washington that Lewis wasn't buying enough goods from him.

In the spring of 1804, Lewis embarked on a final buying spree. He purchased food, liquor, clothing, Indian trade goods, flags, nails, knives, and kegs. About the time the expedition was due to depart, Lewis couldn't find enough kegs — important containers for keeping many of their stocks dry.

Collecting Bugs, Leaves, Stats, and Maps

President Jefferson instructed Lewis to keep meticulous records about the places they were exploring. He wanted detailed accounts of the people and their cultures, the geography, climate, land, minerals, flora and fauna — you name it. Lewis stayed busy collecting boxes of natural-history specimens to send to Jefferson. As the leader of Jefferson's scientific expedition, everywhere the Corps went, Lewis needed to closely observe his surroundings and locate tree cuttings, plants, and animals of interest to (or perhaps even unknown to) scientists. He sent shipments back to Jefferson in March and again in May of 1804.

One of Jefferson's many assignments for Lewis was to collect and record statistics on the Upper Missouri River. To formalize the process, Lewis wrote out a questionnaire to use in his interviews of the locals. He interviewed a number of men, including Antoine Soulard, surveyor general for the Spanish. Based on a survey from 1800, which did not count Indians, Soulard told Lewis that about 10,000 people were living in the newly acquired Upper Louisiana territory and of these, about 2,000 were slaves. Of the whites, two-thirds were American.

The research Lewis conducted in St. Louis included collecting maps from people who'd already been up the Missouri River. Scottish explorer James Mackay was living in St. Louis, so he visited Camp Dubois and gave Lewis and Clark invaluable information and two maps to take on the trip. The first was Mackey's map from his own 1795 exploration of the Missouri up to the Omaha Indian villages. Three years after his own trip, Mackey sent his protégé, John Evans, on an expedition to find the route to the Pacific Ocean. Evans had gone only as far as the Mandan villages, but he had brought back a map of his journey, a copy of which Mackey gave Lewis.

When Lewis wasn't interviewing locals, collecting statistics, studying maps, recruiting men, ordering supplies, and listening to tales about life upriver, he had letters to write, including ones to Jefferson. In January of 1804, Jefferson wrote Lewis to say that he could keep up with the expedition's progress from reading newspaper accounts. "(The Louisiana Purchase) has inspired the public generally with a great deal of interest as to your progress, Jefferson wrote. "The enquiries are perpetual as to your progress."

Worrying about the American Indians

In January of 1803, Jefferson wrote Lewis with instructions on how to deal with the American Indians that the expedition could expect to encounter. The Louisiana Purchase had been finalized in New Orleans on December 20, so the United States now officially controlled most of the territory that Lewis and Clark would be traveling.

Just call me "dad"

Lewis and Clark began to compose the speeches that they would deliver to tribes along their route. Jefferson's advice boiled down to this: Tell the American Indians that they have a new father — me. Tell them I have great plans for them, plans that will work out well for both American Indians and whites.

Lewis and Clark followed Jefferson's instructions, and as Chapter 8 describes, their speeches strike a note of paternalism that's still evident in American Indian policy today.

Psyched out about the Teton Sioux

In March of 1804, Clark was worried about preparations to meet the American Indians upriver. The locals had filled the men's heads with stories about the dangerous Teton Sioux — armed and mean, demanding steep ransoms for passage through territory they controlled on the river. Sergeant Gass wrote in his journal that the locals said the Upper Missouri was "a country possessed by numerous powerful and warlike nations of savages, of gigantic stature, fierce, treacherous and cruel; and particularly hostile to white men."

The expedition's encounter with the Teton Sioux had to be successful. They had to get past the Teton Sioux in order to reach the Mandan villages, but they also needed to start a relationship with the Teton Sioux that would ease tensions on the river and make traveling through their territory safer for Americans. (Chapter 8 discusses more about the Teton Sioux.)

Using the word "Sioux"

Seoux. Souex. Souix. Seoeux. Sciuex. Soues. Souis. William Clark spelled Sioux at least 20 different ways in his journals. Sergeant John Ordway spelled it Zoe.

Sioux is a French pejorative that means "little snake" — a colonial perpetuation of a derogatory term applied to the Lakota, Dakota, and Nakota people by an enemy tribe. Many different bands of Sioux lived — and still live — on the Middle Missouri River.

The Teton Sioux call themselves Lakota (Lakota is a Sioux dialect). Teton comes from the word Tito-wa, meaning prairie dwellers. Lakotas or Teton Sioux in 1804 included the Oglala,

Brules, Two Kettles, Sans Arcs, Miniconjou and Hunkpapa bands.

The modern Sioux reservations along the Lewis and Clark Trail are known as Pine Ridge (Oglala Sioux Tribe), Rosebud, Lower Brule, Cheyenne River, Standing Rock, Yankton (who are Nakota), and Crow Creek Sioux. They continue to use the term Sioux as part of their official tribal names because it's the name they are called in their treaties with the U.S. government — treaties that recognize their sovereignty and that they hold sacred. Therefore, we respectfully use the word Sioux in this book.

It may have been the wildness of the talk about the Teton Sioux that ultimately made the encounter with them so tense. Pondering the highly-charged talk, Clark decided to add a cannon to the keelboat and mounted it on a swivel so that it could be fired in any direction. He added four blunderbusses to the arsenal (heavy shotguns that used a combination of buckshot or scrap iron or musket balls for ammunition). He mounted two on the *keelboat* (large, shallow freight boat) and one each in the *pirogues* (canoe-shaped boats).

Keeping Rank Secrets

While the expedition wintered at Camp Dubois, Lewis was nagged by an important loose end. Clark's commission as a captain had not arrived. Lewis wrote Jefferson and Secretary of War Dearborn to complain in February of 1804. Months passed, but no reply came and neither did the commission. In the meantime, Lewis called Clark "captain," treated him as an equal, and left him in charge of the men for weeks at a time.

Finally, in early May, Lewis had a very unhappy task to perform. He had to tell William Clark that his commission had come through, but as a lieutenant not as a captain. The reason sounded like bureaucratic hoohaw to Lewis. "The peculiar situation, circumstances and organization of the Corps of Engineers is such as would render the appointment of Mr. Clark as a Captain in that Corps improper," wrote Secretary of War Dearborn. He tried to blunt the blow by pointing out that Clark would be paid the same as a captain.

Adding insult to injury, Lewis knew that Jefferson had signed off on Clark's commission as a lieutenant even though he had made it clear to Jefferson that he was asking Clark to be his co-captain and nothing less, and that Clark had accepted under those conditions. Jefferson also knew that they had been operating as co-commanders since Lewis picked Clark up in Kentucky.

Lewis couldn't (or least didn't) tell Clark to his face. He sent the news in a letter from St. Louis to Wood River on May 6, adding "I think it will be best to let none of our party or any other persons know any thing about the grade."

During the expedition, no one but Jefferson and a handful of others knew that they weren't equal in rank. The men didn't know, and Lewis and Clark did nothing on the expedition to dispel the belief that they were co-captains and co-commanders.

Well after the expedition, Clark told an interviewer, "I did not think myself very well treated," but no records or other documentation indicate that he felt bad at the time. Lewis's insistence on keeping the difference in their official ranks secret kept Clark focused on his goal — he wanted the expedition to succeed and he wanted to co-lead it.

Braving the Storms: The Expedition Begins

Nothing was ever easy for the Lewis and Clark team, and they had another obstacle to overcome as they prepared to launch the expedition: violent thunderstorms.

In early May of 1804, Lewis was in St. Louis, trying to obtain more kegs (containers) for the journey. Clark was at Camp Dubois, continuing to pack and repack the supplies and equipment, trying to find just the right balance to ease plying the deeply laden boats up a river running strongly in the other direction. After packing the keelboat, Clark and 20 men took it out for a shakedown ride. Drouillard came into camp with seven more French Canadian boatmen, known as *voyagers* or *engages,* that he had recruited.

On May 13, Clark sent a message to Lewis that all was ready, and on May 14, Clark wrote in his journal that they were "fixing for a start." The keelboat with 31 men and the two pirogues (canoe-shaped boats), one with six men and the other with eight, set out around 4 p.m. on a rainy day. They went six miles upriver and then pulled over at an island to spend the night. On May 16, the expedition pulled into St. Charles to wait for Lewis to come up from St. Louis.

Discovering Lewis and Clark in Missouri

Missouri has a number of spots where you can camp where Lewis and Clark did, and the conditions are almost as primitive! One is the Grand Pass Wildlife Area in Saline County, which offers unspoiled hiking, birding, and fishing. Another is Stump Island Park near Glasgow, Missouri. In addition to allowing free primitive camping, Stump Island Park offers fishing and boating.

Lewis and Clark State Park and Lewis and Clark Lake near Rushville, Missouri, boast prime bird habitat, exhibits on the exhibition, picnic areas, swimming, fishing, boating, and tent and RV camping. This is where the expedition celebrated Independence Day, 1804 and Clark described "great quantities of fish and Gees and Goslings." For more information Missouri state parks, go to www.mostateparks.com/Lewisandclark.htm or call 800-344-6946.

Another beautiful Lewis and Clark spot is in the middle of metropolitan Kansas City, Missouri. Once a wilderness where Clark stood, today it's a small park called Clark's Point, an inner city overlook of the confluence of the Kansas and Missouri Rivers with a statue of Lewis, Clark, York, Sacagawea, and Seaman (see Chapter 2 for details on these members of the Corps). Kansas City is one of the preeminent art cities in the United States, with over 80 art galleries and 40 museums and art centers. It's also a family destination with a major amusement park, zoo, and science center. Find visitor information on Kansas City at www.visitkc.com or by calling 800-767-7700.

Lewis started for St. Charles by horseback on May 20 in threatening weather. He led an entourage that included Stoddard, the temporary military governor of Upper Louisiana and two of his subordinates. More than a dozen other men in business and politics accompanied them. A violent thunderstorm drove them into a cabin where they decided to eat a picnic that they'd brought along. They then went on in a driving rain to reach the French Canadian town of St. Charles in time for supper.

With so many French Canadians in the party, there was a good attendance at the Catholic Mass the next morning — about 20 men, Clark among them. Lewis made the acquaintance of two French and Indian men, Pierre Cruzatte and Francis Labiche, and he hired them on the spot. Cruzatte's mother was Omaha, a tribe they expected to encounter, and Cruzatte knew the Omaha language. Labiche knew several Indian languages.

Even though it was storming and had been storming for three days, Lewis and Clark decided to leave from St. Charles on the afternoon of May 21. They set off cheered by a small crowd, made a little over three miles in the continuing storm, and then camped on an island.

At dawn on May 22, the Corps of Discovery, bound for glory, was finally on its way.

Chapter 7

Traveling on the Big Muddy

In This Chapter

▶ Saying good-bye to white civilization

▶ Struggling up the Missouri River

▶ Falling in love with the prairie

▶ Suffering the discomforts and dangers of the journey

*O*n May 21, 1804, after more than a year of preparations in Washington D.C., Philadelphia, Harpers Ferry, Pittsburgh, Louisville, and Camp Dubois, the Corps of Discovery left all of that behind and began their epic voyage up the untamed Missouri River. The men rowed, poled, and towed the *keelboat* (a large flat-bottomed boat that carried their possessions) and *pirogues* (boats like canoes), exhausting themselves and making slow progress. However, they were passing through beautiful grasslands, which Lewis and Clark pronounced perfect for future American agriculture. They also described vast herds of buffalo and an abundance of animals never before seen by U.S. citizens.

Although the prairie was awe inspiring, the living conditions were harsh. Sergeant Floyd died of a "bilious colic," later determined by scholars and physicians to be a ruptured appendix, and teenager George Shannon, the Corps' youngest member, was lost for over two weeks. Some of the rough and rowdy men rebelled against the demands placed on them, but punishment was swift and severe for those who drank more than their share, neglected their duty, or deserted. This chapter shares the details.

Leaving "Civilization" Behind

On May 21, 1804, at 3:00 in the afternoon, the *Corps of Volunteers for North Western Discovery* — better known to history as the Corps of Discovery — launched its three boats at St. Charles, Missouri, and set off "under a jentle Breese" up the Missouri River. The Lewis and Clark expedition was underway at last. The people of St. Charles lined the river bank and shouted three cheers as the keelboat and the white and red pirogues (canoes) nosed into the swift current.

The Spanish miss the boats

Fearing that the expedition would try to lay claim to areas of New Spain as well as the United States' newly acquired Louisiana Territory, the Spanish governor at Santa Fe sent four different armed companies during 1804 and 1805 to stop Lewis and Clark. The Spaniards never found them.

Two days later, near-disaster struck. Lewis climbed a hill to get a better look upriver and fell 20 feet down a 300-foot rock cliff. "Saved himself by the assistance of his Knife," wrote Clark.

The following day, the expedition passed Boone's Settlement, established by the great Kentucky frontiersman, Daniel Boone, in 1799. Lewis and Clark went ashore and bought butter and corn, but if they met with Boone, neither of them wrote about it. In fact, at that point, Lewis wasn't writing anything in his journals — or if he was, his notes have been lost.

On May 25, the Corps of Discovery passed La Charette, the last white settlement on the Missouri. The party did encounter several groups in either one or two pirogues heading downriver, bearing furs and pelts, hungry fur traders, and voyageurs heading for the markets of St. Louis.

One of those pirogues carried Pierre Dorion, Sr., a French trader who had met George Rogers Clark, William's brother, during the Revolutionary War. He had lived with the Yankton Sioux on the middle Missouri, had a Yankton wife, and spoke her language in addition to French and English. (More on the Yankton Sioux in Chapter 8.) Lewis and Clark persuaded him to join their journey north to translate for them when they reached Sioux country.

Rowing, Poling, and Towing

With the wind at their backs, the explorers could make 20 miles a day upriver. Without the wind, however, they had to fight for every mile they advanced, and sometimes they had to struggle just to keep the heavily laden, cumbersome keelboat from overturning in the swift river. The Missouri was sometimes clogged with submerged and floating logs. It was shallow in places and laced with ever-shifting sandbars. The men sailed, rowed, pushed, and occasionally towed the big boat from shore. Their labor was intense, but they were young, strong, and eager for the adventure.

Clark, the better boatman of the two captains, generally commanded the keelboat while Lewis walked on shore, collecting animal and plant specimens and eyeballing the land's suitability for future farms, forts, and trading posts.

Lewis's Detachment Orders of May 26 provide a good look at how he organized his floating Army company. He ordered all the sergeants to keep journals recording their daily experiences and observations. He divided the men into three "messes," which would cook and eat as groups. Every evening, each mess got the next day's rations. They were not allowed to cook during the day after getting underway, so they ate a lot of leftovers.

Lewis also stationed one sergeant in the bow of the keelboat to watch the river for snags and the shore for Indians, another at the helm to steer and attend the compass, and another in the middle to manage the sails and make sure the men were working.

Viewing the Vast, Bountiful Prairie

At the beginning of the 19th century, before America's great westward migrations, the prairie that Lewis and Clark got to witness abounded in extraordinary numbers of buffalo, elk, deer, bears, and waterfowl. The lush prairie grasses also fed flocks of wild turkeys and vast herds of fleet goats (as Lewis and Clark called them), which were what we know as pronghorn antelopes. They were the first to be described for Western science.

By July 4, 1804, the expedition was traveling through a virtual Garden of Eden, rich in game and raspberries. That morning, the men fired the keelboat's cannon to usher in the nation's 28th birthday. At noon, they went ashore at the mouth of a small tributary that they named Independence Creek. The party camped that night at an abandoned Kanza Indian village near present day Atchison County, Kansas, and Lewis and Clark gave each man an extra gill of whiskey. They fired the cannon again at sunset in honor of the first Independence Day to be celebrated in the Louisiana Territory.

Clark described the Corps's campsite of July 4 as "one of the most butifull Plains I ever Saw, open & butifully diversified with hills & vallies all presenting themselves to the river covered with grass and a few scattering trees, a handsom Creek meandering thro."

Lewis and Clark recorded page after glowing page, extolling the open prairies as a near Garden of Eden. ". . . deer to be Seen in every direction . . . " wrote Clark, ". . . raspberries perple, ripe and abundant." The profusion of wild prairie flowers moved Clark to downright eloquence, generally a characteristic of Lewis's more ornate prose, ". . . nature appears to have exerted herself to butify the Senery by the variety of flours . . . raised above the Grass, which Strikes & profumes the Sensation, and amuses the mind . . . ." He lamented that such beauty was so far from civilization that only the buffalo, elk, deer, bear, and "Savage Indians" could enjoy it.

A prairie dog for President Jefferson

Early in the fall, while walking on shore near present day Boyd County, Nebraska, Lewis and Clark came upon an extensive colony of small burrowing, barking mammals. The French voyageurs called them *petite chien* ("small dog") and Lewis and Clark called them "barking squirrels." They were prairie dogs. Lewis and Clark and their men were fascinated and spent the rest of the afternoon trying to dig the animals out of their holes. Finally, they poured five barrels of water down a burrow and forced out one unfortunate little creature. They took him back to the keelboat to record him for the first time for Western science. The following spring, they sent back with the keelboat a live prairie dog in a cage for President Jefferson.

On August 8, the Corps of Discovery encountered an unbelievable sight: a huge expanse of something white drifting toward them down the river. Lewis measured it to be three miles long and 70 yards across. It was feathers! A vast mass of white feathers! Ahead, the expedition came upon a large sandbar where thousands of white pelicans were preening themselves, sending their molted feathers downriver in a sea of white.

Millions of "buffalows"

Lewis and Clark had been watching for Indians since leaving "civilization," because Jefferson had instructed them to meet with the West's tribal nations, explain that they now had a new white father, establish peace among the tribes, and establish trade relationships between the tribes and the United States. When the party found its first buffalo (shot by Private Joseph Field), the captains thought the Indians wouldn't be far behind. A month or so later, the buffalo were grazing by the thousands and thousands along the river, and Lewis and Clark were meeting with Yankton and Teton Sioux and Arikara leaders (see Chapter 8).

What's for dinner?

The men of the Corps of Discovery were meat eaters. They were working like dogs to move their boats upriver against the Missouri's fast current, and they were traveling through a country that teemed with many species of dinner on the hoof. As a result, to keep up their strength, they ate and ate and ate — nine pounds of meat per day per man. (This was a group of men that didn't think about vegetables; in addition to meat, they ate hominy, lard, salt pork, flour, and cornmeal from their provisions.) Their fine hunter, George Drouillard, went out to hunt every day and added deer meat to the diet. He apparently never hunted for greens or roots in the early days of the expedition. The first exception to this fare came with Clark's 34th birthday feast on August 1. That day, the prairie provided venison, beaver tail, cherries, plums, raspberries, currants, and grapes.

The excessive amount of meat along with the lack of vegetables in the men's diet quickly began to take a toll on their health, as discussed in the following section.

Getting Sick, Lost, Scared, and Busted

The men of the Lewis and Clark expedition may have been traveling through a landscape of breathtaking beauty, but conditions were harsh. Illness was troublesome, and medical treatment was primitive. They were traveling unknown terrain, and even seasoned woodsman could lose track of time. Anxiety about the Indians kept the men unsettled. And the troops themselves were responsible for some of their own problems: drinking more than the allotted amount, neglect of duty, and desertion.

Illness afflicts the troops

By mid-June of 1804, most of the Lewis and Clark party had already felt the pain of dysentery and boils. Lewis and Clark blamed the muddy river water the men had to drink. The disproportionate volume of meat in their diets caused them considerable gastric distress. They were also plagued by thick hordes of mosquitoes and gnats, so they were a collection of digestive and itching misery.

Lewis did what he could to alleviate their symptoms. While studying medicine with Dr. Benjamin Rush in Philadelphia in preparation for the expedition (see Chapter 5), Lewis procured a supply of Dr. Rush's patented purgative pills, sometimes called *Rush's thunderclappers* or *thunderbolts* by the men of the Corps. During the voyage, Lewis copiously prescribed them for his men to cure all manner of digestive complaints. Each pill was a powerful laxative made up of calomel and jalap from the roots of the *Exogonium jalapa* from Mexico.

Lewis couldn't always help his men, given the strenuous labor and his limited medical knowledge. In August of 1804, Sgt. Charles Floyd became ill with what Lewis diagnosed as bilious colic. Nothing Lewis did could relieve him, not even a dose of Dr. Rush's purgative pills. All the men were worried about him, and York was especially attentive.

Captain Clark sat up with Floyd all night on August 20, but the young man from Kentucky was much weaker the next day. The party stopped to prepare him a warm bath, but he never got to partake of its benefits. He died that day at the age of 22 "with a great deel of Composure," according to Clark. Before he died, Floyd asked Clark, his fellow Kentuckian, to write a letter for him.

The Corps of Discovery buried Charles Floyd with full military honors on a bluff overlooking a beautiful river that flowed into the Missouri, near present day Sioux City, Iowa (see Figure 7-1). They also named the river Floyd's River.

Figure 7-1:
Sergeant
Floyd's
monument.

Floyd Monument. Courtesy of National Park Service, Lewis and Clark National Historic Trail.

Modern scholars believe that Floyd died of a ruptured appendix and resulting peritonitis. He was the only member of the expedition to die during the voyage. Unfortunately, given Sgt. Floyd's probable ruptured appendix, the thunderclappers Lewis administered quite likely hastened the young sergeant's death. On the other hand, the finest physicians in the world probably couldn't have saved Floyd: In 1804 medical science didn't know how to treat appendicitis.

A few days after Floyd's death, Lewis and Clark held an election of the men to decide Floyd's successor as sergeant. The party chose Patrick Gass, and on August 26, Lewis issued orders promoting Gass to the rank of sergeant.

George Shannon gets lost

On August 26, Lewis and Clark sent out George Drouillard and teenaged George Shannon, the youngest member of the expedition, to round up the horses. Drouillard returned before nightfall, but Shannon didn't. Lewis and Clark sent Private John Colter to find him, and then sent Drouillard, too. Neither could find the boy.

Two full weeks after Shannon's disappearance, the keelboat's bowman spotted Shannon, weak and nearly starved, sitting on the bank of the Missouri as if waiting for them. The men pulled him aboard, and he explained his disappearance.

By the time he found the horses, he was sure that the boats had moved on upriver ahead of him, so he had been traveling hard trying to catch up. In fact, the boats were behind him. He had run out of bullets but had killed a rabbit to eat by firing a stick from his gun. Mostly, he had subsisted on wild plums and grapes. Finally, he had given up on catching the Corps of Discovery and was waiting on the bank for any boat that might come along headed south.

An incredulous William Clark wrote in his journal that "a man had like to have Starved to death in a land of Plenty for the want of Bulletes or Something to kill his meat."

The men face devil spirits

Lewis and Clark had heard about a cone-shaped hill near the White Stone River (called the Vermillion River in present-day South Dakota) where the Plains Indians believed devils or spirits lived. The devils were reported to be human in form, but with large heads, about 18 inches tall and armed with sharp arrows. Reportedly, they killed everybody who ventured up their hill. All the tribes in the area — Otoes, Omaha, and Sioux — had suffered losses at the hands of these devils, and they wouldn't go near the place.

On a cloudy morning in late August of 1804, the expedition came within sight of the bedeviled hill, and Lewis and Clark decided to explore it. They took with them Privates John Shields, Joseph Field, William Bratton, John Colter, Robert Frazer, Corporal Richard Warfington (who was not a member of the permanent party but would command the keelboat on its homeward journey), *engage* (laborer) E. Cann (also not a member of the permanent party), Sergeant John Ordway, George Drouillard, and Lewis's black Newfoundland dog, Seaman — perhaps to have safety in numbers.

The group hiked for about four hours to reach the top of the hill, which sat solitary on the surrounding flat terrain. The day was so hot that they had to send Seaman back to the boat, and all the men suffered from lack of water. But the view from the top was lovely, revealing great flocks of birds and numerous herds of buffalo grazing in all directions. And they met no devils.

The hill is known today as Spirit Mound, a special stop on the Lewis and Clark National Historic Trail. Located near Vermillion, South Dakota, Spirit Mound Historic Prairie is a new South Dakota State Park. For information about visiting call 605-987-2263 or visit www.state.sd.us/gfp/sdparks/spiritmound/spiritmound.htm.

Drinkers, sleepers, and deserters got the lash

Conditions were strenuous for the men of the Lewis and Clark expedition. It's not surprising that discipline sometimes broke down as the men reacted to the heavy demands placed on them. But violations of the rules brought swift and brutal punishment.

- **Taking a sip:** On June 26, the Corps of Discovery was 400 miles upriver at the mouth of the Kansas River. They stopped there for three days to rest and take river measurements, but while they camped, they suffered a raid on their whiskey supply by their own men.

  Lewis had provisioned the expedition with about 120 gallons of whiskey for the whole trip. Each man got a daily ration of one gill (about ½ cup). While on night sentry duty, Private John Collins decided to tap a keg, just for one sip — who would know the difference? He had one sip, and then another and another. Private Hugh Hall joined him, and pretty soon they were both drunk.

  The next morning, Captain Clark called a court martial with Sgt. Nathaniel Pryor presiding. They charged Collins with stealing whiskey and getting drunk on duty. They charged Hall with taking whiskey contrary to the rules. Collins pleaded not guilty and was sentenced to 100 lashes. Hall, hoping for mercy, pleaded guilty and got 50.

- **Catching some zzz's:** On the night of July 11, Private Alexander Willard fell asleep while on guard duty, and Sgt. Ordway caught him. Lewis and Clark called another court martial. They found Willard guilty of a military crime that could have gotten them all killed

had hostile Indians been nearby, and they sentenced him to 100 lashes a day for four straight days.

- **Making a run for it:** The third court martial on the first leg of the journey occurred on August 18, Lewis's 30th birthday. Private Moses Reed had deserted two weeks earlier, and Lewis and Clark had sent George Drouillard, the company's best tracker and hunter, to find him. On August 18, Drouillard came riding into camp with Reed in tow and with a delegation from the Oto Indians, including their leader Little Thief and the Missouri Indian leader Big Horse (see Chapter 8). Lewis and Clark shared a cordial meal with the Indian leaders, whom they had been anxious to meet, and then convened Reed's trial. They found him guilty and could have executed him according to military law of the day. Instead, they sentenced him to run the gauntlet, whereby the men of the expedition formed two lines and flogged the offender as he ran between them. Reed had to run it four times — the equivalent of about 500 lashes. Lewis and Clark also discharged him from the expedition's permanent party and, after the winter at Fort Mandan (see Chapter 9), they sent him back to St. Louis with the keelboat. They replaced him in the permanent party with Private Robert Frazer.

  The Corps' guests, Little Thief and Big Horse, expressed dismay at the severity of Reed's punishment, saying that their people never beat anyone. Lewis and Clark explained the military custom to the alarmed Indians and sent Reed to his gauntlet.

Chapter 8

Pitching American Trade to the Western Tribes

In This Chapter

▶ Looking for Indians along the Platte

▶ Talking peace and trade with the Otoes and Missouris

▶ Dancing and dealing with the Yankton Sioux

▶ Avoiding violence with the Teton Sioux

▶ Enjoying the Arikaras

*B*y July of 1804, the Corps of Discovery had worked its way past the mouth of the Platte River. Lewis and Clark were diligently fulfilling some of their many directives from President Jefferson. However, one really important one — trade diplomacy with the Western tribes — was eluding them. They couldn't find the Indians!

Finally, the expedition began to encounter some of the tribes. With elaborate military pomp and circumstance, the Corps of Discovery tried to carry out three of its primary missions: announcing U.S. ownership of the Louisiana Territory to the Indians (who thought it was *their* home), securing promises of peace among the tribes, and paving the way for lucrative trade partnerships between the tribes and the United States.

In this chapter, Lewis and Clark finally take their best shot at frontier diplomacy — with mixed results. The Corps held peaceful councils with the tribes of the Oto, Missouri, and Yankton Sioux. However, their diplomatic efforts with the powerful Teton Sioux were unsuccessful, and the dangerous and disastrous negotiation was a failure of historic proportion. The showdown with the Tetons left the Corps wary and wily, but they rallied and enjoyed friendly meetings with the Arikaras.

Poling Past the Platte

By late July 1804, the Corps of Discovery had poled, sailed, pushed, and cursed its way past the mouth of the Platte — a typical prairie river that seemed a mile wide and an inch deep and meandered into the Missouri from the faraway Rocky Mountains. Most rivermen of the day considered the Platte to be the dividing line between the lower and middle stretches of the Missouri.

By the time the expedition reached the Platte in late July, Lewis and Clark had expected to meet Oto, Missouri, Omaha, Ponca, and Pawnee Indians. But they hadn't. And they were getting worried. Where were those Indians? Finally the captains realized, or more likely were told by some of the part-Indian members of the Corps — Labiche, Cruzatte, or Drouillard — that in midsummer, the tribes always left their villages along the rivers and went out onto the prairies to hunt buffalo.

So Lewis and Clark decided to slow up and wait awhile. They set up camp about ten miles beyond the mouth of the Platte on what is now the Iowa side of the Missouri River. They called the spot White Catfish Camp after the big, fat, white, river catfish they had been catching for supper. They stayed there about a week to rest, repair the boats, and look harder for Indians. On July 23, they sent their best scout, George Drouillard (whose name Lewis and Clark always spelled Drewyer), and Pierre Cruzatte, the one-eyed fiddle player (see Chapter 2 for details on both men), out to find the Otoes and neighboring Pawnees. Two days later, Drouillard and Cruzatte returned alone. Disappointed and frustrated, Lewis and Clark broke camp and once again headed up the Missouri.

Uncovering the Loch Ness Monster's brother

Lewis collected specimens for the scientific mission throughout the expedition, and sometimes his diligence was rewarded. While studying in Philadelphia, Lewis had learned from Dr. Caspar Wistar how to look for fossils (see Chapter 5). On September 10, that Paleontology 101 course paid off big time. While scouting a ridge above the river, the explorers made a remarkable discovery. They found a petrified skeleton — 45 feet of vertebrae with some teeth and ribs attached.

Clark recorded it as the backbone of a really big fish. In fact, it was the backbone of a Mesozoic aquatic reptile called plesiosaur — the same creature that many believe lives in Loch Ness in Scotland. At least some parts of the skeleton were later enshrined in the Smithsonian Institution.

Peddling Peace and Prosperity to the Otoes and Missouris

At last, on July 28, while out hunting, Drouillard met a lone Missouri Indian and talked him into coming back to camp to meet Lewis and Clark. The Missouri told the explorers that his band was very small, having been depleted by smallpox, and was now living with the Otoes about four miles from the river. The "great gang" of Otoes, as Clark described them, were hunting buffalo out on the plains.

The next day was dark and rainy, but Clark sent the French *engage* (laborer) La Liberte, who spoke Oto, to accompany the Missouri man back to the Oto camp and invite the tribe's leaders to meet with Lewis and Clark.

On July 30, the Corps of Discovery made camp on a grassy bench above the river and below a higher bluff and waited for La Liberte and the Otoes. The bluffs above camp provided expansive views of the meandering river and sweeping prairie, dotted with groves of willow, cottonwood, mulberry, elm, sycamore, linden, ash, hickory, walnut, coffee nut, and oak trees. Clark also noted in his journal that the soil was of "good quality."

At sunset on August 2, a group of Otoes and Missouris arrived at the Council Bluff camp and set up a camp of their own. Among them were six leaders, but not their principal headmen, Little Thief and Big Horse. Also among them was a white trader who lived with the Otoes and spoke their language. Clark noted the man's name as Mr. Fairfong.

Eating "Water Millions" and preparing for the council on the bluff

Lewis and Clark sent gifts of pork, flour, and roasted meat to the Oto camp and invited the Indians to a council the next morning. The Otoes reciprocated with gifts of watermelons — "Water Millions," as Clark spelled it — and agreed to meet. That night, not sure of what to expect, every man of the Corps of Discovery was alert and sleepless.

The next morning was foggy as Lewis and Clark prepared for their first council with the Western tribes. Lewis drafted his speech. Clark prepared presents for the Indians according to his perception of their status, while the men rigged the keelboat's mainsail into an awning to serve as shade from the summer sun and attached an American flag to a pole to make the meeting official. (Their keelboat was a 55 foot, large, shallow cargo boat.) Excitement was in the air — the Indians were coming. Lewis and Clark would finally get to be diplomats.

What's for dinner?

Dinner for the Corps of Discovery always meant substantial portions of protein (see Chapter 7). During this part of the voyage, the protein was in the form of wild turkeys, geese, catfish, beaver, and elk. Sometimes they added wild plums, grapes, currants, or raspberries. Joseph Field killed a badger, but Lewis and Clark had it stuffed to send back to President Jefferson.

Trotting out the traveling military parade

The Otoes and Missouris and their interpreter, Fairfong, arrived after breakfast. Lewis and Clark subjected them to what would become the expedition's standard U.S. Army traveling show — a military full dress parade by the men of the Corps; the Great White Father speech by Lewis (more in Chapter 2); anointment of tribal leaders as "first," "second," and sometimes "third chiefs" (the Corps' names, not the Indians' — see the Introduction to this book); and the presentation of gifts.

As gifts, Lewis and Clark packaged up fancy American dress coats, red leggings, blue blankets, American flags, Jefferson peace medals (see Figure 8-1), gunpowder, face paint, certificates of good conduct, and whiskey to distribute to the Oto and Missouri leaders that they would appoint as "chiefs," according to the American military custom of the time.

Lewis's speech announced to the Otoes and Missouris that the United States now owned the Louisiana Territory, including the Missouri River and their tribal homelands. He explained that their former French and Spanish "fathers" were gone and would never return. The tribes now had a new Great White Father back in Washington. This new father required his "red children" to make peace with their neighbor tribes and trade only with the Americans.

Lewis said, in part, ". . . the great chief of the Seventeen great nations of America, impelled by his parental regard for his newly adopted children on the troubled waters, has sent us out to clear the road, remove every obstruction, and make it the road of peace between himself and his red children residing there." Lewis promised that the Americans would build a trading post at the mouth of the Platte River and that the tribes would get a better deal there than they had from their first white fathers. He was promising trade for peace.

But he was also threatening. If the Otoes and Missouris did not follow these requirements from their new father, they would be barred from trade with the new sovereign of their lands and would suffer accordingly. He concluded by inviting Missouri and Oto leaders to visit their new father in Washington — where they could see firsthand how rich America was and how happy the Eastern tribes were to be living in compliance with their great father's directives. They'd see how happy these tribes were to be conquered and protected.

Figure 8-1:
The
Jefferson
Peace
Medal.

Courtesy of Dana Linett.

Clark recorded in his journal that the Indians were "well pleased." Several of the Oto and Missouri leaders gave speeches of their own, agreeing to abide by the orders of their new father, expressing happiness to have a new father they could depend on, and hinting that they hoped their new trade partners would be more generous than their old ones. Lewis and Clark gave out more gifts, and Lewis fired the expedition's air gun — that silent novelty weapon that somehow always seemed to "astonish" the natives. (See the "Showing off the cannon and the air gun" sidebar for details.)

Less than overwhelmed by the Indians' words, Clark called them "no oreters" (orators) but was pleased enough with what he and Lewis felt to be a successful first diplomatic effort. The Indians appeared to accept Jefferson's trade policy as fair and good.

Welcoming the elusive Little Thief and Big Horse

After the council on the bluff, Lewis and Clark packed up the boats and proceeded on upriver to make camp among "excessively troublesome Misquitors" (mosquitoes). They sent a copy of Lewis's speech with a bundle of gifts to the principal Oto leader, Little Thief, who, along with Big Horse, principal headman of the smallpox-reduced Missouri Tribe, had not attended the council. Inexplicably (given that Big Horse was the Missouri leader), Lewis and Clark didn't send the speech and gifts to Big Horse. They also sent a request to Little Thief to pledge the Otoes to peace with the Omahas, who were enemies of the Otoes and Missouris.

Showing off the cannon and the air gun

Although the Lewis and Clark expedition was a scientific, exploratory, and diplomatic effort, it was also a mission of the United States Army. It sailed up the Missouri River armed to the teeth. If diplomacy and friendly persuasion failed with the Indians, the Americans could always resort to force. In fact, while at Camp Dubois, Lewis and Clark added a bronze cannon to the keelboat. Lewis purchased the monster gun in St. Louis, and Clark had it mounted on a swivel so that it could be pointed and fired in any direction. The cannon was the expedition's heaviest armament. Up until that time, it was also the biggest, most fearsome weapon ever taken up the Missouri. It could fire a one pound solid lead ball or sixteen musket balls.

Lewis and Clark also purchased four smaller blunderbusses (muzzle-loading firearms, each with flared barrel) and mounted them on swivels, as well — two in the keelboat's stern and one on each pirogue. These four guns could shoot musket balls and buckshot. Together with the cannon, or *swivel gun* as Lewis and Clark usually referred to it, the weapons turned the keelboat and pirogues into gunboats.

In addition to the heavy armaments, Lewis had purchased an air gun in Philadelphia — made by gunsmith Isaiah Lukens. It was a pneumatic rifle whose stock could be pumped full of air to 500–600 pounds per square inch. It was similar to a Kentucky long rifle in power — but it made no noise and produced no smoke. Lewis dragged it out and fired it at every meeting with the Indians who, according to both Lewis and Clark, were generally "astonished." Lewis was the first person to be astonished by his technological toy. On the Ohio River, en route to meeting Clark, he allowed an onlooker to fire it. The man's bad aim hit a woman in the head and nearly killed her (for details, go to Chapter 5).

In mid-August, near the grave of the great Omaha leader, Blackbird, at present day Macy, Nebraska, Lewis and Clark stopped to prepare for an anticipated meeting with the Omahas and the Otoes. They hoped Little Thief would attend. They sent Sergeant Ordway to look for the Omahas. He found the earth lodge village of Tonwantonga, formerly led by Blackbird, but it was completely empty. Rather than waiting to hear about their new Great White Father, all the Omahas had gone buffalo hunting.

In the 1790s, during Blackbird's life, Tonwantonga had housed over 1,000 Omahas. But, as with so many Missouri River tribes, the smallpox epidemic of 1800–1801 cut the Omahas down to a small and devastated group.

On August 18 (Lewis's 30th birthday), Lewis and Clark were just about to despair of ever meeting Little Thief and concluding a peace between the Otoes and Omahas when George Drouillard rode into camp with both Little Thief and Big Horse. Drouillard had been sent out two weeks earlier to find and bring back Private Moses Reed, who had deserted the expedition (see Chapter 7). As usual, Drouillard exceeded expectations. He brought back Reed and the Indian leaders, to boot.

Practicing naked diplomacy

Lewis and Clark court-martialed and punished Reed (which unnerved Little Thief and Big Horse — see Chapter 7). Then the captains turned to the important business of asking the Indian leaders about the dispute between their tribes and the Omahas.

After the discussion, explorers and Indians shared some whiskey and enjoyed some fiddle tunes, and then turned in for the night. They started their negotiation afresh the next morning.

The mainsail awning was reassembled, and Lewis gave his speech to Little Thief, Big Horse, and seven of their warriors.

The Americans gave a *carrot* (twist) of tobacco to each Indian who was present. They gave Big Horse a medal and gifts equal to those previously sent to Little Thief, and gave medals and certificates to the warriors.

After listening to Lewis, Little Thief agreed that peace with other tribes would be a good thing. But he didn't seem to care which Great White Father he was trading with — French, Spanish, or American. He was interested in the best deal for the best goods. With an eye toward the keelboat, which was packed to the gunwales with trade goods, he also wanted generous gifts from this new American father to cement such lofty promises.

Big Horse, who came to the meeting completely naked to demonstrate how poor his people were and how badly they needed to trade goods, took it a step further away from high diplomacy by asking for "a spoonful of your milk (whiskey)," without which he couldn't promise to keep his young men from attacking the Omahas, or the Pawnees either for that matter: whiskey for peace.

Handing out pretty papers

What exactly were the "certificates" that Lewis and Clark were handing out? They were printed papers with the heading, "Thomas Jefferson, President of the United States of America." They stated that the Indian leader who was receiving one was an ally of the United States and would receive U.S. protection as long as he acknowledged and accepted U.S. authority. Lewis and Clark filled in the name of the Indian leader by hand and ceremoniously presented each certificate.

Later makers of federal Indian policy would embrace the effectiveness of whiskey to subdue and control some tribal people, but Lewis and Clark were disgusted by the request. Besides, they had only 120 gallons of grog to get the Corps of Discovery through the entire voyage, and — with only a few exceptions — these men, including Captain Lewis, were enthusiastic drinkers. Little Thief then asked Lewis and Clark to send a delegation to make peace with the Pawnees. The Americans, becoming frustrated at the whole drift of the discussion, refused, and the meeting ended on a sour note.

Meanwhile, Sergeant Charles Floyd was becoming very sick (see Chapter 7), and the expedition parted from the Otoes and Missouris to proceed upriver.

Trying to understand generations of patterns

Lewis and Clark expected that their gifts to the tribes would produce willing, childlike agreement to their talk about peace and Jefferson's ideals. The Otoes and Missouris expected more generous gifts from the explorers' apparent endless supply and wanted whiskey in return for making peace with feuding neighbors. Each side expected too much and understood too little.

The lack of understanding isn't surprising, given the vast difference in perspective. The captains asked Little Thief and Big Horse why there was trouble between their tribes and the Omahas. The dispute came down to horse stealing (or borrowing), fighting, death, and retaliation — an age-old reality among tribes on the river. To Lewis and Clark, these reasons seemed petty. To Little Thief and Big Horse, they were part of ordinary life that had gone on for countless generations and would continue despite Lewis's and Clark's high-falutin' words, promises, and threats.

Wooing the Sioux

Lewis and Clark knew from their investigations in St. Louis that support and cooperation from the Sioux bands was vital to the success of American trade with the Missouri River tribes. Their first encounter with the famed Sioux would be with the Yankton tribe. But Lewis and Clark were eager, and apprehensive, to meet the Teton Sioux, the tribe of powerful warriors who regulated trade on the upper Missouri.

Lewis and Clark had heard a lot of stories from St. Louis fur traders about the Tetons' harassment of river traffic, demands for gifts and tariffs, downright theft of goods from vulnerable traders, and willingness to use force (see Chapter 6 for more information on the Corps' fear of the Tetons and how this may have lead to their adding a cannon to the keelboat). The Tetons' reputation among the whites was terrible. They were militarily proud and powerful, and they controlled the flow of trade. Jefferson knew about the Teton Sioux and was interested in cementing trade relations with such a strong and successful potential ally. He had urged Lewis and Clark to be especially diplomatic and diligent in winning them over.

In his lifetime, Clark had met (and fought) more Indians than Lewis had and was more comfortable and less arrogant with them, enjoying their company and generally respecting their perspectives — albeit from his own 18th-century, ethno-centrist sense of superiority. One major exception was the Teton Sioux, however. Both Lewis and Clark failed miserably to establish rapport with the Tetons.

The encounters with the Yanktons and the Tetons couldn't have been more different. The encounter with the Yanktons was a social and diplomatic success. The negotiation with the Tetons was a diplomatic debacle that continues to affect the relationship between the U.S. government and the Sioux today.

Hitting it off with the Yanktons

Near the end of August, about a week after burying Sergeant Floyd, the only member of the Corps of Discovery to die on the expedition (see Chapter 7), the *keelboat* (flat-bottomed boat for carrying goods) and two pirogues (large canoes) had just passed the mouth of the James River and were into present-day South Dakota. An Indian boy who was on the river bank jumped into the Missouri and swam out to one of the pirogues. Lewis and Clark put ashore and met two more boys — one of the three was Omaha, and the other two were Yankton Sioux. They told Lewis and Clark that located upriver on the James was a Yankton Sioux encampment. The Corps of Discovery had entered Sioux country.

Excited to meet a band of the legendary Sioux at last and happy for another chance to perfect their Indian diplomacy, Lewis and Clark dispatched Sergeant Nathaniel Pryor and Pierre Dorion, who lived with the Yanktons and spoke their language, to go with the youths to invite their leaders to meet with the explorers at Calumet Bluff camp.

The Yanktons received Pryor and Dorion with honor and enthusiasm. They even wanted to carry Pryor into their camp on a buffalo robe, a gesture of great honor, but Pryor declined — explaining that he only worked for the men who owned the big keelboat and all those trade goods. Nonetheless, the Yanktons cooked up a feast for the white men.

Exchanging ideas

On the morning of August 30, the Corps of Discovery put together all the same military hoopla that they had organized for the Otoes and Missouris (see the "Peddling Peace and Prosperity to the Otoes and Missouris" section earlier in this chapter).

Preceded by singers and drummers announcing their arrival, the Yankton leaders Weuche, White Crane, and Half Man regally entered the Calumet Bluff council site. They shook hands with Lewis and Clark and sat down to hear Lewis's Great White Father speech claiming ownership of the territory by the United States and promoting peace and trade. The Yanktons made speeches, too, expressing their desire for peace and need for trade. They promised to answer Lewis and Clark's request the next day.

That night around campfires, Yankton boys competed in bow-and-arrow contests, and the Americans gave beads as prizes to the winners. The Yankton warriors danced and bragged about their bravery and success in battle, while the explorers tossed them gifts of tobacco and knives. The two groups genuinely seemed to enjoy meeting one another, and a good time was had by all.

Getting down to business

The next morning, Weuche told Lewis and Clark that he needed arms to protect his destitute people and asked for immediate relief. He hoped to receive a supply from the keelboat's stock of guns. He also offered to organize peace efforts among the Plains tribes, but he kept returning to the trade goods Lewis and Clark were transporting up the Missouri.

Half Man's speech echoed Weuche's that peace would be good and that his band was poor and needed trade goods. But he also added a warning that "those nations above will not open their ears, and you cannot I fear open them." He was referring to the Teton Sioux.

The meeting ended with the Yankton's agreement to join the American trade alliance, a discharge of the air gun, tour of the keelboat and its wondrous instruments, and gifts of tobacco and corn. The two groups liked one another. Clark described the Yanktons as "Stout bold looking people" and admired an elite society of their warriors who never retreated in battle.

Confusing explorers with traders

Like the Oto and Missouri leaders, the Yanktons remained focused on the abundance of goods that the expedition carried. The Americans explained themselves as explorers and diplomats — advance men for future traders — but the Indians saw the loaded keelboat, concluded that the Americans were traders, and wanted to obtain as many of their goods as possible. They weren't even sure what explorers were. The only white men they had met were traders and trappers, so Lewis and Clark encountered this same misunderstanding with all the Missouri tribes.

The Yanktons, like all the tribes on the lower and middle Missouri, knew that their world was changing. The powerful Teton Sioux completely controlled trade through what is now South Dakota and North Dakota, intimidating Indian and non-Indian traders alike. The adolescent United States of America now "somehow" owned their homelands, so they had a new political balance to get used to.

The Yanktons were worried about their future and wanted to secure their role in whatever kind of trade system all these changes would produce.

Confronting the Tetons at Bad River

In September, three weeks after their pleasant meetings with the Yanktons, Lewis and Clark entered the complex world of upper Missouri trade and the stretch of river controlled by the Brule band of Teton Sioux. The little Army flotilla had made its way halfway through what is now South Dakota. The mornings were getting chillier, and the ever increasing wind was often in their faces. The river was also growing shallower, and the keelboat frequently got stuck on sandbars. On September 12, by late afternoon, the crew had progressed only one mile. The weather was drizzly and the "muskeetors [mosquitoes] verry troublesome," according to Clark.

On September 23, the men observed "a great Smoke" to the southwest — a signal that the Indians had discovered the Corps of Discovery. In fact, the Indians had been watching the Americans for a long time. Lewis and Clark put ashore and made camp. Before long three Teton Sioux youths swam the river to meet the Americans and reported that a camp of 80 Teton lodges was established at the next river, with 60 more lodges a little farther on. The youths had set a prairie fire to warn the Tetons of the boats' approach.

Lewis and Clark gave the boys some tobacco to take to their leaders with an invitation to meet the following day at the mouth of the Bad River — interestingly named considering what lay ahead — opposite present-day Pierre, South Dakota.

Misunderstanding the Tetons

What Jefferson, Lewis, and Clark didn't fully understand was that the Tetons were middlemen between European traders and the Arikara villages upriver. They exchanged European goods and furs for the Arikara's agricultural products (ensuring a dependable food supply for the Teton people). The Americans sought to open direct trade with all the tribes, including the Arikaras. Such an arrangement would negate the Tetons' role as broker, so the Tetons had turf, economic status, and food supply to protect. They didn't see much value, but plenty of threat, in America as a trade partner. So Lewis and Clark had a tricky negotiating job ahead of them.

Beyond all that, two of the three principal Teton leaders who would meet with Lewis and Clark — Black Buffalo and Tortohongar, known to white traders as The Partisan — were themselves engaged in an ongoing struggle for power and prestige within the Brule band of Tetons. Black Buffalo led the largest group of Brule and was a man who commanded much authority and respect. The Partisan was more unpredictable and challenged Black Buffalo whenever opportunity presented. Their one-upmanship was sometimes brutal and dangerous.

Stealing a horse, making a point

On September 24, 1804, Lewis and Clark prepared gifts for the Teton leaders: medals, flags, cloth, knives, American military coats, cocked hats, and tobacco. They also prepared their guns — just in case.

The explorers hadn't yet reached the mouth of the Bad River when Private John Colter, who was ashore hunting, shouted that some Tetons had stolen one of the expedition's horses. Five Tetons showed up on the river bank. Lewis and Clark anchored the boats in the middle of river and told the Tetons that the horse was intended as a gift for their leader. If the five men understood what the Americans were saying, they didn't buy it and left. The meeting with the Tetons was already off to a precarious start.

The boats proceeded on to the Bad River and anchored opposite its mouth. Lewis went ashore on an island where the talks were to be held and shared a ceremonial pipe with some of the Teton leaders. The leaders gave back the horse.

Failing to communicate

On September 25, the customary mainsail-awning was erected and the U.S. flag raised. The Indians arrived — led by Black Buffalo, The Partisan, and Buffalo Medicine (the third Teton leader). Food gifts were exchanged and speeches begun. Then a staggering problem revealed itself. Neither side could understand the other's language.

The only member of the expedition who could speak the Brule Teton language was Pierre Dorion, the French fur trader who had accompanied the Corps to Yankton country. Lewis and Clark had left him there (where his Yankton wife and children lived) to try to make peace between the Yanktons and Omahas. What could they have been thinking? George Drouillard's sign language was inadequate and so was Pierre Cruzatte's command of Sioux. As a result, miscommunication and misunderstanding torpedoed the already complicated and delicate relations.

Trying to accomplish as much as they could without too many words, Lewis and Clark had their fully uniformed men march in parade as usual, and then gave Black Buffalo, to them the obvious headman, lavish gifts. Well, that slighted The Partisan and enflamed the two leaders' rivalry. All of the Tetons complained that their gifts were paltry. So Lewis fired up the air gun for entertainment. This distraction was to no avail — nobody was astonished, as they had been before. Then the Americans invited the Indians onboard the keelboat to show off its technological magic and to offer a few shots of whiskey. Not a great idea.

Hijacking the boat

The Partisan pretended to be drunk and got belligerent. Trying to defuse an increasingly touchy situation, Clark took the Tetons back ashore in one of the pirogues. But as soon as they landed, a few Indians grabbed the bow line as if to take over the boat. At that point The Partisan physically jostled Clark and said the boats could go no farther upriver. Another bad idea. Clark drew his sword. Lewis, onboard the keelboat, aimed the cannon. American soldiers leveled their guns, and Teton warriors strung their bows. Diplomatic disaster was just a trigger finger away.

Black Buffalo saved everybody's bacon — and probably a lot of innocent lives (many Teton women and children were at the gathering). He stepped between the angry men and grabbed the pirogue's bow line away from The Partisan's men. Then he retreated some distance to confer with the other Teton leaders.

A relieved Clark approached them and offered to shake hands. They refused. So he climbed into the pirogue and pushed off toward the keelboat. A minute later, Black Buffalo and a few of his men waded after Clark and asked to come aboard the keelboat. Clark warily agreed, and the whole grouchy bunch proceeded about a mile upriver and dropped anchor for the night near a small island, which Clark named "Bad humered Island" in honor of the day.

Dancing the night away

The next day, September 26, the Tetons decided to take a new approach. They invited the Americans to their village for dinner and a dance. The observant Sergeant Ordway described the village as "very handsome in a circle and about 100 cabbins in number and all white." Clark called the Teton homes "neatly formed, those lodges are about 15 to 20 feet Diametr Stretched on Poles like a sugar Loaf, made of Buffalow Skins Dressed." They were tepees.

The Tetons carried Lewis and Clark into the main village lodge on buffalo robes. The Americans were seated next to Black Buffalo and a circle of about 70 elders and warriors. A space was cleared in the middle of the circle where ceremonial pipes, the flag of Spain, and the new U.S. flag, which the Americans had given as a gift the day before, were placed.

A Teton elder spoke, and then Black Buffalo. The Americans couldn't really understand what the two Indians were saying but recorded later that they "Spoke approveing what we had done." Black Buffalo lit and passed around the ceremonial pipe. Teton women brought on the food — roasted dog and buffalo, *pemmican* (buffalo jerky), and potatoes. Drummers, singers, and dancers performed. The Tetons were holding several Omaha Indians prisoner after a raid, and Clark asked that they be freed in pursuit of peace between the Tetons and Omahas. But Black Buffalo wasn't interested in extending the night's magnanimity that far.

As the evening's festivities wound down and Lewis and Clark were leaving for their boats, the Tetons offered a few young women to accompany them for the night, but Lewis and Clark refused them (even though Clark had earlier described the Teton women as "chearfull fine lookg womin . . ."). The offer was an honor from the Tetons; refusing them was an insult from Lewis and

Clark, who appeared to have understood the custom. Another self-inflicted blow to their own diplomacy. Even so, the evening's fun seemed to cheer everyone and defuse some of the previous day's tension.

Misunderstanding, again

Lewis and Clark spent September 27 visiting in the Teton village, and the evening brought another round of eating and dancing. Afterward, The Partisan and one of his men accompanied the Americans in the pirogue to spend the night on the keelboat. In the dark, the pirogue ran into the bigger boat's anchor line and broke it. The resulting shouting and scramble to save the boats somehow caused the Tetons to think they were being attacked by Omahas (in retaliation for the earlier raid).

In the village, Black Buffalo called out the troops, and 200 armed Teton men lined the shore. This show of force in turn alarmed Lewis and Clark, who thought the Tetons meant to attack and rob them. They posted extra guards that night, and neither Tetons nor Americans got any sleep.

Fearing the worst, again

On September 28, Lewis and Clark were more than ready to leave the Teton Sioux behind and proceed on toward the Arikara villages where they hoped for a fresh diplomatic start. However, the Teton leaders urged them to stay, and many villagers turned up onshore. As the Corps of Discovery was about to set sail, The Partisan's men grabbed the anchor line. Fearing the worst, Lewis and Clark asked Black Buffalo to intercede, but Black Buffalo said the men only wanted tobacco. By now Lewis had had enough and refused: bad move.

The Americans and Tetons grappled over the line. The Indians demanded more gifts. Clark readied the swivel gun. Once again, violence seemed the only recourse for both sides. Finally, Lewis threw some tobacco at the Tetons, and Black Buffalo yanked the anchor line free, releasing the boat to get underway. For the second time, Black Buffalo's cool head calmed a dangerous situation and avoided bloodshed.

Taking a second look at history

For four days, the Americans and the Brule Tetons had misunderstood one another, tested each other, danced and feasted and laughed, lost their tempers, and barely avoided violence. For 200 years since then, American historians have labeled the Tetons as bullies and Lewis and Clark as courageous heroes who backed the savages down. In truth, the whole mess was an utter failure to communicate. It was a failure of Lewis's and Clark's diplomacy, ability to grasp the balance of trade on the upper Missouri, and tolerance for the swagger of other proud men. At the end of it all, only the wisdom and superior diplomatic skills of Black Buffalo averted bloodshed.

A few months later, a still-angry Clark would write of the extraordinary Teton Sioux, "These are the vilest miscreants of the savage race, and must ever remain the pirates of the Missouri, until such measures are pursued, by our government, as will make them feel a dependence on its will for their supply of merchandise." His vindictive suggestion prejudiced American policy toward the Sioux to this day.

Persuading the Arikaras

After their frustrating and dangerous battle of wits with the Tetons, Lewis and Clark, accompanied — believe it or not — by Black Buffalo (who caught up to the boats and asked to come along), proceeded on up the Missouri. The Sioux leader stayed aboard the keelboat until just past an abandoned Arikara village — the first sign of Arikara presence on the Missouri. A cold wind blew down the river, kicking up choppy waves. Either seasickness or fear of drowning made Black Buffalo decide to go ashore and leave the expedition to proceed on, unchallenged at last.

Although relieved to be Teton Sioux-less, Lewis and Clark nonetheless didn't let down their guard. They made their way upriver, certain that a Teton ambush waited around every bend.

Arikara life

The Arikaras were farmers and horse breeders. Like the Mandans and Hidatsas upriver (see Chapter 9), the Arikaras grew corn, beans, squash, and tobacco. Lewis and Clark called them "gardners for the soues [Sioux] . . . ." They lived in substantial earth lodges, also like the Mandans and Hidatsas did. Contrast that with their trade partners the Teton Sioux, who lived in tepees made of buffalo hide stretched over tall poles and took those tepees with them when they moved about.

In an intricate symbiotic relationship, the Arikaras traded corn, beans, dried squash, tobacco, and horses to the Tetons in return for beaver pelts, meat, European manufactured goods and implements, and guns that the Sioux had gotten in trade at the Dakota Rendezvous, held every year on the James River in present-day South Dakota.

The Tetons traded at the Rendezvous, and then brought their goods to the Arikara towns in late summer and early fall for another festive trading session. Thousands of people filled the Arikara villages each year during this feasting, dancing, trading, and flirting season. (The other great market center of the northern Plains was the Mandan villages farther up the river; see Chapter 9.) The Arikaras also traded with the Cheyennes — who were rivals of the Sioux — so the balance was precise.

Going ahead with the plan

On October 8, 1804, the Corps of Discovery arrived at the first Arikara village, Sawa-haini, on Ashley Island in the Missouri River. The 3-mile-long island was intensively planted with corn and tobacco fields. Not knowing whether the Tetons' allies would welcome them or shoot them, the Corps of Discovery was prepared for both possibilities. Lewis and Clark made camp, and then went to Sawa-haini to meet with French trappers Joseph Gravelines and Pierre-Antoine Tabeau, who had lived among the Arikaras for over a decade and spoke Arikara and Sioux. (Too bad Lewis and Clark hadn't met them before the Bad River talks.)

Gravelines and Tabeau assured the Americans that the Arikaras were friendly, and so Lewis and Clark began preparations for their next great council with the Indians. They planned their military parade, readied the air gun for a demonstration, and organized gifts for the leaders that they would make chiefs. Lewis rehearsed his now-familiar speech.

Trying to spite the Teton Sioux

As they anticipated meeting the Arikaras, Lewis and Clark added a new diplomatic, and spiteful, objective to their existing agenda of announcing American sovereignty over Louisiana Territory, urging peace among the tribes, and creating trade partnerships between the tribes and the United States. They added the objective of disrupting the Teton-Arikara alliance.

Lewis and Clark were confident that they could change prairie alliances to suit President Jefferson's wishes and the needs of American trade, but neither Lewis nor Clark understood the Indians' long-standing and complicated alliances.

Pretty much all of the non-Indian traders, including Lewis and Clark, viewed the Tetons as tyrants and the Arikaras as victims getting the short end of the trading stick. But to the Arikaras, the trade alliance was a beneficial relationship, necessary for both partners. It afforded the Arikaras:

✔ Trade goods that they didn't have to travel to get

✔ A market for their crops

✔ The protection of a powerful ally

Teton Sioux protection was no small plus for the Arikaras. In the quarter century before Lewis and Clark's visit, they had been reduced in number by about 75 percent, because of devastating multiple smallpox epidemics and repeated raids by the Mandans (the Arikaras, like the Tetons, sometimes stopped traders from going upriver to the Mandan villages, which are described in Chapter 9). The Arikaras once occupied dozens of large villages, and their population numbered upward of 20,000 to 25,000 people. By 1804, they were refugees of disease and war, living together in three villages near the mouth of the Grand River in present-day South Dakota.

The arrangement also afforded the Tetons, who were not stationary farmers, a steady food supply.

Because each of the three Arikara villages was an amalgam of residents and refugees from other, now-deserted, Arikara towns, political rivalries and neighborly tensions were complicating factors for agreement to the American trade plan. The civil leader of Sawa-haini was Kakawissassa. But Kakawita, the war leader of another devastated village, had recently moved to Sawa-haini and was challenging Kakawissassa's authority. The other two Grand River villages, Rhtarahe and Waho-erha, were led by Pocasse (also known as Hay) and Piahito (Hawk's Feather or Eagle's Feather) respectively, who had their own authority to protect.

Putting on the show

On October 10, everything was ready for the meeting at the explorers' encampment, including Old Glory snapping in the breeze and soldiers in full dress uniform. However, only Kakawissassa showed up, so Lewis and Clark sent the French trapper, Joseph Gravelines, to the other two villages to urge Pocasse and Piahito to join the crowd. The reluctant leaders finally came along. (The Americans apparently overlooked Kakawita altogether and never met him.) Lewis and Clark did understand Pocasse's and Piahito's reluctance: Clark recorded that "a jellousy exists between the Villages for fear of our makeing the 1st Chief from the lower Village." Nevertheless, Lewis and Clark honored American military custom and named Kakawissassa "grand chief" of all the Arikaras anyway.

The soldiers of the Corps of Discovery marched, and Lewis and Clark fired the keelboat's swivel gun — three times for emphasis, or maybe to impress the few Teton Sioux men who were in the crowd — and Lewis delivered his usual speech, interpreted by Joseph Gravelines, announcing American sovereignty over Arikara homelands, urging peace among all the tribes, and requiring trade only with American merchants in exchange for protection from the new Great White Father. Kakawissassa was anointed, and many gifts were exchanged.

Gifts for the "chief's" people included: vermilion face paint, pewter looking-glasses, beads, razors, combs, scissors, knives, tomahawks, and 400 sewing needles. The leader received military coats and cocked hats, medals, and American flags.

As had been their custom, Lewis and Clark also offered the Arikara leaders some whiskey, but the Indians refused it, saying that they were surprised that their "Great White Father" would offer them something that would turn them into "fools."

At the council's conclusion, the three Arikara leaders promised to consider the Americans' propositions and give them an answer the next day. The formalities broke up, and the visiting, sight-seeing, eating, and fun began.

Cutting a rocky deal

At noon on October 11, Kakawissassa arrived at the expedition's camp, bearing gift baskets of corn, beans, and dried squash from his summer gardens. He delivered a carefully drafted speech, during which he declared that the Arikaras

- ✔ Would not block the river to American trade
- ✔ Wanted to become partners in the American trade system
- ✔ Would provide many fine buffalo robes
- ✔ Would intercede on behalf of the Americans for trade with the Cheyenne and Arapaho to the west

He also asked Lewis and Clark to speak well of the Arikaras to the Mandans — a prelude to peace between old enemies.

Kakawissassa would make exceptions to his promises in future years, but for now, Lewis and Clark felt they had gotten what they came for. With Kakawissassa onboard the keelboat, they moved upriver and anchored next to Rhtarahe and Waho-erha, the two other Arikara villages, one of which was led by Pocasse. Pocasse, who had returned home by then, came aboard, and the explorers showed off the boat's magical technology. Everybody ate more corn, beans, and bread, and then moved on to Waho-erha for yet more food. Resumption of the talks were scheduled for the next day.

On October 12, Pocasse expressed interest in peace with the Mandans and even offered to go to Washington to visit President Jefferson — something Lewis and Clark had tried to get virtually every Indian leader to do. Pocasse also injected some reality into the talks: He asked the Americans to stop the Teton Sioux from retaliating against the Arikaras for agreeing to participate in Lewis's and Clark's trade plan.

Piahito, the leader of Waho-erha, was more forthright. He didn't believe hostile Mandan-Arikara relations could easily be healed. But he considered accompanying the expedition to talk peace with his old enemies. In the end, one of the Arikara leaders, unnamed in the journals but possibly Piahito, did travel with the Corps of Discovery to the Mandan villages.

Sharing in Arikara culture

While the Arikara leaders considered Lewis's and Clark's trade for peace plan, the men of the Corps of Discovery were enjoying Arikara food, architecture, and hospitality. Sergeant John Ordway savored their cooking and recorded how delicious it was. The Corps' master carpenter, Sergeant Patrick Gass, visited Sawa-haini and recorded fascinating descriptions of earth lodge construction.

In addition, Lewis and Clark thought that the Arikaras, awed by the expedition's sextant, magnet, and other exploring and navigating equipment, believed the American strangers had spiritual powers. Lewis and Clark thought so, perhaps because of York, Clark's slave. The Arikaras had never met a black man before, and some of them evidently thought he might be a beast or a spirit being. York played it up pretty shamelessly by roaring and chasing the children, who chased him back. He told them he was a people-eating black bear that Captain Clark had tamed, and he growled some more — delighting and scaring them.

Clark was not entirely amused, noting in his journal, "Those Indians wer much astonished at my Servent. They never Saw a black man before, all flocked around him & examind. him from top to toe, he carried on the joke and made himself more turibal than we wished him to doe."

Paint that wouldn't rub off

In March 1805, the powerful and arrogant Hidatsa Indian leader, Le Borgne, paid a visit to the Lewis and Clark encampment. He had snubbed the Americans all winter, effectively rendering ineffective their efforts to establish a desired trade alliance.

During the visit, he noticed Clark's slave, York. (More on York in Chapter 2.) Le Borgne had heard about York's black color and thought that it was paint; after all, Mandan and Hidatsa warriors had the custom of painting their faces black to show power, good medicine, and even grief. So Le Borgne spit on his hand and rubbed York's skin. When the color didn't come off and York removed his cap to show his hair, Le Borgne was captivated, declaring the big slave to be a different species from white men.

The Hidatsa leader left Lewis and Clark "much pleased" with his gifts and feeling warmer toward the Americans. After his visit, other Hidatsa leaders began to visit regularly.

York in the Camp of the Mandans by C.M. Russell. Courtesy of the Montana Historical Society.

The Great Sioux Nation today

More than 62,000 American Indians live in South Dakota, and most are members of the Great Sioux Nation. Tribes living in South Dakota today include five with reservations along the Missouri River and Lewis and Clark National Historic Trail: the Yankton Sioux, living in the southern part of the state along the Missouri River bottom; Crow Creek Sioux and the Lower Brule (Teton) Sioux, living on opposite sides of the river in the middle of the state; and Cheyenne River Sioux and Standing Rock Sioux, occupying a large swath of the northern part of the state.

Each tribe offers opportunities to experience its culture — through museums, powwows, recreation areas, galleries, casinos, and buffalo herd tours.

✔ North of Greenwood on the Yankton Sioux Reservation, two monuments mark Yankton history — the Treaty of 1858 Monument and Struck By the Ree's grave. (Struck By the Ree, a respected Yankton leader, was the baby Meriwether Lewis wrapped in an American flag, saying he would grow up to be a friend of the white man.) The Yankton Sioux Tribe offers guided tours of its bison herd if you call ahead at 605-684-3641.

Lake Francis Case and Fort Randall Dam at Pickstown, along with the Lake Andes National Wildlife Refuge north of Pickstown are also within the Yankton reservation. Lake Francis Case offers swimming, fishing, camping and tours of the large earthen dam. The wildlife refuge is grasslands that are great for birding, with grebes, pelicans, herons and pheasants. The second weekend in July is the tribe's annual rodeo, and the first full weekend in August is the annual powwow at Lake Andes. The Fort Randall Casino and Hotel is located between Pickstown and Wagner. For information, call 605-384-3804.

✔ Bluffs on the Missouri River flank the western edge of the Crow Creek Indian Reservation, and Lake Sharpe stretches from Big Bend Dam at Fort Thompson, the tribal headquarters, to Pierre, the state capitol. The tribe's wildlife department offers guided hunting and fishing trips and maintains a buffalo herd north of Fort Thompson. Call for information at 605-245-2327.

✔ Lower Brule Reservation shares Lake Sharpe with the Crow Creek tribe and features its own wildlife reserve, a home for buffalo and elk to roam. Lower Brule's 80-mile Lake Sharpe shoreline offers superb fishing, swimming, boating, camping, and other recreation. Visitors can stay in style at The Golden Buffalo Resort. For information, call 695-473-5399.

✔ North of Pierre are two huge Indian reservations that border the Missouri River — Cheyenne River and Standing Rock. Both have wide open spaces and long drives with only wildlife for company. Near Swiftbird along Highway 212, visitors can see the Cheyenne River Sioux tribe's buffalo herd (call ahead to schedule a tour). The H.V. Johnson Lakota Cultural Center in Eagle Butte and the Timber Lake Area Museum offer exhibits on Lakota culture, art, and history. Timber Lake also has a large collection of marine fossils native to the area. Twenty miles east of the reservation in Gettysburg is a place where the expedition spent several peaceful days at an Arikara village. Today, at West Whitlock Recreation Area, you can walk inside a replica of an Arikara lodge. More information on the Cheyenne River Sioux Reservation is available at 605-964-4000.

Standing Rock Reservation straddles the South Dakota-North Dakota border on the western side of Lake Oahe, a sprawling Missouri River reservoir. Sitting Bull, one of the Lakota's great warriors, and Sacagawea, the Shoshone woman who traveled with Lewis and Clark (see Chapter 12), are memorialized at a site west of Mobridge overlooking the river. Mobridge is the site where Lewis and Clark found three Arikara villages. Fort Manuel, where Sacagawea died, no longer exists, but you can stand on the river bluffs near Kenel, where the fort once stood. Standing Rock also provides excellent fishing, boating and other water sports at Indian Creek Recreation Area. Deluxe accommodations are available at the Prairie Knights Casino and Lodge in Fort Yates, North Dakota. Powwows are held throughout the summer. For dates or other information, call toll free, 888-210-6115.

If the Arikaras thought that the men of the expedition had unusual spirit energy, York clearly had the most. Because of his color and size, they called him "The Big Medison" (see the "Paint that wouldn't rub off" sidebar for an explanation).

The Arikaras were warm and friendly, open with their hospitality and culinary gifts. Clark described them as "Durtey, kind, pore and extravigent [generous]." Arikara women enjoyed respect and position and were free to make their own decisions about many life choices, including boyfriends — to the delight of the American men. Sexual relations with beautiful Arikara women were the first intimate relationships that the men had indulged in since leaving St. Charles, and they were eager partners. The Arikaras, like the Mandans farther north, believed that sex was a conduit for transmitting spiritual power and hunting prowess from one person to another. Lewis and Clark believed that Arikara women wanted sex with the Americans so that they could receive some of the explorers' perceived spiritual energy and then pass it on to their husbands.

And, because they considered him "The Big Medison," the women especially wanted to spend time with York. On one occasion, recorded by Clark in his field notes, an Arikara man invited York to his lodge to hang out with his wife, and then guarded the door so no one else could enter.

The Corps of Discovery was able to learn much about Arikara life and customs, but sadly, only a few descriptions — such as the tastes of the food, construction of the earth lodges, and beauty of the women — were recorded. One of the Arikara leaders told Clark stories about Arikara legends, beliefs, and oral traditions, but Clark recorded none of them. He believed that they weren't worth mentioning. Jefferson, the ever-curious amateur ethnographer, could not have approved.

All good things must come to an end. So on October 12, after the final council, the Lewis and Clark expedition bid farewell to new friends and girlfriends. Cruzatte played some fiddle tunes, the Arikara leader who agreed to go to the Mandans came aboard (see the "Cutting a rocky deal" section earlier in this chapter), and the boats pushed off into the swift current, heading north once more.

Chapter 9

Enjoying a Cold Winter among Warm Mandans

. . . .

In This Chapter

▶ Meeting the Mandans and Hidatsas

▶ Promoting the American proposal for peace and trade

▶ Wintering at Fort Mandan

▶ Meeting Sacagawea, delivering a baby

▶ Living with the Mandans at 45° below zero

▶ Making maps and writing reports

. . . .

*T*he Lewis and Clark expedition reached the northern plains, and they hoped to get the Mandans and Hidatsas to enter into a trade alliance with the Arikaras, trade allies of the Teton Sioux. (See Chapter 8 for details about the Arikaras and the Tetons.) The goal was to give the Corps some allies against the powerful Teton Sioux and to expand trade for the United States. Lewis and Clark's frontier diplomacy was often naïve, arrogant, and not always well thought out. Nonetheless, the Corps of Discovery enjoyed a warm and happy winter sojourn among the Mandans and Hidatsas, most of it in weather well below zero. They hunted, danced, dated, and dined.

While with the Mandans, the captains signed on Toussaint Charbonneau, an ill-respected French-Canadian trader, and one of his Shoshone wives, the tiny, teenaged Sacagawea, to serve as interpreters. And in an exercise of frontier medicine, Captain Lewis assisted Sacagawea's delivery of a baby boy, who would travel with the Corps to the Pacific Ocean.

In this chapter, we reveal more about how Lewis and Clark's diplomacy worked and didn't work, and what that meant to the Corps of Discovery as they bedded down for the second winter of the expedition.

Promoting the American Trade Plan

The Corps of Discovery continued its diplomatic trade mission up the Missouri River to the villages of the Mandan and Hidatsa tribes (near present-day Washburn, North Dakota). These villages were the great marketplace and trade center of the northern plains.

At the time of the Lewis and Clark expedition, the Mandan and Hidatsa villages were larger in population than St. Louis and nearly as large as Washington, D.C. (which had only just been made the capitol). For generations, they had been the hub of a vast network of commerce for Indian and non-Indian traders. In late summer and autumn, Assiniboines, Arapahoes, Crows, Cheyennes, Kiowas, French, English, and others bartered for Spanish horses, Mandan corn, Cheyenne leather, English guns, meat, furs, blankets, implements, and adornments. The British fur traders — North West Company and Hudson's Bay Company — had both feet in the door, but now that the United States owned the river, Lewis and Clark meant to corner the lucrative market for Uncle Sam.

Lewis's and Clark's objective was to persuade three nations of Indians — the Arikara, Hidatsa, and Mandan — to unite in a trade alliance with the United States and against the powerful nomadic Teton Sioux who controlled trade on the lower Missouri River. (Flip to Chapter 8 for more on the Yankton Sioux, Teton Sioux, and Arikara tribes.)

Lewis and Clark hoped to achieve this alliance despite the fact that the Hidatsas (Lewis and Clark called them big bellies — in French, *gros ventre* — or Minnetarees, after Menetarra, one of their villages) and the Mandans co-existed in an uneasy alliance against the Arikaras as well as the Teton Sioux. The trade mission was important because, if successful, it would

- ✔ Give the Corps of Discovery allies against the dominant Teton Sioux
- ✔ Establish trading partners for the United States
- ✔ Provide a source of food and a winter campsite for the Corps
- ✔ Supply interpreters and other helpers for the expedition
- ✔ Allow the explorers to gather information about their continued route to the Pacific

Visiting the villages

Lewis and Clark had recruited an Arikara Indian leader to join them on the long stretch of their journey from Arikara lands to the Mandan and Hidatsa villages (see Chapter 8) in order to encourage the Mandans and Hidatsas to join the Arikaras in a trade alliance against the Teton Sioux. The Corps of Discovery left the Arikara villages in mid-October of 1804. Bearing the Arikara delegate (who was unidentified by Lewis), the keelboat (cargo boat) and two pirogues (canoes) slowly worked their way upriver past abandoned Mandan villages.

The captains noted a lone ceremonial pole standing ghostlike on the prairie, a particularly poignant, lonely witness to the vibrant life destroyed two decades before by the 1781 smallpox epidemic.

They moved on to two populated Mandan villages and three Hidatsa villages, as shown in Figure 9-1.

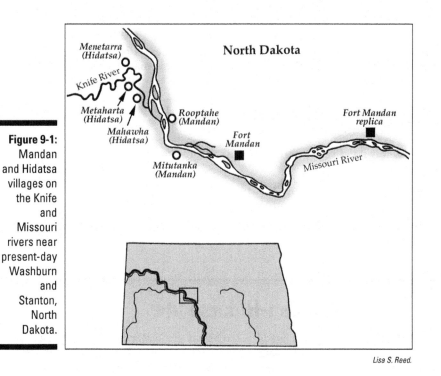

Figure 9-1: Mandan and Hidatsa villages on the Knife and Missouri rivers near present-day Washburn and Stanton, North Dakota.

Lisa S. Reed.

Mitutanka, the first Mandan village

In late October, the 47 men reached the first Mandan village that showed any living human activity. Mitutanka was a group of 40 or so earth lodges that were home to about 400 people. They were led by Sheheke, or Big White, as Lewis and Clark came to call him, because of his light complexion and his portliness. Sheheke more accurately means "coyote." The Corps came upon a nearby Mandan hunting party, and the Mandan and Arikara leaders greeted each other cordially, even smoking a sacred pipe together. Encouraged by such civility between the two leaders of enemy tribes, the Corps made camp. Although suffering from one of his occasional bouts with rheumatism, Captain Clark visited at Mitutanka with Sheheke and his "second chief" (as Clark referred to him), Little Raven, and both expressed eagerness to do business with the Americans. After all, trade was their game.

Rooptahee, the second Mandan village

Pleased with themselves about the success at Mitutanka, the Corps moved on upriver to the second Mandan village, Rooptahee, where Lewis visited with "first and second chiefs" Posecopsahe, or Black Cat, and Raven Man Chief. (The Indians did not actually have first, second, and third chiefs. Those titles were bestowed by Lewis and Clark as they went along.)

The Hidatsa villages (Mahawha, Metaharta, and Menetarra)

Having introduced themselves to Sheheke and Black Cat, the captains turned their energies to calling a council of the Mandan and Hidatsa leaders to announce the new American sovereignty over Louisiana Territory, as they had downriver, to "dutiful Indian children" (Lewis's patronizing term).

The captains sent invitations for the council to the Mandan leaders and to the three as yet unvisited Hidatsa villages:

- Mahawha, directly across the river from Rooptahee, the second Mandan village

- Metaharta, located on the Knife River and home of future expedition members Toussaint and Sacagawea Charbonneau

- Menetarra, also on the Knife River, a village led by the brilliant, one-eyed Le Borgne

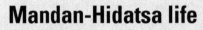

Mandan-Hidatsa life

Mandan and Hidatsa lands were the bread basket of the northern plains. Both Mandans and Hidatsas were, and still are, renowned for their corn — 13 varieties of multicolored, sweet and meal corn. The women were, and still are, the primary farmers, tending fields of corn, beans, squash, and sunflowers in the rich bottom land along the banks of the Missouri River. They boiled and dried sweet corn, shucked and dried beans, and stored squashes for winter use and for trade. They also dried and stored wild foods, such as chokecherries, wild turnips, and Jerusalem artichokes. They grew tobacco, which was often mixed with bearberry, or *kinnikinnik,* leaves for ceremonial smoking.

The homes of the Mandans and Hidatsas, like those of the Arikaras, were made of earth and sod over wood frames and could provide shelter for several families. Sometimes prized horses were even brought inside during especially cold weather. The spaces between the lodges were filled with drying racks and bins to store dried corn, beans, squash, and other foods. A great place to see earth lodges like those used during Lewis and Clark's time is at Knife River Indian Villages, a historic site administered by the National Park Service near Stanton, North Dakota.

The Knife River flows into the Missouri above several villages (see Figure 9-2). Lewis's and Clark's aim was to persuade the Mandans and Hidatsas to ally themselves with their enemies, the Arikaras, against the Sioux. Such an alliance, they hoped, would marginalize the Sioux and open the Missouri River and the great Mandan-Hidatsa trading empire to American merchants.

Figure 9-2:
Knife River
villages.

Big Hidatsa Village from the air with the Missouri River in the background. National Park Service Photo.

Convening the council

On October 29, on the banks of the Missouri River away from the villages, with the keelboat's sail stretched around them to keep out the wind, the Mandan and Hidatsa Indians met with the Lewis and Clark expedition and the Arikara leader.

Lewis began the event by firing the keelboat's swivel gun. Handing out gifts and acknowledging those he believed to be chiefs, he explained that the United States now owned their lands as well as the river itself and would control all future trade, making it advantageous to enter into a trade alliance among themselves and the Arikaras with the United States.

He ended the conference by firing the Corps' air gun. The Hidatsas were not impressed, and Clark noted their restlessness to leave the council. The Mandans were probably bemused by all the military swagger, because both nations viewed the expedition as a trading venture (as did the Arikaras — see Chapter 8). The Indians returned to their villages, promising to consider the

The Mandan, Hidatsa, and Arikara Nations today

The Three Affiliated Tribes of Fort Berthold Reservation is home for descendants of the Arikara, Hidatsa, and Mandan ancestors who welcomed and harbored the Lewis and Clark expedition in 1804–1805. Severely decimated by recurring epidemics of smallpox, the Arikaras moved north in 1862 to share what became the reservation with their historical enemies, the Mandans and Hidatsas. Today, the Three Affiliated Tribes of Fort Berthold operate a campground and RV park, casino resort, marina, and museum on the shores of Lake Sakakawea in New Town, the tribes' administrative headquarters. They also offer golf course packages at nearby courses, arrange for buffalo and elk herd viewings, and host a Lewis and Clark Bicentennial national signature event in 2006 (see Chapter 1). Powwows are held throughout the summer. For information, go to www.mhanation.com or call 701-627-4781.

alliance and decide whether or not to accept it. Before their decisions were made, the unnamed Arikara who accompanied the expedition decided to return home.

Black Cat was the first Mandan leader to accept the Americans' proposal, although he did so cautiously. And even as he accepted, he chastised the captains for not giving his villagers more gifts. On November 1, Sheheke came to visit. He also agreed to peace with the Arikaras and, with an eye toward a winter's supply of trade goods and military protection against potential raids by the Sioux, he shrewdly invited the Corps of Discovery to build its winter garrison near his village, saying " . . . if we eat, you shall eat. If we starve, you must starve also . . . ."

Both Mandan villages had now agreed to the American plan, but there was no response from the Hidatsas.

Building Fort Mandan

In late fall of 1804, while waiting for the Indians to respond to their proposed trade alliance, Lewis and Clark began their search for a site to build the Corps' second winter encampment. The weather was growing colder, and geese, swans, cranes, and ducks were flying south in droves. Lewis and Clark decided to accept Sheheke's invitation to winter near his Mandan village of Mitutanka.

The only trees suitable for fort building, large groves of cottonwood, grew along the river near Sheheke's village, so the men got to work sawing and hammering a rudimentary garrison into existence.

During the fort's construction, scores of curious Mandan men, women, and children became regular visitors, trading corn and meat for the expedition's fascinating new goods. Especially prized was an iron corn mill, which the Indians immediately dismantled for its metal.

The winter garrison took shape, built of and heated entirely with cottonwood (see Figure 9-3). It consisted of two rows of four huts, each room 14 feet square and 7 feet high, with plank ceilings and lofts above. The backs of the huts formed a wall 18 feet high to keep out intruders. Two rooms were allotted for stores and provisions. The men moved into their winter home on November 20 and went to work completing the interior. The little fort sat snug on the east side of the Missouri below its confluence with the Knife River, 164 days' travel and 1,500 miles from the Corps's 1803–1804 winter quarters at Camp Dubois (see Chapter 6). The captains named it Fort Mandan.

Figure 9-3:
Photo of replica Fort Mandan in Washburn, North Dakota.

Aerial shot of Fort Mandan. Courtesy of Fort Mandan, Washburn, ND.

Meeting Sacagawea

The Lewis and Clark expedition had taken up residence in the newly constructed Fort Mandan. But the population of the encampment continued to grow beyond the original troops. Traders and Indians joined the party to act as interpreters for the Corps.

Indian billiards?

In his journal, Sergeant John Ordway described a popular game played by the Mandans that some Europeans later claimed was billiards, because it was played with sticks about 4 feet long resembling billiard cues. The sticks had leather tassels on the ends and four leather markers at intervals along their lengths. The Indians played the game outside in the freezing winter. They laid out a smooth plank floor about 50 yards across; then two men at a time ran down the floor and slid their sticks after a flat hoop made of clay. Scoring was marked according to which marker hit the hoop, although Ordway admitted he did not fully understand how the score was kept.

Hiring a sneaky scoundrel and a man of no merit

The Captains invited French-Canadian fur trader Rene Jessaume, who was living in the village and spoke Mandan, to move into the encampment with his Mandan wife and family to serve as interpreter for the Corps. Jessaume claimed to have served as a spy for Clark's big brother, George Rogers Clark, during the Revolutionary War, but William didn't believe him, nor did he like him very much. The man was disliked by a number of Indians and other traders for being a sneak and scoundrel, and Clark agreed with them. Nonetheless, Clark needed a Mandan interpreter, and Jessaume was the only one.

A few days later, Touissant Charbonneau, another French-Canadian trader living in Metaharta, came to the fort site and asked to hire on as a Hidatsa interpreter. He and his two Shoshone wives, including Sacagawea, moved into the encampment. Sixteen-year-old Sacagawea was six months pregnant; Toussaint Charbonneau was nearly three times her age and "of no peculiar merit," according to the captains.

Sacagawea: An American icon

When Sacagawea was 10 or 11 years old, she had been kidnapped by the Hidatsas on a raiding foray into the Three Rivers headwaters of the Missouri, in present day Montana. She was brought back as a captive to live in the Hidatsa villages. There, Charbonneau either traded for her or won her in a gambling match.

At 16, she was an expectant mother and destined to become one of the most famous women in American history. Her Shoshone and Hidatsa upbringing would have taught her where to hunt for wild foods and how to prepare them, a skill that would come in handy for the Corps of Discovery. Her captivity would have made her tough. She probably drew on both her Indian cultures to become a good mother.

Sacagawea's baby boy

The winter among the Mandans bonded the men into brothers, but one event made them a complete family. On February 11, Sacagawea went into labor and was in violent pain, unable to deliver. The captains were worried about her survival because their hopes were pinned on the prospect of her interpreting for them with her native tribe, the Shoshones (in present-day Idaho and Western Montana), when the time came to trade for horses to cross the mountains. The explorers knew from the Hidatsas that there would be mountains to cross (the fabled Northwest Passage) to reach rivers that flowed into the Pacific. They also learned that the Shoshones, who lived at the base of the mountains, had horses that could be bartered for to help make the crossing.

Jessaume told Lewis that administering a couple of dried rattlesnake rings (the rattles at the end of the snake) often induced birth. Lewis just happened to have some rattlesnake rings, so he broke them into small pieces and mixed them with water. The teenaged Sacagewea drank the potion, and ten minutes later Fort Mandan was filled with the squalls of a healthy baby boy. Charbonneau named his son Jean Baptiste. In less than two months, the infant would be on the river with his mother, accompanying the Lewis and Clark Expedition across the rest of the continent. Clark later became very attached to baby Baptiste, nicknaming him Pomp and often carrying him on his shoulders as the Corps trekked along.

The myths and legends, statues and landmarks bearing Sacagewea's name and acknowledging her value to the expedition (see Chapter 18) were in the future. But in 1805, it was a bitterly cold winter, and Sacagawea had a newborn baby to get ready for a long journey.

Sacagawea's true role

Sacagewea proved to be invaluable as an interpreter and as a symbol of peace. No Indians along the expedition's journey could mistake the Corps for a war party with a woman and baby along. Her bravery in rescuing the captains' journals when the canoe that she, Charbonneau, and Jean Baptiste were riding in was swamped (see Chapter 10) earned her respect and gratitude from Lewis and Clark. Her reunion with her brother in the late summer of 1805 would be one of the most amazing and fortunate episodes of the entire expedition (see Chapter 12).

Although often referred to as a "guide" in early accounts of the expedition, Sacagawea actually guided the Corps only once, over Bozeman Pass on Clark's return down the Yellowstone (see Chapter 16). Her strategic value was as an interpreter. Her personal warmth and selfless, uncomplaining hard work endeared her to all the men, especially Clark, who affectionately nicknamed her Janey.

Bird woman: Sacagawea/Sacajawea/Sakakawea

Her name was recorded phonetically in Lewis's and Clark's journals as Sacagawea, which means bird woman in Hidatsa. Today the Hidatsas, and everyone else in North Dakota, spell it Sakakawea. When Nicholas Biddle edited Clark's journals in 1814, he changed the spelling to Sacajawea, said to mean boat launcher or boat pusher in Shoshone. In recent years, historians have reverted to the expedition journalists' original spelling of Sacagawea, meaning bird woman.

Trying to Manipulate Plains Politics

Because of the Louisiana Purchase (see Chapter 3), Meriwether Lewis understood that the expedition had become a diplomatic venture. The Corps of Discovery needed to communicate the transfer of sovereignty to every Indian tribe and foreign interest they encountered. And Thomas Jefferson had promised Congress that the expedition would result in expanded trade and commerce. He hoped that Lewis and Clark would be able to steal away from the British and others the lucrative trade business with the Indian tribes.

However, the captains' frontier diplomacy was naïve and based more on cultural arrogance than any understanding of the complex relationships between the tribal nations of the northern plains.

Flawed diplomacy

From their many Indian guests, Lewis and Clark slowly began to realize some of the intricate, constantly shifting realities of trade, war, and life on the northern plains.

- ✔ For safety from the Sioux and Arikaras after the smallpox epidemic, the Mandans had moved upriver to be near the Hidatsa villages.

- ✔ The Mandans never went West and allowed themselves to be portrayed as victims of the Sioux and Arikaras, co-existing with their more powerful Hidatsa neighbors in a sometimes suspicious truce.

- ✔ The Hidatsas habitually traveled far to the West to capture horses and sometimes even capture people from the Shoshones and Blackfeet.

- ✔ Although trade partners of the Mandans and Hidatsas, the Assiniboines to the North sometimes raided the villages and stole horses. They're discussed in more detail in Chapter 11.

Although the Mandans and Hidatsas were shrewd and artful traders, always getting the best deals from their bargaining, Lewis and Clark persisted in viewing them as victims of some of their trade partners, especially the Teton Sioux, susceptible to the American peace/trade plan and deserving of the Corps' protection.

The captains also discovered that, upon hearing of their ally's participation in the captains' trade proposal to the Mandans and Hidatsas, the Teton Sioux had retaliated against the Arikaras, beating them and stealing their horses. Potential retaliation by the Sioux for forsaking the Arikara-Teton alliance had motivated the Arikaras to ask Lewis and Clark for protection (see Chapter 8). But Lewis and Clark had no spare guns or men to leave behind to protect anybody.

The captains later discovered that they hadn't seen or heard much from the Hidatsas, because the Mandans had told their neighbors that the Americans would kill any Hidatsa who came around the fort. No sooner had Lewis and Clark straightened that out than they received word of a Teton Sioux attack on a group of Mandan hunters. Captain Clark marched a contingent of heavily armed soldiers across the now-frozen Missouri to come to the aid of the Mandans. Instead, the show of force alarmed the Mandans, who were perturbed by the meddling and thought the Americans were fools to want to chase the long-gone Teton Sioux in such severe cold. Embarrassed, Clark returned to Fort Mandan.

The Mandans forgave the captains for their ill-advised attempt to save the Mandans from the Sioux and, on December 7, they invited the Americans to accompany them on a buffalo hunt. The Mandans provided horses, and Lewis plus 15 of the soldiers joined in. The captain got a lesson in horsemanship that day. The Indian ponies were quick and well trained, and the Mandans, with bows and arrows, could ride at breakneck speed, shooting and evading the huge beasts.

Lewis loved the outing, and the Americans shot and killed many buffalo. In the first of several joint buffalo hunts throughout the winter, the party brought back thousands of pounds of buffalo meat to feed everybody.

Dealing arms

By midwinter, Fort Mandan was running low on meat and corn, and the Indians had already saturated themselves with the Americans' trade goods. In addition, John Shields, the expedition's blacksmith, had already mended all the Indians' broken hoes, knives, and firearms, so there seemed to be nothing further to trade, except for battle axes. These weapons had hatchet blades 7 to 9 inches wide by 5 to 6 inches high on short handles. They weighed under a pound each and were "formed in a very inconvenient manner," according to Lewis. He didn't think the battle axes were well designed for combat use, but because the Mandans wanted a particular design, Shields made that design.

Many of the Mandan warriors sought to trade for guns, but because the expedition was a peaceful mission, guns were out of the question. But battle axes were okay, it was rationalized, because Shields could make them out of sheet metal from an old stove. So he made them, and the Americans traded axes for food. When the warriors later sought permission to use the axes against the Sioux and Arikaras, the captains denied the request. In the spring, however, despite all the captains' preaching about peace, the Hidatsas happily set off for their annual raids in Shoshone and Blackfeet country (see Chapters 11, 12, and 16) with shiny new battle axes in hand.

Neutralizing British fur interests

The British trading companies presented a unique diplomatic problem. Their trade with the villages was well established, and American traders could not yet compete with them. Although Lewis and Clark had the legal authority to throw the British out of northern Louisiana Territory, they didn't have the physical might. So they invited representatives of the North West Company to visit Fort Mandan.

North West Company representatives Francois-Antoine Larocque and Charles MacKenzie arrived in December, and Lewis and Clark issued a warning: When trading with the Indians, don't give them any flags or medals that would signify British sovereignty. Because the North West Company traders had no flags or medals to give, they happily agreed and enjoyed the captains' whiskey.

Living Life at 45° Below Zero

The winter of 1804–1805 was brutally cold. Lewis and Clark recorded temperatures as low as 45° below zero — colder than any member of the expedition had ever experienced before.

The keelboat became trapped in the ice and had to be hacked out. Even the air froze in an ice fog, and Lewis and Clark constantly marveled at the Indians' ability to withstand the sub-zero temperatures. The river was frozen so thick that herds of buffalo could walk across it. The Mandans and the Americans became constant companions, friends and lovers, sharing food, stories, and entertainment. In addition to buffalo, the men hunted and ate pronghorn antelope, deer, elk, beaver, hare, and prairie wolves (coyotes).

As the long, cold winter settled onto the prairie, Lewis became revered as a doctor, and the Indians traded the Corps corn for his services. He treated a

Mandan child's abscess and even amputated the toes of a 13-year-old boy who had been caught out all night with only a buffalo robe to keep him warm. Frostbite was common, too, among the men of the expedition, although no cases were so severe among them as to require amputation.

Venereal disease, a common malady of the frontier areas where the fur trade was well established, also kept Lewis in demand as a doctor. According to Clark, the men of the Corps found the Mandan women "very handsome," and the severe cold fostered much romantic huddling. Lewis treated the complaints with regular doses of mercury and Rush's thunderbolt pills, a powerful laxative (see Chapter 5). Purging and bleeding, however, continued to be his most common prescription for whatever ailed his patients.

Making Maps and Feeling Optimistic about the Northwest Passage

The frigid winter months at Fort Mandan were busy ones. In addition to the visiting trading, hunting, and merrymaking, Lewis and Clark also had to fulfill their fact-gathering mission. Jefferson's requirements included mapmaking, writing reports, keeping records of the Indians' languages, cataloging tools and clothing, and gathering botanical and mineral specimens.

William Clark met often with Mandan and Hidatsa leaders to find out everything he could about the country upriver — a region as yet unvisited by white men. The Hidatsas had frequently been as far as the Rocky Mountains and drew maps on the garrison's floor of wonders such as the Great Falls of the Missouri, whose noise could be heard from a great distance, and the Shining Mountains of the Great Divide (now known as the Continental Divide). They pinpointed the Yellowstone, Milk, Musselshell, Judith, and Marias Rivers. Clark meticulously transferred all the Indians' information onto a map that has become a cartographic legend (see Figure 9-4), a document that guided the explorers' travels right to what they assumed would be the fabled Northwest Passage.

Because the Hidatsas always traveled west on horseback, not in boats, and had never crossed the Divide, their information didn't dispel the myth of a Northwest Passage. Their estimate of how far the Corps would have to portage (carry) the boats and provisions around the Great Falls was half a mile as opposed to the actual 18 miles. In fact, it would take the men nearly a month to get through that 18 miles of prickly pear cactus, troublesome "musquetors" (mosquitoes), blazing heat, and pelting hailstorms. (See Chapter 10.) The Hidatsas estimated that it would take a half day for the Corps to cross the mountains and reach a large West flowing river, as opposed to the eleven hungry, snowy days it actually took. These estimates created wild optimism in the captains' hearts, optimism that would be brutally dashed by midsummer (see Chapters 10 and 11).

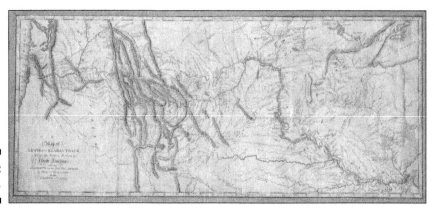

Figure 9-4:
Clark's map.

Writing reports and recording languages

During the winter at Fort Mandan, Clark pored over his mapmaking and Lewis wrote and wrote and wrote. The report he had promised to Jefferson became a tome describing the region's flora, fauna, geography, climate, Indian nations, economics, politics. And it wildly touted the agricultural promise of the northern prairies.

The captains also recorded the Indians' languages and vocabularies as accurately as they could, given the expedition's tenuous system of translation. A Hidatsa speaker would say a word to Sacagawea, who would repeat it to Charbonneau, who would say it in French to Jessaume, who would say it in English to Lewis and Clark. The Hidatsas were suspicious of the captains' motives for recording their languages, and Charbonneau and Jessaume would often argue fiercely over the translation, so the margin for error was probably huge. Nonetheless, Lewis and Clark persevered.

One of the greatest tragedies of American history, especially for American Indians now facing the grim threat of language extinction, is the loss of those painstakingly recorded vocabularies in 1809. Lewis had hand-carried his vocabularies to Jefferson in Washington in 1806. In 1809, as he was leaving Washington for good, Jefferson sent Lewis's Indian vocabularies, plus those Jefferson himself had collected over the preceding 30 years, to Monticello by boat. While en route on the James River, the trunk containing the vocabularies was stolen. The thief, disappointed at finding only papers in the trunk, threw them all overboard. According to Jefferson, a few pages washed up on shore but were "defaced by the mud & water." It was the loss of a lifetime of work, and it broke Jefferson's heart.

Preparing the specimens (and that poor, pitiful prairie dog)

Although it was winter, Lewis gathered a few botanical specimens, including *Arctostaphylos uva-ursi L.* (bearberry or kinnikinnik, which the Indians mixed with tobacco), *Aquilegia canadensis L.* (columbine), and *Nicotiana quadri-valvis* (pursh or Indian Tobacco). Since leaving St. Louis, the captains had gathered corn, tobacco seeds, botanical and mineral specimens, Indian tools and clothing (including a magnificent, painted buffalo robe), as well as an unfortunate prairie dog that they had captured (see Chapter 7). Cut off from his colony and imprisoned in a tiny cage for months, the small creature eventually arrived at Monticello still alive. All of these items would be sent back to Jefferson in the spring along with Lewis's report, his more than 100 catalogued botanical specimens and the Indian vocabularies.

Sharing ceremonies

As the Lewis and Clark expedition wintered at Fort Mandan, the men celebrated Christmas, shared New Year's Day, and participated in an ageless sacred ceremony of the buffalo hunting nations.

New Year's song and dance

By Christmas, Fort Mandan was completed inside and out, warm and cozy. The captains told the always visiting Indians that the holiday was a great medicine day for white people and asked them not to visit the fort on that day. The men fired the swivel gun at daybreak and many rounds from their guns all day long. The captains raised the U.S. flag and distributed whiskey. The Corps drank, ate, danced, and frolicked well into the night. The only Indians who witnessed the merriment were the wives of the interpreters, including Sacagawea.

New Year's was a different story, however, except for the cannons, whiskey, and dancing. Clark, York, and 16 of the men paid a social visit to Mitutanka "for the purpose of dancing." The one-eyed Omaha/Frenchman, Pierre Cruzatte, supplied the fiddle tunes. Francois Rivet danced on his head. Others played the harmonica, tambourine, or *Jew's harp* (a small metal musical instrument held between the teeth and played by finger plucking a projecting rod, producing a twangy sound). Clark ordered York to dance, and the Mandans were delighted that "So large a man should be so active . . . ."

Tunes of the era

Some early American tunes and hymns that Pierre Cruzatte may have played on his fiddle for the Corps' dancing pleasure would likely have included the following:

✔ *Chester* (Revolutionary War hymn)

✔ *Highland Laddie* (traditional Scottish)

✔ *The Gobby-O* (traditional Irish)

✔ *All Mortal Flesh Be Silent* (17th-century French hymn)

✔ *The Rose Tree* (popular 18th century; a favorite of George Washington)

✔ Various hornpipes (traditional)

✔ *A Merry Christmas* (18th-century British)

✔ *Red-Haired Boy* (traditional Irish)

✔ *Whiskey Before Breakfast* (traditional Irish)

Some of these tunes, as well as traditional Indian music of the era, can be found on recordings available from Makoche Recording Company, Bismarck, North Dakota. Call 800-637-6863 or visit the company online at www.makoche.com.

Buffalo calling

In early January of 1805, the Americans were invited to a Mandan dance, a ritual for luring the buffalo. The ceremony fascinated and happily baffled the explorers: The Mandans believed that the prowess of elder hunters could be transferred to the younger men through sex with their wives. During the ritual, the young hunters offered their young wives to the old men, some of whom, Clark observed, could scarcely walk. When the young women later had sex with their husbands, the transfer of hunting power was complete.

According to Lewis and Clark, the Mandans believed that explorers also possessed powerful "magic," so the soldiers were invited to participate in the ceremony in the same role as the old hunters. The men didn't have to be asked twice.

A few days later a herd of buffalo showed up, just as the ceremony provided, and the hunt began.

Part III
Into the Unknown: Fort Mandan to the Pacific

The 5th Wave   By Rich Tennant

"It's just a hunch captain, but I think we may be in for a spot of bad weather."

In this part . . .

You travel with the Corps of Discovery from Fort Mandan to the Pacific Ocean, a trip no white man had taken before. You witness the Corps carrying its boats and supplies around the Great Falls of the Missouri and then finding the Shoshones, Sacagawea's birth tribe, with whom they could trade trinkets for horses to cross the Rocky Mountains.

Staring at a sea of high snow-topped mountains, Lewis realized that there was no Northwest Passage, but they pressed on. You discover how the starving explorers emerged from the mountains into the generous hospitality of the Nez Perce, and then built canoes and floated down the Columbia River to the Pacific. There, they built their third winter fort and spent the season wet, cold, cranky, and homesick.

Chapter 10

Journeying through Paradise and Purgatory on the Northern Plains

In This Chapter

▶ Sending the keelboat home

▶ Harassing grizzly bears

▶ Choosing the right river

▶ Portaging the Great Falls

▶ Abandoning the iron boat

▶ Polishing off the whiskey

*I*n this chapter, we describe the Corps's passage through the wondrous Missouri River valley between Fort Mandan and the Great Falls, where the plains teemed with wildlife and the men had their first encounters with grizzly bears. Both the blowing sand and the mosquitoes were unrelenting, too.

The Corps became confused when the Missouri and the Marias Rivers converged, but Lewis and Clark correctly chose the south fork. They arrived at not one, but five massive waterfalls and were forced to make a horrendous 18-day portage. They maneuvered their boats and tons of luggage overland around the falls in blistering summer heat. Clark, Sacagawea, her son (Jean Baptiste, affectionately nicknamed "Pomp" by Clark for his "little dancing boy" antics), and Charbonneau nearly perished in a flash flood. (More on these Corps' members in Chapters 2 and 9.)

Near the end of this phase of the journey, Lewis's beloved iron boat experiment failed miserably (see the "Getting that sinking feeling" section near the end of this chapter) and the men drank the last of their whiskey.

Closing Up the Fort and Sending the Keelboat Home

On the spring equinox of 1805, the ice on the Missouri River began to break up and float downriver in huge chunks. Also floating along were the carcasses of buffalo that had drowned when they broke through the crumbling ice. The Mandan and Hidatsa Indians (discussed in Chapter 9) were ready for them and nimbly negotiated the ice floes to snag the easy source of fresh meat.

After spending the coldest winter of their lives at Fort Mandan, the men of the Corps of Discovery were more than ready to get on the road again. They were eager to go looking for the Great Falls of the Missouri.

The men repaired the keelboat's ice damage, built dugout canoes, took stock of their provisions and weapons, sewed buckskin clothes and moccasins, and began loading the boats.

Everything was ready by April 7, and the Corps put their oars in the water again after five months in the company of the Mandans. The keelboat — laden with Clark's and Floyd's journals (Lewis hadn't written in his since leaving Camp Dubois), the winter's reports (Lewis had written copious ones), as well as specimens and gifts for President Jefferson — set sail under the command of Corporal Richard Warfington (the expedition's only corporal) and headed downstream. The boat and its fabulous cargo, including the following, arrived at St. Louis six weeks later on May 20:

- Lewis's "Summary View of Rivers and Creeks"
- Clark's "Summary Statement of Rivers, Creeks and Most Remarkable Places"
- Clark's "Estimate of Eastern Indians" (describing the tribes east of the Rocky Mountains that the expedition had met)
- Lewis's dried and preserved botanical specimens (200 of which still reside at the American Academy of Natural Sciences in Philadelphia)
- Maps
- William Clark's journal
- Sergeant Charles Floyd's journal
- Mineral specimens
- Muster rolls
- Accounting records
- Astronomical and weather data

↙ Twenty-five boxes and cages of zoological specimens, including

- Skins, bones, antlers, and stuffed animals

- Four live magpies (long-tailed birds related to the raven)

- One live sharp-tailed grouse

- One live prairie dog

↙ Four boxes and three trunks containing Indian artifacts, including

- Mandan bows and arrows

- A Mandan earthen cooking pot

- Buffalo robes, including one painted by a Mandan artist depicting a battle of the 1790s between the Sioux and Arikaras against the Mandans (this robe still resides in Harvard University's Peabody Museum)

Meanwhile, the *permanent party* (the men selected to go all the way to the Pacific; a handful of men were to go only as far as Fort Mandan then return to St. Louis with the keelboat — see Chapter 2) continued on the journey (see the following section).

Never-Ending Enchantment on the Plains

The heavily loaded red and white pirogues (canoes) and six new canoes carrying the permanent party nosed upriver toward country as yet unexplored by white men. Lewis and Clark could hardly control their excitement. The night before setting out, Lewis wrote his first (and one of his most memorable) journal entry: "we were now about to penetrate a country at least two thousand miles in width, on which the foot of civillized man had never trodden; the good or evil it had in store for us was for experiment yet to determine, and these little vessels contained every article by which we were to expect to subsist or defend ourselves . . . . I could but esteem this moment of my (our) departure as among the most happy of my life."

As the boats pulled away under Clark's command, Lewis walked onshore — as he often did and would continue to do — sometimes covering more than 30 miles a day, and not in waterproof tech hiking boots, either! He stopped at Rooptahee village to share a pipe and say goodbye to his friend Black Cat. Then the Mandan villages and Fort Mandan faded into the distance.

The first few days on the river were idyllic. The boats made good time. After strenuous days, the party spent the evenings laughing, singing, and dancing to Cruzatte's fiddle and enjoying their daily rations of whiskey.

The Corps of Discovery was traveling through country vastly more abundant with wildlife than even the prairies of the lower Missouri. Lewis thought the Northern Plains were paradise — filled with "immence quantities of game in every direction . . . immence herds of buffaloe Elk deer & Antelopes."

Encountering tame wildlife

Not only did enormous herds of game cover the plains, but the animals were virtually unafraid of people. Lewis noted, "the buffaloe Elk and Antelope are so gentle that we pass near them while feeding . . . they frequently approach us more nearly to discover what we are . . . ." In late April, Lewis met a buffalo calf "which attached itself to me and continued to follow close at my heels until I embarked & left it."

It would have been easy to kill the gentle beasts wantonly, as did many white hunters who came after Lewis and Clark. But the captains forbade it; instead, they killed only what they needed for food.

Beaver, the ultimate prize of the fur trade, was everywhere. The party feasted often on beaver tail, one of their favorite delicacies. In addition, herds of buffalo were accompanied by packs of gray wolves, and Lewis admired the predators' cooperative hunting style of chasing prey from one wolf to the next until the object of the chase was too worn down to escape the pack. When they were well fed, even the wolves were unafraid of the explorers. The wolves sometimes jumped into the river and killed swimming antelope. One day, Lewis's dog, Seaman, did the same, dragging the doomed pronghorn ashore to his master.

Exploring the land of milk and honey

The Corps of Discovery made good progress on the now westward-flowing Missouri. On April 25, they reached the place where the Missouri and the Yellowstone Rivers converged. (The Yellowstone was also called Rochejhone River, from the French *roche jaune,* which literally means "yellow stone.") With him, Lewis took Ordway, Drouillard (he almost always took Drouillard), Joseph Field, and Seaman the dog to explore overland and take some navigational measurements. He sent Field up the Yellowstone to explore as far as he could get in a day and wrote happily about the "wide and fertile vallies" and "these delightful tracts of country . . . ." Vast herds of buffalo, elk, and antelope covered the plains, and the terrain was rich with serviceberries, gooseberries, chokecherries, currants, willows, and honeysuckles. That evening, "our little community" camped at the rivers' junction near the present-day border of Montana and North Dakota. They feasted on freshly killed meat, drank a dram of whiskey each, fiddled, sang, and danced the night away.

As the Corps continued on the Missouri River, Lewis and Clark checked off the landmarks — mostly rivers — that the Mandans and Hidatsas had mapped for them (see Chapter 9). On May 3, they passed a clear stream that Lewis named Porcupine River because of all the porcupines in the area. Clark named one tributary 2,000 Mile Creek because the party was now 2,000 miles from the mouth of the Missouri — 2,000 miles and nearly one year from their starting point.

On May 8, the expedition passed another river emptying into the Missouri from the north. The Hidatsas had called it The River Which Scolds All Others. Lewis renamed it the Milk River because of its glacial milky color — and that's what it's still called. (But don't you just love the mystery of the Hidatsas' name better?)

On May 20, the party arrived at the Musselshell River and a sizeable grove of cottonwood trees. A few miles above the mouth, a "handsome river" emptied into the Musselshell, and Lewis and Clark named it "Sah-ca-gar-we-ah's, or bird woman's River after our interpreter the Snake woman."

Exploring "seens of visionary inchantment"

At the end of May, the expedition entered an incredible landscape as remote and pristine today as it was 200 years ago: the Missouri Breaks. For over 150 miles, the Missouri River flows through the Breaks and on through an even wilder, more beautiful, and rugged canyon known as the White Cliffs (see Figure 10-1) — all in central Montana, east of present-day Fort Benton. On May 25, Lewis recorded the first bighorn sheep of the journey, and on the 26th, he climbed the bluffs and beheld, far in the distance, his first glimpse of the Rocky Mountains.

A beautiful river flowing into the Missouri from the south was named Judith River by Clark for his cousin and future wife, Julia Hancock, who was also known as Judith.

The expedition made slow progress through the White Cliffs because of rocks, strong wind, and shallow water. But Lewis sounded like a one man Chamber of Commerce: "The hills and river Clifts which we passed today exhibit a most romantic appearance. The bluffs of the river rise to the hight of from 2 to 300 feet and in most places nearly perpendicular; they are formed of remarkable white sandstone. . . . The water in the course of time in descending from those hills and plains on either side of the river has trickled down the soft sand clifts and woarn it into a thousand grotesque figures, which with the help of a little immagination and an oblique view at a distance, are made to represent eligant ranges of lofty freestone buildings, having their parapets well stocked with statuary . . . . As we passed on it seemed as if those seens of visionary inchant-ment would never have and end . . . ."

Figure 10-1:
The White
Cliffs of the
Missouri.

White Cliffs of the Missouri River. Courtesy of Travel Montana.

Eating, drinking, and breathing sand

Lewis and Clark witnessed the breathtaking beauty and wildness of the Northern Plains. While they were enjoying the "seens of visionary inchantment" described by Lewis, they were also pestered by blowing sand and merciless mosquitoes. And they were thumping their chests at the prospect of meeting majestic grizzly bears.

The wind on the plains was nearly constant — bringing relief from the mosquitoes and pushing the boats along nicely. However, it had its drawback: It drove fine particles of sand into everything — eyes, ears, gear, even Lewis's pocket watch. Lewis noted that "Soar eyes is a common complaint among the party. I believe it originates from the immence quantities of sand which is driven by the wind . . . so penitrating is this sand that we cannot keep any article free from it; in short we are compelled to eat, drink, and breath it very freely." (The men's sore eyes were treated with white vitriol [zinc sulfate] and lead acetate.)

The wind didn't abate until the party reached the mountains months later — nor does it abate to this day on the treeless Northern Plains.

TRAIL TIPS
NORTH
SOUTH

The Upper Missouri River Breaks National Monument

If Lewis and Clark were alive today, they would recognize few places from their journey. One stretch of the Missouri River in Montana, however, offers the same sights described in the journals as "seens of visionary inchantment." The White Cliffs worn into "a thousand grotesque figures" are now protected within the Upper Missouri River Breaks National Monument. For 149 miles, the Upper Missouri National Wild & Scenic River meanders through sagebrush, cottonwoods, and steep sandstone cliffs, arches, and castles in many colors. You can take a motorized day tour of the Missouri Breaks and enjoy a picnic on the banks or a take a tour by canoe. Managed by the Bureau of Land Management, the monument welcomes anglers, hikers, hunters and picnickers to its prime wildlife habitat.

Beyond the monument on the river is the Charles M. Russell National Wildlife Refuge. Extending 125 miles (as the crow flies) up the Missouri River from Fort Peck Dam in north-central Montana, the Charles M. Russell National Wildlife Refuge contains approximately 1.1 million acres of native prairies, forested coulees, river bottoms, and badlands. It's the kind of landscape often portrayed in the paintings of Charlie Russell, the colorful western artist for whom the refuge is named.

Boating, swimming, primitive camping, fishing, and big-game hunting are permitted in the refuge (with some restrictions), and hiking and horseback riding are the only way to reach the more remote areas of the refuge (there are no marked trails, so expertise with maps and compass is highly recommended). Although the damming of the river has altered the environment from when Lewis and Clark traveled the river in Montana, the refuge is a wild place offering plenty of challenges for modern explorers. And most of the area above the river is private ranch lands grazed by cows herded by Montana cowboys, who are harassed by descendants of the "musquetors" that plagued Lewis and Clark. For more information, go to www.visitmt.com or call 800-VISITMT (800-847-4868).

Dealing with "troublesom musquetors"

One of the most ferocious beasts on the plains was also one of the smallest: the ever annoying mosquito. Along with gnats and prickly pear cactus, the mosquitoes made the men feel constantly stuck and sucked on. The men had all been issued mosquito nets, one of their most critical pieces of equipment, but it was only the wind and sometimes the still cool night temperatures that offered relief.

Mosquitoes had plagued the expedition since it set out from St. Charles, but these pests of the Northern Plains swarmed in huge clouds and made life miserable. The expedition's journal keepers wrote some version of "musquetors troublesom" nearly as often as they wrote "we proceeded on." And they spelled mosquito nearly as many different ways as Clark spelled Sioux (see Chapter 6).

Harassing grizzly bears

Lewis and Clark had been awed by the tame manner of the animals on the plains. However, one animal never acted tame, and the Corps of Discovery took it personally. The Mandans and Hidatsas had told them about grizzly bears. The Indians had so much respect for the great bear — *Ursus horribilis horribilis* (see Figure 10-2) — that they ceremonially prepared themselves to hunt it as if they were preparing to go to war.

Lewis openly scoffed at the Indians' descriptions of grizzlies' "strength and ferocity," certain that the natives were afraid of the bears because of inferior hunting weapons. The beasts would be no match for the explorers' long rifles.

Stalking bears

The men of the expedition were all full of testosterone, ready to confront their first grizzly.

On April 29, Lewis and one other hunter got their chance. They came upon two grizzlies and shot and hit a bear apiece. Although mortally wounded, one of the bears charged Lewis for 80 yards before the captain could reload and kill it. These two bears were apparently juveniles, but bigger and "much more furious and formidable" than the black bears Lewis had encountered back home. He was impressed by the severity of injury that they could endure before dying. But he was still arrogant, convinced that his guns would render them less dangerous than the Mandans described.

On May 5, Clark and Drouillard killed another grizzly. With ten shots in it, the great bear still swam halfway across the river, dying on a sandbar 20 minutes later and roaring terribly all the while. Clark estimated this bear, an adult, at 500 pounds. Lewis was starting to lose some of his cockiness about the bears when he wrote, "I find that the curiosity of our party is pretty well satisfied with rispect to this anamal."

Viewing bears as enemies

On May 11, Private William Bratton shot a grizzly through the lungs, but the powerful beast chased him for half a mile before he could hail the pirogue for help. Lewis ordered the crew of the pirogue ashore to hunt the enemy bear. They tracked it another mile and finally killed it with two shots to the head. "These bear being so hard to die reather intimedates us all," Lewis wrote, "I do not like the gentlemen and had reather fight two Indians than one bear." He was at least beginning to respect the magnificent "gentlemen" — creatures who were at the top of the Plains' food chain and had no natural enemies except other bears. From this point on, the men thought of the bears not so much as animals, but as enemies, and they strategized their bear hunts like battlefield skirmishes.

Figure 10-2:
John F. Clymer painting of a grizzly and the expedition.

John F. Clymer, Hasty Retreat. Courtesy of Mr. John F. Clymer and the Clymer Museum of Art.

Less than a week after Bratton's narrow escape, the men saw a bear on the river bank and went ashore to ambush it. Six men attacked and wounded the bear. Still, it chased them into the river and jumped in after them. Finally, someone shot and killed it.

The explorers' next great bear war occurred in early July when they were camped at White Bear islands above the Great Falls of the Missouri. Grizzlies were starting to hang around the camp. Seaman barked at them all night, and nobody was getting any rest. Lewis decided to take out his frustrations on the "enemy:" He led a 12-man commando attack across the islands, but the squad only found one bear. It chased Drouillard, who shot and killed it.

 And so it went. The ursine lords of the plains were anthropomorphized into enemies — challengers of expeditionary manhood. The bears repeatedly paid for the distinction with their lives, and they never killed even one member of the expedition in retaliation. Some Indians will tell you that the reason grizzlies — the few that remain in Montana and Idaho — are so aggressive today is because of Lewis and Clark's constant harassment.

Appreciating Sacagawea

Although the grizzly bears were ferocious and unapproachable, most of the animals on the Northern Plains showed no fear of humans. This quality, as well as the sheer abundance of game, made hunting easy. The successful hunts ensured that the men continued their tradition of consuming nine pounds of meat, per man, per day (see Chapter 7 for details). Needless to say, this diet was not nutritious. (The men took Rush's pills, a powerful laxative, for the constipation resulting from such a heavy meat diet.)

When Sacagawea began to travel with the Corps, she immediately made a positive difference in the health of the men by adding to the supper menus. She dug wild Jerusalem artichokes out of mice burrows, gathered wild licorice, and collected a root she called white apple. She contributed a necessary and tasty variety to an otherwise all-meat diet, probably helping to avoid a problem with scurvy and other diseases.

On May 14, 1805, Sacagawea contributed more than roots and berries. She and her 3-month-old baby, Jean Baptiste, were riding in the white pirogue, under sail, with Charbonneau (who couldn't swim) at the helm. Suddenly a fierce gust of wind nearly capsized the big, clumsy canoe. Charbonneau, described by Lewis as "perhaps the most timid waterman in the world," panicked and steered the boat broadside to the wind instead of into it — all the while praying to God for mercy.

Lewis and Clark were both walking onshore, which they usually didn't do at the same time. (Clark normally commanded the boats while Lewis walked.) They watched in horror while the pirogue filled with water, and precious items washed overboard. The boat was carrying journals, maps, books, and instruments. A disaster was happening before their eyes. The one-eyed Cruzatte — probably the Corps of Discovery's best boatman — finally brought Charbonneau to his senses by threatening to shoot him if he didn't grab the tiller and right the boat, which the terrified Frenchman finally did. Cruzatte and the crew bailed out the water and paddled to shore.

But in the eyes of Lewis, the real hero of the day was Sacagawea. Throughout the debacle, and with imminent danger to her infant, she remained calm, snagging and retrieving articles as they floated away. Lewis praised her in his notes, "the Indian woman to whom I ascribe equal fortitude and resolution, with any person onboard at the time of the accedent, caught and preserved most of the light articles which were washed overboard."

Boudin Blanc

Sacagawea's husband, Toussaint Charbonneau, contributed to happy taste buds. He was a good cook and regularly made *boudin blanc* or white pudding. It was a sausage he created using buffalo intestines, buffalo meat, kidney suet, salt, pepper, and flour, boiling and then frying them in bear grease. Lewis loved "this white pudding we all esteem one of the greatest delacies of the forrest" and devoted extensive lip-smacking description to it in his journal.

Deciding Which River Was the Missouri

By June 1, 1805, Lewis and Clark were listening hard, hoping to hear the distant roar of waterfalls. According to the Hidatsa's estimations, the Corps of Discovery should have been nearing the Great Falls of the Missouri. Instead, the Missouri River split into two rivers! That was one river more than the Corps had bargained for; the Hidatsas hadn't even mentioned that another river converged with the Missouri at this point, creating a fork. Jefferson had explicitly directed Lewis to follow the Missouri. But which river was the Missouri? The expedition camped where the two rivers met and pondered their next move.

Standing at a fork in the river

The unexpected river was about the same size as the Missouri and joined it on the north side. It was deep and muddy like the Missouri had been for over 2,000 miles. The south fork was swifter and ran clear. The Hidatsas' information about rivers and landmarks had been completely accurate up to this point. But they made their westward excursions overland on horseback, not in boats on the river, so they apparently always bypassed this fork.

Every member of the party — except for Lewis and Clark — believed that the Missouri was the muddy north fork. The captains believed it was the clear south fork, because a river coming out of the mountains should be clearer. They sent Sgt. Pryor to scout the north fork and Sgt. Gass to the south. Both returned with no conclusive findings.

Lewis and Clark then decided to explore the rivers themselves for a day and a half — Lewis to the north and Clark to the south. It rained hard, and the terrain became slick and dangerous footing. Private Richard Windsor, who was with Lewis, slipped and nearly fell to his death.

Trusting a hunch

When the two scouting parties returned to the camp, both Lewis and Clark were more convinced than ever that the south (or left) fork was the Missouri, although the men didn't agree. Even Cruzatte, the veteran riverman, believed that they were wrong. Lewis and Clark directed the Corps of Discovery to prepare for travel up the left fork, which they did in spite of their disagreement. Lewis wrote that the men "very cheerfully . . . were ready to follow us any wher we thought proper to direct but that they still thought that the other was the river . . ." — a nice commentary on the men's trust in Lewis and Clark's leadership.

Lewis named the river not taken the Marias River in honor of his cousin Maria Wood. Because the river they did choose to take was shallow, the Corps needed to travel lighter, so they *cached* (concealed and stored for later use) the big red pirogue on an island at the mouth of the Marias. They also cached tools, pelts, skins, kegs of dry corn, pork, salt, and even a couple of rifles. A year later they would retrieve nearly everything in fine shape except for the red pirogue, which was ruined by high water.

As it turned out, Lewis and Clark were right, and the Corps of Discovery proceeded correctly up the Missouri.

Hearing the Roar of the Great Falls at Last

June 13 was a magical day for Lewis. He hiked ahead of the boats and before long, heard the sound that he had long anticipated: "a roaring too tremendious to be mistaken for any cause short of the great falls of the Missouri." He hurried down to the river and drank in "the grandest sight I ever beheld." He was certainly enraptured, pouring out hundreds and hundreds of words in his journal to describe the sight. It also confirmed that he and Clark had made the right choice and followed the Missouri River where the Marias and the Missouri converged.

He and his small party — Drouillard, Goodrich and a few others — camped at the falls, and Lewis resumed his hike the next morning. He was searching for the best route for a *portage* (carrying the boats over land) that the Hidatsas had estimated would take half a day. Five miles from the Great Falls, Lewis came upon a second smaller falls and again struggled to find adequate words for "one of the most beatifull objects in nature . . . " He named the second cascade Crooked Falls and walked on.

Altogether, Lewis discovered five waterfalls that day, covering 12 miles of river — not just one "great falls" as the Hidatsas had told him. He was so enchanted by "this ravishing prospect," that he kept on walking to the next tributary, which the Hidatsas called the Medicine River (now named the Sun River). It came into the Missouri from the northwest, above the falls.

On his way to the Medicine River, Lewis came upon a huge herd of buffalo and shot one for his supper. He hadn't yet reloaded his rifle when a grizzly bear approached him. Without a loaded gun, Lewis ran (not a smart thing to do when a grizzly is coming at you). The bear charged, and Lewis jumped into the Missouri. He pointed his *espontoon* (sort of a spear and walking stick combination, also called a *half-pike*) at the bear in a feeble effort to defend himself. The bear — a cousin to all those fearsome beasts throughout the voyage that eight and ten musket balls through the lungs and heart could barely stop — was cooperative. It turned and ran away. Lewis was lucky as well as enchanted.

Bringing back the Great Falls

Between 1891 and 1930, the five glorious waterfalls (see the following figure) — those "most beatifull objects in nature" that made Lewis's heart sing — were submerged or at least reduced by a series of five dams, one for each waterfall. The dams were built to generate electrical power for the City of Great Falls, Montana, and communities and industries as far away as the copper mines of Butte. In fact, because of the dams, Great Falls became known as the Electric City.

In recent years, the Montana Power Company sold the aging dams to conserve costs, and there is now a growing citizen demand to carefully dismantle the dams and give the river back its roar.

Travelers on the Lewis and Clark Trail can visit Great Falls' premier attraction, the Lewis and Clark National Historic Trail Interpretive Center. The Center overlooks the Missouri River below some of the falls, currently diminished by a dam. Other historical attractions in Great Falls include the Ulm Pishkun Buffalo Jump Education Center, the C.M. Russell Museum of Western Art, and Paris Gibson Square Museum of Art. The Sun and Missouri Rivers offer float trips and fishing, while the Little Belt Mountains and the Highwood Mountains offer hiking, biking, and camping. For more information, go to `www.greatfallscvb.visitmt.com`.

Falls on the Missouri River.
Courtesy of Donnie Sexton/Travel Montana.

On his return hike from the Medicine River, Lewis got charged again — this time by three buffalo bulls. However, they, too, stopped, and then ran away. Lucky, indeed.

Sailing Boats over the Prairie

Lewis's walk to the Medicine River was enchanting, magical, and fortunate, but it was also sobering. He realized that the Corps of Discovery would have to portage the boats more than 16 miles around all those waterfalls. It ended up taking 18 days, far more than the half day predicted by the Hidatsas. And many things went wrong, including nearly losing one of the expedition's most valuable and beloved members.

Curing Sacagawea

While Lewis was discovering the Great Falls of the Missouri, Sacagawea, back at the camp, was deadly ill. Clark described her condition as "Somewhat dangerous." She had a high fever, hardly any pulse, and her arms and hands were twitching oddly. Clark bled her (a staple of early 19th-century medicine) and applied bark poultices to her pelvic area, where she had the greatest pain. But the young woman was getting worse.

Lewis administered opium and "barks," which strengthened the girl's pulse. Lewis also had the men bring water for her from a sulfur spring that discharged into the Missouri near their camp. Benefiting from the sulfur water, opium, laudanum, and poultices, Sacagawea began to recover, and the sulfur spring has been called Sacagawea Spring ever since. Lewis wrote that he believed that she had "an obstruction of the mensis [Lewis meant menses or menstrual period] in consequence of taking could [cold]."

By the next day, his patient was nearly free of pain, and Lewis fed her some broiled buffalo meat. She even went out to gather white apples and was hungry enough to eat them raw. The raw fruit made her sick again. Lewis treated her with more opium and sulfur water, and then he bawled out Charbonneau for letting her eat the raw tubers.

Surviving hail, heatstroke, and cactus

While Lewis was treating Sacagawea, Clark scouted the south bank above the river for a good portage route. He established a base camp on a pretty, cottonwood-lined creek that entered the Missouri from the south (now called Belt Creek but named Portage Creek by Lewis and Clark). After surveying the waterfalls and observing the Missouri's bend toward the south after the falls, Lewis had determined that the best route for the portage was across the prairie on the south side of the river. Clark set off to survey the route and map out the path they would have to take.

Lewis found a huge old cottonwood tree, nearly two feet in diameter, along the creek. He had the men cut it down, saw it into cross sections, and shape those sections into wheels. The men cut up the white pirogue's mast to make axles and, with the wheels, fashioned two ingenious wagons — Lewis called them "trucks" — to carry the canoes up the ravines, across the prairie, and back to the Missouri.

Planning the portage

Lewis and Clark cached the white pirogue and some of its cargo at the Portage Creek base camp. They planned to take Lewis's lighter iron-frame boat (a collapsible iron boat frame of his own design — see details in Chapter 4) over land with them to replace the pirogue once they got back on the river.

The men went hunting for meat for the portage and hides to cover the iron boat after it was assembled.

Clark decided to supervise the portage, so that Lewis could go ahead to the next camp at a group of islands that Clark had named White Bear Islands (after the legendary grizzly bears). White Bear Island camp would be the end of the portage and the beginning of river travel once more. While the men were transporting the canoes, Lewis would prepare the iron boat for the next leg. That was the plan, anyway.

Rocking and rolling, cruising and bruising

The portage began on June 22. It was completed on July 2 and was unbelievably hard work. The strong, young men hauled the heavy wheeled canoes up and down ravines with every ounce of strength they had. Upon reaching the White Bear Island camp, they would deposit their load, and then go back for the next one.

The prickly pear cactus that was everywhere pierced their "mockersons" and their feet. Sharp rocks cut and bruised the same feet. The heat was overpowering and the mosquitoes "exceedingly troublesome," as always. Thunderstorms roared across the portage route, with huge hailstones pelting the men bloody and covering the ground. The rain arrived in heavy sheets, which made the ground slick, and mud stuck to the wheels of the trucks. The men were often faint and near collapse from exhaustion, but, incredibly, they remained cheerful and loved the adventure.

And the winds did blow. However, this time the men turned them to advantage. They sometimes rigged up sails on their "trucks" and sailed them across the prairie.

Surviving a flash flood

On June 29, the prairie was so wet from rain that Clark allowed the men to rest a little. He took York, Charbonneau, and Sacagawea with Jean Baptiste (also called Pomp) and walked back to the Great Falls. A black heavy cloud blew in, and the little group hurried to find shelter before the next deluge began. Clark and Sacagawea found a ravine with some sheltering rocks and took cover. It was a bad choice. Soon "the rain fell like one volley of water falling from the heavens," and a flash flood thundered down the ravine.

Clark grabbed his gun and pushed Sacagawea, carrying Pomp in her arms, ahead of him up the slope to higher ground. Charbonneau was above them, frozen with fear (which seemed to be his natural response to life-threatening danger), and York was on the prairie, searching for them all. Clark and Sacagawea barely got out of the ravine before the torrent became 10 feet deep, and then 15. Clark lost his compass, a tomahawk, and his shot pouch, and Sacagawea lost Pomp's *cradle board* (a rigid, wooden Shoshone version of a backpack baby carrier). They were all soaked to the bone. Clark worried about the child and feared Sacagawea would have a relapse of her recent illness because of the chill. He made them all run back to camp as fast as they could go for dry clothes and some grog that York had in a canteen, "which revived verry much."

Clark, Sacagawea, Pomp, and Charbonneau were able to change into dry clothes after the storm at the Great Falls because their part of the camp actually had a roof over it. Lewis and Clark had procured a buffalo skin tepee before leaving Fort Mandan, which was put up each night for Lewis and Clark, plus civilians Sacagawea, Pomp, Charbonneau, and George Drouillard to sleep in. (The rest of the Corps of Discovery had to sleep in the open.) The tepee traveled to the Pacific Ocean and back with them, serving as home to the family grouping until they reached the Mandan villages again in 1806.

The men fared as badly or worse. The hail was so big and fell with such force that it bruised and bloodied their heads and bare backs. Clark refreshed them with a little grog, too.

Launching the Experimental Boat

While Clark and the men struggled and suffered with the physical hardships of the portage, Lewis was doing some mental suffering (as he was inclined to do). At the White Bear Island camp, Lewis had his cherished iron-frame boat (see Chapter 4) assembled, and he prepared the 28 elk and 4 buffalo hides that would be needed to make its hull. The men called the boat *The Experiment.*

The collapsible vessel was the marvelous invention that Lewis and Jefferson had designed in early 1803 and that Lewis had ordered built in Harpers Ferry (see Chapter 4). Once assembled, the iron boat was 36 feet long and 4½ feet wide. It was supposed to carry up to 8,000 pounds.

Pining for pine trees

What Lewis suffered about was the camp's complete lack of pine trees, with the gooey pine tar he had counted on for all these miles to seal the seams holding the hides together to make *The Experiment* water tight.

To substitute for pine tar or pitch, Lewis tried a lot of different concoctions, finally settling on a mixture of charcoal, beeswax, and buffalo tallow.

On the Fourth of July the men raised the boat on a scaffold and built fires under it to dry the neatly sewn hide covering. They coated the hull with the beeswax and tallow, and things looked promising.

Getting that sinking feeling

On July 9, Lewis launched the boat, happily proclaiming that it "lay like a perfect cork on the water." The men loaded it and the canoes they had hauled across the prairie and prepared to get underway at last. Nearly a month had passed since they arrived at the Great Falls of the Missouri, and summer travel weather was a-wasting.

Alas. The wind kicked up, and they had to unload the boats to keep the river's whitecaps from swamping them. After the storm blew through, Lewis examined his new boat. It was sinking. The holes punched by the sewing needles would not hold the beeswax seal. Lewis was devastated. But he had to accept defeat; he didn't have time to try again.

Harboring new canoes but no hard feelings

Now the expedition had another problem to solve before they could proceed on. Abandonment of the iron boat would leave them short on carrying capacity for getting all their goods up the river. They had to replace *The Experiment* with something.

Clark later told Nicholas Biddle — in 1810 he was the first editor of the journals — that he had anticipated the problem and had already scouted around for cottonwood trees big enough to make a couple of replacement canoes. The men took five days to turn the tree trunks into two new boats.

This predicament may have been the first real difference of opinion between the expedition's co-commanders. The romantic Lewis was obsessed with the iron boat and used up precious traveling time to make it work. Pragmatic Clark seems to have had his doubts all along. When the iron boat failed, he had a replacement solution ready. But, no matter how he may have felt, Clark never wrote a word of blame about Lewis.

Savoring the Last Gill of Whiskey

The Corps of Discovery spent its second Independence Day west of the Mississippi working on the iron boat. But they did celebrate. That evening, they ate bacon, beans, dumplings, and buffalo, and Cruzatte played his fiddle. Lewis and Clark measured out the last of the whiskey and gave each man a final gill.

Lewis and Clark generally measured out the whiskey rations in drams or gills. A fluid *dram* equals $\frac{1}{128}$ of a pint, a small amount. A *gill,* however, which is what the men got for their final ration on July 4, 1805, is equal to ¼ of a pint or half a cup.

Available for your home garden

Some plants and trees recorded by Lewis and Clark are ones you can plant in your own garden, and they're available from regional garden centers, nurseries, and mail-order catalogs. They include:

Trees and shrubs:

- Osage orange
- Wood's rose
- Serviceberry
- Narrow-leafed cottonwood
- Rocky Mountain maple
- Paper birch
- Mountain ash
- Whitebark pine
- Huckleberry
- Oregon grape

- Big leaf maple
- Gooseberry
- Currant

Wildflowers:

- Blue flax
- Montana bitterroot
- Lupine
- Larkspur
- Showy phlox
- Columbine
- Mariposa lily
- Scarlet gilia
- Penstemmons
- Jacob's ladder

They were halfway through the Voyage of Discovery. It was the last whiskey they would taste until their return trip from the Pacific more than a year later. And keep in mind that these were drinking men. Captain Lewis was an alcoholic and suffered from what was then called melancholia (probably today's bi-polar syndrome). Yet Lewis, like the others, would have to spend the next 14 months completely sober. He no doubt could have ferreted away a little grog for his own private use, but he didn't. If the men had to go whiskey-less, so would he.

Chapter 11

Searching for Snakes and Horses

. . . .

In This Chapter

▶ Passing through the gates

▶ Fearing the Assiniboines

▶ Searching for the elusive Shoshones

▶ Facing the awesome truth about the Northwest Passage

. . . .

*I*n July of 1805, the Lewis and Clark expedition was running short of summer traveling weather. They desperately needed to find Sacagawea's birth tribe, the Shoshones (or Snakes as Lewis and Clark sometimes called them) and trade for horses to cross the mountains.

The expedition floated through a remarkable set of cliffs and finally reached the headwaters of the seemingly endless Missouri. They searched and searched and searched some more for the Shoshones. Clark got sick. George Shannon got lost — again (see Chapter 7). And Lewis climbed to the top of the Continental Divide, beholding a sea of mountains that stretched to the far horizon.

In this chapter, we share the trials and tribulations of Lewis and Clark as they prepared to cross the mountains — mountains higher and vaster than they and Jefferson could ever have dreamed.

Sailing through the Gates of the Mountains

On July 15, 1805, after spending a month hauling their boats around the Great Falls of the Missouri and trying to make the iron boat work (see Chapter 10), the expedition resumed travel at last. Captain Lewis and Privates Potts and LePage (see Chapter 2 for details on these two men) walked onshore to lighten the loads of the canoes. Lewis was so happy to be underway again that he even described the prickly pear cactus that had been destroying the men's feet in terms slightly less than miserable resentment: "the prickly pear is now in full blume and forms one of the beauties as well as the greatest pests of the plains." The wild sunflowers and other wildflowers were also in bloom. The sweeping summer prairie was — and still is — sublime along that eastern edge of Montana's Rocky Mountain Front.

Lewis also described the geography, including Square Butte, the massive solitary butte southwest of modern day Great Falls, Montana (made famous by artist C.M. Russell). Lewis called it Fort Mountain, and said: "this mountain has a singular appearance it is situated in a level plain, its' sides stand nearly at right angles with each other . . . and rise perpendicularly to the hight of 300 feet."

The first day back on the Missouri, Drouillard shot and wounded a deer, which ran into the river. Lewis's dog, Seaman jumped in and caught it, and then delivered it to his master. Good dog, Seaman!

Gates of the Mountains and Helena area today

Surrounded by the grandeur of the Rocky Mountains, Helena is a city with an amazing variety of outdoor recreation and wildlife-viewing opportunities.

As Lewis and Clark traveled up this part of the Missouri River in 1805, Lewis was awed by the steep limestone walls and noted the splendor of what he named Gates of the Mountains. You can see the same sights today by motorboat tour offered in the summer at Gates of the Mountains Wilderness Area, 20 miles north of Helena on Interstate 15. The wilderness area also offers camping, swimming, fishing and hiking.

If you're a trout-fishing enthusiast, you'll love the Helena area's many lakes and streams, where rainbow, brook, brown, bull, yellowstone cutthroat, and westslope cutthroat abound. Nearby Holter and Hauser Lakes are perfect for camping, fishing, swimming, wind surfing, water-skiing, and boating. Those activities are also available at Canyon Ferry Lake, a large reservoir on the Missouri River just 20 minutes east of Helena. Or you can enjoy the same variety of recreation at local favorite Spring Meadow Lake, just a few miles west of downtown Helena and open year round.

The largest city park, Mount Helena, includes 630 acres of trails, offering spectacular views of the city and gulches around Helena. The Blackfoot Meadows and Continental Divide Trail offers hikers potential encounters with moose, elk, black bears, mountain goats, and bighorn sheep. The 1.5-million-acre Bob Marshall Wilderness Complex, with 1,800 miles of hiking trails, begins a few miles north of town and stretches all the way to Glacier National Park. You can downhill ski at Great Divide Mountain, just 20 miles from town, with more than 60 runs, 30 for advanced skiers. You also find three major snowmobile trail systems within a 30-minute drive of Helena. For information about the Helena area, go to www.helenacvb.visitmt.com or call 800-743-5362.

In those first days of resumed travel, Lewis and Clark named a couple of rivers that flowed into the Missouri — the Smith River for Robert Smith, who was Jefferson's Secretary of the Navy, and the Dearborn River for Secretary of War Henry Dearborn.

The Missouri itself had become winding and increasingly shallow and rocky. Poling, rowing, towing, and pushing the canoes up it was backbreaking work. The men spent hours each day wading up to their waists in cold water, and everybody was constantly exhausted. The Missouri was no longer a muddy prairie river. It had become a clear, cold, swift mountain current, which meant only one thing: The expedition had reached the foothills of the Rocky Mountains.

On July 19, the canoes entered a deep, narrow canyon. Lewis named this extraordinarily beautiful stretch the Gates of the Mountains (see Figure 11-1), and that's what it's still called today. Lewis's description may have reflected his own mood more than the landscape: "this evening we entered much the most remarkable clifts that we have yet seen. [T]hese clifts rise from the waters edge on either side perpendicularly to the hight of 1200 feet. every object here wears a dark and gloomy aspect. The tow(er)ing and projecting rocks in many places seem ready to tumble on us . . . from the singular appearance of this place I called it the *gates of the rocky mountains* . . . musquetoes less troublesome than usual."

You can take a summer tour boat through the Gates today, You can also kayak through or go hiking around and above the cliffs. The area is a 6-mile-long canyon of the Missouri that opens to a lovely valley just north of present-day Helena, Montana. The Gates of the Mountains are still beautiful and still fairly pristine.

Figure 11-1:
Gates of the Mountains.

Gates of the Mountains. Courtesy of National Park Service, Lewis and Clark National Historic Trail.

Avoiding Assiniboines

The original diplomatic objectives of the Corps of Discovery included meeting with as many tribes along the Missouri as they could in order to

- Explain American sovereignty over Louisiana Territory
- Urge peace among the tribes
- Establish trade agreements between the tribes and Uncle Sam

After their near disastrous encounter with the Teton Sioux (see Chapter 8), the Lewis and Clark agenda also included disrupting the Teton-Arikara trade alliance (see Chapter 9), thus marginalizing the Sioux.

From Fort Mandan to the Great Falls, however, Lewis and Clark made a temporary but radical change in their mission. Instead of seeking out the tribes in that area, they worked hard to avoid meeting them. That's because the expedition was traveling through Assiniboine country, and Lewis and Clark had heard that the people of that nation were like the Sioux, playing a dominating role in their trade and social arrangements. The Corps feared that this tribe would present a threat to the expedition. Lewis and Clark tended to view the tribes as either good or evil, and in a typical snap judgment, they concluded that the Assiniboine were "a vicious illy disposed nation" with a "turbulent and faithless disposition." And they hadn't even met them.

From Sacagawea, Lewis and Clark knew to expect the Shoshones — and their horses — anytime after the Great Falls of the Missouri and before the Missouri's headwaters at the Three Forks. They wanted to get to the Shoshones without any delays. As the expedition traveled through present-day eastern Montana, they saw many recent signs of the Assiniboines, including hunting camps, sweat lodges (small structures for taking purifying steam baths), prayer offerings, distant smoke, and tepees. One day, a dog drifted into the explorers' camp, and a general alert ran through the Corps that the Assiniboines were close and no doubt ready to attack.

During the portage around the Great Falls, Lewis and Clark decided not to send one of the canoes and some of the men back to St. Louis with news of the expedition's progress. That had been their earlier plan, but with all those Assiniboines out there *somewhere,* the captains decided to keep all the men together. And keep all the rifles nearby.

Despite the Indians' signs and the Corps's wariness, Lewis and Clark never met any Assiniboines. Instead, the hidden Indians observed the expedition's progress through their territory and preferred not to spend time making contact with the explorers, whose reputation for arrogance and ineptitude was growing among the sophisticated Plains tribes.

TRAIL TIPS

NORTH
SOUTH

Don't avoid the Assiniboines in your own travels

Of the seven Indian reservations in Montana, two of them are home to the Assiniboine tribe that Lewis and Clark did their best to avoid. Don't make the same mistake if you're traveling the Lewis and Clark trail.

Fort Peck Reservation is made up of 2 million acres in the northeastern corner of Montana, fifty miles south of the Canadian border. It is home to Assiniboine and Sioux tribes. If you follow Lewis and Clark's water trail through Montana, you'll pass by over 100 miles of the Fort Peck reservation. Attractions on the reservation include the Assiniboine and Sioux Culture Center and Museum in Poplar and the Assiniboine Village in Wolf Point, a traditional village where visitors can observe the everyday cultural practices of the tribe. Fort Peck also hosts several powwows, rodeos, and festivals throughout the summer. For more information, call 406-768-5155.

If you're traveling west through Montana on the Lewis and Clark Trail of 1805, the next reservation you will come to is Fort Belknap in north-central Montana, home to Assiniboine and Gros Ventres tribes. The Fort Belknap Tourism Office runs an information center in Harlem, Montana, where the tribe sells native crafts and offers tours of Snake Butte and Mission Canyon. Snake Butte (named for its resident rattlesnakes) overlooks the tribal buffalo pasture and ancient tepee rings. Mission Canyon south of Hays is a scenic recreation canyon that's a popular camping destination. Deer and antelope are common sights. Annual events include Milk River Indian Days and Hays Powwow, both held in July. For information on Fort Belknap, call 406-353-2205.

Continuing along the westbound Lewis and Clark Trail, Rocky Boy Reservation is near the Canadian border in north-central Montana. Rocky Boy is home to the Chippewa-Cree tribe, not the Assiniboine, and the Bear Paw Mountains. Bear Paw Ski Bowl is a popular attraction, as is the annual powwow, held the first weekend in August. Information on Rocky Boy reservation is available at 800-823-4478.

Desperately Seeking Shoshones

After leaving the White Bear Islands, the Corps's diplomatic goal of avoiding Indians changed to one of desperately seeking Indians, namely the Shoshones.

The expedition was depending on the Shoshones to meet two urgent needs:

- ✔ **Horses:** The Corps couldn't pack all their goods over the Rockies without them.
- ✔ **Guidance:** Unlike some men, Lewis and Clark weren't reluctant to ask for directions. And they needed them big time. They wanted Shoshone input on what route to take over the upcoming mountains.

While Lewis and the canoes were rowing through the inspiring, albeit dark and gloomy, Gates of the Mountains, Clark was hiking ahead overland. He took York, Joseph Field, and John Potts with him, all of them watchful and alert for any sign of the Shoshones. Clark and Lewis had agreed that the whole party might frighten the Indians away with all the gunshots they would be firing as they hunted their way along, which would make the Shoshones mistake them for a raiding party from their traditional enemies, the Blackfeet. (The very powerful and well armed Blackfeet had European guns. The Shoshones did not.) Clark's smaller party would, they hoped, appear less threatening.

Both contingents of the Corps of Discovery — Clark's advance group and Lewis's larger party in the canoes — strained hard to find signs of the Shoshones.

Throbbing feet and frayed nerves (but no Shoshones)

Clark saw smoke signals and began to leave little signs of his own that he hoped the Shoshones would find and realize that the explorers were friendly white men, not dangerous Blackfeet. He scattered bits of cloth and paper, but lured no Shoshones. Finally his feet were hurting so badly that he stopped and waited for Lewis to catch up.

Having walked about 30 miles during the day over sharp rocks and spikey vegetation, that night Clark wrote, "my feet is verry much brused & cut walking over the flint, & constantly Stuck full Prickley pear thorns, I puled out 17 by the light of the fire to night."

The going had been rough and exhausting, and the men — for the first time — were starting to complain. Once again, Sacagawea came to the rescue.

On July 22, Sacagawea, originally a Shoshone, began to point out familiar landmarks from her childhood. She told Lewis that the expedition was following "the river on which her relations lived, and that the three forks were at no great distance." According to Lewis, her news "cheered the sperits of the party who now begin to console themselves with the anticipation of shortly seeing the head of the missouri yet unknown to the civilized world." (This comment revealed an interesting cultural bias, considering all the rich and complex civilizations Lewis had traveled through for 14 months.)

Lewis had the men fly small American flags from the canoes to show any Indians who were out there that the party was friendly. Clark set out overland again, this time with Joseph and Reuben Field, Robert Frazer, and Toussaint Charbonneau. Despite the condition of Clark's feet, he "deturmined to proceed on in pursute of the Snake Indians." And Lewis wrote, "altho' Capt. C. was much fatigued his feet yet blistered and soar he insisted on pursuing his rout in the morning nor weould he consent willingly to my relieving him . . . finding him anxious I readily consented to remain with the canoes."

Clark's determination and Lewis's ready consent illuminate one of the few tense moments between the two captains even hinted at in their journals. So Clark walked on, and Lewis rowed.

Three days — and five sets of swollen prickly pear tortured feet later — Clark's advance party reached the Three Forks of the Missouri. They found the prairie blackened by fire and saw lots of recent horse tracks, but no Shoshones. Clark left Lewis a note stuck to a tree branch and proceeded on up the westernmost of the three forks.

When Lewis and the canoes arrived at the Three Forks, the expedition was growing genuinely desperate to get some horses. If they didn't find the Shoshones soon, they might have to spend another winter east of the mountains. They couldn't pack all their supplies and trade goods over the Rockies without horses, nor did they even know the route to take. They really needed to find Sacagawea's people — and soon. Lewis wrote, "We begin to feel considerable anxiety with rispect to the Snake [an early fur trader name for Shoshone] Indians."

One thing working against Lewis and Clark was the fact that the Shoshones didn't normally leave their summer fishing camps on the Lemhi and Salmon Rivers, on the west side of the Continental Divide, and travel eastward to the Three Forks area until the September buffalo hunting season. So, the expedition camped at the Three Forks (where Sacagawea had been captured by Hidatsa Indians five years before), mended their clothes, and doctored their aches.

Naming the Three Forks

While camping in the beautiful Three Forks valley, Lewis and Clark named a few geographic features, including each of the forks of the Missouri's headwaters.

✔ They named the eastern fork the Gallatin River, for Secretary of the Treasury Albert Gallatin.

✔ They named the middle fork the Madison River, after Secretary of State and later President, James Madison.

✔ The southwest fork, the one leading into the mountains, they named the Jefferson River in honor of "that illustrious personage."

Dealing with illness, note-eating beavers, and a lost man (but no Shoshones)

The Corps stayed at the Three Forks for three days. They were almost 3,000 miles upriver from St. Louis. Lewis described the country as opening "suddenly to extensive and beatifull plains and meadows which appear to be surrounded in every direction with distant and lofty mountains." The streams were clogged with beavers and otters, and Lewis estimated that the spot would be perfect for a fur-trading post. In fact, in only a few years, the Three Forks would become the center of the American fur trade — as soon as businessman Manuel Lisa (see Chapter 6) could get there.

Feeling bilious

After following the western fork of the Missouri for some miles and then doubling back and exploring the middle fork for a short distance, Clark returned to the Three Forks and the expedition's camp on July 27. And he was pretty sick. He had a high fever, chills, and muscle cramps. He reported that he was also "somewhat bilious and had not had a passage for several days." Nine pounds of meat a day and scant dietary fiber would tend to cause that — even with all that walking.

Lewis prescribed a dozen of Dr. Rush's thunderclappers, a powerful laxative pill that Lewis prescribed for all kinds of digestive complaints. Clark took five of them, bathed his feet in warm water, and got some badly needed rest.

While Clark recovered his health, Lewis recorded more birds (blue grouse and pinon jay), picked currants, and named two more small rivers, Wisdom and Philosophy (later called Big Hole and Ruby). When the party got underway again, the captains reversed roles. Lewis took Drouillard, Gass and Charbonneau and went overland; Clark managed the canoes.

Cussing beavers

The expedition followed the Jefferson to a fork with the Wisdom River. In advance of the boats, Lewis wrote a note to Clark saying that he was continuing up the main tributary of the Jefferson, which is now called the Beaverhead River. He stuck the note on a green willow twig. Clark and the canoes arrived at the fork and proceeded to grunt and pull and push their way up the Wisdom. But that stream was even shallower and more choked with willows than the Beaverhead, and before long, canoes were overturning and filling with water.

When Lewis returned to help dry out the expedition's goods, he asked Clark why he hadn't proceeded as directed in the note. What note? It had disappeared. After much surmising, Lewis and Clark agreed that a beaver must have chewed through the twig and carried it away for supper, note and all.

Getting lost again

Clark had sent George Shannon on up the Wisdom to do some hunting. When the canoes swamped and turned back toward the Jefferson, Clark sent Drouillard to find Shannon. He couldn't.

The men fired their rifles as a signal and waited for the young explorer until the next day, August 7. Then they stashed one of the canoes (having consumed its load of provisions) and started up the Beaverhead. They made only a few miles a day. They were exhausted, sick, and sore. Shannon, who had improved his ability to get found after getting lost (see Chapter 7), turned up three days later.

Sacagawea once again lifted the men's "sperits." She pointed out a ridge of land that the Shoshones called the Beaver's Head, because to them it looked like a swimming beaver (see Figure 11-2). She told Lewis and Clark that they would find her people soon — if not on the Beaverhead, on the river immediately to the west of it.

Figure 11-2: Beaver's Head Rock.

Beaverhead Rock. Courtesy of National Park Service, Lewis and Clark National Historic Trail.

Misunderstanding tab-ba-bone

Certain now that the Shoshones and their horses were oh-so-close, Lewis set out on foot again. This time he was accompanied by Drouillard, Hugh McNeal, and John Shields. Clark had developed a painfully infected boil on his ankle and so continued laboring upstream with the canoes.

Craving currants

Lewis made written records on massive numbers of water birds along the river and wetlands: "curlooes" (curlews), sandhill cranes, geese, mergansers, plovers, and trumpeter swans. He mentioned pheasants on the plain. He also noted botanical specimens, such as box elder, choke cherries, narrow leafed cottonwoods, currants (black, red, "perple," and yellow), red and black gooseberries, honeysuckles, wild roses, sage, service berries, southernwood, and broad leaf and narrow leaf willow.

Lewis especially liked the wild yellow currants, and the botanist in him got carried away describing them: "the perianth of the fructification is one leaved, five cleft, abreviated and tubular, the corolla is monopetallous funnel-shaped; very long, superior, (permanent tho') withering and of a fine orrange colour . . . the fruit is a berry about the size and much the shape of the red currant of our gardins."

Oddly — given the care they had hitherto taken with their Indian diplomacy — Lewis and Clark don't appear to have developed any kind of strategy for approaching the Shoshones, who were now close. Or, if they made a plan, they didn't record it. They did think to ask Sacagawea what the Shoshone word for white man was. Well, the Shoshones had never met any white men, so they didn't have a word. The best she could come up with was "Tab-ba-bone," which meant stranger, someone other than a relative or friend. It could also have meant enemy in the right context. So armed with "Tab-ba-bone" and a few trade trinkets, Lewis set out to find the Shoshones.

Lewis's small party followed "a plain Indian road" until it petered out at a lovely little valley that Lewis called Shoshone Cove, "one of the handsomest coves I ever saw, of about 16 or 18 miles in diameter." They camped for the night and feasted on venison. Shoshone Cove is now inundated by the Clark Canyon Reservoir, near scenic present-day Dillon, Montana.

Scaring Away a Shoshone

On August 11, Lewis sent Drouillard afield to his right and Shields to his left. McNeal walked with Lewis, and thus spread apart, the men tried to find the Indian road they had located the day before. About five miles along, Lewis spied a Shoshone Indian! They saw a man on horseback about two miles away, riding in their direction. Through his spy glass, Lewis "discovered from his dress that he was of a different nation from any that we had yet seen, and was satisfied of his being a Sosone." The Indian was "mounted on an eligant horse without a saddle, and a small string which was attached to the under-jaw of the horse which answered as a bridle." The Shoshone carried a bow and quiver of arrows, but no rifle. Lewis was overjoyed.

Sending mixed signals

The mounted Indian stopped about a mile from the white men, and Lewis stopped, too. He took his blanket out of his pack and "mad him the signal of friendship known to the Indians of the Rocky mountains and those of the Missouri, which is by holding the mantle or robe in your hands at two corners and then throwing up in the air higher than the head bringing it to the earth as if in the act of spreading it . . . this signal of the robe or skin for ther gests to set on when they are visited."

The signal must have been unknown to the Shoshone on the "eligant" horse. His attention was on Drouillard and Shields approaching on Lewis's flanks. Lewis, fearing that his men would frighten the Indian away, left his rifle with McNeal and took some beads and trinkets and a looking glass out of his pack and started walking toward the Indian again. When Lewis got to within 200 yards of him, the Shoshone turned his horse and started moving away.

Now even more desperate, Lewis started shouting loudly, "Tab-ba-bone, Tab-ba-bone," and holding up the trinkets for the Indian to see. He also signaled for Drouillard and Shields to stop. Drouillard did. But Shields didn't see the signal and kept moving forward. Lewis pulled up his shirt sleeve so the Shoshone could see his white skin and kept shouting "Tab-ba-bone." When Lewis was about 100 yards from him, the Indian sped away on his horse, disappearing into the willow brush. He was putting fast distance between himself and a stranger who openly identified himself as a foreigner and potential enemy and who had two men carrying rifles closing in on each side.

Casting blame

Lewis was mortified, disappointed, and angry. And he did an ugly thing for a commanding officer. He blamed his men, instead of his own lack of planning or miscommunication. He believed that the Shoshone would have talked with him if Drouillard and Shields had only had the wits to stop sooner and "could not forbare abraiding them a little for their want of attention and imprudence on this occasion."

The men tried to follow the horseman's tracks, but a rain shower obliterated every trace, and Lewis was forced to give up and try again the next day.

Realizing the Awesome Truth about the West

On August 12, Lewis and his party set out early. They passed brush lodges and places where women had been digging roots. The men eventually followed a well used Indian road. They didn't find any Shoshones, but they did see a wolverine, "a different animal from any that we have yet seen."

Celebrating the end of the Missouri

The Indian road began to get steeper, and the stream they were following, the smallest tributary of the Missouri so far, shrank to a rivulet. Lewis wrote, "the road took us to the most distant fountain of the waters of the mighty Missouri in surch of which we have spent so many toilsome days and wristless nights." The Lewis and Clark expedition had succeeded in following the Missouri to its source. Lewis took a long cold drink. McNeal stood with one foot on each side of the tiny brook and "thanked his god that he had lived to bestride the mighty & heretofore deemed endless Missouri."

After indulging in the significance of the moment, Lewis pressed on up the trail, which wound ever higher. The group was traveling up what is known today as Lemhi Pass, about to reach the Continental Divide — that magical spine of the continent that divides the rivers flowing into the Atlantic Ocean from the ones flowing into the Pacific Ocean.

A recipe for sunflower seed bread

Meriwether Lewis had cultivated taste buds and often wrote in his journal about new foods he found or was offered by the Indians. Here is a recipe for sunflower seed bread that he detailed on July 17, 1805:

"The Indians of the Missouri particularly those who do not cultivate maze [corn] make great uce [use] of the seed of this plant for bread, or use it in thickening their soope [soup]. they most commonly first parch the seed and then pound them between two smooth stones untill they reduce it to a fine meal. to this they sometimes mearly [merely] add a portion of water and drink it in that state, or add a sufficient quantity of marrow grease to reduce it to the consistency of common dough and eate it in that manner. The last composition I think much best and have eat it in that state heartily and think it a pallateable dish."

Shattering a myth

Since the earliest days of North American exploration and colonization, Europeans had believed that a convenient Northwest Passage connected the east flowing rivers, over the crest of the continent, to the west flowing rivers. It's what Christopher Columbus was looking for in 1492, but he found a giant continent, instead. Alexander MacKenzie had crossed Canada in search of it, a decade before the Lewis and Clark expedition; he didn't find it, either. Jefferson had instructed Lewis to follow the Missouri to its headwaters, where he hoped Lewis would find it. Jefferson and Lewis believed that it would be a narrow crossing from one broad river plain to another.

At the top of Lemhi Pass, Lewis was forced to accept an earthshaking truth. "[W]e proceeded on to the top of the dividing ridge from which I discovered immence ranges of high mountains still to the West of us with their tops partially covered with snow" (see Figure 11-3).

Figure 11-3:
The view from Lemhi Pass today.

Lemhi Pass. Courtesy of National Park Service, Lewis and Clark National Historic Trail.

Nobody in Lewis's and Jefferson's world ever dreamed that east and west would be separated by hundreds of miles of endless mountains — or that the mountains could be so much higher than the familiar Appalachians. On August 12, 1805, Meriwether Lewis discovered that there was no Northwest Passage and shattered a long-held dream.

Chapter 12

Making a Cold, Hungry, and Dangerous Trek across the Mountains

In This Chapter

▶ Finding the Shoshones and holding on for dear life

▶ Clinching the deal and getting the horses

▶ Giving up on the River of No Return

▶ Falling up the Great Divide

▶ Meeting "Welsh" Indians

▶ Enduring the Bitterroots crossing

▶ Staggering out of the mountains

*H*aving gone to the top of Lemhi Pass and seen the immense mountain range the expedition had yet to cross, Lewis had intensified his search for the Snake Indians — the Shoshones — and their horses. He finally found the Shoshones, but had a difficult and tense time trying to convince them of his friendly intentions. (Chapter 11 has all the details of Lewis's first Shoshone encounter.)

In this chapter, you find out that Shoshone leader Cameahwait and a party of warriors accompanied Lewis to meet Clark and the Corps of Discovery coming up the Beaverhead River. Luckily for the Corps, Cameahwait turned out to be Sacagawea's brother as well as a friend, and the expedition successfully acquired the horses and arranged for a Shoshone guide.

You also discover that while Lewis and Clark had maintained hope that they could ride the rivers across the mountains, their hopes were dashed when Clark saw the impassable River of No Return. They faced the chilling reality that they'd have to make the mountain crossing on foot. This chapter follows the Corps on the harrowing journey over the Bitterroot Range of the Rocky Mountains, as they lost their way and came close to starvation before finally emerging on the open prairies in Nez Perce country.

Needing the Shoshones (but the Shoshones Need to Leave)

History grants you a unique vantage point on the voyage of the Corps of Discovery. You can understand events from the perspective of Lewis and Clark *and* from the view of the American Indians. In the late summer of 1805, the Shoshone tribe and the Lewis and Clark expedition were both in big trouble. The Corps needed to find the Shoshones, but the Shoshones — in danger of starvation and attack by rival tribes — didn't want to be found.

Depending on Shoshone guides and horses: The Corps

In August of 1805, Lewis and a party of men reached the top of 7,373-foot Lemhi Pass, along the Continental Divide in the Beaverhead Mountains (a Rocky Mountains sub-range on the border of present day Montana and Idaho). Although it was summer by the calendar, Lewis had seen snow-capped and seemingly endless Rocky Mountains to the west. He knew that the fate of the expedition depended on convincing the Shoshone tribe to provide horses and guides to cross those mountains. And they had to make the crossing soon or wait until spring.

During the trek over the pass, Lewis and his men had seen a Shoshone on horseback, but the man was frightened and fled (see Chapter 11). Lewis was dismayed and angered at this bungled first contact. He descended from Lemhi Pass with a new urgency. He had to find the Shoshones fast.

Starving, afraid, and anxious to travel: The Shoshones

The Shoshones weren't easy to find, and they had good reasons to be elusive. They were a plains tribe who hunted buffalo, but they had been driven off of the plains and into the mountains by other tribes who had guns — the Blackfeet and Atsinas to their north and the Hidatsas to their east. Skilled horsemen, the Shoshones had hundreds of horses but only two or three guns and no ammunition.

Raids by the Knife River Hidatsas were common and without guns, the Shoshones were at their mercy. Sacagawea, who accompanied the expedition (see Chapter 2), had been kidnapped in a Hidatsa raid on the Shoshones when she was 12 years old. The Atsinas had attacked the Shoshones the previous spring, capturing warriors, stealing horses, and burning down all but one tepee.

Game was scarce in the mountains where the Shoshones were forced to live, so the tribe was surviving on berries, roots, a few fish, and small game animals. As Lewis approached their territory, they were in fact slowly starving and were anxious to begin a dangerous but necessary trip onto the plains to hunt buffalo.

Hooking Up with the Shoshones

On August 13, Lewis and his small party approached three Shoshone women gathering roots a few miles from their Lemhi River village (in today's Idaho, a few miles north and west of Lemhi Pass). One woman fled, but a young girl and an old woman froze as if terrified. Lewis and his men were sunburned and dressed in buckskins and moccasins, so the women may have thought they were from an enemy tribe. Lewis laid down his rifle and pulled up his sleeve to show them his white skin.

Lewis slowly won them over, pulling gifts from his saddlebag — mirrors, beads, and moccasin awls. He took out vermillion, a color that Lewis had been told meant "peace" to the Shoshone. He painted their faces with it. The new friends had begun to walk toward the Shoshone village when 60 warriors on horseback rode full tilt to the women's rescue. While the women explained that Lewis was not an enemy, he produced gifts and presented an American flag.

Getting an overwhelming welcome

The Shoshones, as relieved as Lewis must have been, "embraced me very affectionately," Lewis wrote, putting an arm over his shoulder and touching his left cheek with theirs. "Bothe parties now advanced and we were all caressed and besmeared with their grease and paint till I was heartily tired of the national hug."

Cameahwait, one of the Shoshone leaders, led them to the only skin tepee that the tribe had left after the Atsinas' latest raid and seated them ceremonially on antelope skins. After a ritual smoke in what Lewis described as a "little magic circle," Lewis talked and Drouillard signed in translation. The Shoshones gave them food — serviceberry and chokeberry cakes — that they couldn't really spare. Later, they offered Lewis a small piece of salmon, which he mistakenly thought meant that they were near the ocean. They also gave Lewis a bitterroot, a staple food of the tribe. He hated it. The root was "naucious to my palate," he wrote. After eating one, he never cared to eat another. Because he was the first white man to record its existence, the plant was named after him anyway: *Lewisia rediviva*. (It was named *rediviva* because a year after Lewis collected, dried, and preserved it — a year without moisture of any kind — the specimen he sent back to Jefferson began to sprout new growth!)

Lewis went to bed early that night while Drouillard, McNeal, and Shields stayed up until after midnight dancing with the Shoshones. The next day, Lewis tried to get a party of Shoshones organized to go with him to meet Clark, who was coming up the Beaverhead River on the other (Montana) side of Lemhi Pass.

Resorting to promises and insults

Many Shoshones suspected that Lewis and the Corps were setting a trap for them. The afternoon of August 14, Lewis pressed for Cameahwait to organize a party to meet Clark. After a long speech to his warriors, Cameahwait signaled that they'd be ready to go the next morning. But the next morning, they still weren't ready. Even Cameahwait seemed reluctant to go. Finally, Lewis asked what the problem was. Cameahwait replied that "some foolish persons" thought Lewis was in league with the Blackfeet tribe and was leading them into an ambush. Cameahwait said that he wasn't worried himself, but he didn't act anxious to get going, either, that day or the following day.

Lewis, meanwhile, resorted to promises and insults.

Lewis wrote in his journal that "Cameahwait, with his ferce eyes and lank jaws grown meager for the want of food. . .[said] "If we had guns, we could live in the country of the buffaloe and eat as our enemies do, and not be compelled to hide ourselves in these mountains and live on roots and berries as bears do."

Lewis, desperate, said what he needed to say. "I told [Cameahwait] . . . that after our finally returning to our homes towards the rising sun, whitemen would come to them with a number of guns and every other article necessary to their defence and comfort."

That was nice for the future but didn't move Cameahwait to act in the present. When that assurance didn't appear to move him, Lewis questioned the warrior's manhood. That worked. Cameahwait even cajoled a handful of warriors to go with them the following day.

As they were leaving the village, "several old women were crying and imploring the great spirit to protect their warriors," Lewis wrote, "as if they were going to inevitable destruction." After a couple hours, more warriors joined the travelers. As the day wore on, it appeared to Lewis that all of the men of the village had joined them and quite a few of the women. The journey (west to east) over Lemhi Pass took on a celebratory air. Over the next two days, the pattern reversed itself. Whether from fear or hunger, the Shoshones began to drift away from the group.

Feeding the famished Shoshones

The Corps and the tribe were still communicating only in sign language, and the Shoshone were deeply suspicious of Lewis's party and its intentions. Lewis sent Drouillard out to hunt and asked the Shoshones to be quiet so the game wouldn't be scared off. The Shoshones thought they were being asked to be quiet because *they* were being hunted. Two Shoshones went off to see what Drouillard and Shields were *really* up to. After a while, one warrior rode back at full tilt. Lewis feared "some unfortunate accident." The excitement turned out to be that Drouillard had bagged a deer and there would be meat for lunch. The Shoshones were so hungry that they ate the raw organs that Drouillard discarded.

Lewis wrote ". . . when they arrived where the deer was . . . they dismounted and ran in tumbling over each other like a parcel of famished dogs each seizing and tearing away a part of the intestens which had been previously thrown out . . . each one had a piece of some description and all eating most ravenously . . . I viewed these poor starved devils with pity and compassion."

Two more deer and a prong horn sheep were killed and eaten. Although the Shoshones' hunger was temporarily tamped down, their apprehension wasn't. As they proceeded toward the promised rendezvous with Clark, the tension was thick enough to cut. Cameahwait put *skin tippets* (a kind of mantle) around the necks of Lewis and his men to disguise them as Shoshones. Going along with his distraction, Lewis gave Cameahwait his cocked hat with a feather to put on. Now, from a distance, Cameahwait looked like the party's leader and Lewis's buckskin shirt, deep tan, and Shoshone tippit made him look like "a complete Indian in appearance," Lewis wrote.

Missing Clark

Cameahwait and Lewis's crafty maneuvers helped keep everyone calm until they got to the Montana side of the Continental Divide on the Beaverhead River where Clark and the expedition were supposed to meet them. But from two miles away, Lewis could see that Clark's party had not arrived. The Shoshones slowed, and then halted, clearly suspicious. Lewis began to panic, not knowing what to do but knowing he had to do something dramatic or the Shoshones would bolt. To assure them that they were not being ambushed, he gave Cameahwait his rifle. Then Lewis's men followed his lead and gave their rifles to Shoshone warriors, as well.

Lewis saw the note that he had left for Clark at the spot where they were to meet, and made up a lie on the spot, saying that the note had been left there by an advanced scout from Clark's party, and the note said that Clark was "coming up slowly" — that is, Clark had not yet arrived.

To keep the Indians from leaving that night while they waited for Clark, Lewis kept up a good front, although he was feeling glum, and regaled the remaining Shoshones with descriptions of York, Sacagawea, and goods that were arriving with Clark. He went to bed but didn't sleep much, anticipating failure and blaming the Shoshones for it. The expedition, he wrote, seemed "to depend in great measure upon the caprice of a few savages who are as fickle as the wind."

By morning, another group of Shoshones had left. Twenty-six Shoshone men and three women remained. Despite all of Lewis's efforts, some of the warriors continued to berate Cameahwait for putting them in danger. Lewis worried that if Clark didn't show up by the following day, no Shoshones would be left to greet him. They'd leave for their buffalo hunt or hide in the mountains, driving their precious horses in front of them, and the expedition would be sunk.

Reacting to tense times: Lewis's writings on the Shoshones

Lewis's tension while he waited with the Shoshones for Clark made him churlish. In the journals, he berates the Shoshones for being "cheerful and gay" one minute and "sirly as so many imps of satturn" the next. He slights them for having a "capricious disposition" even thought he knows what's made them moody and skittish — they have no defenses against their enemies who raid and ambush them continually. Due to the recent losses they'd suffered at the hands of the Blackfeet, both men and women had cut their hair, part of their ceremony of mourning that's still a common practice among some tribes today.

Lewis tells Cameahwait that among "whitemen it was considered disgraceful to lye or entrap an enimy by falsehood." On the other hand, Lewis lies to the Shoshones, his new friends, about a note he left for Clark. Lewis appears to think that it's okay for "whitemen" to be dishonest with their friends but not their enemies.

Lewis complains that the starving Shoshones are not waiting for the game to be cooked but are eating meat raw, including intestines, and ruining his appetite. He calls them brutes for the practice. But he probably ate his meat cooked very rare and had eaten Charbonneau's recipe for *boudin blanc* (stuffed intestines) with relish.

Despite Lewis's *ethnocentric* comments (biased in favor of a particular ethnic group — his own), he actually liked the Shoshones as much as his world view permitted him to like Indians. "They are frank, communicative, fair in dealing, generous with the little that they possess, extreemly honest, and by no means beggarly," he wrote. But he was willing to do whatever was necessary, including manipulate, lie, and condescend to them, to get their horses. He was reacting to his circumstances, just as the Shoshones (and all the other tribes encountered by the expedition) were reacting to theirs.

Celebrating the reunions

Clark, meanwhile, was battling up the shallow Beaverhead River and by midday the next day, was close to the forks where Lewis waited. Clark, Sacagawea, and Charbonneau walked on the riverbank ahead of the boats.

A mile from the forks, they saw Indians on horseback riding toward them. Clark realized that Lewis and Drouillard, dressed in the manner of Shoshones, were with them. Sacagawea and Charbonneau, Clark wrote "began to dance and show every sign of joy." She began to suck her fingers, a sign she belonged to this tribe.

Clark was greeted as if he had descended from the heavens. Clark received a round of "national hugs" and shells for his hair. The Shoshones were delighted by the boats, clothing, guns, dog, and most of all, York. As the baggage was being unloaded from the canoes, one of the women, Jumping Fish, recognized Sacagawea. She was called Jumping Fish because she had escaped the Hidatsa during the same raid in which Sacagawea was captured.

After Clark had been greeted with a pipe ceremony at the camp Lewis had set up below the forks, the men began to talk. "Glad of an opportunity of being able to converse more intelligently," Clark wrote, "Sacagawea was set for; she came . . . sat down, and was beginning to interpret, when, in the person of Cameahwait, she recognized her brother. She jumped up, ran & embraced him, & threw her blanket over him and cried profusely." Lewis wrote that the reunion was "really affecting."

Promising Guns in the Future for Horses Now

Lewis, Clark, Cameahwait, and other Shoshone leaders began a formal council — interrupted at times by Sacagawea's tears of joy. Communication was labor intensive. When the Shoshone spoke, Sacagawea translated into Hidatsa for Charbonneau, who rendered it into French for Labiche, who passed it on in English for Lewis and Clark. Then the order was reversed when a captain spoke.

The expedition was desperate for horses and didn't have much to give the Shoshones in trade. Lewis emphasized that their mission was to open a trade route for American merchandise to flow to the Shoshones (and others) and they couldn't get that started unless they made it over the mountains to the west. Cameahwait's personal war name was "Black Gun." He and the other tribal leaders wanted a supply of manufactured goods, especially guns and ammunition.

After the usual speeches, Lewis promised that the Shoshones would get guns in future trades, and Cameahwait replied that the expedition could have horses and whatever else they needed. There weren't enough horses in camp to carry the expedition's baggage over Lemhi Pass, so Cameahwait volunteered to go to his village at Lemhi River, on the other side of the pass, to recruit more Shoshones from his band to come help with the portage. The council ended with the distribution of peace medals to the Indian leaders (see Chapter 8) and gifts to the crowd. The ever-popular air gun (also discussed in Chapter 8) was shown off.

In relief and gratitude and presumably in honor of Sacagawea's reunion with her brother (which the journals don't have much to say about), the captains named the place where they camped with the Shoshones "Camp Fortunate." (Today, Camp Fortunate is under the water of Canyon Ferry Reservoir south of Dillon, Montana, due east of Lemhi Pass.)

Returning from The River of No Return

Lewis and Clark were between a rock and a hard place. Between them and the Pacific Ocean stood a vast expanse of snow-capped mountains. The Corps could walk across the mountains or they could ride the river. They were really, really hoping to ride.

Clinging to hope for a river crossing

During his first meeting with Cameahwait, Lewis had inquired about going west over the mountains by following the nearby creek (today's Agency Creek) that emptied into a river (today's Lemhi River) that led north to another river (today's Salmon River) that went west through the mountains. Cameahwait said that it couldn't be done because the river that went west (the Salmon) was impassable by canoe. Lewis refused to believe him, writing "this account had been exaggerated with a view to detain us among them."

But no one was making up stories about the Salmon River to keep Lewis around. And Lewis may not have been aware of the tribe's ambivalence about his party's presence. Shoshone oral history says that some members of the tribe thought that Lewis and his men were "children of the great spirit," but others believed that they were sent by the Shoshones' enemies. And until Lewis and his men started supplying game for the famished tribe, the expedition was a drain on limited foodstocks.

Lewis's state of denial was understandable. What Lewis and Clark really wanted to do was proceed by water and *not* be forced to climb those "rockey" mountains (as Clark spelled it). Neither Lewis nor Clark wanted to believe that their preferred path was blocked without first checking it out. So the captains decided to split up again, Lewis staying at Camp Fortunate on the east side of the Continental Divide and Clark taking eleven men and canoe-building tools back across Lemhi Pass to the west of the Divide to scout out the river. Clark also took Sacagawea and Charbonneau with him so that while he was gone checking out the river, the two of them could help Cameahwait bring more Shoshones with horses back across Lemhi pass to Lewis. (Those horses were needed to help haul the expedition's goods from Camp Fortunate back over the Continental Divide to the Shoshone village.)

Finding a guide (and understanding why Lewis's River was called the River of No Return)

Clark's party included three or four Shoshones and left on August 18, Lewis's birthday. In two days, they reached Cameahwait's village at Lemhi River, about three miles north of today's Tendoy, Idaho. Clark was invited into the only remaining skin tepee in the village — the others were made of brush, a reflection of the Shoshones' poverty. Clark was fed some salmon and berry cakes before starting a council talk with Cameahwait and some of his villagers. Clark asked Cameahwait's advice on a practical way to get over the Rocky Mountains from there, and Cameahwait gave him a detailed relief map showing the rivers — Lemhi, Salmon, and Bitterroot — and the Bitterroot Mountains (a sub-range of the Rocky Mountains). Cameahwait told Clark about the route taken by the Nez Perce, who made the trip over the mountains annually to hunt buffalo. Cameahwait warned that the "the road was a very bad one," wrote Clark, and had no game. But Clark figured that if the Nez Perce could cross every year without food, the expedition could, too.

In the council, Clark told the Shoshones that the expedition had made peace for them with the Mandan, Hidatsa and Arikara. Cameahwait once more brought up the Shoshones' need for weapons. Clark promised Cameahwait he would get the weapons he needed.

Clark asked all the villagers to take their horses across the Continental Divide to the eastern (Montana) side and help Lewis's crew and baggage back across Lemhi Pass to the western (Idaho) side. He found an elderly Nez Perce man to guide them in their exploration of the Salmon and for their later trip over the Bitterroot Mountains. The captains called their guide Old Toby, although his name was Pi-kee queen-ah or Swooping Eagle. The name Toby may have been short for Tosa-tive koo-be, or "furnished . . . white man brains." Old Toby and one of his sons stayed with the Corps of Discovery for the following eight weeks.

IN THEIR WORDS

Taking time out for a midlife crisis

Lewis appears to have had a mini-midlife crisis on his 31st birthday. His journal entry that night is moody, hypercritical, and serious as a heart attack. "This day I completed my thirty first year," his journal entry begins. "I reflected that I had as yet done but little, very little indeed, to further the happiness of the human race, or to advance the information of the succeeding generation. I viewed with regret the many hours I have spent in indolence, and now soarly feel the want of that information of the succeeding generation which those hours would have given me had they been judiciously expended."

Then he seems to pull himself up. "I dash from me the gloomy thought and resolved in future, to redouble my exertions and at least indeavor to promote those two primary objectives of human existence (furthering the happiness of the human race and advancing the information of the succeeding generation)." He ends by promising to "to live for *mankind,* as I have heretofore lived for *myself.*"

Clark went down today's Lemhi River, reaching today's Salmon River (which Clark named Lewis's River) on August 21. The next four days took Clark far enough along the Salmon River to see that the Shoshones had been right — the Salmon had incredible falls and rapids and couldn't be canoed. Even if the river had been passable, no trees were big enough for canoe-building, and no game was available for food. Old Toby said that conditions worsened as the river flowed west. The Salmon's nickname became and remains today The River of No Return. Clark and his men turned back and after two days, camped near today's town of Salmon, Idaho.

Clark sent Private Colter to Lewis on August 24 with a message that the Salmon River was not their route west.

Unfortunately, by the route that Lewis and Clark eventually followed, the expedition would have to cross two mountain passes before they could again travel by water. The Corps had a long hike ahead of them.

Preparing for a Long Walk

While Clark and his party went to check out a river passage over the mountains, Lewis stayed at Camp Fortunate observing and writing about the Shoshones while the Corps who stayed with him made preparations to depart. Lewis's party was to cross over the Lemhi Pass going west and then meet up with Clark at the Shoshones' Lemhi River village a few miles to the north. If Clark found that the Salmon River was impassable, he would meet Lewis at the village and they would seal the deal with the Shoshones for the necessary horses to carry their baggage. Then the expedition would trek north along the spine of the Divide and the Bitterroot River for a hundred miles, turning west and south across the Bitterroot Mountains over the Lolo Trail (also known as Nimiipuu or Nez Perce Trail) for nearly a hundred more miles.

Caching goods and leaving Camp Fortunate

Lewis cached the expedition's excess equipment and baggage at Camp Fortunate. He had the men create 20 packsaddles out of rawhide and wood.

Lewis spent six days at Camp Fortunate observing Shoshone life and language. On the fourth day, Sacagawea and Charbonneau came into camp with the Shoshones who had volunteered to help Lewis and Corps cross the Continental Divide — Cameahwait and 50 Shoshone men plus many women and children. The Shoshones were ravenously hungry and were happy to divide the Corps' recent catch of 528 fish and a little game. Cameahwait was especially delighted by the dried squash the Corps had brought from the Mandans — the best thing except sugar he'd ever tasted, he told Lewis.

The group left Camp Fortunate on August 24, stopping for a drink at the head of the last spring-fed creek before the Continental Divide. Lewis called the creek "the extreme source of the Missouri" (although it wasn't), and Sergeant Ordway wrote that after drinking from "the head of the Missouri," he'd walked a mile west and drank from the "head Spring of the Columbian River."

Scaring Lewis

Cameahwait was under tremendous pressure from the Shoshones to abandon Lewis's portage across Lemhi Pass and head for buffalo country. Charbonneau reported to Lewis that Sacagawea heard Cameahwait ask his men to tell the rest of the band to meet him at Lemhi Pass, and they'd head for the Missouri River and the buffalo hunt from there. Lewis yelled at Charbonneau for not telling him sooner, then called for a smoke with Cameahwait and two other tribal leaders.

Confronted, the two other leaders denied responsibility and blamed Cameahwait. Lewis shamed him for breaking his word. Cameahwait said that he'd done wrong, "induced . . . from seeing all his people hungry," wrote Lewis, and he would keep his word in future.

Lewis didn't write in his journals that he understood the enormous sacrifice Cameahwait and the Shoshones were making on his behalf. He did go without his own supper that night, directing that the one deer shot that day go to the women and children. And he ordered the fiddle to be played that night for dancing.

Haggling for horses

Private Colter arrived in Cameahwait's village about the same time as Lewis's party. He had been dispatched by Clark to bring the bad news that the Salmon River was impenetrable. Clark's message meant that the expedition would be crossing the Rocky Mountains on foot and that Lewis should start negotiating for horses. Lewis wanted 30 horses, enough for all the gear that hadn't been cached and to let the party ride at times. But the Shoshones were reluctant to sell that many horses unless they got some guns and ammunition out of the deal, and Lewis refused to sell them guns.

When Clark arrived in the Shoshone village, the captains double-teamed the Shoshones with promises and threats. They succeeded in trading for 29 young and poorly fed horses, but none that had ever worn a packsaddle. To reach that number, Clark had to give up a pistol and rifle, ammunition, and powder (and break the general rule about not giving guns to Indians, a measure of their extreme need to get going) before the Shoshones would trade them the last few horses they needed.

Slipping, Sliding, and Hacking Their Way Up the Divide

By the route that Lewis and Clark chose, the expedition would have to cross two mountain passes before they were able to get back on a river that would take them to the ocean.

On August 30, the expedition said their goodbyes to the Shoshones and followed Old Toby and three of his sons north down the Lemhi River to the Salmon River, up today's Tower Creek and then cross-country over an Indian road to the North Fork of the Salmon. And that's where the fun started.

In addition to Old Toby and his sons, the party included an unknown and unheralded number of Shoshone women who carried the expedition's baggage. Lewis's journal on August 24, 1805, mentioned that "the Indian women took the balance of the baggage."

Leaving the Indian road on September 2, they had to axe their way forward through the brush next to the North Fork. They started to climb hillsides so steep that the horses, unused to packsaddles, began to slip, slide, and even tumble and roll down the hillsides. They hacked their way north up on the Montana side of a spine of mountains that divide today's Montana and Idaho.

TRAIL TIPS
NORTH
SOUTH

Traveling Lost Trail Pass today

The entire expedition traveled in the vicinity of today's Lost Trail Pass in 1805 and Clark crossed to the near north in 1806. Today, the pass is U.S. Highway 93 and is accessible to everyone. True, you may not see *exactly* where they crossed because historians hotly dispute where that was, but you get a good sense of what a

challenge it was to get pack horses up those steep slopes.

You can travel Lost Trail Pass in the winter, and great skiing is nearby. But you'll need chains and/or four-wheel drive for safety's sake — the snow gets deep at times.

No one knows their exact path the following day (but it was in the area of Lost Trail Pass, named not by Lewis and Clark but by a later settler who'd read the expedition journals). The horses were stiff, and the path was very steep. Food was scarce, and the men were hungry, cold, and sometimes wet. The conditions were so bad and the effort so exhausting that the men became disoriented, and their journals at this point are confusing.

Meeting "Welsh" Indians

The night of September 3, it began to snow. After it snowed two inches, it started to rain. When the men were wet to the skin and freezing, it began to sleet.

Moving on the next day with the ground covered in snow, the expedition crossed today's Idaho-Montana border and went down the north side of the Salmon-Bitterroot divide to Ross's Hole (a *hole* is a trappers' term for a broad, flat, mountain-rimmed valley). There they met the Salish Indians, whom the captains called Flathead Indians.

The expedition didn't actually meet Indians who flatten the heads of their infants — Flathead Indians — until they got to the Columbia River valley. Because the Salish didn't practice that custom, no one knows why the captains concluded that the Salish were "flatheads."

The Salish had 33 lodges at their village at Ross's Hole, housing about 400 to 500 people and 300 horses. (Each Salish man had 20 to 100 horses.) Lewis noted that the Salish were well-dressed, stout, and fair-skinned. Their greeting was gracious — they "threw white robes over our shoulders," wrote Lewis, offered the ritual pipe, and invited the Corps to camp with them. Lewis and Clark gave them some American tobacco, which they liked better than their own.

Visiting the Salish today

The Flathead Indian Reservation, home of the Salish, Pend d'Oreille, and Kootenai Nations, is located in the northwestern part of Montana on the western slope of the Rocky Mountains, beginning a few miles north of Missoula, Montana, and extending to the borders of Flathead Lake. Over 4,000 of the 7,000 tribal members live on 1.2 million acres with tribal headquarters at Pablo, Montana.

At the Flathead Indian Reservation, make your first stop The People's Center, a living museum that provides a cultural bridge for visitors to find out what tribal life was like before contact with white men, during the white settlement era, and today. Native Ed-Ventures Tours, located in The People's Center, offers educational outings, river float and scenic boat tours, customized itineraries, traditional encampments, and guided visits to powwows.

Follow State Route 212 to the National Bison Range and Visitor Center, where you can take a driving tour of the 20,000 acres of elk, buffalo, pronghorn deer, and bighorn sheep habitat.

For more information on visiting the Flathead Indian Reservation, go to www.peoples center.org or call toll-free, 800-883-5344.

Communication was difficult at first. The Salish language, Clark wrote, was "a gurgling kind of language, spoken much through the throat." A Shoshone boy who was living with the Salish turned out to be the missing link in the by-now familiar translation assembly line — he turned Salish into Shoshone for Sacagawea, who translated into Hidatsa for Charbonneau, who rendered it into French for Labiche, who translated into English for the captains.

The next day, with the help of all their translators, Lewis and Clark delivered their standard drill — speeches about the Great White Father and the coming of U.S. trade, and then a distribution of gifts according to rank or status. (See Chapter 8 for an overview of Lewis and Clark's first run-through of this presentation.)

The captains bought 11 horses from the Salish and exchanged an additional seven for "a fiew articles of merchendize," Lewis wrote. Salish women gave them berries and roots for the journey, and the principal Salish leader, Three Eagles, gave them animal skins — badger, otter, goat, and antelope.

On September 6, before the Salish headed off to meet the Shoshones at the Three Forks for the annual bison hunt, the captains bought two more horses and wrote down some Salish vocabulary.

Examining the Welsh Indians myth

In Lewis's and Clark's day, it was commonly believed that a Welsh prince named Madoc had discovered America in 1170. According to the legend, the prince returned to Wales and recruited thousands of colonists and brought them back to Newfoundland (or Florida or South America, depending on the version). The Madocians moved across the continent, assimilating with the Indian tribes. Some of the more ludicrous variations on the myth included the assertion that the Madocians were the force behind the great Aztec, Mayan, Incan, and Moundbuilder cultures — any Indian culture that had been extremely accomplished or had created a monumental civilization.

These Welsh Indians were extremely elusive. No matter where someone traveled, they were still one tribe away from discovery. They were said to have blue eyes, blond or red hair, light skin, and a language that resembled Welsh. It was common, until a tribe was known, to imagine that they were the descendants of the Welsh tribes. It happened to the Shawnee, Pawnee, and Comanche tribes until they became known to explorers or trappers and were found to be not remotely Welsh.

In the late 1700s, an American con artist named William Browles traveled to London and created a sensation claiming to be a Welsh Indian with knowledge of the Madocians on the upper Missouri River. Some Welsh raised money and sent an explorer named John Evans to find Browles' Madocians in 1795. He found the Mandans, instead, and not a blue eye or blond head among them.

At the time Lewis and Clark departed on the expedition, people believed (Jefferson among them) that the Corps of Discovery might very well find some Madocians in their travels.

Sergeant Ordway noted "we suppose that they are the welch Indians if there is any such" because of the sound of their language and their fair skin. Patrick Gass wrote that the Salish were "the whitest Indians I ever saw." Joseph Whitehouse wrote that they spoke in a "brogue." Lewis took down the names of things in their language to find out whether or not "they Sprang or origenated first from the welch or not."

Resting for the Next Climb

After leaving the Salish Indians at Ross's Hole, the expedition headed north along the Bitterroot River. They continued to suffer from lack of food. It "rained this evening," Lewis wrote on September 6, "nothing to eate but berries, our flour out, and but little Corn, the hunters Killed 2 pheasants only." On the 8th of September, they hiked through an open valley, an untaxing day for a change. But a hard rain fell all evening. On the 9th, Old Toby told them it was time to leave the Bitterroot River along a creek Lewis named Travelers' Rest (today's Lolo Creek, ten miles south/southeast of Missoula,

Montana). The place they camped that night was where the Nez Perce often camped and is known today as Travelers' Rest. From there, the expedition would proceed straight west along the creek, said Old Toby, and then over the formidable Bitterroot Mountain Range.

In anticipation of a long, hard haul over the highest mountains yet, the Corps stayed at Travelers' Rest on September 10 to rest and hunt. The mountains they could see from the camp looked ominous. Private Joseph Whitehouse wrote, "Though the day is warm, the Snow does not melt on the mountains a short distance from us . . . . The Snow makes them look like the middle of winter."

Visiting the Missoula/Lolo area

Missoula is an abbreviated version of the Salish name for this area of Montana — *Nemissoolatakoo* — meaning "near cold waters." This area is the heart of the ancestral homelands of the Salish and Kootenai tribes. Settlers arrived and began to displace the tribes in 1860.

Missoula is called the Garden City for its mild climate and lush landscapes. The city lies in the heart of the northern Rockies of western Montana, and three major rivers run through the area: the Blackfoot, Bitterroot, and Clark Fork of the Columbia River. These natural resources offer great hiking, fishing, whitewater rafting, and mountain biking.

Near the town of Lolo, a few miles south of Missoula, is Travelers' Rest State Park, the location of the expedition's camp before they ascended the Bitterroot Range. The park, which was recently acquired from private owners, is open April through September and features a self-guided interpretive walk.

Straight west from the town of Lolo is Lolo Hot Springs, now a resort called Lolo Trail Center, where you can soak, swim, explore, and tour the interpretative center.

If you want to retrace some of the most challenging paths of the Lewis and Clark expedition — the Lolo Trail and Lolo Pass — several options are available from mid-July through October.

Snow doesn't clear from the Lolo Trail corridor until mid-July, and it can start snowing again in October, sometimes earlier. You can drive U.S. Highway 12 (be sure you have a full tank of gas) or if you have four-wheel drive, travel the Lolo Motorway (during the Bicentennial, 2003–2006, you'll need a permit in advance from the U.S. Forest Service). For information, go to www.lewisandclarktrail.com/section3/idahocities/lolotrail/permit.htm. If you're truly adventurous, you can make part of the trip on foot or horseback (don't forget to take water). Consider using one of the local outfitters to guide you over; the place is almost as wild as when Lewis and Clark traveled it. If you're interested in spending the night, the Forest Service rents fire lookouts and cabins; a campground is also in the area.

Before setting out, stop in at the Lolo Pass Visitor Center for information and exhibits on the expedition and the Nez Perce Tribe. Packer Meadows (an open field where the expedition stopped to camp in September of 1805 and to cook dinner in June of 1806) can be reached from Forest Service Road 373, one mile south of the Visitor Center. For more information, go to www.lewisandclark.state.mt.us or call toll-free, 800-VISITMT.

While out hunting, Private John Colter came upon three Nez Perce Indians and brought them into the camp at Travelers' Rest that afternoon. (Nez Perce means pierced nose in French. Lewis and Clark called the Nez Perce "Choppunish," and the Nez Perce' name for themselves is Nimiipuu.) One of the three said that he would travel with them to "introduce us to his relations . . .," wrote Lewis. The Nez Perce man said his people lived on a plain on the Columbia River just over the mountains. From his village, he told Lewis, the expedition could navigate all the way to the sea by canoe. This was great news. To get to the Nez Perce village "would require five sleeps wich is six days travel, to reach his relations . . . ." This also sounded good to Lewis.

The bad news, the Nez Perce told them, was that there were at least two better routes across the Rockies than the one they were on.

As the expedition enjoyed their rest and anticipated the climb, Old Toby had another revelation to share with the captains. He said that to the east, *just four days away,* was the Great Falls of the Missouri River. That couldn't have been welcome news to Lewis and Clark, who had just spent *fifty-three days,* nearly two months, getting from Great Falls to Travelers' Rest.

Freezing and Starving over the Bitterroot Mountains

Having so far escaped the Teton Sioux (see Chapter 8), mosquito and grizzly attacks (see Chapter 10), a horrendous portage (also in Chapter 10), illness, and exhaustion, the Corps of Discovery started the hard part of the journey. On September 11, 1805, the expedition began to climb "the most terrible mountains," Patrick Gass wrote, "that I ever beheld."

Getting a rough start

It was an inauspicious beginning. Following the Nez Perce Trail (or Nimiipuu Trail, part of which is known today also as the Lolo Trail), they climbed up beside Lolo Creek in the Bitterroot Mountains (See Figure 12-1). That night, two horses strayed from camp and weren't caught until 3 p.m. the next day. The Nez Perce who said that he'd help guide them lost patience and left. The Corps made only seven miles before camping for the night.

The next day, the trail was "verry bad passing over hills & thro' steep hollows over falling timber," Clark reported, "most intolerable . . . on the sides of the Steep Stoney mountains." Clark made camp at 8 p.m. after 11 hours of climbing. Men continued to straggle into camp over the next two hours.

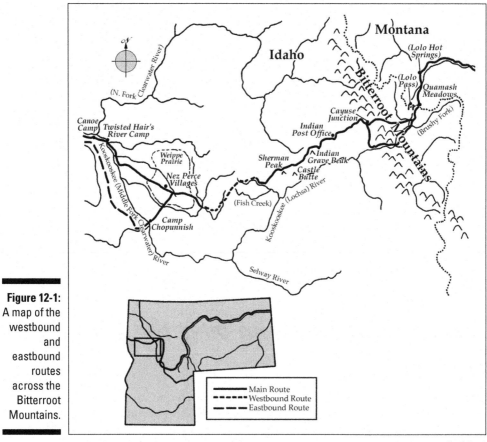

Figure 12-1:
A map of the westbound and eastbound routes across the Bitterroot Mountains.

Lisa S. Reed.

Lewis's and four other men's horses strayed the night of September 12, and Lewis and the men stayed behind to look for them while Clark and the others went on. Clark stopped at a hot springs (today's Lolo Hot Springs) to wait for Lewis.

When Lewis arrived, the expedition followed a "tolerabl root" crossing the Continental Divide into today's Idaho via Lolo Pass. They camped in an open glade. Still pristine, the field is known as Packer Meadows today.

The men were in good spirits, even though the only view from the glade was more snow-capped mountains. If the Nez Perce man was right, in four days they'd be on the other side of those mountains.

Suffering terrain unfit for men or horses

On September 14, it rained, then it hailed, and then it snowed. Old Toby got disoriented and led the party down to an Indian camp that had been recently used, so no grass was left there for the horses. Clark said the road was "worst than yesterday . . . excessively bad . . . Steep and Stoney." The hunters had nothing to offer for supper, so they killed and ate a colt and named the place "Colt killed Creek."

After four miles of following the Kooskooskee River (today's Lochsa River) downstream, Old Toby realized that he was going the wrong way and directed the expedition to cut across the mountains to the ridgeline to get back on the right path. Going to the ridgeline from where they'd started was nearly impossible — incredibly steep and over an "emence quantity of fallen timber," Clark wrote.

Horses fell and tumbled down the mountainside, "which hurt them verry much," Clark wrote in understatement. The horse carrying Clark's *field desk* (larger but similar to a lap desk) tumbled for 40 yards down the slope, stopped only by a tree. The desk was ruined but the horse, much to Clark's bemusement, was unscathed.

The meal that night was leftover colt boiled in melted snow.

Dining on colt and candles

It began to snow and continued to snow all of September 16 until an accumulation of eight inches. The expedition was not dressed or equipped for a snowstorm. Clark walked in front to try to keep the men from wandering off the track, but he sometimes had to backtrack, slowing the expedition down.

At noon, the group stopped to build a fire to warm themselves and dry out. "I have been wet and as cold in every part as I ever was in my life . . .," Clark wrote. With only moccasins on his feet, he was afraid he would lose some toes to frostbite. They couldn't hunt, because the area offered no game. That night, they killed a second colt for food.

It took the Corps until 1 p.m. the next day to gather the horses that had strayed from camp to find some grass to eat. It snowed hard on the steep trail, and two more horses were injured. The Corps was able to make ten only miles. They saw no game and had to kill another colt for supper.

By September 18, the Corps' remaining provisions were a small amount of bear oil, a little portable soup (a dried vegetable-and-bean mixture), and 20 pounds of candles. To fill the deepening void in their guts from days without food, some of the men ate candles. Because candles in those days were made of *tallow,* or animal fat, this hard culinary choice was not without its nutritional benefits.

They ate the last of the previous day's colt for breakfast. Clark took six hunters and went on ahead of the others to try to find some game, while Lewis force marched the remaining party 18 miles. Patrick Gass wrote about "this horrible mountainous desert."

Clark and the hunters went 36 miles that day but didn't find anything to shoot. There was nothing to eat. Clark called his camp that night "Hungery Creek."

Descending Joyfully to Level Ground

On September 10, Clark and the hunters arrived at today's Sherman Peak, and when Clark looked down, he saw open prairies, including the Camas and Nez Perce prairies of today's Idaho.

Lewis, traveling behind Clark, saw the same sight, "To our inexpressible joy . . . . [We] discovered," Lewis wrote, "a large tract of Prairie country lying to the S.W. and widening. . .through that plain the Indian (Old Toby) informed us" ran the Columbia River. It looked to be about 60 miles away, but Old Toby assured Lewis that they could reach it the next day.

But before the Corps could enjoy level ground, they had to navigate the path that they were on, which was a steep precipice and extremely dangerous. Private Frazer's packhorse fell and rolled 100 yards into a creek. Miraculously, when they fished the horse out of the creek, he was unhurt and got back into line to carry on. "This was the most wonderful escape I ever witnessed," Lewis wrote, "the hill down which he roled was almost perpendicular and broken by large irregular and broken rocks."

As Clark and his hunters were finally descending the mountains weak with hunger, they still hadn't found any game. But they did find a Nez Perce horse, which they killed and ate for breakfast. They left some of the meat for Lewis and the rest of the men to find and move down the mountain into the warmth of rising temperatures.

Lewis found the horsemeat on September 20, along with a note from Clark that the hunting party was proceeding as fast as it could for level country (and food).

Seeing Weippe Prairie today

The National Historic Landmark Weippe Prairie is a swath of *camas* (edible root) prairie near today's town of Weippe, Idaho, along state Highway 11. Weippe Prairie has been the traditional gathering place for the Nez Perce for thousands of years. Its significance to the Nez Perce includes associations with the 1877 Nez Perce War, as well as the place where the Corps of Discovery emerged from the mountains into Nez Perce country. Although the exact meeting site of Clark's encounter with the Nez Perce is now on private property, Weippe Prairie remains undeveloped and is easily visible from a roadside turnout with interpretive signage. (See Chapter 13 for more information on Nez Perce country.)

On September 20, Clark's party was the first to stagger out of the mountains onto an upland plain. He and the hunters emerged in today's Clearwater County near Weippe Prairie in the homeland of the Nez Perce Indians. They could see many Nez Perce lodges in the distance, which they moved toward. When they were about a mile away, they came upon three frightened Nez Perce boys, who hid in the grass from them. Finding two of the boys, Clark dismounted and approached them slowly, holding out some ribbons as a gift. Then he sent the boys to the village to announce the expedition's arrival.

Lewis and the rest of the men staggered down from the mountains the following day, September 21. The only things on their minds were food, more food, and rest.

On September 22, 1805, an ebullient Lewis wrote "[T]he pleasure I now felt in having triumphed over the rocky Mountains and descending once more to a level and fertile country . . . can be more readily conceived than expressed."

Chapter 13

Recording "Ocian In View! O! The Joy"

In This Chapter

▶ Being saved by the Nez Perce

▶ Riding the Columbia: new landscapes and unfamiliar tribes

▶ Passing through the great trade center of the Northwest

▶ Taking a lesson in trading from the Chinooks

▶ Getting a first look at the Pacific Ocean

After 11 days crossing the great snowy divide, the starving Corps of Discovery stumbled out of the Bitterroot Range of the Rocky Mountains and onto Weippe Prairie in what's now northern Idaho. They met the Nimiipuu, or Nez Perce Indians, who — at the urging of one of their women elders — spared the Americans' lives and welcomed them warmly. The hungry explorers gorged themselves on unfamiliar Nez Perce food — camas cakes (from a tasty root) and dried salmon — and every one of them ended up with a killer bellyache.

The Corps exchanged their horses for canoes once again and shot down the Snake River to the Columbia. At last headed downstream toward the Pacific, the Corps of Discovery met landscapes and people like none they had ever seen before. On November 7, 1805, William Clark was able to record his famous exclamation, "Ocian In View! O! The Joy."

Escaping the Mountains: Clark Reaches the Weippe Prairie

On September 20, 1805, Clark and his advance party of hunters set foot on the level ground of Weippe Prairie, delivered at last from the high, cold, foodless Bitterroot Mountains (see Chapter 12). The grassland was an ancient gathering place for the Nimiipuu people. The French traders called them Nez Perce or Pierced Nose Indians. Lewis and Clark called them Chopunnish and met only a few people with pierced noses living among them. The Nez Perce were, and still are, widely renowned for their horses. When Clark arrived, Weippe Prairie was abuzz with Nez Perce activity.

Chowing down on Nez Perce food

Clark and his men rode toward a grouping of lodges and came upon three young Nez Perce boys, who immediately hid in the grass. Clark jumped off of his horse and rustled the tall grasses until he found two of the kids. To the boys' surprise, the big, gaunt redhead gave them small gifts and urged them to let their village know that visitors had arrived.

Like most tribes along Lewis's and Clark's route, the Nez Perce knew that the explorers were coming. They had heard about the white strangers and often sent scouts out to learn more about such rumors. Even with a lot of espionage and advance information, reality doesn't always live up to anticipation. In the flesh, the bearded, blue-eyed, light-skinned, unwashed vagabonds may have been fascinating, but maybe also a little, well . . . stinky.

A few minutes after the boys left, a Nez Perce man approached Clark and cautiously invited him to a large tepee belonging to the group's headman, Broken Arm, who was away from the village at the time. The women brought out dried salmon, camas root bread, and some buffalo, and the hungry explorers ate heartily. They reciprocated with a few gifts and rode on to the next village.

Once there, Clark found time to record a few observations about the Nez Perce — the men were "portly" and the women were "handsome featured." Clark paid special attention to the cooking methods for camas root bread, which he relished. Camas are round, onion-like roots that have been a food staple of the Nez Perce for hundreds of years. They are sacred and protected. Clark described camas as "Some round and much like an onion which they call *(Pa she co)* quasmash the Bread or Cake is called Pas-she-co Sweet, of this they make bread and Supe." The journals show that the explorers loved their taste but not their digestibility.

That evening, the delicious but unfamiliar menu began to result in painful gas and bad diarrhea for everyone in Clark's party. Lewis and the rest of the expedition had yet to experience this phenomenon.

Dodging death, thanks to Watkuweis

To say that the Lewis and Clark expedition was lucky would be a tremendous understatement. Their lives had been repeatedly saved by Indian generosity and wisdom — by Black Buffalo (see Chapter 8) and Sheheke (Chapter 9), Sacagawea (Chapter 9) and Cameahwait (Chapter 12), Old Toby (Chapter 12), and Three Eagles (Chapter 12). In this case, an elder Nez Perce woman, Watkuweis (which means "returned from a far country"), made the difference between life and death for Clark's small contingent. Watkuweis was living in Twisted Hair's camp when Clark arrived, and he noted her in his journal as having "formerly been taken by the Minitarries of the north & Seen white men."

Watkuweis had once been captured by the Blackfeet or Atsinas and taken to what is now Canada. A white trader purchased her, and she lived among whites for a number of years. The whites treated her well and after returning to her own people, she remembered their kindnesses.

Like the Shoshones, the Nez Perce desperately wanted to acquire guns to defend themselves against raiding Blackfeet and other tribes. Killing the weak, starving, and now sick explorers for their weapons would have been easy. But Watkuweis urged the Nez Perce to "do them no hurt." The explorers were like the people who helped her, and she wanted to help them. The Nez Perce leaders also had an eye to future trade and complied with their elder's request by welcoming the expedition with famous hospitality.

Bonding with Twisted Hair

The second day after arriving in Nez Perce country, Clark consulted in sign language with the village leader about a route to the Pacific. The Nez Perce man drew a map of the Clearwater and Snake Rivers. The Columbia lay beyond the Snake. The Indians also told Clark about Celilo, or Wy-am, the vast fishing and market center at the great falls of the Columbia.

Clark's host directed him to the third Nez Perce village on the prairie — the camp of an elder leader named Twisted Hair. Clark sent Private Reuben Field back to meet Lewis and the main party, who were just coming out of the mountains. Then Clark set out to find Twisted Hair.

It was late when he started out, and Clark got lost in the growing darkness. Lucky for him, he ran into a Nez Perce passerby who, for a small fee, directed the lost explorer to Twisted Hair's fishing camp. Despite not being able to understand each other, the elder Twisted Hair and the younger Clark struck up a friendship and smoked late into the night. Clark described the leader as "a Cheerful man with apparent siencerity."

Getting a Camas Bread Welcome: Lewis Joins Clark and the Nez Perce

On September 22, Lewis and the rest of the Corps of Discovery stepped out of the mountains and onto Weippe Prairie, where Clark has been for two days. Reuben Field was there to meet them. He led them to the first Nez Perce village where the malnourished men were offered their first meal of camas bread.

Throwing caution to the wind: Let 'em eat cake

Clark had spent the morning with Twisted Hair and his son and traveled back with them to Broken Arm's camp just as Lewis and the hungry gang bit into their first taste of camas. Clark, who had experienced digestive horror just two days before, "cautioned them of the consequences of eating too much," but to no avail. Lewis especially savored the bread-like cakes. The evening was friendly and joyful despite the rigors of communicating through sign language — and despite impending severe gastrointestinal distress.

That sweet evening in the absent Broken Arm's camp, before their intestinal systems would betray them, the lucky-to-be-alive Lewis and Clark expedition learned much from Twisted Hair and his people. Twisted Hair drew for Clark on white elkskin what proved to be a remarkably accurate map of the river route to the Columbia as far as Celilo Falls. Clark also gathered similar maps and directions from other Nez Perce men and noted that the accounts "varied verry little." The Nez Perce had been trading as far as Celilo for generations.

Nursing a collective bellyache

Every member of the Corps of Discovery came down with the same intestinal distress that got Clark upon his arrival. Lewis — who apparently enjoyed the camas root cakes more than anybody — was in the roughest shape.

TRAIL TIPS
NORTH
SOUTH

Visiting Nez Perce National Historical Park

If you want to experience Nez Perce country and find out more about the tribe, be sure to visit the National Park Service's beautiful Nez Perce National Historical Park.

The park consists of 38 heritage sites across four states — Idaho, Oregon, Washington, and Montana. The visitor center at Spalding, Idaho, just east of Lewiston on Highway 95, has wonderful exhibits about Nez Perce culture and legends. Log on to www.nps.gov/nepe or call 208-843-2261.

Clark, who was less ill than the others, administered the ever effective Rush's thunderbolt pills (a powerful purgative developed by Dr. Benjamin Rush, whom Lewis studied with prior to the expedition — see Chapter 5). Because the pills were laxatives, Clark probably prolonged everybody's diarrhea.

Lewis was still sick nearly two weeks after arriving in Nez Perce country. But the hunters were not finding any game, so their diet remained camas and dried salmon. On October 4, in Clark's straightforward narrative, the two captains ate a supper of "roots boiled, which filled us So full of wind, that we were Scercely able to Breathe all night felt the effects of it."

Talking business and politics with the Nez Perce

Lewis and Clark called another of their Indian councils (see Chapter 8) to explain U.S. trade policy and sovereignty over Indian land. Given the uncertainty of signed translation, no one can be sure who understood what from that effort.

In his journal, Clark noted how different the Nez Perce language sounded from the Salish he had heard at Ross's Hole. The Nez Perce spoke a Sahaptian language that turned out to be more similar to the languages spoken by tribes that Lewis and Clark would meet on the Columbia than it was to the Salish or Shoshone languages that they had recently heard. The Corps of Discovery had passed from one ancient linguistic sphere to another.

From their meager remaining stores, Lewis and Clark distributed gifts of clothing, tobacco, flags, and medals — but not the guns the Nez Perce really needed.

During the days with the Nez Perce, the members of the expedition traded vigorously for camas, dried salmon, and berries. For these food staples, they swapped cloth, metal, and the blue beads that were always favored by the Indians. Despite his friendliness, Clark whined that the Nez Perce were "very selfish and stingey" in their trading. (If he thought that the Nez Perce were stingy, he would soon be astounded by the virtuoso Chinook traders on the Columbia. See the "Loving to Hate the Chinookan Tribes" section later in this chapter.)

The Nez Perce — and many of the other tribes that the Corps would soon visit — were accustomed to trading for European goods with Europeans or the Columbia River tribes. Without John Ordway's keen eye, historians would know far less than they do about the human world that Lewis and Clark passed through. Thankfully, however, during the Nez Perce sojourn, Ordway noticed and recorded European trade goods — the first he'd seen since leaving the Mandan Villages. He noted copper kettles and other metal objects.

Ordway also noted mat lodges among the plains-style tepees. The mat lodges were made of tules (pronounced TOO-lees) — the large reeds that grow in the wetlands of the Columbia and her tributaries. The river tribes made their houses of them.

Getting Back on the Water

Despite their friendly surroundings, Lewis and Clark could not stay long with the Nez Perce. The expedition was now in the Columbia River watershed, facing the Pacific, and they were in a hurry to get there. The Nez Perce agreed to look after the group's horses while they proceeded on to the Pacific in canoes. The explorers would pick up the horses the next spring on their return trip.

Making new canoes

The Corps had to construct new boats for the ride to the ocean. Initially, work on the canoes was slow. The weakened men had been hatcheting out the canoes — a task they were ill-equipped and too sick to do effectively. But the Nez Perce had a quicker method. Twisted Hair showed Clark how to burn out the centers of big ponderosa pine logs. Using the Indians' burning technique, the digestively crippled Corps (see the preceding section) crafted five canoes in ten days.

On top of the help with the canoes, Twisted Hair and a younger leader, Tetoharsky, promised to travel with the Corps of Discovery down the Columbia and to intercede for them with the Sahaptian-speaking tribes who lived on the river. They would meet them downriver in a few days.

Lewis and Clark bade farewell to the Nez Perce villages as they had the Yankton Sioux, Teton Sioux, Arikaras, Mandans, Hidatsas, Shoshones, and Salishes before them (see Chapters 7 through 12) — in a happy evening of fiddle music, dancing, and eating.

On October 7, Clark cached the saddles and a few other supplies. The rest was loaded into the new canoes, and the party left Canoe Camp, as they called their camp among the Nez Perce, and set out on the Clearwater. They were headed downriver for the first time since leaving the Ohio River two years before.

Saying goodbye to Old Toby

Just a couple of days later, the Corps of Discovery paddled into its first of many river rapids. They could have portaged the rough water, but they were in a hurry and gave it a shot in the boats. They made it, but that was the last straw for Old Toby. The elder Shoshone had brought Lewis and Clark over the mountains to the Nez Perce. He was ready to turn around and head back to his Shoshone lands.

In a hand off, as soon as Twisted Hair and Tetoharsky showed up to accompany Lewis and Clark downstream, Old Toby took off — not even waiting for his pay. Patrick Gass speculated that the rapids scared him. Whatever it was, Lewis and Clark were now in the hands of their Nez Perce companions, headed for the Columbia.

Heading down the Snake River

On October 10, the Corps of Discovery left the Clearwater and turned downstream on the Snake River. They camped that night near present-day Lewiston, Idaho, and Clarkston, Washington. While everyone else in the Corps dined on dogs (which they were forced to eat by then) and more dried salmon bartered from local tribal fishermen, Clark hunted ducks and "had a good dinner of Blue wing Teel." Clark was not a fan of eating dogs.

The Corps of Discovery was leaving the dense forests of Nez Perce country and emerging onto the vast, nearly treeless Columbia River Plateau in eastern Washington and Oregon. Firewood grew scarce. The rapids grew bigger. Canoes capsized and swamped.

The expedition passed numerous small fishing camps made of brush lodges. They particularly noted the graveyards — burial sites surrounded by picket fences — that were so different from the raised burial scaffolds of the plains. Lewis and Clark had left the world of buffalo and had entered the realm of salmon.

Meeting the Salmon People: Wanapums, Yakamas, Walla Wallas, and Umatillas

As the Lewis and Clark flotilla approached the great Columbia, Twisted Hair and Tetoharsky (the Nez Perce leaders who had agreed to travel with them) scouted ahead to the first sizeable villages. On October 14, 1805, the expedition arrived at the Deschutes River just above the junction of the Snake and the Columbia and set up camp. But their arrival was not without observation. The riverbanks quickly became lined with curious Yakama (or Chimnapams, as Lewis and Clark called them) and Wanapum (Sokulks, to Lewis and Clark) spectators. Lewis and Clark prepared once again for a council with tribal leaders.

Holding a grand council

That evening, the Wanapum leader, Cutssahnem, arrived gloriously at the explorers' camp in a regal, grand entry behind 200 drumming and singing Wanapum men. The huge gathering greeted each other and smoked together, and then Lewis tried to explain American sovereignty and trade policy. He spoke of his "joy in Seeing those of our friendly Children." George Drouillard translated Lewis's words in sign language to Twisted Hair and Tetoharsky, and the Nez Perce leaders translated in Sahaptian to Cutssahnem. The Wanapum's words were translated via the reverse process. Who knows how much was understood?

Lewis and Clark distributed gifts — a large medal, a shirt, and handkerchief to Cutssahnem and small medals to other leaders. The men traded for Wanapum salmon and dog meat.

Lewis and Clark stayed a few days at the junction of the Snake and Columbia — near modern Washington State's Tri-Cities of Pasco, Kennewick, and Richland and close to the beautiful Sacajawea State Park. The area had always been a fishing and trading place for the Wanapums and Yakamas.

Being astonished by salmon

Lewis collected vocabulary from the Wanapum leader Cutssahnem. Clark took some lunar observations and then explored further down the Columbia in one of the canoes. He described tule-mat fishing lodges, fish-drying racks, "emenc quantities of dried fish," and dying salmon — everywhere. The river was full of thousands of decaying fish. He was astonished by it and couldn't explain it. He didn't realize that he was witnessing the Pacific Northwest's great salmon spawning season — millions of salmon swimming up the undammed Columbia, spawning and dying as they had for millennia.

Like buffalo on the plains, the salmon was— and is — sacred. For the tribes of the Northwest, it is Creator's great gift — the wellspring of spiritual, economic, and social life. At the time of Lewis and Clark, before the Columbia River was dammed and obstructed, the salmon runs were a wonder of nature. Fishing and trading fish for other foods and goods sustained a large, wealthy native population. Life was bountiful. Now, only 200 years later, some species of salmon recorded by Lewis and Clark are extinct; others are severely endangered. But salmon is still a dietary staple of the Northwest tribes and the center of ceremonial life. Through modern tribal organizations, such as the Columbia River Inter-tribal Fish Commission, Columbia River tribes are working hard to bring back the salmon. To find out more, log on to www. critfc.org.

Barging in on the locals

Clark stopped at one Wanapum lodge and basically invited himself inside for lunch — some tasty boiled salmon served on a reed platter "neetly made." He had something of a habit of barging in on local residents all along the expedition's route. His hosts had always been polite, and the Wanapums were no different.

They told Clark that they used dried salmon for food and fuel, which made sense to him because there were no trees and, therefore, no wood for fuel.

Their mat houses were an entirely new architectural form to Clark. He wrote, "The Houses or Lodges of the tribes of the main Columbia river is of large mats made of rushes, Those houses are from 15 to 60 feet in length generally of an Oblong Square form, Suported by poles on forks in the iner Side, Six feet high, the top is covered also with mats leaving a Seperation in the whole length of about 12 or 15 inches wide, left for the purpose of admitting light and for the Smok of the fire to pass which is made in the middle of the house. — The roughfs are nearly flat, which proves to me that rains are not common in this open Countrey."

Floating and noting

On that day of his gentle exploratory float, Clark recorded much about Wanapum and Yakama appearances, dress, and fishing gear. He described the people as being "of a mild disposition." "The Dress of those natives differ but little from those on the Koskoskia and Lewis's rivers, except the women who dress verry different in as much as those above ware long leather Shirts which highly ornimented with beeds Shells &c. &c. and those on the main Columbia river only ware a truss or pece of leather tied around them at their hips and drawn tite between ther legs and fastened before So as barly to hide those parts which are So Sacredly hid & Scured by our women."

Clark noted that the men and women of the river tribes seemed to share their workloads fairly evenly and that the people deeply respected and honored their elders.

Revitalizing American Indian languages

In the 19th century, Indian boarding-school students were punished for speaking their own languages. This was part of the United States' Indian policy, which sought to eradicate tribal languages. According to recent estimates, of the 300 original native languages in North America, only 175 exist today. Of these, 125 are no longer learned by children and 55 are spoken by only one to six elders, which means that when they die, their language will disappear.

Without action, only 20 languages will survive the next 50 years. According to The Indigenous Language Institute, ". . . loss of the language means loss of all the accumulated knowledge of culture, spiritual practice, medicinal knowledge, custom, and history; a unique world view, and expression of a whole people. Such loss means loss of diversity, and it is an irreplaceable loss." The tribal nations whose homelands Lewis and Clark explored are aggressively stemming that tide. They are currently teaching their languages in tribal universities and community programs through formal classes, immersion camps, mentor-apprentice programs, and salvage interviews with elders.

Lewis and Clark also gathered geographical information from Cutssahnem. He drew them a charcoal map on animal hide, showing the Columbia's tributaries and the locations of river villages. A Yakama leader contributed a second map. On October 18, the travelers headed their canoes downstream on the great Columbia — the River of Life.

Taking a rain check with the Walla Wallas

The Corps of Discovery met the Walla Walla Indians and their leader, Yelleppit, at the mouth of the Walla Walla River. Yelleppit welcomed them with a basket of berries. The captains distributed medals, strings of *wampum* (beads used as currency), and handkerchiefs and explained American trade policy and "friendly intentions."

Taking good note of the Americans' guns and goods, Yelleppit urged Lewis and Clark to stay longer so that "his people might come down and See us." Now that the Pacific was within grasp, however, the explorers were in an even bigger hurry. They declined Yelleppit's invitation and "promised to Stay with him one or 2 days on our return."

As the expedition moved on down the Columbia, Clark "assended a high clift about 200 feet above the water . . . from this place I discovered a high mountain of emence hight covered with Snow, this must be one of the mountains laid down by Vancouver, as Seen from the mouth of the Columbia River, from the Course which it bears which is *West* I take it to be Mt. St. Helens." The peak was actually Mt. Adams, but Clark knew that he was gazing at the east flank of a peak whose west side could be seen from the Pacific.

Scaring the Umatillas

Near the mouth of the Umatilla River, the Americans began to meet Indians who seemed to be afraid of them. As the Corps of Discovery's canoes floated by, the Umatillas abandoned their villages and hid.

Watching the Umatillas flee from him, Clark canoed over to their village and announced himself. He found 32 people in one large mat lodge "crying and ringing there hands." He shook hands with each one of them, gestured his friendly intentions, offered the men his pipe to smoke, and handed out some small articles. Thus, he went from lodge to lodge creating goodwill. Lewis drew the other canoes up, and the American and Umatilla men smoked and chatted in sign language.

TRAIL TIPS

Touring tribal museums

A delightful way to find out more about the Wanapums, Yakamas, Walla Wallas, and Umatillas as well as the unique salmon and horse world of the Columbia River Plateau is to visit the museums and cultural centers of the four tribes. These facilities are located in eastern Oregon and Washington, along or near the Lewis and Clark National Historic Trail:

✔ **Wanapum Dam Heritage Center:** This center is located at the Priest Rapids Dam on the Columbia River in Ephrata, Washington, about 60 miles northwest of the Tri-Cities area in the ancestral home of the Wanapum People. Log on to www.tcfn.org/tctour/museums/Wanapum.html or call 509-754-3541.

✔ **Yakama Nation Cultural Center:** This beautiful facility is located in Toppenish, the seat of government for the Yakama Nation. The center has a museum, restaurant, gift shop, library, theater, and RV park. The exhibits, collections, and dioramas illustrate Yakama culture and legends. Go to www.tcfn.org/tctour/museums/Yakama-center.html or call 509-865-2800.

✔ **Tamastslikt Cultural Institute:** The extraordinary Tamastslikt Cultural Institute is located at the foot of the Blue Mountains near Pendleton, Oregon. It is the interpretive center for the Confederated Tribes of the Umatilla Indian Reservation: Cayuse, Umatilla, and Walla Walla. World-class exhibits portray tribal history and culture. The Institute is also a critical resource for helping to document, preserve, and revitalize tribal languages and traditions. Log on to www.tamastslikt.com or call 541-966-9748.

✔ **The Museum at Warm Springs:** This magnificent facility has been nationally acclaimed for its interactive multimedia exhibits, treasured artifacts, and stunning architecture. It was created by the Confederated Tribes of Warm Springs as a living legacy of the Wasco, Walla Walla, and Paiute Peoples. Go to www.warmsprings.com or call 541-553-3331.

From the convoluted translations, Clark tried to understand why the Umatillas reacted with fear instead of welcoming hospitality like the other tribes of the region. He had shot a crane earlier in the day, and he surmised that the Umatillas had heard the gunshot and watched the dead bird fall from the sky. Clark's theory: The Umatillas had concluded that the explorers also came from the clouds and were not men. At least that's how he recorded the story later that night.

The atmosphere didn't really become relaxed until the Umatillas saw Sacagawea and her son, nicknamed Pomp (see Chapter 2). Clark wrote, "as Soon as they Saw the Squar wife of the interperters (wife) they pointed to her and informed those who continued yet in the Same position I first found them, they imediately all came out and appeared to assume new life, the sight of This Indian woman . . . confirmed those people of our friendly intentions, as no woman ever accompanies a war party of Indians in this quarter."

Going to the Super Market

In late October 1805, Lewis and Clark reached the melding point between the upper and lower Columbia. The landscape and vegetation changed from the barrenness of the plateau to the big tree rain forest of the coast. Tule mat villages gave way to plank houses. The explorers noticed more Indians wearing European clothing and adornment and using metal tools and cookware. Here, The Dalles cascades and Celilo Falls — the two great falls of the Columbia — were the centers of the river's vast fishing and trading networks. Fishing and trading were big business, and this area was the mega-store of the Northwest.

Tribal traders from upriver (Nez Perce, Wanapum, Yakama, Walla Walla, and Umatilla) and downriver (Chinookan language speaking tribes — see the "Loving to Hate the Chinookan Tribes" section later in this chapter) came together at The Dalles. They traded dried salmon, wappato, berries, other foodstuffs, buffalo hides, sometimes horses, guns, European blankets, kettles, sailor jackets and other clothing, adornments, beads, stories, games, music, and dances.

Trade was controlled by the upper Chinookan Wishram (called the Echeloot, by Lewis and Clark) and Wasco merchants who lived in villages between The Dalles and Celilo. The most prominent Wishram village, Nixluidix, had so many fish stacks that Clark estimated them to hold 10,000 pounds of dried fish. The air of the marketplace smelled like dead fish and hosted swarms of fleas.

The Dalles market was an ancient and prosperous economic and social institution. Economic and political relationships had evolved over thousands of years and were complex. The Wishrams' and Wascos' control of trade through The Dalles was a role similar to that of the Teton Sioux on the Missouri (see Chapter 8). Lewis and Clark didn't fully understand or appreciate the balance of trade on the Missouri. They understood even less about Columbia River trade. And they often vilified the Columbia River people, especially the Chinooks (see the "Loving to Hate the Chinookan Tribes" section), as vigorously as they vilified the Teton Sioux.

Running the Falls: Extreme Canoeing in the Columbia Gorge

On October 22, the expedition's canoes reached Celilo Falls and the beginning of a spectacular and dangerous stretch of the river through the Columbia Gorge. They reached the Deschutes River just above the Falls and scouted around for a good portage route. The river shot down a 38-foot-high waterfall, through the narrow gorge with cliffs rising 3,000 feet above.

Drinking beer and shooting the rapids

Clark drew a map in his elk-skin-bound journal of the junction of the Columbia and the Deschutes, showing the beginning of the Celilo Falls. Below the map he recorded, "one of our party J. Collins presented us with Some verry good *beer* made of the *Pa-shi-co-quar-mash* bread." The root bread acquired from the Nez Perce many days earlier had fermented, and Collins capitalized on nature by making beer.

Lewis and Clark hired local Indian men to help carry the expedition's baggage around the Falls. They also sent the members of the party who couldn't swim around the Falls, carrying the most valuable items — journals, field notes, Jefferson's letter of credit, guns, ammunition, and scientific instruments. The others ran the rapids in the canoes. The Indians were certain that the crazy white men were going to kill themselves and gathered in throngs to watch. As their luck would provide, Lewis, Clark, and the rest of their party made it through.

Saying goodbye to Twisted Hair and Tetoharsky

The expedition stayed for three days below the Falls at a camp they called Fort Rock Camp (now the modern city of The Dalles, Oregon). They repaired the canoes and dried out their gear.

Now on the rapid downriver side of Celilo Falls, Twisted Hair and Tetoharsky (the Nez Perce leaders who came along as guides) were a long way from home. They began signing persistently of expected dangers from the "nations below" and wanted to start for home. In parting, Lewis and Clark gave each friend a medal, and Twisted Hair and Tetoharsky turned east toward Nimiipuu (Nez Perce) country once again.

The expedition ran rapids, hired local pilots, and even lowered their canoes with elkskin ropes to get through the next 50 rushing miles of the Columbia.

Loving to Hate the Chinookan Tribes

During the trip down the Columbia River, William Clark recorded much information about the river's Chinookan-speaking tribes, who included the Skilloots, Cowlitz, Multnomahs, Kathlamets, Wahkiakums, Clatsops, and Chinooks. Despite the language barrier and the difficulty with translation, he chronicled their clothing, houses, canoes, burial practices, and trading habits.

These tribes were accustomed to trading for the products of whites, so the explorers were not exotic to them. The people of the Columbia River were amazing traders — always getting the best of their deals with the explorers. Clark often complained about their high prices.

Salmon fishermen — then and now

The tribal fishermen who pulled in the big chinook salmon at Celilo Falls were strong, highly skilled, and surely fearless. They plied their trade from atop lofty platforms constructed out over the Falls — the precarious-looking but strong platforms were built using ancient engineering techniques, passed along for generations, and provided access to the most productive fishing spots. The fishermen then lowered nets into the water below the platforms and hauled up tons of salmon.

The descendants of those fishermen that Lewis and Clark admired are still fishing — still using the same techniques and the same ancestral fishing spots. Some as commercial fishermen, some as weekend anglers. Fishermen on the smaller streams fished (and still fish) using long-handled dipnets. The nets were historically made of hemp twine, attached to wood hoops with sinew and mounted on long pine saplings up to 25 feet long. Today, traditional materials have been replaced with steel, plastic, fiberglass, and aluminum.

Early European and Yankee traders

By the time Lewis and Clark arrived at the mouth of the Columbia, European sailing ships had been stopping to trade for over a decade. In 1805, European-made goods were commonplace throughout the Chinookan villages.

In 1792, one American and two British ships brought the first Europeans to the Columbia River trade mecca. In May, American Captain Robert Gray sailed the *Columbia Rediviva* up the great river that he named for his ship. He was after sea otter pelts, and the entrepreneurial Chinooks traded him plenty for American hardware and cloth.

Later, two British ships — *Chatham* under Lieutenant W.R. Broughton, and then *Jenny*, commanded by Captain James Baker — crossed the Columbia River Bar and sailed and traded upriver.

By 1805, the area was a major center for the sea otter fur trade, and hundreds of ships had come to call every summer since the *Columbia Rediviva*. But when Lewis and Clark arrived in November, the summer's last ship was long gone.

Treasuring a Chinook canoe

At the beginning of November, the expedition reached Beacon Rock and the first rising tides. They were well into territory dominated by the powerful Chinookan tribes. In addition to their trade prowess, the Chinooks were distinguished by their extraordinary water craft and skill in using them.

Lewis and Clark were taken with the graceful design, marvelous craftsmanship, and light weight of the Chinook canoes (see Figure 13-1). Clark wrote "these Canoes are neeter made than any I have ever Seen and calculated to ride the waves and carry emence burthens." Lewis traded the expedition's small canoe, a hatchet, and some trinkets for one of the Chinook's canoes. The "Indian canoe" became his favorite, and during the oncoming wet winter, he would describe it as "so light that four men can carry heer on their sholders a mile or more without resting; and will carry three men and from 12 to 15 hundred lbs."

Figure 13-1: Chinook canoe from Clark's Journal.

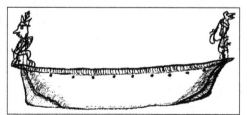

Lewis and Clark Journals Codex J:53 (canoe with carved images).
Courtesy of the American Philosophical Society.

Struggling for federal recognition

To be recognized by the United States government as an official Indian tribe carries sovereign nation status and innumerable benefits: health care, schools, housing, and the authority to build tribal businesses. The powerful Chinook Indian Tribe, who once controlled the vast, lucrative, multi-national Columbia River trade network, has been trying since 1979 to get Congress to recognize them.

In 1997, the Bureau of Indian Affairs found "insufficient grounds" to grant recognition. The Bureau reversed itself in 2001, when it determined that the Chinooks were in fact a tribe and would be recognized. The Chinooks hardly had time to celebrate. In 2002, the BIA reversed itself again and revoked recognition. And so the saga continues.

It is one of the sad legacies of westward expansion following Lewis and Clark. Some nations who met the explorers have since been removed from their homelands. Some have been consolidated with other tribes. Some were recognized by treaty as sovereign nations. Others were not.

Among those tribes that were crucial to Lewis and Clark's success, the Chinook, Clatsop/Nehalem, Wanapum, Agaideka'a Shoshones, Shawnee United Remnant Band of Ohio, and Monacan Indian Nation are not recognized as tribes today by Uncle Sam. But they are all still here, and most continue to live on their ancestral homelands.

Misunderstanding Chinook customs

The forests were towering with massive firs and spruces. The river was often foggy, and Indian visits were frequent. The Chinooks liked York and enjoyed Cruzatte's fiddle music. However, one of the visiting Indians' customs deeply distressed the Americans: their inclination to take things.

The explorers were beginning to lose numerous small items to petty theft by the Indians. It was a custom of the trading tribes that Lewis and Clark never understood, and it annoyed them to distraction. The Indians viewed what Lewis and Clark called theft as taking appropriate payment for services provided. Or as gifts befitting their importance. It was a problem that would persist throughout Lewis's and Clark's stay in the Pacific Northwest. And it was a source of much cultural misunderstanding and resentment.

Lunching with the Skilloots: A good day turns bad

In early November, near the modern cities of Portland, Oregon, and Vancouver, Washington (not to be confused with the similarly named

Vancouver, British Columbia, Canada), the Lewis and Clark expedition floated the now wide and placid Columbia into Skilloot territory. The explorers stopped at a village and bought four bushels of wappato.

The broad-leaved arrowhead — or wappato — grew in swampy areas along the Columbia and was a staple of the Chinookan diet — much as camas was for the Nez Perce. The roots were egg-sized and when cooked, tasted like potatoes. Lewis and Clark liked wappato as much as they did camas — and suffered less for it. According to Clark, "this root they call *Wap-pa-to* which the Chinese cultivate in great quantities called the *Sa-git-ti-folia* or common arrowhead (*we believe it to be the Same*) it has an agreeable taste and answers very well in the place of bread." On the Columbia River, wappato was nearly as big a trade item as salmon and blue beads.

After stopping at the village, the Corps continued on downstream and stopped for lunch. A group of Skilloots followed, and Lewis and Clark invited them to join in. What started out as an apparent friendly visit, however, turned a little ugly when Clark discovered that his prized pipe tomahawk — the one they had been smoking — was missing. Drouillard's capote (a long, woolen, hooded blanket coat worn by Canadian fur traders) was also missing. Clark searched all the Skilloots and their canoes. He found the capote but not his beloved pipe. The angry explorers ran the Skilloots off and proceeded on their journey. They made good time, but with a watchful eye toward the natives.

On the final stretches of the Columbia, Clark recorded lots of cultural details about Wahkiakum (another Chinookan-language tribe) houses and Chinook trade jargon — the unique, hybrid Chinook-English language of trade at the mouth of the Columbia. Lewis and Clark even learned to speak a few words of it.

The expedition was now meeting enormous Chinook coastal canoes, which Lewis and Clark both sketched in their journals. The ocean couldn't be far away.

Visiting Portland

Put Portland, Oregon, on your don't-miss list. Cited by *Walking Magazine* as one of America's best walking towns, Portland is a people-friendly, flower-bedecked walker's paradise, with excellent public transportation. Include a leisurely stopover in The Rose City during your bicentennial travels. Enjoy the coffee, roses, books, dining, and art. This green and hilly city on the Willamette and Columbia Rivers in old Skilloot country is 80 miles from the Pacific Ocean and 65 miles from the snows of Mt. Hood. For visitor information, visit www.pova.com or call toll-free, 800-962-3700

Celebrating an Ocean View

November 7, 1805, started out foggy. By afternoon the mists had cleared, and an exultant William Clark recorded his most famous (and emotional) journal entry, "Ocian In View! O! The Joy."

The explorers hadn't quite arrived at the sea, but they could hear the breakers. Their muscles filled with excitement, and they powered on. That night, camped in the rain that would be never-ending for the next four months, Clark calculated how far they had come from the mouth of the Missouri: 4,142 miles. "Great joy in camp we are in *view* of the *Ocian*, this great Pacific Octean which we been So long anxious to See."

Animals and plants new to Western science

Throughout the exploration, as Jefferson had directed, Lewis and Clark collected and described many species of animals and plants for the first time for Western science (that is, for non-Indians; Indians, of course, had known, hunted, and revered these western species for millennia). While preparing for the exploration in Philadelphia, Lewis was taught the *Linnean* system for recording plants and animals, and so named the hundreds of species that were "new" to science. Among them were some wildlife much more familiar to you today:

✔ **Clark's nutcracker:** *Nucifraga columbiana*

✔ **Coyote:** *Canis latrans latrans*

✔ **Cutthroat trout:** *Salmo clarkii*

✔ **Grizzly bear:** *Ursus horribilis horribilis*

✔ **Lewis's woodpecker:** *Asyndesmus lewis*

✔ **Mule deer:** *Dama hemionus hemionus*

✔ **Prairie dog:** *Cynomys ludovicianus ludovicianus*

✔ **Pronghorn antelope:** *Antilocapra Americana Americana*

✔ **Bitterroot or rock rose:** *Lewisia rediviva* (Montana's state flower)

✔ **Lewis's wild blue flax:** *Linum lewisii*

✔ **Narrow-leafed cottonwood:** *Populus angustifolia*

✔ **Ponderosa pine:** *Pinus ponoderosa*

✔ **Western red cedar:** *Thuja plicata*

Chapter 14

Coping on the Coast

. . . .

In This Chapter

▶ Voting on a site for the winter fort

▶ Moving into Fort Clatsop

▶ Getting stingy and hostile with the neighbors

▶ Being homesick and touchy

▶ Making salt and visiting a whale

▶ Mapping, drawing, and hoping for the ships to arrive

. . . .

*T*he Corps of Discovery had traveled, by Clark's estimate, 4,142 miles from the mouth of the Missouri to the mouth of the Columbia. They had crossed the Bitterroots (see Chapter 12) and shot through the rapids on America's western rivers (see Chapter 13). Now they stood in view of the Pacific Ocean.

Because it was already November, the Corps scouted for a location for their winter camp and took a historic vote to decide on which side of the Columbia to build it. The wind and rain were unrelenting, and the explorers hunkered in their new quarters, which weren't all that comfortable because fleas covered everything.

This chapter describes how the wet, bored, itchy, and homesick explorers spent the long winter months at Fort Clatsop. They traded with and visited on tense terms with their Clatsop and Chinook neighbors and waited in vain for trading ships to arrive.

Holing Up at Cape Disappointment

The 33 people of the Corps of Discovery had traveled over 4,000 miles, experienced countless amazing adventures, and had reached the Pacific Ocean. When Clark exclaimed, "Ocian in View!," what he actually saw was the Columbia River Estuary. But, close enough.

Lewis and Clark believed, from Indian reports, that white trading camps were located on the coast, so they hurried to get there. They got as far as Point Ellice when one of those drenching Pacific storms rolled in, turning the very air to water. They were stuck on the rocky shore for five days. For shelter, they cobbled together some lean-tos, using mats and boards that they pilfered from a nearby deserted Chinook camp.

Waiting for the storms to clear

On November 15, the expedition left their makeshift shelter and moved four miles down the river to an abandoned village at Chinook Point. They hunkered in there for another nine days of steady heavy rain. The storms were (and still are) merciless — and would only get worse as the winter progressed. The pitiful party was "all wet & disagreeable," living in cold, soaked, rotting leather clothes, unable to get dry or warm. On November 22, 1805, Clark wrote, "O! how horriable is the day." They were pinned down and couldn't get out until the storms let up.

All the same, Lewis and Clark both found time to explore Cape Disappointment (so named in 1788 by British sea captain and fur trader John Meares), on what is now the Washington State side of the Columbia, and up the coast for some distance. They found no white trading settlements, despite the rumors of their existence. Both Lewis and Clark did, however, carve their names on a tree at the Cape. To his signature, Clark added "By land from the U. States in 1804 & 1805."

While the weather made the explorers miserable, the Chinooks (see Chapter 13) and Clatsops (the gentle Chinookan tribe who lived — and still live — mainly on the Pacific coast south of the Columbia), who were as intimate with the rain as eagles with the air, traveled cheerily around in it in their big coastal canoes. They came visiting often, bringing wappato (a root discussed in Chapter13) and fish, and even women, to trade.

Staring at the ocean

When the weather finally cleared on November 24, there stood — right before the explorers' eyes — the actual Pacific Ocean. They were looking at Point

Adams on today's Oregon side of the Columbia and Cape Disappointment on the Washington side, the awesome Columbia River Bar and the giant rollers of the Great Western Sea.

How many worlds away they were from where they began! From the sweeping prairies, vast buffalo herds, and mosquito swarms of the Northern Plains to the snows and soaring peaks of the Rocky Mountains to the treeless Columbia Plateau, the cascades, and astounding salmon runs of the Columbia River, through mountains and forests to the wet, shaggy rainforest of the northwest coast. Jules Verne couldn't have imagined a journey through more fantastic worlds.

The journey had been long and winter was coming, so finding warm lodging was critical. Visiting Clatsop traders told the ill-prepared Americans that the south bank of the river offered better protection from the weather, along with more game, than did the north bank. As had been the case many times, the expedition was saved by the Indians again.

Voting and making history

On November 24, 1805, a truly historic little event took place on a sandy beach looking out at the endless Pacific. The Corps needed to find a spot to build a shelter for the winter. But which side to build on: the south bank of the Columbia River or the north bank? As Army captains in command of a military exploration unit, Lewis and Clark could have made the decision to cross and ordered the canoes loaded. But they didn't do it that way. Instead, they consulted each member of the Corps of Discovery about which side of the river to spend the winter and recorded their votes.

York (Clark's slave) and Sacagawea voted, and Clark recorded their preferences, along with everyone else's including Lewis's and his own. In his journal entry of November 24, a Sunday, Clark listed York's vote as "do do" — or ditto to cross and examine. He recorded Sacagawea's vote as "Janey in favour of a place where there is plenty of Potas." By this time — nine months after the birth of Jean Baptiste Charbonneau, the infant explorer — Clark had become quite fond of Sacagawea and her child. His terms of endearment for them were "Janey" and "Pomp."

York's vote happened 65 years before the 15th Amendment to the U.S. Constitution guaranteed former slaves the right to vote. Sacagawea voted 115 years before the 19th Amendment guaranteed women the right to vote. And American Indians couldn't vote in their own land until 1934, when U.S. citizenship was bestowed upon them.

Visiting Fort Clatsop today

In 1948, National Park Service archaeologists first studied the Fort Clatsop site for evidence of Lewis and Clark. Nearly 50 years later, in 1996, the Park Service resurrected those efforts and mounted a modern excavation. Archaeologists found credible evidence of a corner of a structure and a long-burning fire — possibly a latrine or trash pit. They also found a brass bead from the era 1793–1820 and a lead musket ball. Research is still proceeding on the bead and musket ball. In 1997, a blue bead, like those most preferred by the Clatsops and Chinooks, was excavated.

The National Park Service keeps the spirit of Lewis and Clark's damp and boring winter alive and inviting at Fort Clatsop National Memorial (see the following figure). The park in the beautiful rainforest centers around a 50 x 50-foot replica of Fort Clatsop built in 1955. Fort Clatsop National Memorial is located on the approximate site of the original garrison, just a few miles from the lovely town of Astoria, Oregon. The park also includes a salt works site and a wonderful visitor center with exhibits, a theater, and a bookstore. For visitor information, log on to www.nps.gov/focl or call 503-861-2471.

The picturesque nearby towns of Astoria, Warrenton, Seaside, and Cannon Beach offer extraordinary Oregon coastal views, museums, hiking, great seafood, local cruises, old Victorian homes, beachcombing, boating, clamming, fishing, bicycling, camping, great coffee, and — of course — fog, rain, and history. For a visitor guide, go to www.oldoregon.com.

Fort Clatsop Replica. Courtesy of the National Park Service.

Building Fort Clatsop

The Corps voted to spend the winter of 1805–1806 on the south side of the Columbia River. The Chinooks lived on the north side of the river, where the Corps of Discovery had been camped, and the Clatsops lived on the south side. The Chinooks drove harder bargains — Lewis called them "great higlers in trade," and their food prices were higher. Besides, Lewis and Clark liked the Clatsops better. Of them, Clark wrote, "This nation is the remains of a large nation destroyed by the Small pox or Some other which those people were not acquainted with, they Speak the Same language of the Chinooks and resemble them in every respect except that of Stealing, which we have not Cought them at as yet." (See Chapter 13 for some insight into Chinook customs.)

Picking a spot

Taking advantage of the good weather, the expedition went back upriver for two days, looking for a shorter and safer spot to cross the Columbia. From there, Lewis took the "Indian canoe" (see Chapter 13) and with George Drouillard, Reuben Field, George Shannon, John Colter, and Francois Labiche, crossed the river to the site of present-day Astoria, Oregon.

The hunters shot several deer and some waterfowl — an encouraging sign. From there, Lewis explored up the Netul River, a tributary now called the Lewis and Clark River. About three miles from the Netul's junction with the Columbia, Lewis found his spot. It had a spring, it offered plenty of large coastal trees — towering firs, spruces, and hemlocks for lumber — and it had game.

Getting to work

The place became a construction site as Lewis put the men to work sawing logs. The first thing they built was a smokehouse, hoping to find a way to preserve meat in the soggy climate. Many distractions made the work slow: It rained, the winds blew ferociously, the men got hurt or sick. And the fleas drove them all nuts. The Clatsops came often, visiting and trading.

Nonetheless, Fort Clatsop got built, and even though the roof wasn't completely on, the Corps of Discovery moved in on December 23. The snug little garrison was about 50 feet square, with two 15 x 50-foot buildings facing each other, separated by a 50 x 20-foot parade ground. A high wall surrounded the entire compound, with one main gate and a smaller rear gate that led to the spring. On one side, the log structure was divided into three rooms for the men's barracks. The other side had four rooms — one was the smokehouse, one an orderly room, one was for the Charbonneau family, and one for Lewis and Clark.

Lewis and Clark's nearest neighbors were the Clatsops, who lived in several sizeable villages near the fort. La't'cap, a Clatsop village led by a young leader named Cuscalar, was about seven miles away and the closest to Fort Clatsop (see the following section). Neahkeluk, another Clatsop village, was led by Coboway and located at Point Adams. Farther south on the coast was a smaller Clatsop village. Farther south still at Tillamook Head were the Tillamook villages. The Chinooks and Wahkiakums (another Chinookan tribe) lived across the Columbia.

Getting to Know Cuscalar

On December 8, as construction on the fort began, Clark went looking for the best route to the ocean so that the men could establish a salt-making camp (a goal he later achieved; see the following). The next day, he met a small group of Clatsops loaded with fresh salmon. They signed to Clark that they had a town on the coast and invited him to join them there for lunch. Together, they proceeded down the creek to the ocean and a small group of houses, called La't'cap or Dried Salmon Village, that sheltered 12 families.

The men smoked with Clark while the women prepared a tasty meal, uniquely presented: "[I]n the eveng an old woman presented a bowl made of a light Coloured horn a kind of Surup made of Dried berries which is common to this Countrey which the natives Call *Shele wele* . . . this Surup I though was pleasant, they Gave me Cockle Shells to eate a kind of Seuip [soup] made of bread of the *Shele well* berries mixed with roots in which they presented in neet trenchers made of wood."

Clark was a guest of Cuscalar, a Clatsop leader, and the two developed a friendship of sorts. While it rained and blew outside, Clark enjoyed good food and company inside and even learned some Clatsop games. He wrote, "those people have a Singular game which they are verry fond of and is performed with Something about the Size of a large been . . . which they pass from, one hand into the other with great dexterity dureing which time they Sing, and ocasionally, hold out their hands for those who Chuse to risque their property to guess which hand the been is in."

Later, when Cuscalar was sick, Clark sent him a piece of cinnamon to cheer him up. However, the relationship eventually turned sour when Lewis and Clark offended Cuscalar by refusing the feminine companionship that the Indian leader offered them.

Making Salt

On December 8, 1805, Clark departed the Fort Clatsop construction site in search of the most convenient route to the ocean. Clark's intention was to set up a salt-making operation, although he did so skeptically and reluctantly. He wasn't any more fond of salt than he was of dog meat (see the story in Chapter 13). But everyone else wanted salt, so he took a stroll to find a path to the sea. Clark returned the next day having found his route to the coast and its salt — a one-way trip of about seven miles from Fort Clatsop.

On December 28, Lewis and Clark dispatched to the coast George Gibson, William Bratton, and the Kentucky salt maker Joseph Field, along with five of the expedition's largest kettles, to start making salt.

The three men selected a site near present-day Seaside, Oregon, in Clatsop County, and set up shop and living quarters. They kept fires going under the kettles and boiled sea water in them until the water evaporated, leaving behind the salt. They scraped it out and stored it, and then filled the kettles with sea water to start again. Usually, three men manned the salt works, and the duty rotated. The operation lasted for about two months and produced three or four bushels of salt (see Figure 14-1).

Figure 14-1:
Making salt.

John F. Clymer, Salt Makers. Courtesy of Mr. John F. Clymer and the Clymer Museum of Art.

On January 5, the salt makers brought their first salt to Fort Clatsop, and Lewis pronounced it "excellent, fine, strong, & white . . . a great treat to myself and most of the party." Except Captain Clark, who preferred his food unsalted.

Being Out-Maneuvered in Trade and Diplomacy

The Chinooks and Clatsops were extraordinarily successful traders, who loved the business, art, and sport of bargaining. Lewis and Clark were stingy novices by comparison. The coastal tribes had a stable trading economy, and ships reliably arrived every summer, carrying both European and Yankee goods. The Chinooks were sailors and traders, not warriors. They were astute businessmen and market analysts. Theirs was a thriving community — vital and cheerful, living in abundance and harmony on a bountiful land and sea. In the same land, Lewis and Clark were wet, miserable, sometimes hungry, whiny, ineffectual traders, who were battened down out of the weather in a fortified garrison full of fleas, seven miles from the nearest neighbor.

Lewis and Clark complained bitterly because — unlike the early part of the journey when the expedition had boats laden with cargo — the Corps were now the ones who were running out of goods.

The Clatsops, Chinooks, and others weren't even impressed with York (see Chapter 8); they had seen black sailors. And they had seen plenty of navigational instruments and gadgets on the big ships. Lewis and Clark were less unique than they had been on the plains.

Trading goods for food

To the Indians, Lewis and Clark appeared to be stingy amateurs at trade negotiations. But they had to be stingy. After a year and a half of trading their way along the trail, the explorers had only a small handful of useful trade goods left — mostly fish hooks and a few metal files.

But, despite the American hunters' best efforts to supply elk meat, the Corps had to trade with their neighbors for food on many occasions. Mostly, they bought dried fish and wappato. The members of the expedition apparently did little fishing of their own, and wappato didn't grow near Fort Clatsop, so they were dependent on the Indian grocers.

Trading Sacagawea's blue beads for pelts

The Americans did sometimes buy other necessities, such as mats to sleep on, and a few maybe not-so-necessary pelts — sea otter, lynx and a panther (mountain lion). Coboway, leader of the principal Clatsop village at Point Adams, brought lynx and otter skins, which Lewis and Clark readily bought.

On November 20, while hunkered down at Chinook Point before crossing the river to build Fort Clatsop, Clark wrote of meeting Comcomly, the legendary Chinook leader, and Chil-lar-la-wil, another Chinook leader. The prominent Chinooks had come to visit the explorers at their rain-besieged campsite. (As far as historians know, the great Comcomly never visited the Corps at Fort Clatsop, and Lewis and Clark never plied their diplomacy with him.)

A member of Comcomly's party wore a beautiful sea otter robe, and Lewis and Clark both tried to buy it from him. They finally got it in exchange for the belt of blue beads that Sacagawea wore. In return for the belt, Lewis and Clark gave her "a Coate of Blue Cloth."

Failing to cross the cultural divide

To Lewis and Clark, there were good Indians and bad Indians. The Mandans (Chapter 9), Shoshones (Chapter 12), and Nez Perce (Chapter 13) were examples of good Indians. The Teton Sioux (Chapter 8) and Assiniboines (Chapter 11) were bad. Lewis and Clark were stymied by the Chinooks — a rich and powerful tribe that controlled trade at an international seaport. The Chinookan tribes were successful business people, living in prosperity. They didn't fit the Americans' stereotypes. Plus, the two groups could barely communicate with each other through sign language and Chinook trade jargon. The result was a cultural divide too deep to cross.

The Chinookan tribes also violated the captains' cultural conditioning. Lewis and Clark thought that the Indians were ugly. Lewis described them as "low in statue reather diminutive, and illy shapen; possessing thick broad flat feet, thick ankles, crooked legs . . . ." The moody explorer was especially repulsed by Chinookan women's dress, calling it "the most disgusting sight I have ever beheld." Like the men, women wore brief clothing made of woven cedar bark, "silk-grass" and furs — "of sufficient thickness when the female stands erect to conceal those parts usually covered from formiliar view, but when she stoops or places herself in many other attitudes, this battery of Venus is not altogether impervious to the inquisitive and penetrating eye of the amorite."

Despite their dislike of the Chinooks, Lewis and Clark admired some aspects of their lives. Highest on the list were the Chinooks' beautiful canoes — the seafaring ones often over 50 feet long (see Chapter 13) — and the natives' skill at piloting them through big seas and forceful weather. The Americans also admired the Indians' water repellent woven cedar hats, which were far more effective in keeping out rain than any Army-issue or other hat. Clark drew several in his journal and purchased at least one. Lewis and Clark also admired the Chinooks' sense of family harmony and general cheerfulness.

Abandoning diplomacy

Until that rainy winter, diplomacy had been one of the expedition's foremost missions. But at Fort Clatsop, Lewis and Clark barely mentioned the Great White Father or American trade policy. For one thing, they were no longer in the United States. They had left the newly annexed Louisiana Purchase at today's Montana/Idaho state line. So perhaps they were just uncertain of their authority.

Whatever the reason, they never pursued diplomacy. Although they met the legendary Comcomly — the most powerful tribal leader in the area — they never arranged a council with him. And they offended other Clatsop and Chinook leaders, such as Cuscalar (see the "Getting to Know Cuscalar" section earlier in this chapter) and Taucum (see the "Restricting Indians" section later in this chapter).

Pierre Cruzatte, the one-eyed Omaha/Frenchman, never took his fiddle to the Clatsop villages to provide music for dancing (as he had with the Mandans — see Chapter 9). Instead, the Corps mostly stayed at Fort Clatsop, dreaming of going home.

Suffering through the Winter: Oh, How I Wanna Go Home

The Corps experienced a radically different winter from the one before at Fort Mandan (discussed in Chapter 9), when their adventure was still new. Instead of 45° below zero, the Corps of Discovery had to contend with constant heavy rain and wind. Everything was wet. The only dry place was inside their quarters, and that's where they stayed most of the time.

Because they ventured out only when necessary and seldom visited with the Indians, the Corps of Discovery had fewer adventures to record than they had the previous two winters (see Chapters 6 and 9) — no buffalo hunts, no raids by the Sioux, no frostbite, no communal dances, not even any fist fights.

They were bored stiff. Their journal entries often noted "Not any thing transpired desering particular notice." At any given time, many of the party were sick or injured. Mostly colds and chills, plus strains from lifting heavy logs and such. Clark noted that York had "Cholick & Gripeing." Others had dislocated shoulders, strained knees, diarrhea, and many sniffles.

The hunters went hunting for elk; sometimes successfully, sometimes not. The men sewed elk hides into new clothes and moccasins by the dozens of pairs. And they were tortured by fleas — everywhere — in their clothes and sleeping mats.

Missing home and family during the holidays

They were homesick, too. They had been away from home a long time. The approaching holidays worsened their longing for home and family.

On Christmas morning 1805, the captains were awakened by a discharge of firearms and a song and a shout "under our winders" from the men. Then, just like Christmas everywhere in America, they all exchanged gifts. Clark recorded the presents he got — an Indian basket from Silas Goodrich, a pair of moccasins from Joseph Whitehouse, "a fleece hosrie Shirt Draws and Socks" from Lewis, and two dozen white weasel tails from Sacagawea.

Lewis and Clark divided the remaining tobacco in two and gave half to the men who used it. To those who didn't, they gave handkerchiefs. Clark didn't record whether or not he gave anything to Sacagawea.

New Year's Day came and went. As was their custom, the men fired their weapons at day break and shouted "Happy New Year!" That was it. No dancing, no feasting.

It never stopped raining — of the Corps of Discovery's three months at Fort Clatsop, only 12 days were rain-free. The soggy Americans couldn't wait for spring to arrive so that they could head for home.

Writing again: Lewis revealing his thoughts

The one really big thing that happened on New Year's was that Lewis again began writing journal entries. Lewis had acknowledged and described every natural milestone of the journey in wonder-filled poetic flourishes — the White Cliffs, the Great Falls of the Missouri, and Gates of the Mountains (all discussed in Chapter 10). However, when the Corps reached the coast and Clark recorded his famous "Ocian in View!," Lewis's journal was empty on that date.

You may wonder what Lewis's reaction was when the expedition arrived at the Pacific. Nobody knows what Lewis thought. He was silent, and Clark recorded nothing about his partner's state of mind or emotions, only some of the things Lewis did — such as carving his name in a tree and directing the construction of Fort Clatsop. Lewis hadn't recorded much in his journal in over three months, ever since the expedition came out of the Bitterroots into Nez Perce country in late September (see Chapter 13). Or if he had been writing, his journal from that time has been lost.

During the exploration, Lewis had several lapses in his journal writing, and inquiring minds have often speculated why. Lewis was prone to melancholia (what was likely today's manic-depression or bipolar disorder). He was a heavy drinker and by New Year's had been six months without alcoholic beverage, except for Collins' beer in October (see Chapter 13). The Corps of Discovery had drunk the last of its whiskey on the Fourth of July 1805.

On January 1, 1806, Lewis once again put pen to paper, and his first words revealed a mood: "our repast of this day tho' better than that of Christmass, consisted principally in the anticipation of the 1st day of January 1807, when in the bosom of our friends we hope to participate in the mirth and hilarity of the day, and when with the zest given by the recollection of the present, we shall completely, both mentally and corporally, enjoy the repast which the hand of civilization has prepared for us. [A]t present we were content with eating our boiled Elk and wappetoe, and solacing our thirst with our only beverage *pure water*."

Restricting the Indians

On January 1, when Lewis began writing in his journal after a long stretch of recording nothing, one of the first things he wrote was an "order for the more exact and uniform dicipline and government of" Fort Clatsop.

The order provided strict controls for the comings and goings of the Indians. A guard, consisting of a sergeant and three privates, was to be posted at all times. "It shall be the duty of the centinel also to announce the arrival of all parties of Indians to the Sergeant of the Guard, who shall immediately report the same to the Commanding officers." Lewis and Clark instructed the men "to treat the natives in a friendly manner; . . . . Nevertheless it shall be right for any individual, in a peaceable manner, to refuse admittance to, or put out of his room, any native who may become troublesome to him . . . ."

At sunset every day, the Sergeant of the Guard, accompanied by Charbonneau and two privates, were to round up any visiting Indians and put them out of the fort, unless they had permission from Lewis and Clark to stay overnight.

One of the reasons for the no-Indians-after-sunset rule was to minimize petty theft. The Chinooks thought the explorers were inferior traders, but the explorers thought the Chinooks were thieves (see Chapter 13). Lewis and Clark were ever watchful of their guns and tools. At one point, Clark threatened to shoot any Indian who got near the Corps' baggage.

The new rules caused predictable tension between the Corps and the Indians. In February, a curious Chinook leader, Taucum, and 25 Chinook men arrived at Fort Clatsop to see what the reclusive little American community was up to. Lewis and Clark welcomed them respectfully and shared food and smoke. They gave Taucum a peace medal (see Chapter 8). The two groups enjoyed each other's company until sunset, when Lewis and Clark had the Chinooks abruptly ushered out the gate.

Taucum and his men had paddled across the Columbia River Estuary to see the Americans, and the distance was too far to go back home that night. But Lewis was unrelenting.

Lewis refused to allow the Chinook leader Taucum to stay in the fort overnight. That evening in his journal, Lewis unleashed a vicious, paranoid, even racist, tirade against "savages:" "notwithstanding their apparent friendly disposition, their great averice and hope of plunder might induce them to be treacherous. [A]t all events we determined allways to be on our guard as much as the nature of our situation will permit us, and never place our selves at the mercy of any savages. We well know, that the treachery of the aborigenes of America and the too great confidence of our countrymen in their sincerity and friendship, has caused the distruction of many hundreds of us."

In light of the endless native generosity and hospitality that benefited Lewis throughout the voyage, his words — written by a man whose nerves were clearly frayed — are saddening. He worried about the trust his men had in the natives, being so long accustomed to "friendly intercourse" with them, and vowed to instill the belief "that our preservation depends on never loosing sight of this trait in their character, and being always prepared to meet it in whatever shape it may present itself."

Waiting for their ship to come in

Lewis and Clark hoped, even expected, to encounter a European or American trade ship sometime during their Pacific winter. They hoped to be able to replenish their dwindling supplies and send back important documents and journals (and especially letters to Jefferson and loved ones).

They didn't realize that summer was the trading season at the mouth of the Columbia. Ships wouldn't be expected to sail over the Columbia River Bar into the bay until after the Corps of Discovery departed in March. All the same, one ship reportedly did arrive at the mouth of the Columbia, but Lewis and Clark never knew about it.

Altogether, it was a wet, paranoid, itchy, depressing winter for the expedition. They yearned to be back in the bosom of their own culture.

Going whale-watching

Sometime around New Years' Day, the Clatsops told Lewis and Clark about a whale that was beached near Tillamook Head, a few miles south of the expedition's salt-making camp. On January 6, Clark and a party of 12 set out in their canoes to see the whale, and they hoped to trade for some whale meat and oil.

Sacagawea got to go along. In one of the journals' rare glimpses into her heart, Lewis wrote, "the Indian woman was very impotunate to be permited to go, and was therefore indulged; she observed that she had traveled a long way with us to see the great waters, and that now that monstrous fish was also to be seen, she thought it very hard she could not be permitted to see either (she had never yet been to the Ocean)."

That night, the little party made camp on the beach and warmed themselves with bonfires. Clark recorded, "the evening a butifull Clear moon Shiney night, and the 1st fair night which we have had for 2 months."

The group hiked up and over Tillamook Head to the whale site near present day Cannon Beach, about 35 miles from Fort Clatsop. When they got there, they found only a whale skeleton. The nearby Tillamooks had stripped the great beast clean and had an oil rendering operation going full steam. Clark measured the skeleton at 105 feet.

He bargained with the Indians for some of their product, but all he could get was "about 300 wt." of blubber and "a fiew gallons of oil."

While not as much as he'd hoped, Clark was grateful for what he got from the whale and had a sense of humor about it. He wrote, "Small as this Stock is I prise it highly; and thank providence for directing the whale to us; and think him much more kind to us than he was to jonah, having Sent this monster to be *Swallowed by us* in Sted of *Swallowing of us* as jonah's did."

Laughing at McNeal's folly

On their way back to Fort Clatsop with the whale blubber, Clark's party stopped for the night at the expedition's salt-making camp. Clark dispatched a few men to go duck hunting, and then paid a call on a neighboring Clatsop house at the Necanicum River. Clark and his hosts were sharing a pipe when, about 10:00 p.m., they heard frantic shouting from houses across the Necanicum. Clark's Clatsop host signed to him that someone's throat had been cut. Alarmed, Clark checked on his men and found one missing: Hugh McNeal. The Captain sent Sergeant Pryor and four men to find him. Before they got far, they met McNeal "comeing across the Creek in great hast."

What happened? An Indian man of another village had invited McNeal to one of the lodges across the river to eat. When the man tried to get McNeal to go with him to another lodge, a woman tried to warn the explorer that the man intended to kill him for his blanket. When McNeal failed to understand the warning, the Chinook woman, "an old friend of McNeals," ran outside and started shouting. The attempted murderer ran away, and McNeal escaped with his life.

Clark, still in good spirits over the whale junket, nicknamed the Necanicum River "McNeal's Folly Creek."

Mapping and Drawing

Confined to quarters by the weather for long stretches, Lewis and Clark had a lot of time to work on their maps and record their zoological, botanical, and ethnographical observations. What they produced is an astounding wealth of information — accompanied by some pretty good art.

As he had the previous winter with the Mandans, Lewis recorded page after page of ethnographic description about the Columbian and coastal tribes, their houses, foods, clothing, and trading methods. He recorded a rich array of animal and bird life, 100 or so in all, and many minute botanical details, including profiles of the magnificent climax forest trees — red cedar, Sitka spruce, western hemlock, Douglas fir, and western white pine. Lewis was awed by the size of the trees in the coastal rainforest and recorded their dimensions — some "as much as 36 feet in the girth or 12 feet diameter . . . they frequently rise to the hight of 230 feet."

But Lewis and Clark didn't only write profusely about the things they were observing, they drew them, too.

Lewis drew leaf varieties, condors, gulls, brants (ducks), white salmon trout, Chinookan canoes of various types (see Chapter 13), sage grouse, and much more. He was always attentive to the foods he sampled along the trail, and at Fort Clatsop, one of his favorites was eulachon or candle fish. Lewis called them anchovies, "they require no additional sauce, and I think them superior to any fish I ever tasted." He drew several versions of the 7-inch delicacy (see Figure 14-2).

Figure 14-2:
Lewis's drawing of a eulachon or candle fish.

Lewis and Clark Journals Codex J:93
(Eulachon). Courtesy of the American
Philosophical Society.

Clark illustrated the Clatsop art of head flattening (see Chapter 13). He drew swords, paddles, woven cedar Chinookan rain hats, pine cones, flounders, and floor plans. But mostly, Clark drew very good maps. Clark completed his map of the journey from Fort Mandan to Fort Clatsop. When he put it together with his map of the previous winter showing the route from St. Louis to Fort Mandan, he produced the first complete topographic record of the West. Geographers consider it the most important product to come out of Fort Clatsop.

By February, Lewis's journal entries increasingly alluded to "counting the days" before the expedition could depart. Together, Lewis and Clark studied Clark's map and determined that there was a shorter route over the mountains that they could follow on their return trip. On February 14, 1806, Lewis wrote, "we now discover that we have found the most practicable and navigable passage across the Continent of North America." They had accomplished Jefferson's primary objective. But the passage, although shorter than the way they had come, was not the Northwest Passage of myth (see Chapters 3 and 11).

IN THEIR WORDS

What's for dinner?

Through the winter of 1804–1805 at Fort Mandan, the Corps of Discovery dined mainly on buffalo and corn. At Fort Clatsop, on the other hand, they ate dried and fresh salmon, wappato roots, Lewis's favorite *eulachon* (also called candle fish), edible thistle, sturgeon, berries (salal, evergreen huckleberry, cranberry, bearberry, and wild crab apples), occasional beaver, dogs, and elk (boiled, roasted, dried, and sometimes spoiled).

Lewis described the local method of cooking sturgeon: "a brisk fire is kindled on which a parcel of stones are lad. When the fire birns down and the stones are sufficiently heated, the stones are so arranged as to form a tolerable level surface, the sturgeon . . . is now laid on the hot stones; a parsel of small boughs of bushes is next laid on and a second course of the sturgeon thus repating alternate layers of sturgeon and boughs . . . it is next covered closely with matts and water is poared in such manner as to run in among the hot stones and the vapor arising being confined by the mats, cooks the fish."

Part IV
Bound for Home

In this part . . .

The Corps of Discovery heads for home. After recrossing the Rocky Mountains, the company split into two units, with Clark exploring the Yellowstone country, while Lewis surveyed the Marias River. By this time, Lewis had been without a drink of whiskey for a year and was often short-tempered; in fact, you find out about his run-in with some young Blackfeet that resulted in the death of two of them.

Despite all that, plus getting shot in the bum, you read up on how Lewis reunited with Clark on the Missouri and they proceeded on to the Mandans where they said goodbye to Sacagawea. In this part, also find out what happened to everybody after the expedition.

Chapter 15

Stealing Away and Climbing Every Mountain (Twice)

- -

In This Chapter

▶ Leaving the Columbia River and its tribes behind

▶ Relaxing with the Walla Wallas

▶ Waiting out the thaw with the Nez Perce

▶ Trying twice to climb the Bitterroots

- -

*T*o say that the Corps were ready to leave the Pacific Coast and head for home is an understatement. Lewis and Clark were physically depleted and emotionally frayed, and they were definitely showing the strain. On March 23, 1806, the Corps departed Fort Clatsop (for details on the winter fort, see Chapter 14) and began the long journey home.

This chapter takes you through the expedition's ups and downs (mostly downs) as they travel the first leg of the trip home. Just about everybody involved behaved badly. The Corps started the journey by stealing a canoe from the Clatsops. Reaching today's Portland area, Clark took a side trip and tricked the local natives out of some food. During the first portage around the Cascades of the Columbia River, Indians stole Seaman (Lewis's dog). The coveted pooch was recovered, but the Cascade portages and the dealings with the Chinookan Indians were tension-filled and dangerous.

Lucky for the Corps, their stays with the Walla Wallas and the Nez Perce were warmer and more productive. But their luck ran out when they tried to climb the Bitterroots too soon. They had to wait out the winter snows before they could successfully cross the mountains.

Fleeing the Columbia River and Its Peoples

By mid-March at Fort Clatsop, members of the Corps of Discovery were in a hurry to leave for home, perhaps mostly to escape the incessant cold rain. The Corps wanted to travel from the fort to St. Louis in one travel season and to do that, they needed to reach the Nez Perce before the tribe left to hunt buffalo, and they had to get through the upper Missouri River before it froze.

The expedition faced four challenges on the first leg of the trip home:

- The scarcity of food in early spring
- The peskiness of the Chinookan tribes
- The portages around the Columbia's waterfalls during high water
- The need to find horses to take them overland to the Nez Perce

Needing food but running out of trade goods

The Corps had dried all the meat that they could find at Fort Clatsop and were counting on the spring run of salmon on the Columbia to provide the rest of the food they needed. They planned to purchase pounded salmon from the Wishrams and Wascos (see Chapter 13) when they reached the Cascades of the Columbia.

But the expedition was running low on trade goods and what they had left was unimpressive. "Two handkerchiefs would not contain all the small articles of merchandize we possess," wrote Lewis. They also had five blue robes, one red robe, five robes made from the expedition's large U.S. flag, a few old clothes, and one old uniform and hat. With so little of value to bargain with, it would be tough to buy salmon or anything else from savvy Chinookan traders along the route.

Going from bad to worse: Corps-tribal relations sink to a new low

The tribes along the river from Fort Clatsop to The Dalles on the Columbia River were tribes of the Chinookan-language group, related to each other and sharing a similar language. They included the Chinooks, Clatsops, Watlalas, Multnomahs, Skilloots, Eneeshurs, Kathlemets, Wahkiacums, Wishrams, Wascos, and others.

Judging the Indians

The Chinookan tribes were in British, not U.S. territory (that is, they were beyond the Louisiana Purchase), so they weren't considered part of the expedition's diplomatic mission. The Corps had no way to communicate with them beyond sign language. And the captains were exasperated by what they perceived to be petty thievery. Several of the Chinookan tribes viewed what Lewis and Clark called "theft" as taking appropriate payment for services rendered, a tax on unimpeded passage through their territory or appropriate gestures of respect. Because the expedition didn't display the appropriate etiquette, the Chinookan tribes may have been demonstrating their own annoyance by pilfering.

Lewis and Clark also resented Chinookan trading skills. The Chinookans were practiced at driving hard bargains with British sea-traders (and with each other, as well). They saw that the expedition had few supplies and great need and set their prices high, knowing that Lewis and Clark often had no choice but to pay them.

Four months earlier at Fort Clatsop, Lewis had said that the tribes were "a mild inoffensive people but will pilfer." By April he was at his wit's end: "I . . . believe this trait in their character," Lewis wrote, "proceeds from an avaricious all grasping disposition."

In February, some Clatsops stole the expedition's dinner of six elk. Later that month, a party of 25 Chinooks and their headman, Taucum, visited Fort Clatsop. That night, although the Chinooks expected to stay the night, Lewis ordered them to go, despite the distance and difficulty of crossing the mouth of the Columbia at night. Lewis's reaction caused hard feelings among the Chinooks. That night, explaining why he hadn't invited Taucum's party to spend the night at the fort, Lewis wrote, "We well know that the treachery of the aborigines of America and the too great confidence of our countrymen in their sincerity and friendship, has caused the destruction of many hundreds of us." Unmentioned, of course, is the destruction of many thousands of Indians east of the Mississippi River by Americans prior to 1806. Lewis continued, ". . . our preservation depends on never loosing sight of this trait [treachery] in their character, and being always prepared to meet it in whatever shape it may present itself."

However, at that time, no Chinook or other Columbia River Indian had harmed even one of the "hundreds of us" (the Americans) to which Lewis referred, so historians have had trouble understanding what set him off so harshly against American Indians in general and the Chinooks in particular. Perhaps Lewis was once again unwell, physically and mentally. By March of that year, many men complained of feeling ill and weak. Lewis believed the problem was "want of proper food" but it was probably also from braving the cold, wet climate and having been away from home so long.

Rationalizing theft

In March of 1806, the Corps of Discovery needed two canoes or they weren't going anywhere. Canoes were the most highly prized objects in Chinookan culture and were often carved works of art as well as transportation. On March 17, Lewis reluctantly gave his flashy dress uniform coat to Drouillard, so that he could trade the Clatsops for one canoe, but Drouillard couldn't persuade the Clatsops to sell a second one. Following their usual methods, the captains would have patiently and persistently pressed the Clatsops for what they needed until they got it, but Lewis's patience was at a low ebb. Some of the men suggested that they steal a canoe from the Clatsops, and Lewis, in an uncharacteristically disreputable move, agreed with them.

"We yet want another canoe, and as the Clatsops will not sell us one at a price which we can afford to give," Lewis rationalized, "we will take one from them in lue of the six elk which they stole from us in the winter." What Lewis doesn't say in his journal entry is that after the Clatsops had stolen the elk, the Corps accepted three dogs as restitution for the theft. The Corps was not owed an additional valuable canoe.

While Clatsop headman Coboway was entertained all day at Fort Clatsop, four men went "over to the prairie near the coast" and stole a Clatsop canoe, and then hid it in the fort until Coboway left.

The theft foreshadowed a trend in bad behavior by Lewis and Clark. In future dealings with the Columbia River tribes, the two explorers lied, tricked, bullied, and threatened lethal violence in order to acquire the food and horses they needed and secure their passage along the route. Lewis, in particular, had trouble controlling his temper. He beat one Chinook for petty theft, threatened to kill Indians and burn their homes, and menaced with a tomahawk a Nez Perce man who was teasing him. (See the "Losing Control: Lewis snaps over his pilfered pooch" section later in this chapter.)

Leaving Fort Clatsop and making the first portage

On March 23, the Corps officially gave Fort Clatsop and its furnishings to Coboway (knowing that the Clatsops would take it over anyway). One of the Corps' last acts was leaving with the Clatsops several copies of a complete list of expedition members, along with instructions to give a copy to the first white parties that arrived after the Corps left. On the back was a map of the route the Corps had come and intended to return.

About 1 p.m., during a momentary break in the rain, the Corps started up the Columbia in five canoes, including the one stolen form the Clatsops. Clark wrote that the Corps ". . . left Fort Clatsop on our homeward journey . . . at this place we had wintered . . . and lived as well as we had any right to expect . . . not withstanding the repeeted fall of rain. . . ." They'd spent 20 weeks and a day at Fort Clatsop. They had seen only 12 days without rain and only six when the sun shone in clear skies.

They'd only gone a mile when they met a band of Chinooks who'd heard they needed a canoe and had brought a nice one with them to sell. The next day, a Clatsop who guided them through some islands said the stolen canoe was his. Lewis offered him an elk skin for it, and whether or not he felt it was a fair price, he was seriously outnumbered, and he accepted.

Retracing their route, the Corps headed back up the Columbia. The trip was slow-going compared to the trip downstream: The water was high; the current was swift; and the weather was cold, wet, and often windy. They made only 15 miles or so a day.

Every day, the Corps encountered Indians from various Columbia River tribes, and they both gathered information and traded when they could for food. The day after leaving Fort Clatsop they stopped at a Kathlamet village among what Lewis called the "seal islands" (today's Lewis and Clark National Wildlife Refuge). Leaving the village, the expedition took the wrong route, and a villager pursued them and directed them into the right channel.

The Indian encounters continued to be congenial. On March 26, they were joined by some Clatsops during their noontime dinner. On March 27, they were joined by some Skilloots, who sold them fish and roots. By March 28, they reached Elalah (Deer Island), a haven for ducks, geese, swans, sandhill cranes, deer, eagles, snakes, and the California condor (a bird the journals called "vultures," with a nine foot wingspan and the capability of felling a deer). On March 29, the Corps met three men from what the journals call the "Clan-nah-min-na-mun nation" and stopped in the afternoon at Cathlapotle, a Chinook village, where they exchanged deer skins for dogs, a sea otter robe, and some wappato roots.

They began to encounter people from various other tribes upriver near The Dalles who were in search of food. These Indians told the explorers that all the nations north of them had consumed their winter supply of food and were hungry.

Terrorizing the Watlala

Reaching Indian Island near today's Portland on April 1, some men from the Watlala tribe signed to the captains that the expedition was too early for the salmon run, which was not expected to begin for another month. "This info," Lewis wrote, "gave us much uneasiness with respect to our future means of subsistence." They wouldn't be able to wait on the Columbia River for the salmon run. By April 2, the captains' had decided that the Corps would need to stop and hunt for several days below The Dalles and dry enough meat to last them until they reached the Nez Perce. While the hunters were sent out to stock up on game, Clark did some exploring.

The Watlala gave Clark a sketch and directions to a large river called the Multnomah they'd missed on the way downstream — today's Willamette River. Clark hired one of the Watlalas as a guide in exchange for a *burning glass* (a lens for focusing the sun's rays to start a fire) and took seven men to explore the river.

While exploring the Multnomah, Clark and the men landed at the Neerchekioo village and entered a large *plank house* (a communal house divided into apartments; in this case, the house was 226 feet long divided into 30-square-foot apartments). Clark was hoping to bargain for some wappato roots (a potato-like food much enjoyed by the Corps) and tried to arrange a swap, but the Watlalas "positively refused to sell any," Clark reported.

To persuade the Indians that he wasn't going away without the roots, Clark took a piece of cannon fuse out of his pocket, cut an inch off, and threw it into their fire, where it burned "vehemently" and changed the fire's color. He also pulled out his compass and used a magnet to make the needle spin. The women present were "astonished and alarmed" and an old blind man began to pray "with great vehemence." The children hid and the women begged him to "take out the bad fire" just before the fuse consumed itself. Needless to say, several bundles of wappato were instantly Clark's.

Recovering Seaman, the kidnapped canine

Spring snowmelt was raising the water level of the Columbia to flood stage. It was already 12 feet higher than in the autumn of 1805, making paddling against the current a struggle. They continued to hunt in every direction, finding elk, deer, and bear and drying the meat. On April 6, Beacon Rock (see Chapter 13) came into view. They camped three nights in what's now Sheppard's Dell State Park, east of Rooster Rock, to hunt and dry meat, and then moved on to their first portage at the Cascades of the Columbia. On April 9, in a steady rain, they faced the entrance of the Cascades of the Columbia. The south side of the river was impassable, and the north side treacherous, so they had to tow one canoe at a time along the shore. That night, one of the canoes drifted away and a nearby villager returned it; Lewis rewarded the man by giving him two knives.

Even in low-water conditions, a Cascades *portage* (travel overland around or between bodies of water while carrying boats and other goods) was dangerous. One false move, and canoes and goods could be lost and people could be injured or killed. Clark was in charge of the Corps' portage operation begun in the rain on April 11, while Lewis and some of the men stayed in the base camp at the lower end of the Cascades with the tents and baggage. If it stopped raining, the baggage would be carried along the shore that afternoon to the canoes. Clark and the men guided the empty canoes through the rapids by rope lines from the shore. The goods were hauled over a narrow, slippery path about 3,000 yards long.

The Watlalas controlled the river at the Cascades, and the toll they extracted was meant to communicate that they were in charge. The captains were not feeling patient, however. Their indifference to a protocol they didn't know or understand apparently roused hostility in the tribe. Several Watlalas confronted John Shields walking along on the path with a dog he'd bought for dinner. As they pushed him around and attempted to steal the dog, Shields drew his knife and threatened them until they ran off.

As the day wore on, four men working the portage were "lamed by various accedents." Two Watlalas watching from above on the cliffs rained down stones on them. Clark and the men finished dragging four of the five canoes up the river, but were too exhausted to portage the fifth and decided to wait until the next day to drag it up.

The tribe surrounded the camp that night and three Watlalas snuck into camp at dusk and stole Seaman. Lewis, more than furious, ordered three men to chase them down and use whatever force necessary to get the dog back. Confronted by armed men, the Watlalas gave the dog up. The Watlala headman told Lewis that the incident was just two "very bad men" acting alone, but Lewis didn't care. He ordered sentries to shoot any Watlala caught trying to steal any Corps' property.

The portage the next day was guarded by men with short rifles, and the Watlalas gave the Corps no problems, although the Corps lost a canoe when it slammed into a large rock and sank.

Looking for horses and portaging The Dalles

By April 15, the Corps was established in Rock Fort Camp (at the lower end of the Long Narrows) preparing to portage The Dalles. The captains decided that the water was too high for the portage at Celilo Falls, and after they got past The Dalles, they would travel overland to the Nez Perce. To do that, they would need at least 12 horses.

Finagling for horses

Clark took Drouillard, Charbonneau, and nine other men to the north side of the river to set up a forward camp and sent men out to find tribes with horses to trade. When the Skilloots they encountered refused to sell horses for the small bundles of goods that the Corps was offering, Clark sent a note by runner advising Lewis that he was not having any luck. Lewis sent back a note counseling Clark to double the offering price.

Clark accepted an invitation to an Eneeshur (another tribe living on the north side of the Columbia) leader's village and found great-looking horses, but no one was in a hurry to trade for them. Clark laid out the goods that he had packaged very carefully in bundles, hoping to trade for one horse per bundle. He eventually got three horses, but only one was worth keeping.

Clark tried a different tack with another reluctant band: distributing salve for the headman's sores, offering small gifts for his children, and putting camphor and flannel on the sore back of his wife. That day's work gained him two more horses.

Using every trick in the book to get horses

While packhorses hauled the Corps' goods over The Dalles portage, Clark went to another Eneeshur village and used "every artifice decent and even false statements to enduce those pore devils to sell me horses." The band drove a hard bargain; they'd trade one horse for one cooking kettle and would take nothing less. Clark offered his own large blue blanket, his military coat, his sword, and his hat plume, instead. The answer was no.

At this point Clark was exasperated with the Eneeshurs and resorted to name calling. He wrote in this journal that the people of The Dalles were "poor, dirty, proud, haughty, inhospitable, parsimonious, and faithless in every respect." Then he traded them two kettles for two horses.

Bidding farewell with violence and vengeance

On April 21 and 22, the last two days at The Dalles, the Corps gave up any semblance of goodwill toward the local natives. For several nights, tomahawks and knives had disappeared even after Lewis warned the Skilloots that anyone caught stealing would be severely beaten. Waking up to news of another stolen tomahawk, Lewis ordered the canoes, poles, and paddles that the expedition no longer needed burned "so not a particle should be left to the benefit of the Indians."

When one man tried to take an iron socket from a soon-to-be-burned canoe, Lewis hit him several times and had him thrown out of camp. Lewis told the Skilloots that the next thief would be shot and that the Corps was "not afraid to fight them, that [I] had it my power at that moment to kill them all and set fire to their houses."

The Lewis and Clark expedition completed the portage and put The Dalles behind them. Lewis joined Clark at an Eneeshur village, where Clark had had no luck buying horses.

The next morning, a saddle and buffalo robe were appropriated by a villager from a runaway horse, and Lewis wanted men sent back to find the goods or, if they couldn't be found, to burn the village houses down. Fortunately, after a search, the saddle and robe were found.

The expedition put as much baggage as they could on the horses and proceeded on foot along the north side of the Columbia River through dry, rocky country. They were led by an unnamed Nez Perce who had shown up in Clark's camp in a Skilloot village on April 18, bringing a bag of balls and powder that Clark's party had misplaced days before. The Nez Perce guided them back to his country; he lived near the place they'd boarded their horses the previous autumn (see Chapter 13).

Seeking Respite with the Walla Wallas

Finished with The Dalles portage and free from the Columbia and what the Corps perceived to be its troublesome tribes, the Corps marched gratefully toward Walla Walla country and its friendly leader Yelleppit (see Chapter 13). The journey was difficult. They had little to eat and too few horses to carry their gear and supplies over the rocky terrain.

Hardships were mitigated by overnight camps among tribes that the captains called Wahhowpum (probably Klickitat Indians) and Pishquitpahs (probably a band of Umatilla or Cayuse Indians), who were on the river awaiting the salmon run. They spent an evening with the Klickitats, dancing to the fiddle and trading pewter buttons, strips of tin and twisted wire for roots, dogs, and wood for fuel. The Corps acquired three horses and rented three more from the Nez Perce man who accompanied them.

When the expedition camped the next day near the Pishquitpahs, the journals reported that the tribesmen were famous hunters and excellent riders (men and women) who had never seen white men before and flocked around the explorers.

Reuniting with Yelleppit

Four days, many sore feet, and several twisted ankles later, the Corps sat down to the last of their food, a meager meal of boiled jerky. At this new low point, Yelleppit arrived with an invitation to join him in his village for several days. "He appeared much gratified at seeing us return," Lewis wrote, and assured the captains that the Walla Wallas could help them out with food and horses for their journey to the Nez Perce.

In the village, Yelleppit gathered wood and food and presented it personally to the Corps, urging his people to follow his example. With their gifts of food and four purchased dogs, "the party Suped heartily," Clark wrote.

Even luckier, the Walla Wallas told the captains about a shortcut to the entrance of the Kooskooskee River (today's Clearwater and Lochsa rivers) that would reduce their trip to the Nez Perce by 80 miles. Yelleppit gave Clark "a very elegant white horse," indicating that he'd like to have one of the Corps' kettles in return. Unfortunately, the expedition had just traded all the kettles it could spare. When told they couldn't give up another kettle, Yelleppit "said he was content with whatever [Clark] thought proper to give him." Clark gave him his sword, which Yelleppit had previously admired, along with some ammunition and gunpowder.

Gift-giving: One good turn deserves another

The Corps prepared to leave, asking Yelleppit for two canoes to ferry their baggage across the river, but the headman insisted that they stay at least one more day. He had invited his neighbors the Yakamas (see Chapter 13) to visit and dance that evening, and he wouldn't take no for an answer. The captains argued that they needed to get going in order to bring the trade goods back that they knew the chief wanted. The chief's counter — that one day wouldn't make any difference — was too true to fight, and the captains said that they'd spend another night.

To pass the time, a Shoshone woman prisoner and Sacagawea helped trans-late a conversation with the Walla Wallas that lasted several hours, and Clark treated several sick people. At sunset, 100 Yakama men, women, and children came into camp and, along with the Walla Wallas, formed a huge half circle and watched the Corps dance to fiddle tunes. Then the two tribes, about 550 people, danced until 10 p.m. with some of the Corps joining in.

As the expedition prepared to leave the next day, another round of gift-giving ensued, with the captains presenting small medals to tribal leaders. In response, Yelleppit presented the captains with horses. Seriously one-upped, the captains responded with additional gifts of "Sundery articles" including one of Captain Lewis's prized dueling pistols and several hundred rounds of ammunition. (The captains' rule against giving Corps guns to Indians had been abandoned.)

The Corps spent the next morning canoeing their gear to the other side of the river and got stuck there another night because they couldn't corral their horses in time to leave before dusk. Clark continued to care for the sick.

The next day, the expedition ". . . took leave of these friendly honest people the Wollahwollahs. . ." The second night away, three Walla Walla boys caught up with them to return a steel trap that had been left behind. Lewis was impressed. "I think we can justly affirm . . . that they are the most hospitable, honest, and sincere people that we have met with in our voyage."

Returning to the Nez Perce

The Corps now had 23 excellent horses, most of them acquired from the Walla Wallas. After traveling two days in high winds, rain, hail, and snow, they were met by a Nez Perce named Apash Wyakaikt, or Flint Necklace.

Although the journals don't mention his role until 1806 on the return trip, Flint Necklace had preceded Lewis and Clark in October 1805 to the junction of the Columbia and Snake Rivers to announce the expedition's arrival. Lewis believed that Flint Necklace was "very instrumental in procuring us a hospitable and friendly reception among those natives."

On May 4, the expedition arrived at the camp of Tetoharsky (see Chapter 13), another Nez Perce leader who'd helped the expedition the preceding fall. Cold and out of food, the Corps crowded into Nez Perce lodges. That afternoon, they encountered Neeshneparkkeook (also called Cutnose, named for the wounds to his face from a battle with the Shoshones) and his band. With them was a Shoshone prisoner who could help communicate with the Nez Perce beyond sign language (because Sacagawea spoke Shoshone).

Food was scarce as they traveled east along the Clearwater River with the Bitterroot Mountains looming in the distance as a silent, snow-covered reminder of what lay ahead. The Nez Perce gave them "unwelcome intelligence" that no crossing could be attempted until mid-June or later. The hunger to get to the "fat plains of the Missouri" was palpable.

Breaking up a squabble

When the Corps reached the lodges of Twisted Hair, the Nez Perce leader they had left in charge of their horses the preceding autumn, they heard rumors that the horses were scattered and the saddles and tack damaged. Cutnose and Twisted Hair got into a long, heated argument that the captains couldn't understand, and the Shoshone interpreter wouldn't get involved. Trying to break it up, the captains told them that they were leaving and invited both men to come along. Drouillard was called in as an interpreter to try to sort things out. They talked to each man separately.

The elderly Twisted Hair explained that as soon as he took charge of the horses, Cutnose and Broken Arm (another Nez Perce village headman — see Chapter 13) came back from a Shoshone raid and were jealous of Twisted Hair's assignment and harassed him until he was worn down and neglectful of the horses. Cutnose said that he and Broken Arm had intervened because Twisted Hair was "a bad old man" and two-faced and had allowed some young Nez Perce to mistreat some of the horses. He and Broken Arm had tried to protect the horses but couldn't.

Over the next few days, the Corps recovered 21 horses, half the saddles, and some of the ammunition that had been cached. They had promised Twisted Hair a gun for his services, but were not overjoyed with the job he'd done, so the captains gave him an old British trading musket that Lewis had acquired from a Chinook for two elk skins. The ill will between the Nez Perce men evaporated as soon as the horses were returned.

Deliberating at council

The Corps slogged through eight inches of snow to Broken Arm's village, a warning that they were in for a long wait until the snow melted in the Bitterroots. They asked Broken Arm to trade them one of their lean horses for a fat horse so they could eat it, but Broken Arm said that he was "revolted" by the idea of a trade, because he preferred to give them meat in friendship. He said the captains could have as many colts as they wanted and gave them two fat ones, asking nothing in return. Lewis said that this was the "only act which deserve the appellation of hospitality which we have witnessed in this quarter."

Two more important Nez Perce headmen arrived in Broken Arm's village: Hohots Ilppilp (Bloody Chief) and Yoomparkkartim (Five Big Hearts). Lewis decided that it was an ideal time to hold a grand council with the Nez Perce.

Crowded into the council tepee on May 11 and 12, the captains drew a map of the United States with charcoal on a stretched hide. Lewis didn't use the usual "red children" and "Great White Father" rhetoric and talked about the Nez Perce's becoming part of the American trade system and its planned trading posts. He stressed peace among the tribes, and asked the Nez Perce to send a delegation to Washington. The "tedious" translations — English to French to Hidatsa to Shoshone to Nez Perce — took all morning. At the end, the power of the United States was demonstrated by showing the tribe the magnets, spy glass, compass, watch, and air gun.

The Nez Perce deliberated before answering. After several hours, Broken Arm came out of the tepee and took flour made from cous roots and turned it into a thick mush. He ladled it into "the kettles and baskets of all his people" and explained the decisions made by the council. He asked everyone who agreed with the decisions to eat their mush. "All swallowed their objections if any they had very cheerfully with their mush," Lewis wrote, although some women cried and tore their hair.

It turned out that the captains had not been as persuasive as they'd hoped. The tribe was about 4,000 strong and had a larger horse herd than any other tribe in the country, but they were continually attacked by the Blackfeet and Atsinas who were better armed. The bottom line, the Nez Perce said, was guns. If the Americans could deliver them, then the Nez Perce might send a delegation to Washington. They might go to the Missouri to trade if the Blackfeet and Atsinas stopped being a threat to them. They were willing to try again to make peace with the Shoshones, but only because they had recently avenged the deaths of the peace party that they'd already sent to the Shoshones.

If the captains were disappointed in the Nez Perce response, they didn't write about it in their journals.

Passing the Time at Camp Chopunnish

Lewis and Clark turned their attentions to the trip ahead and gathered enough food to get them over the Bitterroots. The reports from the Nez Perce — the Lolo Trail would be impassable for another month — continued to be unwelcome. To wait out the winter weather, the Corps moved to a camp site along the north bank of the Clearwater River near today's Kamiah, Idaho. They didn't name the camp but the place has become known as Camp Chopunnish. ("Chopunnish" was Lewis and Clark's name for the Nez Perce. It may have been an adulteration of the Salish name for Nez Perce that means, "those who live to the south.")

While waiting through most of May and early June at Camp Chopunnish for the snowmelt, the Corps developed close relationships with the Nez Perce, and the camp became second only to Fort Mandan for the rapport that developed between the Americans and the Indians. The Corps admired the physical and emotional natures of the Nez Perce, appreciated their hospitality, and respected their intelligence. Hunting, trading for food, music, dancing, treating the sick, gambling, and racing brought them together constantly. There were no Nez Perce prohibitions against sex with whites and although the journals are silent on sexual relations with the Nez Perce, it's assumed that a number of liaisons were formed. Some evidence also exists that Clark fathered a child while at Camp Chopunnish (see the "Clark's Nez Perce son?" sidebar).

Clark's Nez Perce son?

When western photographer William H. Jackson encountered a Nez Perce band before the 1877 Nez Perce War, he photographed an elderly, blue-eyed, sandy-haired man who was said to be William Clark's son.

When Chief Joseph's band surrendered to General Miles in 1877, one of the older Nez Perce prisoners was pointed out to the Americans as Clark's son. The Nez Perce never doubted that the man was fathered by Clark, but his paternity remains a mystery that can't be proved one way or the other. (Although this book has a rule — see the Introduction — about not using the English word "chief" to describe a tribal leader or headman, Nez Perce leader Joseph became famous in U.S. history as "Chief Joseph," and the name has stuck.)

Hard bargaining

Bargaining with the Nez Perce was tough. They weren't interested in trade goods, such as beads and ribbon, the only items the Corps had left. They wanted tools, knives, kettles, and blankets, things the expedition couldn't afford to sell. Necessity being the mother of invention, some men used links from a chain to make moccasin awls for trade. Men also cut buttons off their clothes.

A series of accidents on the Clearwater by small parties traveling to trade in outlying villages — a horse and pack falling in, a canoe and cargo lost — were disastrous for the dwindling supply of goods. "Having exhausted all our merchandize," Lewis wrote, "we are obliged to have recourse to every subterfuge in order to prepare in the most ample manner in our power to meet that wretched portion of our journey, the Rocky Mountains, where hungar and cold in their most rigorous forms assail the wearied traveler." He didn't explain what he meant by "every subterfuge," but it doesn't sound like a good deal for the Nez Perce.

Doctoring

While they waited and gathered food, Clark provided medical attention to Jean Baptiste (Sacagawea's baby son), who was sick with a throat infection, and to countless Nez Perce men, women, and children. Clark had cured a man on the westward journey and established his reputation with the Nez Perce as a doctor. Many of Clark's simple medicines and remedies cured their milder afflictions (such as his salve for sore eyes, which Clark mentions was common to tribes west of the Rockies). Laudanum (tincture of opium) eased the pain of those who couldn't be cured.

Clark tried everything he could think of to help a headman brought to the village who had been paralyzed for five years. Nothing worked. Finally, Clark observed that Private Bratton's chronic back problems were eased by intense sweat baths and recommended one for the paralyzed leader. According to Clark's journal, when the first bath failed to improve him, Clark tried to get his family to take him home, but they wouldn't, so Clark ordered sweat baths for several consecutive days. To the amazement of everyone, the man slowly regained use of his arms and hands. By the end of May, he was also moving his legs and toes.

Shooting, racing, and dancing

Games and gambling were popular between the Nez Perce and the men of the Corps and helped pass the time. They held a shooting match, which Lewis won at 220 yards, but the Nez Perce won hands down shooting with bows and arrows, both standing and on horseback. Footraces were frequent, usually won by George Drouillard, Reuben Field, or one young Nez Perce, and frequent horse races were regularly won by the Nez Perce. (See Chapter 2 for more on Drouillard and Field.) "It is astonishing," Lewis wrote, "to see these people ride down those steep hills which they do at full speed."

Some nights there was music and entertainment, the Corps providing fiddlers and the American version of dancing, and the Nez Perce providing songs and drums and their own style of dance.

The warm relationship with the Nez Perce and the merriment in the camp was a welcome distraction from the daunting task ahead — making the return climb over the frozen Bitterroot Mountains.

Facing the Bitterroots Again

On May 31, Lewis noted that the expedition had accumulated 65 horses, which meant that on the climb through the Bitterroots, each person could ride and lead his or her own packhorse, with several animals left over for food. Despite continued warnings from the Nez Perce that the Bitterroots couldn't be crossed yet, the Corps prepared to leave. On June 10, they moved to Weippe Prairie (see Chapter 13) and camped for several days to make their final preparations.

Both captains had doubts about the wisdom of trying the crossing against Nez Perce advice. "Even now," Clark said, "I shudder with the expectation [of] great difficulties in passing those Mountains." Lewis wrote that bad weather and hunger would stalk them at least four days of the climb.

Disregarding Nez Perce advice

The climb was worse than they feared. The expedition started out from Weippe Prairie on June 16, and everyone was soon knee-deep in snow, a fact that Lewis wrote "augurs but unfavorably with respect to the practicality of passing the mountains."

On June 17, they completely exhausted themselves climbing in drifts that were 12 to 15 feet in places. It became clear that continuing in such impossible conditions would risk their lives and everything they had accomplished so far. "Melancholy and disappointed," and "a good deel dejected," the Corps stowed some of their baggage, turned around, and went back to Weippe Prairie. It was the first time, Lewis noted, that the Corps had been "compelled to retreat or make a retrograde march."

On June 18, Lewis and Clark dispatched Drouillard and Shannon to return to the Nez Perce villages and arrange for guides for their second climb through the Bitterroots. They sent one rifle to offer as payment for a guide and promised two more rifles and ten horses after the job was done (an unprecedented reward offered because of their desperate circumstances). As the remaining group descended, Private Potts badly cut his leg with one of his own knives, and Lewis had trouble stopping the bleeding. Colter and his horse fell and rolled over each other down the rocky slope for "a considerable distance," wrote Lewis, but were, miraculously, unhurt.

On June 21, the Corps, still descending and hoping to see Drouillard and Shannon, met two young Nez Perce on their way to visit the Salish (see Chapter 12), who told them that Drouillard and Shannon were two days behind the two Nez Perce and were bringing guides, three horses, and a mule that had strayed down the mountains. The captains left Patrick Gass and a squad of men to wait with the two Nez Perce until the expedition's second climb. Later that day, the remainder of the Corps was back at Camp Choppunish on Weippe Prairie.

Drouillard and Shannon arrived at the camp two days later, along with three young Nez Perce who would guide the expedition at least as far as Travelers' Rest (see Chapter 12). They also brought news of a peace plan arranged between the Nez Perce, Walla Walla, and Shoshone tribes.

Putting the mountains and snow behind them: Hello, hot tub!

Led by the Nez Perce, the Corps started at daybreak the next morning (June 24) and made it back to where they'd left Patrick Gass and his squad. They reached their abandoned baggage by June 26, repacked, and then followed the trail along the ridge dividing (today's) North Fork of the Clearwater and the Lochsa River. On June 27, Lewis wrote that they were entirely surrounded by mountains with no clue except the advice of their guides, "most admirable pilots," on how to proceed. Those mountains would "damp the sperits of any except such hardy travellers as we have become."

They made 28 miles that day and camped on the side of Spring Mountain at 6,500 feet. That night, with no meat left, the Corps ate boiled roots mixed with bear oil. The horses had no grass to graze on, so the horses spent their only hungry night under Nez Perce guidance. The next morning, by 11:00, the Corps covered thirteen miles and were back in abundant grass.

They said goodbye to the snow on June 29, descended the mountain to the Lochsa River, and went up the trail to a camas field (today's Packer Meadows) on the Continental Divide between the Clearwater and Bitterroot rivers. After the men again dined on boiled roots for dinner, they marched on toward the Bitterroot River for seven miles to today's Lolo Hot Springs. Clark wrote that they had put "those tremendious mountains behind us — in passing of which we have experienced Cold and hunger of which I shall ever remember."

That night they were in "the baths" of Lolo Hot Springs (see Chapter 12), soaking their weary muscles. The next day, they reached Travelers' Rest (near present-day Lolo, Montana, and now the site of a state park), where they planned to stay for several days before beginning the journey's next phase.

Chapter 16

Exploring Far Horizons

. . . .

In This Chapter

▶ Going separate ways at Travelers' Rest

▶ Following the Yellowstone and autographing Pompy's Tower

▶ Scouting the Marias and bringing death to Two Medicine

▶ Reuniting the Corps and paddling on

. . . .

After 4,142 miles and their "wet and disagreeable" winter, as Clark put it, in the coastal mists of Fort Clatsop (see Chapter 14), the homesick Corps of Discovery began the journey home, a bit shamefully, on March 23, 1806. Against their own rules, they stole a Clatsop canoe, and then they made their way back to the friendly and kind Nez Perce (see Chapter 15). They crossed the Rocky Mountains using a different, shorter route and arrived at their old Travelers' Rest Camp on June 30 (also in Chapter 15).

In this chapter, you find out how Lewis and Clark split the company into four groups to explore new areas and complete the portage around the Great Falls of the Missouri. Clark explored the Yellowstone, while Lewis went north to the Great Falls and overland to the Marias River. Clark's trip was relatively peaceful. Lewis's, on the other hand, progressed from paranoia to misunderstanding to death for two Blackfeet teenagers. One of Lewis's own men even shot Lewis in the behind.

Somehow, the two captains managed to reunite the Corps at the junction of the Yellowstone and Missouri Rivers — one month and one week after parting at Travelers' Rest.

Splitting Up at Travelers' Rest

While at Fort Clatsop, Lewis and Clark had decided to divide the company into four smaller units to conduct additional explorations before making final tracks for home. They calculated that, if they split up, they would have enough time to achieve two goals:

- ✔ Follow the Yellowstone River and deliver their diplomatic message to tribes in that area.
- ✔ Follow the Marias River far enough to find out whether or not it flowed down from Canada.

Lewis and Clark had an important economic incentive for wanting to follow the Marias River. Jefferson believed that ownership of the Louisiana Territory included the watersheds that contributed to it. If the source of the Marias was north of the 49th Parallel — the disputed boundary between British Canada and the Louisiana Purchase — Lewis and Clark surmised that trade from those fur-rich Canadian headwaters could legitimately be diverted to St. Louis.

The Corps of Discovery arrived at their old campsite of Travelers' Rest on June 30, 1806, and stayed three days. They caught their breath, mended their equipment, and finalized their plan — a complicated and extremely risky one.

Saving Travelers' Rest

In September 1805 and early July 1806, the Lewis and Clark expedition camped in a beautiful valley between the Bitterroot and Sapphire Mountains in what is now Montana. The campsite was a centuries-old resting spot for tribes crossing the mountains. Lewis and Clark called the pure cold stream Travelers' Rest Creek. It's now Lolo Creek.

In the 200 years since the members of the Corps of Discovery refreshed themselves in its waters, the area west of Missoula and near fast-growing Lolo, Montana, was nearly lost to residential and commercial development. Concerned citizens and historians fought to preserve the location as a historical site on the Lewis and Clark National Historic Trail. In early 2001, they were able to purchase the site and donate it to the State of Montana for a state park, and in 2002, archaeologists confirmed traces of a latrine and cook fires left by the expedition.

The park is open seven days a week, offering a self guided trail, interpretive programs, and guided tours. For information, log on to www.travelersrest.org or call 406-273-4353.

Making Clark's to-do list

According to the plan finalized at Travelers' Rest, Clark would take some members of the Corps (including York, Sacagawea, Jean Baptiste [Pompy], and Charbonneau — see Chapter 2 for more on these Corps members) and head overland back to Shoshone Cove and the Three Forks of the Missouri. There they would uncache the canoes stored during the trip to the Pacific (see Chapter 12).

Clark's party would then split into two groups:

- ✔ Sergeant John Ordway and part of Clark's party would take the canoes down the Missouri to White Bear Island, meet some of Lewis's men, and help with the portage around the Great Falls.
- ✔ The rest of Clark's group would proceed down the Yellowstone River.

Planning Lewis's agenda

Lewis intended to take George Drouillard, Patrick Gass, John Thompson, Hugh McNeal, Silas Goodrich, William Werner, Robert Frazer, plus Reuben and Joseph Field and travel overland to the Great Falls of the Missouri. There, they would retrieve the boats, specimens, and goods cached at White Bear Island the previous year.

Then Lewis's party would also split into two groups:

- ✔ One group would repack the goods and wait for a contingent from Clark's party to help portage them around the Great Falls.
- ✔ The other group would go with Lewis to explore the Marias River to its northernmost point.

Lewis's two groups would reunite later at the mouth of the Marias and head together down the Missouri to meet up with Clark's party.

The entire Corps were to reconnect in a month at the junction of the Missouri and the Yellowstone Rivers.

Since leaving Travelers' Rest in 1805, Lewis and Clark had learned a lot from the Shoshones and Nez Perce about available routes across the mountains, and they were clearly confident in the abilities of their men, enough so to divide them into small units that would travel hundreds of miles from each other. It was a huge gamble, filled with the potential of meeting grizzly bears, prickly pear cactus, and fearsome Blackfeet Indians — and who knows what else along the Yellowstone River (or Rochejhone River, as the French traders called it).

Exploring the Yellowstone: Clark Leaves His Mark

On July 3, Lewis and Clark parted company and hoped that the parting would be temporary. Lewis worried, "All arrangements being now completed for carrying into effect the several schemes we had planed for execution on our return, we saddled our horses and set out I took leave of my worthy friend and companion Captain Clark and the party that accompanyed him. I could not avoid feeling much concern on this occasion although I hoped this seperation was only momentary."

Making good time to the Three Forks

Clark and his party, with 50 horses, made good time from Travelers' Rest up the Bitterroot River. By July 6, they were at Ross's Hole where the expedition had met the Salish the year before (see Chapter 12). From Ross's Hole, Clark took a shortcut over what is now Gibbon's Pass to the Wisdom (now Big Hole) River and then made a beeline to Shoshone Cove following Indian and buffalo trails. Two days later the party was at Shoshone Cove, where they had cached tobacco, medicines, and plant specimens in 1805. The tobacco-chewing men "became So impatient to be chewing it that they Scercely gave themselves time to take their Saddles off their horses before they were off to the deposit."

The party cleaned and repaired the canoes and other cached items and took off again the next day down the Beaverhead and Jefferson Rivers to the Three Forks of the Missouri. The distance that had taken them three weeks to travel upriver the summer before (see Chapter 11) took only three days going downstream. River travel is always easier when you go with the flow.

From the Three Forks, Sergeant John Ordway, with Collins, Colter, Cruzatte, Howard, Lepage, Potts, Whitehouse, Willard, and Weiser, manned the canoes and headed downriver to the Missouri and a rendezvous with Lewis's party at the Great Falls. Clark, with Pryor, Bratton, Gibson, Hall, Labiche, Shannon, Shields, Windsor, York, and the Charbonneau family, went overland by horseback to the Gallatin River and stopped for the night.

Following Sacagawea

Many fictitious accounts and faulty history have portrayed Sacagawea as the expedition's guide. She was not. Her invaluable contribution to the Corps of Discovery was as an interpreter. After all, when the Hidatsas captured her at the Three Forks and took her to their earth lodge villages in today's North Dakota, they traveled overland, *not* via the Missouri River. Now on the journey to the Yellowstone, Clark was essentially following the Hidatsa's route, and Sacagawea remembered it. She explained the route the Hidatsas had taken, and Clark trusted her memory.

After leaving the Gallatin River, Sacagawea told Clark of a buffalo road that crossed a gap in the mountains. The gap is now known as Bozeman Pass. "The indian woman who has been of great Service to me as a pilot through this Country recommends a gap in the mountain more South which I shall cross." Clark followed her route and, on July 15, came out on the Yellowstone River at modern day Livingston, Montana.

Sewing horse moccasins

Clark's party had made a quick trek over rocky trails, and their unshod Indian ponies were getting sore feet. When they got to the Yellowstone, Clark sent the hunters out to shoot some buffalo — not only for supper but also for their hides to make moccasins for the horses. According to Clark, the horse moccasins relieved "them very much in passing over the stoney plains."

Soon after, Charbonneau's horse threw him, and Gibson fell off his horse, landing on a sharp stick that penetrated his thigh. So the party halted to mend, and while they were idle, Clark located some cottonwoods big enough to make some new dugout canoes. He found trees big enough to make two canoes 28 feet long and 18 inches wide — enough room for everyone in the party. For stability, he had them lashed together.

Missing the heisted horses

On July 21, the explorers awoke to find 24 of their 50 horses missing. They were in Crow Indian country and assumed that the Crows took the horses. Expecting, therefore, to meet the Crows any day, Clark drafted a speech for them about American trade opportunities and horse stealing. But he never got to deliver it. He never saw those elusive Crows.

Three days later, the canoes were ready to go. At the Yellowstone's junction with the Clark's Fork of the Yellowstone, Clark sent Pryor, Shannon, Hall, and Windsor plus 12 horses on to the Mandan villages, and everyone else piled into the boats. Pryor was to deliver a letter for the captains (see the sidebar, "Planning a takeover," later in this chapter) and trade horses for sugar, coffee, tea, and "Sperits."

Christening Pompy's Tower (now Pompeys Pillar)

The canoes, steered by Clark's party, sped down the Yellowstone River, making as much as 80 miles in a day. On July 25, 1806, about 30 miles downstream from today's Billings, Montana, the boat party "arived at a remarkable rock Situated in an extensive bottom on the Stard. Side of the river & 250 paces from it. This rock I ascended and from it's top had a most extensive view in every direction. This rock which I shall Call Pompy's Tower is 200 feet high and 400 paces in secumphrance . . . . The natives have ingraved on the face of this rock the figures of animals &c. near which I marked my name and the day of the month & year."

Clark named the rock (see Figure 16-1) for his favorite toddler, Jean Baptiste Charbonneau, whom he called "my boy Pomp." The child was two and a half years old and had spent all but the first two months of his life traveling across the continent. Pompy's Tower is now called Pompeys Pillar (because Nicolas Biddle changed the name when he edited the journals — see Chapter 18) and is protected as a National Monument.

Figure 16-1:
Pompy's Tower, now called Pompeys Pillar.

Pompeys Pillar. Courtesy of Donnie Sexton/Travel Montana.

Visiting Pompeys Pillar National Monument

The 200-foot-high Pompy's Tower, named by William Clark for Sacagawea's child, Jean Baptiste "Pomp" Charbonneau, is now Pompeys Pillar National Monument. The massive butte 30 miles east of Billings, Montana, has been a landmark for local tribes for centuries. It is composed of sandstone and siltstone of the Hell Creek Formation dating from the Late Cretaceous Epoch. Indian people engraved animals and other drawings into its soft walls. Clark also signed it with his name and the date his party stopped there.

Today, the Monument, which is on the Lewis and Clark National Historic Trail and administered by the Bureau of Land Management, is open to the public from Memorial Day through September and offers interpretive tours, exhibits, wildlife viewing, picnicking, hiking, and a gift shop. For more information log on to www.mt.blm.gov/pillarmon/index.html or call 406.875.2233. For more information about the Lewis and Clark National Historic Trail itself, visit www.nps.gov/lecl or call 402-514-9311.

Clark's autograph — the only physical evidence of the expedition's passing — is still there (see Figure 16-2). The next day, the party arrived at the mouth of the Bighorn River — where just a year later St. Louis merchant Manuel Lisa would build a fur trading post.

Figure 16-2:
Photo of Clark's signature on Pompy's Tower, now Pompeys Pillar.

Clark's signature on Pompeys Pillar. Courtesy of Donnie Sexton/Travel Montana.

Losing sleep because of bellowing buffaloes

Game was becoming more and more plentiful as the party proceeded on toward the Missouri. The buffalo were in rut and the bulls kept everyone awake at night with their bellowing. One day, the explorers had to stop the canoes and wait an hour for a huge herd to cross the river in front of them.

The buffalo were plentiful, and so were the grasshoppers. Clark noted that they had stripped the prairie of all grasses for miles on one side of the river. And the mosquitoes were even more "troublesome" than they had been two years earlier (see Chapters 7 through 10).

Clark noted great flocks of passenger pigeons — later driven extinct by the tide of westward settlement — and large numbers of geese, eagles, hawks, ravens, and swallows. The party continued the practice it developed on the outward journey of shooting at every grizzly bear they met (see Chapter 10). Clark also recorded a description of sweetgrass "which the Indian plat and ware around their necks for its cent which is of a strong sent like that of the Vinella."

On August 3, Clark's party arrived at the Missouri and Yellowstone River junction where they were to meet Lewis. But the mosquitoes were so terrible that Clark left Lewis a note and moved on down the Missouri seeking relief. Clark marked the distance from the Rocky Mountains to the junction of the Yellowstone and the Missouri as 837 miles. The company had covered it in 35 days.

Improvising boats to replace the horses

On August 8, Clark and his party were awakened by two bull boats (see the "Constructing bull boats" sidebar for more information) arriving from upriver and carrying Sergeant Pryor and Hall, Shannon, and Windsor — who were

Constructing bull boats

In his journal, Clark described the process for making a bull boat that Mandans had taught them: "2 Sticks of 1¼-inch diameter is tied together So as to form a round hoop of the Size you wish the canoe, or as large as the Skin will allow to cover, two of those hoops are made one for the top or brim and the for the bottom the deabth you wish the Canoe, then Sticks of the Same Size are Crossed at right angles and fastened with a throng to each hoop and also where each Stick Crosses each other. then the Skin when green is drawn tight over this fraim and fastened with throngs to the brim or outer hoop So as to form a perfect bason. one of those Canoes will carry 6 or 8 Men and their loads."

Planning a takeover

While at Travelers' Rest, Lewis and Clark drafted a long letter to Hugh Heney, an agent of the British North West Company, who lived among the Assiniboines. Heney had befriended the Americans two years earlier, and Lewis and Clark wanted him to help with their manipulation or neutralization of the Teton Sioux.

In the letter, the captains asked Heney to persuade the Teton Sioux to abandon their relationships with British traders and join the American trade network. They wanted him to take a delegation of Sioux leaders to Washington to meet Jefferson and see for themselves the economic and military power of the United States, which Lewis and Clark were sure would subdue the Tetons into ceasing to resist and allow the free flow of American trade up the Missouri. Lewis threatened that the United States "will not long suffer her citizens to be deprived of the free navigation of the Missouri by a fiew comparatively feeble bands of Savages." Feeble? Had Lewis forgotten the Teton's show of power at the Bad River in 1804 (see Chapter 8)?

In return for these services, Lewis promised to pay Heney a dollar a day and expenses and to

see that he was appointed to the American post of Indian agent for the Sioux. Lewis also promised that the United States would establish trading posts in Sioux country. Lewis's letter asked Heney to meet the expedition at the Mandan villages.

What the letter proposed amounted to an astounding corporate takeover. If it worked, the United States would control a fur trade empire from the Mississippi to the Pacific Ocean. An ambitious and aggressive Lewis would be the primary broker of the deal.

When Clark sent Pryor and the men to the Mandan villages, he instructed Pryor to contact Hugh Heney and deliver the captains' letter. If Heney accepted Lewis's proposal, Pryor was to give him three horses. But Pryor and his men never made it to the Mandan villages, because the Crow Indians took all of their horses. As a result of Pryor's aborted trip, Hugh Heney did not receive Lewis's and Clark's letter, and so Heney never got to decide whether to coax and threaten the Teton Sioux into becoming an American trade partner.

supposed to be well on their way to the Mandans by then. Barely two days after leaving Clark, they had awakened to find that during the night every single one of their horses had been taken, presumably by the Crows. Pryor and the others tracked the Indians for five miles before giving up.

Pryor and the men went back to the Yellowstone, arriving at Pompy's Tower, and killed a couple of buffalo. With the hides they made two bull boats (this included a spare one, in case one capsized), loaded their gear, and hurried on after Clark. In the round buffalo-hide craft, Pryor and his three men caught up to Clark's party in 12 days.

As a result of Pryor's aborted trip, the captains' letter was not delivered (see the "Planning a takeover" sidebar). And without the horses, Clark had nothing to offer the Mandans in exchange for corn when the expedition arrived at the Knife River Villages (see Chapter 9). As the party made its way down the Missouri, the men hunted in order to get hides to trade instead.

On August 11, the explorers met two American trappers, Joseph Dixson and Forrest Hancock, coming upriver, heading for the Yellowstone. The men reported that the Mandans and Hidatsas were again at war with the Arikaras. So much for Lewis's and Clark's peace efforts of two years before (see Chapter 9).

Bringing Tragedy to Two Medicine

While Clark was exploring the Yellowstone, Lewis had his own river to scout, the Marias. Clark was pursuing diplomacy, but something else was driving Lewis's mission: money.

The United States had purchased the Louisiana Territory. Thomas Jefferson believed that the sale entitled the United States to claim all of the rivers (and the watershed land surrounding them) that flowed *into* the Territory. If the Marias River began north of the 49th Parallel (the disputed boundary between British Canada and the Lousiana Purchase, which was finally resolved in 1818), Lewis and Clark thought that the United States could legally claim that land and the fur trade from those headwaters could be redirected to St. Louis.

The bottom line: The captains hoped that this legal technicality would allow the United States to take some of Britain's huge fur trade. So it was in the national economic interest that Lewis and his party left Clark and set out on July 3, but it was a trip filled with disappointment, as well as wrath and reprisal — and, ultimately, lethal violence.

Getting back on the plains where the buffalo roam

Lewis and his party of nine explorers and five Nez Perce guides had traveled down the Bitterroot River. On the morning of July 4 — the third Independence Day the expedition had spent west of the Mississippi — and at a spot near the beautiful modern-day college town of Missoula, Montana, Lewis bade a sad farewell to the Nez Perce guides — all of them young men not yet 20. Lewis called them "a race of hardy strong athletic active men" and had his hunters shoot some meat for them to take on their homeward journey.

On July 6, Lewis's group noted fresh Indian signs and "*much sign* of beaver." The small party took turns standing guard day and night. They followed what is now the Big Blackfoot River — which the Nez Perce called the Cokhlarishkit or the "river of the road to buffaloe," as Lewis recorded it. The well-established trail led up through heavy timber and came out at a gentle treeless pass — today called Lewis and Clark Pass — at 6,284 feet above sea level. From there, Lewis could see Square Butte south of the Great Falls of the Missouri and out across the endless sweeping northern prairies.

The party crossed the Dearborn and Medicine (now the Sun) Rivers (see the "Medicine and Two Medicine" sidebar for information) and reached the Missouri just eight days after leaving Travelers' Rest. The route over Lewis and Clark Pass (see Figure 16-3) was 600 miles shorter than the route the expedition had taken west over Lemhi Pass two years earlier (see Chapter 11 for a description). The pass is an old Indian trail and is a fairly low path over the Continental Divide with the Blackfeet River on the other side. The Blackfeet leads to today's Clark Fork River (near Missoula, Montana), which flows to the Columbia River. Today, Lewis and Clark Pass is still accessible as a foot trail.

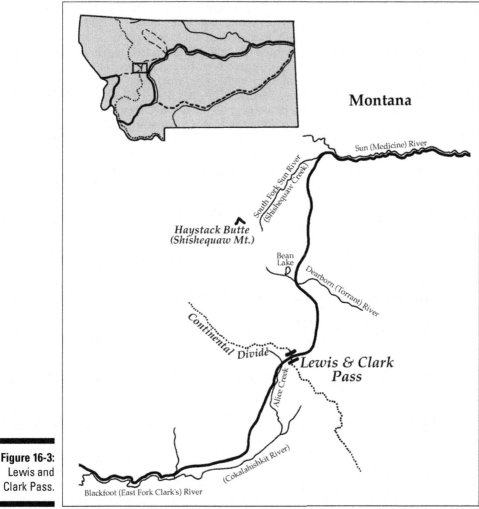

Figure 16-3:
Lewis and
Clark Pass.

Lisa S. Reed.

Medicine and Two Medicine

The Medicine (now the Sun) River flows into the Missouri from the west, above the Great Falls, a good distance upriver from the Two Medicine River. The Two Medicine flows into the Marias River, which flows into the Missouri from the north, below the Great Falls. The Corps of Discovery traveled both rivers.

On the way, Lewis recorded great numbers of passenger pigeons, wild horses, and a few moose. The rutting, bellowing buffalo bulls kept Lewis and his men awake all night, just as they did Clark's party on the Yellowstone. "[I]t is now the season at which the buffaloe begin to coppelate and the bulls keep a tremendious roaring we could hear them for many miles and there are such numbers of them that there is one continual roar." The roaring eve frightened the horses and agitated Seaman, Lewis's dog. The great herds were always followed by packs of wolves. "[T]he wolves are in great numbers howling around us and loling about in the plains in view at the distance of two or three hundred yards. I counted 27 about the carcase of a buffaloe," Lewis wrote. And, as in the year before, the mosquitoes were "excessively troublesome" — "my dog even howls with the torture he experiences from them."

The men were "much rejoiced" to be back on the plains and in buffalo country. Lewis happily wrote "the plains looked beautifull . . . the air was pleasant and a vast assemblage of little birds which croud to the groves on the river sung most enchantingly."

Dealing with spoiled specimens and stolen horses

Lewis's party got to their old portage camp at White Bear Island almost exactly a year after leaving it in 1805 (see Chapter 11). They shot a couple of buffalo, and they made bull boats to cross the Missouri to the cache where they had left supplies the year before.

To Lewis's great distress, water had penetrated the cache and ruined all of the plant specimens he had collected and preserved between Fort Mandan and the Great Falls. The specimens represented an enormous amount of work and care by Lewis, and their loss was a significant blow to botanical research. But there was more bad news that morning. Seventeen of the party's horses were missing and presumed stolen in the night by Indians. Now Lewis could take only three men with him to explore the Marias, instead of the six that he had planned to take. All the same, Lewis insisted on carrying through with the reconnaissance.

He had toyed with the idea of seeking out the Blackfeet and delivering his American trade policy speech, but now, with his party so reduced in number, he decided against it. Despite the extraordinary risk involved in splitting up the party and meeting the Blackfeet, whom he considered "a vicious lawless and reather an abandoned set of wretches," Lewis was obsessed with contributing to American empire building. Not that Lewis had any first hand knowledge of the Blackfeet. He knew only that the "good" Indians (in his opinion) — Nez Perce, Shoshones, and Salish — feared the Blackfeet, and that was enough for him to categorize them as "bad" Indians.

On July 17, Lewis made a drawing of the Great Falls (which has since been lost). He left Sergeant Patrick Gass and most of the men to finish packing up the usable items from the cache and wait for Ordway's party to arrive from the Three Forks to help portage it all around the falls. That combined force would then proceed on down the Missouri in the canoes and meet Lewis at the mouth of the Marias. Then, Lewis set out over the high plains with Drouillard and the two Field brothers. He left the two best horses and the two worst with Gass and took the rest. With such a tiny party, Lewis posted a lookout every night and took his "tour of watch with the men."

Following the Marias to disappointment

On July 18, Lewis reached the Marias River and followed it for three days until the river forked. Cut Bank Creek flowed into it from the north, and the Two Medicine River (which flows out of today's Glacier National Park) flowed into it from the south. Because Lewis wanted to find out how far north any tributary of the Missouri reached, he followed the Cut Bank. Two days, later his party arrived at a beautiful valley where the creek's route veered west. Like the Two Medicine River, Cut Bank Creek was coming out of the mountains. A disappointed Lewis wrote, "I now have lost all hope of the waters of this river ever extending to N Latitude 50° . . . ." Because the water didn't flow from the north into the Louisiana Territory, the United States couldn't legally claim the rights to any British Canadian watershed land — or its lucrative fur trade.

The party made camp at a stand of cottonwoods, and Lewis tried making celestial observations to confirm the latitude. But the weather was cloudy, and the party stayed at the camp for four days, hoping for clear skies. It rained. With clouds obscuring the sun and the moon and the stars, Lewis couldn't take a navigational reading, and he finally gave up. The mosquitoes tormented the group, and huntable game — so plentiful in previous days — appeared to have vanished. They took the lack of game as a sign that Indians were hunting in the area. Fortunately, just when their food was running out, a giant flock of passenger pigeons settled onto the cottonwood branches — so the men shot enough for supper.

On July 26, Lewis named their campsite Camp Disappointment (a different place than *Cape* Disappointment at the mouth of the Columbia River, which was named by a British sea captain in 1788 and discussed in Chapter 14) and packed up to head south once more. Camp Disappointment was about a dozen miles east of present day Browning, Montana. It was the northernmost point reached by the expedition, coming or going.

Running into Blackfeet

Lewis's party rode southeast, crossed the Two Medicine River and followed it — Lewis and the Field brothers heading for the ridge above the river, Drouillard riding in the river bottom. When Lewis got to the top of the ridge, he was surprised to see a herd of 30 or so horses, some with saddles, about a mile away. But he got a real alarm when he saw through his looking glass several mounted Indians watching Drouillard in the valley below. Lewis erroneously identified the Indians as "Minnetares of Fort de Prarie," but they were Piegan, one of the three major bands of Blackfeet.

With that many horses, Lewis assumed that there were as many men and decided it would be futile to run. He told Joseph Field to unfurl the American flag, and Lewis began riding slowly toward the Indians. One of the Piegan riders suddenly rode at full speed toward Lewis, and Lewis dismounted, beckoning to the rider. The Piegan turned his horse around and went back to his party. There were eight Piegans altogether — teenage boys herding horses — but Lewis feared that others were hidden from view. He melodramatically vowed to go down fighting — "preferring death to that of being deprived of my papers instruments and gun . . ." and made Joseph and Reuben Field vow the same.

Lewis cautiously approached the Piegan and shook his hand. Everyone dismounted, and using sign language the Indians asked for tobacco to smoke. Lewis gave a peace medal (see Chapter 8), a flag, and a handkerchief to three of the boys, making them "chiefs" and proposed that they camp together that night.

The combined group rode together to a beautiful grassy bank of the river, where three big cottonwoods grew, and stopped for the night. With Drouillard interpreting in sign language, Lewis learned that a large group of Blackfeet were at the foot of the mountains — about a half day to the west — and that a white man was with them. Another large band was to the south, hunting buffalo in the Marias River area. The Blackfeet traded at a British trading post on the Saskatchewan River for arms, whiskey, and blankets. This meant that Canadian fur traders were already in business not far north of the 49th Parallel — another blow to Jefferson's plan for an American trade empire extending into Canada.

Killing two Piegan youths

Lewis made a naïve and fatal mistake. He gave the Piegan teenagers his peace and trade speech and invited their tribe to join the American trade network as other tribes in their region had. He asked for a council with the Blackfeet at the mouth of the Marias and promised horses and tobacco if the boys would arrange it. The boys did not respond. What he had just told them, in essence, was that the Americans led a trade alliance of Blackfeet enemies — Nez Perce, Shoshones, Salish, and others — and would be trading, among other things, guns to those partners. Like the Teton Sioux, the Blackfeet's control of trade and arms would be jeopardized.

Taking lives

At first light the next morning, Lewis was awakened by a scuffle between Drouillard and one of the Piegan youths over Drouillard's gun. Another Indian youth had taken Lewis's gun and others had the rifles of Reuben and Joseph Field. In the ensuing, confusing struggle, Reuben stabbed and killed one of the Piegan boys. The Indians then dropped the rifles and went after the explorers' horses. Lewis ran after them, shouting that he would shoot unless they let the horses go. One of the Piegans turned to face Lewis. Lewis fired and killed him. Before falling dead to the ground, the Indian also fired, missing Lewis by inches.

Lewis and his men caught three of their horses and stole four of the Indians', saddled up and hightailed it out of there. But before going, Lewis retrieved the flag he had given one of the youths the night before and took some of the Piegans' buffalo meat. He deliberately left the peace medal around the neck of the boy he had shot so "that they might be informed who we were." It was an arrogant and insulting gesture. One of the dead Piegan boys was called Calf Looking. He was 13 years old.

Lewis's exploration of the Marias had been a reckless mistake for Jefferson's trade empire aspirations, and especially for two young Blackfeet. Because of the Americans' alliance with Blackfeet enemies, for decades after the incident, the Blackfeet Nation was hostile to Americans but remained friendly to Canadians. In his journal accounts of the fight, Lewis called the Piegans "warriors," but, according to the Blackfeet, they were boys — horse herders, not fighting men. Conversely, Lewis and his three men were U.S. soldiers, well armed.

Riding hard

Lewis and his men rode south as hard as they could, night and day, believing that a vengeful Blackfeet war party was on their heels. The six remaining terrified and ashamed Piegan boys rode just as hard in the opposite direction. No Blackfeet were chasing Lewis. But, not taking any chances, he drove men and horses 100 miles before he let them stop and rest.

Today's Blackfeet Nation

The Blackfeet Nation reservation, with 1.5 million acres, straddles the border between Montana and Alberta, Canada, in the eastern shadow of Glacier National Park in Montana and Waterton National Park in Alberta. The seat of tribal government in Montana is the town of Browning at the eastern entrance to Glacier. The Blackfeet Nation is actually a confederacy of three bands — the Siksika (meaning Blackfeet), the Blood, and the Piikani or Piegan. The Piegan are based primarily in Montana, the Blood and Siksika primarily in Alberta. The name Blackfeet derives from the unique black color of their moccasins, which were either painted or blackened by prairie fires.

The Blackfeet — the most powerful nation on the upper Missouri during Lewis's and Clark's time, are no longer hostile to visitors but welcome them warmly. The Blackfeet have numerous visitor attractions — visitor museums, historic sites, tourist camps, and cultural and scenic tours, including tours of Glacier National Park from the perspective of the Blackfeet, whose homeland it remains. Trout fishing on the Blackfeet reservation is among the best in the world. Rainbow, brown and brook trout abound (a tribal permit is required).

The Museum of the Plains Indians in Browning, the tribal headquarters, exhibits the creative achievements of the Plains tribes. Next door to the museum, you can tour the re-creation of an encampment called "In the Footsteps of the Blackfeet." Half-day and full-day Blackfeet Historic Site Tours originate at the museum and include Lewis and Clark event sites. Recreation camps are also offered — participants sleep in tepees, build smokeless fires, and eat traditional food. Twelve miles from Browning is Camp Disappointment, the farthest point north reached by the Lewis and Clark expedition. Near the town of Cut Bank, you can tour the Two Medicine Fight site, where Lewis shot a Piegan Blackfeet boy in a fatal misunderstanding.

For more information on the Blackfeet today, including their rich culture and tourist opportunities, log on to www.blackfeetnation.com or call 406-338-5425.

Lewis reached the Missouri River on July 28 and soon heard rifle shots coming from upriver. It was Gass and Ordway and the rest of that party (but not Clark, York, Sacagawea, and the others with Clark) in the canoes and the white pirogue. The men's joyous reunion was quick. Still fearing Blackfeet reprisal, the group loaded Lewis's baggage into the boats, turned the horses loose on the prairie, and took off down the Missouri. They stopped briefly at the mouth of the Marias to retrieve goods left in other caches the year before (see Chapter 10). Again, a number of items were damaged, including some prized grizzly bear skins. The big red pirogue was decayed beyond repair. The men left it there and hurried on.

For five days Lewis and his party of now 16 men zoomed down the Missouri. They cooked only the evening meal and ate cold meat during the day so they wouldn't have to stop. On August 7, they reached the mouth of the Yellowstone where they had planned to meet Clark.

Taking a bullet in the buttock from a nearsighted, one-eyed fiddle player

Clark was not at the specified meeting place on the Yellowstone. He had left a note saying that he was moving on down the Missouri looking for a campsite with fewer mosquitoes.

Four days later, Clark was still ahead of the rest of the group, but Lewis stopped to rest and hunt elk. He and Pierre Cruzatte, the one-eyed, near-sighted fiddler, took their rifles and pursued their prey into the willows along the river. With each hunter partly obscured by the bushes, Cruzatte mistook Lewis's buckskin britches for an elk and fired. His bullet hit Lewis just below the left hip and passed through his buttocks, coming out the other side and lodging in his leather pants. Lewis shouted at Cruzatte, but got no answer, which convinced him that he had been shot by Indians. He ran as hard as he could manage back to the canoes. Cruzatte denied having shot his captain, but the bullet that had lodged in Lewis's pants was from a U.S. Army rifle.

Back at the canoes, Sgt. Gass dressed Lewis's wound, and the party headed downriver again with Lewis lying on his belly in the pirogue. Lewis spent that night with a fever and a Peruvian bark poultice on his behind.

The next day, August 12, his party met the same two white trappers (Dixson and Hancock) that Clark had met, traveling upriver to the Yellowstone country. In the coming month, the expedition would meet a steady flow of adventurers. Manifest Destiny (the idea that the United States could and should grow westward, although that term itself had not yet come into usage) had already descended on the West.

Reuniting the Corps

On August 12, Meriwether Lewis and his party caught up to Clark, and the Corps of Discovery was whole again. Every member of the expedition was once again traveling together.

From the standpoint of diplomacy, Clark's trip down the Yellowstone was a bust. He had hoped to meet the Crow in the flesh, not just as horse-borrowing phantoms in the night. But he never met them.

On the other hand, Lewis had hoped to avoid meeting any Indians during his exploration up the Marias River drainage — deep into Blackfeet country. Clark failed to meet Indians, and Lewis failed to avoid them. Two Piegan youths were killed by Lewis and his party. And the exploration had shown that the Marias River and its tributaries didn't extend into present-day Canada (squashing hopes of diverting some of that country's fur trade to the United States). Lewis's exploration was also a dismal failure.

That evening, Lewis could hardly write in his journal because of the pain of his gunshot wound (see the preceding section). But, ever the botanist, he recorded a description of the pin cherry, "the bark is smooth and of a dark brown colour. the leaf is peteolate, oval accutely pointed at it's apex . . . finely or minutely serrate, pale green and free from bubessence. the fruit is a globular berry about the size of a buck-shot of a fine scarlet red . . . the pulp of this fruit is of an agreeable ascid flavour and is now ripe." It was the last journal entry he would write.

Two days later, the expedition arrived at the Mandan villages.

Chapter 17

Heading Home

. . . .

In This Chapter

▶ Trying one more time to push the American plan on the Indians

▶ Saying good-bye to Sacagawea, Pomp, Charbonneau, and Colter

▶ Leaving the wilderness and entering the limelight

▶ Enjoying acclaim from the president and the nation

▶ Splitting up and moving on

. . . .

*I*n August of 1806, the Lewis and Clark expedition was going home. As the canoes arrived back at the Hidatsa and Mandan villages, Clark was in command, because Lewis was recovering from an unfortunate friendly fire gunshot wound to the backside (see Chapter 16).

In this chapter, we tell you what happened when the Corps revisited the Indian nations of the Northern Plains. Clark redoubled his efforts to impose the plan for a peaceful tribal alliance (between the Hidatsa, Mandan, and Arikara) against the Teton Sioux and to convince the tribes to send delegations to Washington. The expedition also bid farewell to Sacagawea, her husband Charbonneau, and their son, as well as to Private John Colter (the captains granted him permission to head back west). In a dangerous bit of *déjà vu,* the Corps had another tense brush with the powerful Teton Sioux, but escaped unscathed. Traveling as fast as they could, the expedition also met boatloads of fur trappers headed north.

In the communities along the shore, the Corps were received like conquering heroes. Jubilation at their survival greeted them in St. Louis, where Lewis immediately wrote President Jefferson and Clark's brother in order to get the word out to the American public of their successful return. They returned home to national attention and acclaim, but within weeks, they disbanded and scattered into history.

Trying Again to Impose the American Trade Plan on the Indians

In August of 1806, the expedition reached the Northern Plains on the journey back from the Pacific. The Corps of Discovery had two goals to achieve on this return visit to the plains tribes:

- ✔ **To get the tribes to send high-ranking individuals or delegations to Washington to meet with President Jefferson.**

- ✔ **To secure the peace among the Mandan, Hidatsa, and Arikara tribes.** The captains still wanted the three tribes to form an alliance against the Teton Sioux to minimize Sioux influence on the Missouri River and clear the way for American commerce.

This was going to be a tall order for the Corps to fulfill, because to Lewis and Clark's dismay, the news from the tribes was awful. The peace plan they had outlined for the tribes during the winter of 1804–1805 had failed as soon as the expedition left the Mandan villages. Fighting had broken out between the Mandans and the Arikaras. The Teton Sioux had raided the Mandans. The Hidatsas had raided the Shoshones.

As the Corps revisited the tribes of the Northern Plains, Clark took one last shot at getting the Indians to comply with the American trade proposal. His tactics included promising, begging, threatening, and manipulating the tribes. Of course, his hopes for the Teton Sioux were less lofty. The expedition just wanted to hustle through that tribe's territory as fast as possible.

Giving up a cannon and getting lectured by the Hidatsas

When the expedition arrived at the Hidatsa and Mandan villages on August 14, 1806, "those people were extreamly pleased to see us," wrote Clark. The expedition fired the *blunderbuses* (large guns with flared muzzles) in greeting. The Corps was embraced by White Buffalo Robe Unfolded, principal leader of the Mahawa village, and Black Moccasin at the Metaharta village. Black Moccasin, Clark reported, was in mourning and "cried most immoderately" as he told Clark about the death of his son, who'd recently been killed by the Blackfeet Indians.

Lewis was still out of commission from an accidental gunshot wound (see Chapter 16). He wasn't able to walk for another eight days and didn't fully recover until mid-September.

Clark sent Charbonneau to invite all the Hidatsa leaders to a council and sent Drouillard to fetch the trader and interpreter René Jessaume to the expedition's camp above the Mitutanka village.

During the council, Clark tried to persuade the tribal leaders to go with the expedition to Washington. To help convince the Indians, Clark made promises that would be difficult to keep. He assured them that

- ✔ No harm would come to them while crossing Teton Sioux territory.
- ✔ They would get federal protection for the return trip and continued protection afterward.
- ✔ Anyone making the trip would receive many significant gifts.

Clark's pitch was interrupted by the arrival of the Hidatsa leader Le Borgne (One Eye), a leader who had not been particularly friendly to the expedition when they appeared two years earlier (see Chapter 9). Le Borgne said pointedly that when the powerful Americans had subdued the Teton Sioux and the trip presented no unnecessary risks, he would make a trip to Washington.

When Le Borgne showed up in Clark's camp with other leaders on August 16, Clark offered him one of the keelboat swivel guns to soften him up to pleas for a Hidatsa delegation to Washington. He also chastised the Hidatsa leaders about raiding the Shoshones. Clark said that they had to stop the raids, and that he was giving the Hidatsa the cannon to defend themselves and other American friends, which included the Arikaras.

An elderly leader blasted Clark for meddling in Hidatsa business. The captains' insistence that they make peace with the Arikaras was a mistake, the leader said, because the Arikaras were their enemies for good reasons, including the Arikara alliance with the Teton Sioux. The Teton Sioux were as big a problem as ever, and no Hidatsas were going through their territory. And furthermore, they weren't going to make promises that they couldn't keep with the Arikaras about peace and cooperation. Clark was crestfallen. Le Borgne got to keep his cannon, and Clark got nothing in return.

Failing with the Mandans

When Clark's negotiations with LeBorgne and the Hidatsa leaders turned sour, he gave up on them for the time being and began working on the Mandan leader, Black Cat, the Rooptahee village headman. Clark had sought the friendly Black Cat out upon his arrival in the Mandan villages (Rooptahee and Mitutanka) on August 14. He and Black Cat had eaten some summer squash together and smoked a pipe. Clark hoped that his old ally would cooperate and accompany them to Washington to meet with Jefferson.

Sorry to disappoint him, Black Cat offered Clark twelve bushels of corn but said he would not go with the expedition through Sioux Country. A young man in his band stepped forward during the negotiation to say that he would go to Washington, but Private George Gibson confronted him and accused him of stealing Gibson's knife, causing a near-riot and breaking up the discussion in Black Cat's village.

On August 15, Jessaume reported that Little Raven, the Mandan second in command (at Mitutanka village), was saying that he would go to Washington. Clark hurried to the village to close the sale but Little Raven wasn't going to commit until he'd mulled it over with his family and friends.

After some consideration of the idea, Little Raven said that he'd changed his mind and wouldn't be going after all. Clark tried to bribe him with a flag, but nothing doing. The reason appeared to be that the Mitutanka headman, Sheheke, was jealous and didn't want Little Raven to go. Exasperated, Clark told translator Jessaume that if Sheheke wouldn't let Little Raven go, he should get Sheheke himself to go to Washington. Jessaume came back with a proposition that Clark couldn't refuse. Sheheke would go on the condition that he could take his wife and children *plus* Jessaume as his translator and Jessaume's wife and children. Not being in a position to bargain, Clark agreed, although he didn't know how all the additional people and baggage would fit in the boats.

The Corps stayed with the Mandans and Hidatsas for three days, and then departed to continue downstream and visit the Arikaras. When Sheheke and his family were leaving, his people "Cried out loud," fearing that they would never see their leader again.

Deceiving the Arikaras

Lewis was still recovering from his gunshot wound and could neither walk nor sit down, so he continued to ride in a canoe on his belly. By August 21, the expedition reached the Grand River and the Arikara villages. A number of Cheyenne Indians were camping and trading with the Arikaras. Clark was given a friendly greeting by both tribes, so he decided to call an immediate council. The Mandan leader Sheheke, sticking close to Clark for protection, attended in order to make a plea for reconciliation between the Mandans and the Arikaras.

Sheheke gave out Mandan tobacco as a goodwill gesture, and Clark presented a running narrative on the expedition so far, translated by Joseph Garreau, a trader. Clark was introduced to a new Arikara leader, Grey Eyes, who gave a rousing speech denouncing the Teton Sioux; primarily, one may assume, for Clark's and Sheheke's benefit.

Lewis and Clark's strategy of aligning the Arikaras to the Mandans and the Hidatsas — away from the Teton Sioux — was doomed. The Arikaras were farmers, and the Teton Sioux were hunters. The Arikaras enjoyed strong trade and homeland security advantages by staying on the Sioux's good side. Clark's speeches and promises couldn't change that fact. The bottom line was that the Arikaras weren't sending a delegation, and they weren't joining an alliance against the Teton Sioux.

Later, a serious shouting match broke out between the Mandan leader Sheheke and the Arikara leader One Arm. Thinking that the argument may turn violent, Clark intervened and said that Sheheke was now under American protection and the Corps would kill if need be to protect him.

That pronouncement broke up the fight, but the Arikaras were firm about not sending a delegation. They "wished to see the Chief who went down last summer return first." Unfortunately, that Arikara leader had fallen ill in Washington and died.

Clark knew about the Arikara leader's death because fur-trappers Joseph Dixson and Forrest Hancock had told him about it, but the tribe didn't yet know that the leader had died, and Clark didn't tell them. If they had been told, the Arikaras might have taken out their considerable grief on the members of the expedition. After they learned of their leader's death, they were enemies of Americans traveling upriver for years.

Before the expedition left the Arikaras and before the Arikaras found out what had happened to their leader in Washington, One Arm and other leaders placated Clark by pledging allegiance to the United States and cooperation with the Mandans, although they also said that they would have to continue to trade with the Teton Sioux for guns and ammunition. Within a few weeks, however, the Arikaras found out that their leader was dead and their promise to the United States was null and void.

Coaxing the Cheyenne

Giving up on the Arikaras, Clark turned to the Cheyenne and smoked with their leader in his white-skinned tepee. Clark tried to give him a small peace medal (see Chapter 8), but the Cheyenne refused to take it. The Cheyenne leader said that white people were "all medicen," meaning that white people and their gifts carried disease. Clark argued strenuously that flags and medals were symbols of status full of good intention, not diseases, and put the medal back around the leader's neck.

While Clark was present, the leader appeared to overcome his anxiety and accept the medal, which pleased Clark, who'd had few successes so far with any of the tribes on his return trip. He was also pleased when the Cheyenne asked him the next day to send traders so his tribe could learn American trapping techniques.

Reviling and riling the Teton Sioux

After passing the mouth of today's Cheyenne River on August 25, 1806, the Corps saw signs of the "Troubleson Tetons," Clark wrote, but the expedition needed food so it stopped and sent hunters out. They also needed to gather specimens for their collection, especially mule deer, pronghorn sheep, and prairie dog. They were on the plains at a particularly good time of year to find wildlife in abundance. Clark climbed a hill south of today's cities of Chamberlain and Oacoma on August 29 and saw "nearly 20,000 [buffalo] feeding on this plain. . .a greater number of buffalow than [he] had ever seen before at one time."

Throwing a fit

August 30 began pleasantly, with the Corps collecting plums along the river and killing a fat elk. Lewis continued to mend from his gunshot wound. Clark sent the two Field brothers and George Shannon in a canoe to collect "barking squirrels" (prairie dogs) to take back as specimens, and later in the day, the expedition pulled over to shore to wait for them.

As they rowed into shore, 80 to 90 well-armed Indians appeared on the opposite river bank a quarter mile below them. The Indians fired a friendly salute, so Clark was confused about who they were; they could be Yankton Sioux, Ponca, or Omaha, maybe even Teton Sioux. He rowed the three Frenchmen who spoke Ponca, Omaha, and a little Sioux out to the sandbar in a small canoe, which got them close enough to talk to the Indians but not close enough to be attacked. Three young Indians swam over to the sandbar. They turned out to be Teton Sioux warriors, and their leader happened to be the man who had diffused the confrontation on the expedition's first encounter with the Teton Sioux in 1804: Black Buffalo.

Even though there was no way to translate what he was saying into Sioux beyond a few words, Clark angrily berated the three young men about the Teton Sioux detaining them two years earlier and about abusing whites coming up the river since then. He refused them some corn that they spotted in the canoe and asked for. (Clark's anger may have been sincere, but it also could have been pure show for the 90 warriors waiting for the expedition to come to shore.)

Getting cursed by Buffalo Medicine

Several more Teton Sioux men swam across, including one who understood Ponca, so Clark, sufficiently warmed up, repeated his angry accusations to them. He told them that he viewed them as bad people and that he had given the Hidatsas a cannon to defend themselves against the Teton Sioux. He also told them to go away and leave the Corps alone, and if they didn't stay away from the river, the Corps would kill every one of them. Then he said that they should go repeat what he'd told them to their leaders, which they did.

The Teton Sioux retreated from the shore up a high hill toward their camp on the other side. Seven of them halted and *blackguarded* the Corps (abused them verbally). Fortunately, the Field brothers and Shannon showed up, so the Corps got underway down the river.

Before they were out of sight, Buffalo Medicine (see Chapter 8) came down the hill and invited the expedition to land. Clark ignored him. Greatly offended, Buffalo Medicine went back up the hill to the top, turned and cursed the Corps with a gesture, a "great oath among Indians," striking the ground three times with his gun.

The expedition went six more miles before camping on an island that had little to recommend it except that the Teton Sioux could not sneak up on them in the night.

Feeling relieved to see the Yankton Sioux

Two days after their encounter with the Teton Sioux, the expedition passed another group of Indians on shore and saluted them, but their salute was not returned. The Field brothers and George Shannon had been left behind to hunt on an island. After seeing the Indians and assuming that they were Teton Sioux, Clark pulled over to wait for his men and make sure that they weren't molested. Gunshots rang out, and Clark assumed that the straggler canoe was under fire. He picked 15 men and they ran back upstream to do battle with the Teton Sioux. Lewis, still hurting, organized the rest of the men to defend the boats.

Clark and company ran full tilt around the bend, but the canoe was still too far away to be a target of the Indians. Their target, it turned out, was an empty keg that someone in the expedition had thrown overboard. Litter. And the Indians turned out not to be Tetons, anyway, but Yankton Sioux, a tribe that had been very friendly to the expedition two years earlier. The Yanktons informed Clark that they had even sent one of their leaders to Washington.

Parting with Sacagawea, Pomp, Charbonneau, and Colter

When the Corps left the Mandan and Hidatsa villages in August, they said goodbye to Sacagawea, her son, Pomp (Jean Baptiste), and her husband, Charbonneau. Lewis and Clark paid Charbonneau $500.33⅓ (in a government draft) on August 17 for his services as an interpreter. Sacagawea was paid nothing. Clark offered to help Charbonneau, Sacagawea, and Pomp settle in Illinois country, but Charbonneau said that the move wouldn't work because he didn't have a way of making a living there. Clark, who had grown extremely fond of Sacagawea's little boy, asked to take Pomp to bring him up "in Such a manner as [he] thought proper." But the 19-month old Jean Baptiste wasn't yet weaned. Charbonneau told Clark to wait a year for when "the boy would be sufficiently old to leave his mother."

The parting may have been emotional for Clark, Pomp, and Sacagawea, but Clark's journal entry for that day shows no indication that it was. Three days after departing, Clark did mention one regret in a letter to Charbonneau: "Your woman who accompanied you that long dangerous & fatigueing rout to the Pacific Ocian and back diserved a greater reward for her attention and services on that rout than we had in our power to give her."

The Corps also said goodbye to Private John Colter. Wanting to skip the homecoming and return to the west, Colter asked and got permission to quit the expedition and the Army before his enlistment expired (which was scheduled to be October, 1806). Colter said he would be "lonely" in St. Louis and had had an offer from the "two men from the Illinois" — fur trappers Dixson and Hancock, whom they had met on the upper Missouri river. The captains gave their permission, as well as enough ammunition, powder, and other gear for Colter to survive two years as a trapper.

Returning to "Civilization"

After leaving the Teton Sioux behind, the Corps traveled down the Missouri River for the next three weeks. They met nearly 150 traders and others who were working their way up the Missouri. The first trading party the Corps encountered was led by James Aird, a Scotsman living in Wisconsin, who held a license to trade with the Sioux. Camping together through a thunderstorm, Aird gave them flour and held them in thrall with two years worth of news from the United States.

They learned that Jefferson had been re-elected, two Indians had been hung for murder in St. Louis, Vice President Aaron Burr had killed Secretary of the Treasury Alexander Hamilton in a duel, and the United States had fought and won a war with Tripoli.

On September 4, they climbed the hill to Sergeant Charles Floyd's grave to pay their respects (Floyd's death is detailed in Chapter 7), found the grave disturbed and restored it. The trip proved to be a little too strenuous for Lewis and set back his recovery.

Opening the trader floodgates

On September 6, the captains bought a gallon of whiskey from a trading boat owned by their friend in St. Louis, Auguste Chouteau. Each man was given a dram of whiskey (a sixteenth of an ounce), the first taste of liquor they'd had since July 4, 1805.

The expedition was traveling downstream an average of 70 miles a day. "The men ply their oars," Clark wrote, "and we descended with great velocity." They met a four-man party on September 10, and then two days later, a two-canoe party sponsored by the Chouteaus of St. Louis. They told the captains that U.S. Army Lieutenant Zebulon Pike (the explorer Pike's Peak is named for) had gone up the Arkansas River two months earlier with the aim of returning via the Red River.

Coming back from the dead

The Corps encountered a large party bound for the Arikara villages to tell the tribe about the death of their leader, who had died in Washington of disease while on his visit to meet President Jefferson. Interpreters who had accompanied their leader to Washington, Joseph Gravelines and Pierre Dorion, were returning to the Arikaras under Jefferson's instructions. The large, armed party was accompanying them in case they had trouble getting past the Teton Sioux.

The following day, the Corps met more traders sponsored by the Chouteaus, who gave them more whiskey and some food. On September 15, Lewis and Clark climbed a hill with a commanding view. The spot is now a park in downtown Kansas City, Missouri.

They met a large boat on September 17, and on board was John McClallen, an old army buddy of Lewis's, who gave them chocolate, sugar, more whiskey, and the latest gossip. McClallen also told them that the public — although not President Jefferson — feared that they had all been killed, or that the Spanish had captured them and put them to work as slaves in a mine. They had been gone over a year past the date when they were expected to return. McClallen said that even he had believed they were dead and was dumbfounded to find them alive and well.

By September 18, the expedition was completely out of supplies, but the men went hungry rather than slow down to hunt for game. The men were living on paw paws, a fruit that could be picked close to the shore. "The party being extremely anxious to get down[,] ply their ores very well," Clark wrote on September 20.

Cow-spotting

To their joy, the men spotted two grazing cows that afternoon on the river-bank, their first cow sighting in two and a half years, and they shouted in celebration for their return to "civilization." They arrived at the settlement of La Charette and fired a salute of three rounds, which was returned. When the townfolk realized that they were greeting the Corps of Discovery, they were astonished and jubilant.

The next day, the Corps rowed with all their might for St. Charles, firing a salute when they reached the town. Citizens welcomed the men into their homes for the night and fed them the next morning. The expedition stopped next at Fort Bellefontaine, a fort that was built in St. Charles after they'd left in 1804. The folks at Fort Bellefontaine gave Sheheke and his family some American clothes. Before arriving in St. Louis, the Corps passed Camp Dubois, their winter camp of 1803–1804.

Reaching Cheering Crowds in St. Louis

News of the Lewis and Clark expedition's arrival in St. Charles swept down the river. When the Corps reached St. Louis at noon on September 23, the residents — as many as 1,000 people — were lined up on the bank waiting for them.

"The people gathered on Shore and Huzzared three cheers," wrote Sergeant John Ordway, "then the party all considerable much rejoiced that we have the Expedition Completed."

"They really have the appearance of Robinson Crusoes," wrote a witness, "dressed entirely in buckskins." Everyone in the Corps became an instant celebrity in St. Louis. A ball was held in their honor in St. Louis the night after they landed. People hung on their every word and spread the tales of their most dangerous adventures. Lewis and Clark became the guests of Auguste Chouteau and his family (see the "Opening the trader floodgates" section for more on Chouteau).

Basking in Praise from the President, the Press, and the Public

As soon as the Corps of Discovery reached St. Louis, Lewis jumped off the boat to write and mail a letter to President Jefferson. The day's mail had already left, so Lewis sent a message to the postmaster in Cahokia to please hold the mail going east until noon the next day. Lewis also wrote to either George Rogers or Jonathan Clark (historians aren't sure which) on behalf of William Clark, expecting that the letter would be printed in the local newspaper. And Lewis continued to write letters to the press announcing the expedition's surprising return.

Newspapers, not all-news cable channels, carried the announcement of the expedition's success across the nation, and soon Lewis and Clark were the toast of the towns. Gala balls were held over the next few months in Lewis's and Clark's honor in Indiana territory, Kentucky, Virginia, and Washington. They were acclaimed everywhere they traveled. Newspapers carried accounts, true and false, of their exploits. One senator remarked that it was like they were returning from the moon.

Briefing a joyful Jefferson

In his letter, Lewis told Jefferson that the Corps had arrived safely and had discovered the most direct convenient route to the Pacific Ocean, although he had to report that there is no all-water route linking the East and West coasts. From the Missouri River to the Columbia River, Lewis wrote Jefferson, it is 340 miles. Of those, 200 miles are good, and 140 are formidable. Sixty of the formidable miles were across tremendous mountains "covered with eternal snows."

Lewis assured the president that the fur trade potential was stupendous. The United States can collect furs from the Northwest and send 90 percent of them to the mouth of the Columbia for shipment to the Orient, Lewis urged. (This plan was opposite from Jefferson's idea that furs from the Pacific Coast be shipped to the Missouri River and brought down to St. Louis.)

Lewis's grand fur trade scheme continued. A great market would be held every July in Nez Perce country. A permanent market would be set up at the mouth of the Columbia River. Lewis assured the president that more beaver and otter were on the upper Missouri River than anywhere on earth.

The next section of his letter reported to the president that he had collected numerous plants and nine new Indian vocabularies. He was also sending the Mandan leader Sheheke (also called Big White) to visit him. Lewis promised to also come to Washington soon after visiting his mother in Virginia.

Lewis's letter was effusive in its praise for Clark. It read: "With respect to the exertions and services rendered by that esteemable man Capt. William Clark in the course of [our] late voyage I cannot say too much; if sir any credit be due for the success of the arduous enterprise in which we have been mutually engaged, he is equally with myself entitled to your consideration and that of our common country."

Lewis closed his letter by telling the president that everyone who left with him from the Mandan villages had come back alive.

As soon as Jefferson received Lewis's letter, he replied: "Washington. I received, my dear Sir, with unspeakable joy your letter. . . . The unknown scenes in which you were engaged, & the length of time without hearing of you had begun to be felt awfully. . . . I salute you with sincere affection. Thomas Jefferson."

Writing to Clark's brother and the newspaper

Newspapers were the fastest way to spread news in 1806. Because the captains agreed that Lewis had the better mastery of language and political spin, Lewis wrote a letter on Clark's behalf to one of his brothers, either George Rogers or Jonathan Clark, knowing that he would have it published in the Frankfort, Kentucky, newspaper.

The letter Lewis wrote for Clark was more dramatic than the one he had sent the president. The Clark letter told about some of the exploits and dangers: near starvation, encounters with wild animals and with hostile tribes, devastating treks over the mountains, and portages around falls.

Clark's letter to his brother was published in the Frankfort, Kentucky *Palladium* on October 9 (before Lewis's letter to Jefferson was even summarized in a Washington paper). The *Palladium*'s editorial statement was "we are persuaded all think and feel alike, on the courage, perseverance and prudent deportment displayed by this adventurous party. They are entitled to, and will receive the plaudits of their countrymen."

Priming the press and lobbying for a reward

Lewis continued to write letters to newspapers throughout the next months, primarily to raise support and to pressure Congress to give expedition members an appropriate reward for their efforts.

On October 27, 1806, an item appeared in the newspaper *National Intelligencer* in Washington, the unofficial mouthpiece of the Jefferson administration: "It is with the sincerest pleasure, that we announce to our fellow citizens, the arrival of CAPTAIN LEWIS, with his exploring party, at St. Louis." It was followed by a summary of Lewis's letter to Jefferson.

The same article was reprinted in the Norfolk paper on November 3, the Boston paper on November 6, and a London paper on December 3.

Lewis didn't give many details in his accounts of the expedition, though, because he was saving those for his publication of the journals. Jefferson had agreed before the expedition's departure to let Lewis publish and profit from journals kept on the journey.

Disbanding the Corps

Although he knew that Jefferson wanted him to come east as quickly as he could, Lewis stayed in St. Louis for a month to raise hard currency to give his men an advance on the pay that was owed them. Money in the quantities he needed was very hard to find. Lewis wrote *drafts* (checks) on the War Department account to 16 different merchants to get enough cash to pay the men.

The captains also auctioned off rifles, kettles, axes, and other equipment from the trip to raise $480.62. Today, those items would be priceless.

Lewis had promised the men that they would receive a parcel of land in addition to their wages. Although they didn't have the land yet, or any deed or promise in writing, the men of the Corps began selling *land warrants* (future claims on government land). Privates Whitehouse and Collins sold their claims to Drouillard. Drouillard then sold the three allotment claims, his and theirs, for a huge profit.

As soon as the men had some money, they scattered.

Chapter 18

Exploring the Fate and Lessons of the Corps of Discovery

. . . .

In This Chapter

▶ Experiencing opposite fates: the captains

▶ Taking their places in history: the Corps

▶ Suffering in the aftermath: the American Indians

▶ Declining over the decades: the environment

▶ Shaping the future: the United States

. . . .

*1*n this chapter, we tell you what happened after the Lewis and Clark expedition ended and the members of the Corps went their separate ways. For many involved in the expedition, the struggle didn't end when the Corps triumphantly reached St. Louis.

Meriwether Lewis found life after the expedition daunting. He floundered as governor of the Upper Louisiana Territory and failed in business. Beset by debt, alcoholism, and paranoia, his life ended tragically when he committed suicide in a remote area of Tennessee. William Clark lived a long and prosperous life in St. Louis as a territorial bureaucrat, the instrument of an Indian policy that devastated tribes east of the Mississippi during his lifetime and others long after he died. Sacagawea died a few years after the expedition but lives on as an icon of three cultures. York pressed Clark for his freedom until Clark finally gave in — ten years after the expedition. The majority of the men in the Corps of Discovery died young, although Patrick Gass lived to be 98.

After the expedition, the American Indian tribes and the land and rivers of the West underwent radical change. Jefferson's dreams of slow growth and peace with the Indians were doomed, but the lessons of the expedition offer renewed hope for harmony among people of all races and between humans and the natural world.

Arriving in Washington

The Corps of Discovery disbanded in October of 1806, less than three weeks after returning to St. Louis. Lewis and Clark stayed a month in St. Louis and then packed up and went east with an entourage that included the Mandan leader Sheheke and his family, the interpreter Jessaume and his family, Sergeants Gass and Ordway, Privates Labiche and Frazer, and an Osage delegation led by St. Louis fur trader Pierre Chouteau. They stopped to visit with Clark's brother, George Rogers Clark, and attended a banquet and ball in their honor.

They split up in Frankfort, Kentucky, on October 13. Lewis, Sheheke, and his party went to Charlottesville and then on to Locust Hill to visit with his friends and family. Clark went to Fincastle, Virginia, to ask Julia (also referred to as Judith) Hancock to marry him. Pierre Chouteau and the Osage delegation went on to Washington.

Every place that Lewis traveled, the citizens wanted to throw a banquet or ball in his honor. When he finally reached Charlottesville, he received a reception at the Stone Tavern. His speech that night praised Clark and the Corps and said that success of the expedition "is equally due to my dear and interesting friend captain Clark, and to those who were the joint companions of our labours and difficulties in performing that task."

Lewis arrived in Washington on December 28, 1806. "Never did an event excite such joy," Jefferson wrote. Lewis, Sheheke, and company attended the theater and some of the Indians danced for the crowd during the intermission. The self-named Great White Father (President Jefferson) received and entertained Sheheke and the Mandans on New Year's Eve. A large Washington banquet and ball was given in honor of both captains on January 14, 1807, although Clark was still in Virginia courting Julia Hancock and couldn't attend.

All historians know about the reunion of Jefferson and Lewis is that they spread Clark's map on the floor and got down on their hands and knees to look it over and talk about it together. The president was thrilled with the news that the expedition had discovered 179 plant species new to science and 122 animal species and subspecies. And he was delighted with the nine new Indian vocabularies that Lewis had compiled.

Dying Young: Meriwether Lewis

Three years and a month after the expedition's safe return to St. Louis, Meriwether Lewis was dead by his own hand.

Lewis was a red-hot celebrity after the expedition and was honored and celebrated everywhere he went on the east coast — Charlottesville, Washington, and Philadelphia — the year the expedition returned. But for reasons we can only guess, including theories that he was very seriously ill with syphilis, and/or malaria, and/or chronic severe depression, post-expedition life became impossible for him.

Reaping rewards and lobbying for land

In March of 1807, Jefferson sent seeds collected on the expedition to his naturalist friends. "On the whole," Jefferson wrote, "the result confirms me in my opinion that [Lewis] was the fittest person in the world for such an expedition." As a special reward, the president arranged Lewis's election into the American Philosophical Society, a very high honor not usually bestowed on a man of modest education. Jefferson declared Lewis to be "a valuable member of our fraternity [returned] from a journey of uncommon length and peril."

Lewis stayed with the president all winter and lobbied the Secretary of War and Congress for an award of land for each of the men of the expedition (except York), equal compensation with himself for Clark, and extra compensation for Labiche, the Field brothers, John Shields, and Drouillard.

Lewis lobbied Secretary of War Dearborn to give Clark a share equal to his own. But it was Dearborn who'd messed up the captain's commission for Clark in the first place, and he refused to rectify it now. (In fact, it took Clark 195 years to get his commission. In 2001, President Bill Clinton finally promoted Clark to captain.) Dearborn proposed that Lewis receive 1,500 acres, Clark 1,200, and the men 320 each. An appropriations bill introduced in late January in the House of Representatives by Congressman Alston, however, used Lewis's figures and asked for 1,600 acres each for Lewis and Clark, along with double pay ($1,228). The men of the Corps, plus Drouillard and Charbonneau, received double pay, as well, plus 320 acres of land.

The appropriations debate was contentious because the potential cost of the land warrants (which meant that they could buy land in the future) could be very expensive if the men chose the most valuable land in the country. The bill took a month to pass the House, and then passed the same day in the Senate. Lewis's total compensation came to $7,262.

Failing to publish the journals

"The humblest of [U.S.] citizens had taken a lively interest in the issue of this journey, and looked forward with impatience for the information it would furnish," Jefferson wrote in 1807, underscoring the importance of publishing the journals and furnishing the information as soon as possible. Lewis left for Philadelphia at the end of March 1807 to find a publisher.

Hatching a good plan

Lewis had an ambitious plan for an expedition publication in three volumes — Clark's map, a narrative of the day-to-day events, and a separate volume on the scientific findings. The plan required hiring some of the best scientists and artists of the day with the costs for preparing the materials to be split equally between the captains.

He hired botanist Frederick Pursh to draw the plants, portraitist Charles Peale to draw the animals, and painter Saint-Memin to draw the Osage and Mandan delegation now visiting Washington. He advanced mathematician Ferdinand Hassler $100 to do the celestial calculations. The estimated publishing costs — separate from the expenses for art, editor's fees, and marketing — came to $4,500. He also bought Sergeant Ordway's journal for $300 and planned to have it incorporated into the narrative.

Neglecting to follow through

What Lewis didn't do in Philadelphia (or ever) was hire an editor, someone to correct the spelling and grammar and merge his, Clark's, and Ordway's reflections. It was the first step in manuscript preparation, and he failed to take it.

Lewis intended to publish the definitive account of the expedition. But to Lewis's dismay, Patrick Gass published a *prospectus* (a solicitation for advance subscriptions) of a book based on his own journal. At the same time, Robert Frazer also intended to publish and had Lewis' permission to do so. The description of Gass's book was so close to what Lewis planned to publish that Lewis panicked and wrote an open letter to the Washington newspaper to warn people off Gass's unauthorized book and to warn readers that while Frazer had Lewis' permission, he "was only a private" and "entirely unacquainted" with the knowledge needed to write on scientific matters. Gass's publisher answered the letter by publicly calling into question Lewis's right to profit from the government expedition. The Gass book was published in 1807 and sold well. Frazer's book was never published, and his journals were lost.

Lewis announced that he would publish a map of the West and the route of the expedition in the spring of 1807 and then bring out the first of a three-volume account in January of 1808. When neither happened on time and then never happened at all, publishers reprinted Gass's book to meet demand and pieced other books together from Gass's account, Clark's letters, and made-up stories.

By the time the excellent history of the Lewis and Clark expedition was finally edited by Nicholas Biddle and published in 1814, public interest in the expedition had waned, and sales were disappointing.

Drifting, drinking, and descending into madness

On February 29, 1807, President Jefferson appointed Lewis to be governor of the Upper Louisiana Territory, and the Senate ratified the appointment. But Lewis was in no hurry to go to St. Louis and didn't much care what was going on there. The acting governor, Frederick Bates, wrote him increasingly frantic letters about territorial problems and assumed that Lewis would show up any minute to deal with them.

Expected in St. Louis, Lewis stayed in Philadelphia. He drank too much. He worried about publishing the expedition history but made no move to find an editor. From April to August 1807, he worked on a final financial accounting for the expedition. There were 1,989 drafts for expenses totaling $38,722.25.

In July, Lewis left Philadelphia and went home to Locust Hill. In September, he went to Richmond to attend the treason trial of Aaron Burr (former vice president of the United States). Then he went back to Locust Hill and worked on a land deal in the Ohio valley. Money began to come in from subscribers for the expedition publication. Lewis still carried the journals around with him. No one had started to edit them.

Lewis wanted to be married and met many eligible women but remained single. How a tall, decent-looking national hero with property and income failed to find a mate is a mystery. Visiting friends in Virginia, he fell for a young woman named Lettitia Breckenridge, but she left town rather than encourage him. Of course, if Lewis did suffer from syphilis, he may not have married for fear of transmitting an infectious disease to his wife.

Flopping as governor

In March 1808, a year after his appointment, Lewis finally arrived in St. Louis to begin his new job. He took over from the acting governor and territorial secretary, Frederick Bates, who couldn't leave the post fast enough. "The difficulties . . . are numberless," he wrote, "and almost insurmountable."

St. Louis was a frontier town, a place barely under the rule of law. The governor before Lewis had made money by illegally granting trading licenses. A large part of the governor's role was negotiating land titles, soothing wounded egos, settling disputes, and keeping a lid on a place that had very rich and very poor people and few in between. Lewis had neither the temperament for the role nor the patience required.

He aspired to be wealthy himself and began speculating in land. He continued to drink too much and to take opium for various ailments. He rented a house that he planned to share with Clark and his new bride, but that arrangement didn't work out. He moved into rooms at Pierre Chouteau's house and an office to conduct his business.

He asked for troops to put down a rebellion by a band of Osage Indians, and Secretary of War Dearborn refused. Jefferson wrote him to ask about the journal publication. Lewis didn't answer him.

Making mistakes

Lewis was a man on the make with no experience in business. In the second half of 1808, one of Lewis's responsibilities was to arrange for the safe return of the Mandan leader Sheheke to his people. One attempt had already failed. Lewis and his friends Clark, Manuel Lisa, and the Chouteau brothers formed the St. Louis Missouri River Fur Company to take Sheheke back (at government expense) and then go on to the Yellowstone River where the company would trap under an exclusive license awarded by Lewis, a silent partner. The plan was a clear conflict of interest. In order to further his own and his friends' business, Lewis used government money as well as the authority of his office to grant licenses.

Lewis made other mistakes. He sent men to capture some Sauk and Fox Indians who had allegedly murdered some whites, and he publicly declared that the Indians would be hanged after their trial (but they weren't). Jefferson, alarmed, wrote a letter advising Lewis that arresting them had been a bad idea and hanging them was out of the question. You could not hang Indians for murder, Jefferson said, because "our juries have never yet convicted the murderer of an Indian."

Lewis dismissed territorial officials and made them enemies. The territorial secretary, Frederick Bates, was for settlement of the territory but Lewis wanted to develop the fur trade and keep settlers out. Bates had resented Lewis, his tardiness, and his closeness to the president from the beginning. When Jefferson left office and James Madison became president, Bates began working behind the scenes against Lewis with the new administration. The contract giving his friends monopoly fur trade rights on the Yellowstone made Lewis unpopular and gave Bates a chance to complain about him to Washington. By April of 1809, Lewis and Bates had a complete falling out and were not speaking to each other.

Sinking into debt

The new Secretary of War, William Eustis, wrote to Lewis in August and very reluctantly approved his contract with the St. Louis Fur Company and its plans for Sheheke. But they refused to pay some of his vouchers (claims for reimbursement of expenses), which implied that they thought the expenditures were either a mistake in judgment or a fraud. The largest of the claims was $500 for an advance paid to the St. Louis Missouri Fur Company to buy gifts for Indians who might try to stop the Mandan leader Sheheke from going home to his Mandan village. The gifts had already been purchased, so Lewis was forced to cover the debt personally.

When word leaked out that Lewis's drafts were being refused by the government, all of his creditors began showing up at his door clamoring for their money immediately. Angry and humiliated, Lewis spent the next three weeks, with Clark's help, trying to clear up his debts. He gave back land that he'd bought on credit and sent the land warrant he'd received as a reward for the expedition to New Orleans to sell. But he couldn't raise cash as fast as he needed it in order to satisfy his hectoring creditors. Clark wrote to his brother declaring that Lewis "is ruined."

Dying hard

Lewis had taken a blow to his finances and to his honor, but his sanity was also a casualty. Lewis decided that he and Clark must go to Washington in person to explain the legitimacy of Lewis's vouchers and get the Secretary of War to reverse his decision and reimburse Lewis for his expenses. Lewis packed up his belongings and the journals, borrowed money to buy opium and some other drugs for the journey, and left St. Louis on September 3, 1809. Lewis was traveling by boat, while Clark went overland.

Becoming deranged

On the boat from St. Louis to Fort Pickering, near today's Memphis, Tennessee, Lewis drank heavily and took leave of his senses. He wrote his will on September 11, leaving everything to his mother, and then tried to kill himself twice (the crew of the boat reported afterward). When Lewis arrived at Fort Pickering, the commanding officer said that he was drunk and in "a state of mental derangement." (Advanced syphilis, a fatal venereal disease, results in the symptoms Lewis was displaying when an inflammation in the brain leads to complete mental impairment.)

The commander took the liquor away from Lewis and detained him at the Fort to force a recovery. For five days, Lewis showed no improvement and was kept under a suicide watch. To pass the time, Lewis wrote President Madison a largely incoherent letter. On the sixth and seventh day, Lewis seemed better and vowed to stop drinking. Borrowing $100 and buying two horses on credit from the commander, Lewis left on horseback over the Natchez Trace with James Neely (an Indian agent), Neely's servant, and Lewis's servant, John Pernia. Neely dropped behind to hunt for stray horses while Lewis rode on to a traveler's rest cabin called Grinder's Stand, arriving at sunset on October 10, 1809.

Surrendering to despair

Discovering Lewis "to be deranged," Mrs. Grinder tried to feed Lewis dinner, gave up the main cabin to him, and went to sleep in the kitchen. The servants slept in the stable. Mrs. Grinder reported that at about 3 a.m. she heard two pistol shots in Lewis's cabin.

In a letter to Jefferson, James Neely wrote that Lewis "had shot himself in the head with one pistol and below the breast with the other — when his servant came in he says; I have done the business my good servant give me some water." Lewis stumbled out of the cabin, and then stumbled back in and collapsed. Mrs. Grinder said that later as Lewis lay dying he begged the servants "to take his rifle and blow out his brains, and he would give them all the money he had in his trunk." Some of Lewis's last words were reportedly, "I am no coward; but I am so strong, [it is] so hard to die."

When Clark heard the news, he cried, "I fear O! I fear the weight of his mind has overcome him."

Meriwether Lewis was dead at the age of 35. He had survived a fall from a bluff, hunger, thirst, fevers, extremes of heat and cold, malaria, bear attacks, Teton Sioux deprecations, backbreaking portages, a skirmish with the Blackfeet, and a gunshot wound to his backside. He led men past their own endurance and lived life full to its edges, but for reasons we do not understand, he could not outlive his own despair.

The case for a diagnosis of advanced syphilis has been made in recent years by Dr. Reimert Ravenholt, an expert in infectious diseases. It would explain Lewis's behavior, especially the suicide. But it can't be proven without exhuming the body. Others who believe Lewis's death was murder have pushed for exhumation. In either case, it's unlikely to happen.

Lewis was buried in Hohenwald, Tennessee, near Grinder's Stand. The inscription is adapted from Thomas Jefferson's eulogy for Lewis: "His courage was undaunted; his firmness and perseverance yielded to nothing but impossibilities."

Living Long: William Clark

After the expedition, Clark accompanied Lewis back east as far as Louisville, where he stopped to visit his family before moving on to Fincastle, Virginia, to ask the 16-year-old Julia (also known as Judith) Hancock to marry him. He turned up in Washington after the formal celebration of the expedition's return. Having failed in an attempt to appoint Clark a lieutenant colonel in the

Army (the Senate had to agree to the military promotion, and it felt he lacked seniority), Jefferson appointed him Superintendent of Indian Affairs for the Louisiana Territory with the rank of Brigadier General of the militia.

Clark returned to St. Louis to begin his new job and distribute land warrants and money to the men of the Corps. He married Julia Hancock in January of 1808. They eventually had five children, naming their eldest son Meriwether Lewis Clark.

Serving as Indian agent

As Superintendent of Indian Affairs, Clark succeeded in reducing the number of unscrupulous traders who were cheating Indians, but he was also part of a not-so-scrupulous scheme in 1808 to form a fur trading company with his friends Manuel Lisa and the Chouteau brothers. They used Lewis's authority as governor to assign the new company an exclusive license for furs trapped on the Yellowstone River.

Clark seemed to many an ideal man to be the territorial Indian agent. Clark liked Indians and felt protective of them, even fatherly. He believed in the mission Jefferson had given the expedition concerning Indians and the Great White Father speeches he and Lewis gave to the Indians again and again.

On the last leg of the expedition, Clark wrote "we have been to the great lake of the west and are now on our return to our country. I have seen all my red children quite to that great lake and talked with them, and taken them by the hand in the name of their great father the Great Chief of all the white people."

Clark had made a lot of friends on the expedition, and that would help him in his work of keeping the tribes under control. Many Indians liked and trusted Clark and believed that he was their advocate even when, as the government's Indian agent, he carried out harsh Indian policies that were not in their interest. He'd gained a reputation among tribes on the expedition as a good person and a compassionate doctor. It helped Clark get the treaties and other concessions the government wanted from the tribes and to become well-regarded by his own culture as an Indian agent.

Clark forced a treaty on the Osage in 1808 that ceded almost all of Missouri, millions of acres, for $1,400 in gifts, a $1,800 annual payment, some farm tools, and use of a blacksmith and grist mill. Clark regretted the shamefully inadequate terms later, saying that if he was "damned thereafter, it would be for making that treaty."

In September, 1809, despite Clark's efforts to help him cope with his debts and his depressions, Lewis committed suicide, and Clark lost his best friend. Clark called it a "turble Stroke to me, in every respect."

Publishing the journals

Clark went to Washington in December after Lewis's death to commiserate with Jefferson at Monticello and talk to him about getting the journals published. In Philadelphia, he found the perfect editor, Nicholas Biddle, a young, well-educated man with time on his hands.

They brought out the *History of the Expedition Under the Command of Captains Lewis and Clark* in 1814, publishing 1,417 copies for $6 apiece. But interest in the expedition had peaked years earlier, and the publication sold slowly.

Policing the tribes

During the War of 1812, Clark persuaded the Lower Missouri River tribes not to take the British side and led a military campaign to the upper Mississippi to fight the British and the eastern tribes. The Osage he'd wronged in an 1808 treaty volunteered 500 warriors for the campaign.

In 1813, President Madison appointed Clark to be governor of the newly formed Missouri Territory. His job had three responsibilities:

- ✔ Strengthening the territory's defenses against hostile Indians
- ✔ Maintaining diplomatic relations with the tribes of the Missouri and upper Mississippi
- ✔ Preparing the territory for statehood

In the decade after the Lewis and Clark expedition, Missouri River tribes became alarmed by wave after wave of trappers, adventurers, and settlers passing through their territories. By 1814, to stop encroachment on their land, Indians were attacking whites on the frontier.

In 1815, to stop the violence against whites in the territory, Clark and other federal officials met 46 leaders at Portage des Sioux at the junction of the Mississippi and Missouri Rivers. It was a meeting orchestrated to show off federal power and persuade tribes to sign treaties relinquishing some of their lands and rights. Many of them did. Black Hawk, leader of the Sauk and one of the prime disturbers of the peace in Clark's view, failed to show up for this Grand Council.

The Sauk leader's absence infuriated Clark, who announced that either Black Hawk would come in to sign the treaty or "blood would be spilt for their disobedience." Thirteen of the Grand Council tribes signed treaties with the United States giving up land in exchange for the promise of U.S. protection in holding onto their remaining land. The 13 tribes split $30,000 in gifts and whiskey.

As a result of these treaties, settlers swept across the Mississippi River in droves, putting more pressure on tribes, creating the need for additional treaties, and leading to the removal of the tribes from their remaining land. Not realizing that he was ratifying terms he'd rejected for ten years, Black Hawk came to St. Louis as Clark demanded and signed the treaty, giving up millions of acres along the Upper Mississippi for $2,234.50.

Losing a race for governor

William Clark was reappointed twice to serve as governor of the Missouri Territory. The post became an elective office in 1820 (because of Missouri's impending statehood) and Clark ran for the job and lost. Several factors contributed to his defeat:

- ✔ During the race, his wife, Julia, died, and mourning kept him from campaigning.

- ✔ He was opposed by businessmen who wanted to abolish the *factory system,* a chain of government trading posts, and replace them with privately-owned posts.

- ✔ He was opposed by people who thought him to be soft on Indians.

- ✔ Euro-American settlers thought he was too close to "French" families, like the Chouteaus.

Embracing the policy of removal

After the defeat for governor of the Missouri Territory, Clark married Harriet Kennerly Radford and returned to the post of Superintendent of Indian Affairs at St. Louis. By 1822, he agreed with Jefferson's philosophy that the only way to save tribes from complete destruction was to move them beyond the limits of the United States and its territories, "where they could rest in peace and in perpetuity reside on the lands. . . ." Maybe Clark actually believed that this strategy would work, but the policy left tribes bereft in body and spirit. Clark oversaw treaties with the Shawnee, Potawatomi, Kickapoo, Sauk, Fox, Delaware, and Chickasaw that gave up hundreds of millions of acres in Ohio, Illinois, Missouri, and Arkansas and forced the Indians to move west of Missouri.

Clark did try to get some financial assistance for tribes removed to the West, but was generally unsuccessful. Cut off from their traditional sources of food, water, trade, and ceremony, tribes removed from their homelands found no rest and no peace. New Indian policies, equally damaging, would keep them down for the next 150 years.

After his second wife died in 1831, Clark's health began to fail, and he moved into his son Meriwether's home, where he died in 1838 at the age of 68.

Having led the most important expedition in U.S. history and having spent 30 years in government service, Clark came to be a widely known and admired as a peacemaker. He had done what the government asked — get the tribes out of the way of U.S. growth — and done his part thoroughly. His funeral was the largest ever held up to that time in St. Louis.

Expecting Freedom: York

York, Clark's slave, tasted almost three years of freedom and celebrity on the expedition. The celebrity continued when the expedition returned to St. Louis. One observer said, "Even the negro York, who was the body servant of Clark, despite his ebony complexion, was looked upon with decided partiality, and received his share of adulation."

York couldn't adjust to being Clark's slave again. After the expedition, York married a slave in Louisville while Clark was visiting there. In 1808, York asked for his freedom to go live with his wife. Clark refused. York asked Clark to let him go to Louisville to live near his wife. Clark said York could go for a visit only.

When Clark said the visit was up, York resisted coming back. He asked to hire himself out and send Clark the money. Clark said no again, and angrily wrote his brother Jonathan to send York back and that if York should "refuse to proform his duty as a Slave" or runs off, he should be sent to New Orleans to be sold, "or hired out to Some Sevare Master untill he thinks better of Such conduct. . . ."

Refusing to take no for an answer

York no longer understood "no" for an answer. Clark wrote to Jonathan and declared, "I do wish to do well by him, but as he has got Such a notion about freedom and his emence Services [on the expedition], that I do not expect he will be of much Service to me again." Clark hired York out (to another slave-holder) as punishment, hoping that he'd get a "Severe" master, "give over that wife of his," and come back to St. Louis.

York returned against his will to St. Louis in May of 1809. York brought home a horse, Clark wrote, but he was "very little Service to me, insolent and sukly, I gave him a Severe trouncing (beating) the other Day and he has much mended."

About ten years after the expedition, York wore Clark down, and Clark gave York his freedom. Clark told the writer Washington Irving in 1832 that he'd given York a wagon and six horses so he could enter the freight business between Nashville and Richmond. (The law at the time required that any slave who was freed had to be given the means to make a living.) Clark told

Irving that all of his slaves had failed as free men and wanted to come back to him, including York.

There's no proof about that assertion one way or the other, but it's true that freed slaves who fared poorly and asked to come back helped relieve their former owners of any guilt that they had about the immorality of slavery. It's also true that free blacks had to compete with slaves and immigrants in a crowded pool of cheap labor. They often lost to the competition. It's believed York died of cholera by 1832, while living as a free man in Tennessee.

Considering a happier fate for York

Some historical records suggest another, happier version of York's fate. In 1832, a trapper named Zenas Leonard said that he met a black warrior leader in the Crow tribe who claimed that he had first come to Crow country with the Lewis and Clark expedition and had returned with a trader in 1822 or 1824. Leonard reported that the black man spoke the language fluently, understood Crow traditions, was treated like a leader, and had four wives. Two years later, Leonard wrote that the black man was still with the Crow and enjoyed a high status.

This version of York's life, no matter how unlikely, is the one we can only hope was right.

Becoming a Legend in Three Cultures: Sacagawea

Sacagawea did almost everything that the men of the expedition did, only she did it carrying and caring for an infant child.

For a long time, popular history made Sacagawea the girl guide of the expedition, and on the return journey, she did show Clark the Hidatsas' route through Shoshone country, where Clark called her his "pilot." But today, she is acknowledged as having been an interpreter, not a guide, and she's also credited as being a key symbol to the tribes they encountered, a sign that the expedition came in peace.

Sacagawea is claimed and embraced by three cultures:

- ✔ The culture of her birth: Shoshone
- ✔ The culture she adopted after her capture: Hidatsa
- ✔ The culture whose expedition she joined: American

In 2000, she was chosen as the face of a golden dollar coin (see Figure 18-1), often called the *Sacagawea Dollar*. Demand for the coin has been high; in fact, people preferring to keep or collect the Sacagawea coin have created a challenge for the U.S. Mint in keeping the coin in circulation.

Figure 18-1:
The
Sacagawea
Dollar.

Courtesy of Ron Guth.

In addition, more statues have been erected in her memory than any other American woman. Figure 18-2 shows one such statue.

Lewis and Clark called her "squar" (squaw) at first, meaning that she was a person of so little consequence, they didn't even bother learning her name. But after the two captains helped her deliver her baby and Sacagawea had became a valuable member of the expedition, Clark affectionately called her "Janey" and watched out for her and her "little dancing boy," whom he nicknamed "Pomp" or "Pompy."

So little is known about Sacagawea that celebrating her as an icon or legend has been easier than writing her biography. Evidence suggests, however, that she lived only six years after the expedition, dying at Fort Manuel where her husband was working for the Missouri Fur Company, just six months after giving birth to her daughter, Lisette. She was only 25.

Early in the 20th century, a librarian at the University of Wyoming put forward the theory that Sacagawea had not died in 1812 but had come home to the Shoshones and the Wind River Indian Reservation in Wyoming, living until 1884 to the age of 100. The woman was called "Sacajawea," Shoshone for "boat launcher." Research from census records and her death certificate list her name as "Bazil's Mother," born in 1784, making her 21 years old in 1805, too old to have been the girl on the expedition.

Figure 18-2:
Statue of
Sacagawea.

C1110 Sakakawea statue in sculptor's studio.
Courtesy of the State Historical Society of North Dakota.

Traveling Happy: Jean Baptiste (Pompy)

Jean Baptiste, the son of Sacagawea and Toussaint Charbonneau, was 55 days old when the expedition left the Mandan villages, and he was a toddler when the expedition returned to the Mandan and Hidatsa villages. He'd been called "Pomp" and "Pompy" by the men and indulged by Clark, who adored him and wanted to take him and raise him as his own child. But Pomp wasn't weaned, so Clark left him with his parents, hoping that Charbonneau would bring the boy to St. Louis the next spring.

Clark didn't get his wish for Jean Baptiste until 1809, when Charbonneau brought Sacagawea and Jean Baptiste to St. Louis to pick up the 320-acre land warrant that Charbonneau had earned for services to the expedition. Clark offered to give the family land and set them up on a farm, but Charbonneau didn't want to farm. He traded Clark the land warrant for $100, and he and Sacagawea returned to upper Missouri country, leaving Jean Baptiste with

Clark, who eventually adopted him. When Sacagawea died at Fort Manuel in 1812, six months after giving birth to a girl, Lisette, Charbonneau brought the infant to Clark, and he adopted her, as well.

The details of Jean Baptiste's life are sketchy but historians do know the outline. He left St. Louis at age 18 to live as a trader at the mouth of the Kansas River. A duke, Paul Wilhelm of Wuerttemberg, visited the area on a scientific expedition and offered to sponsor Jean Baptiste in Europe, where he lived at the Wuerttemberg court for six years, learning to speak four languages fluently and becoming one sophisticated frontiersman.

Back in the United States in 1829, he became a mountain man, known for reciting Shakespeare around the campfire. He served as a U.S. troop guide in the Mexican-American War, worked with mountain man/soldier/Indian scout Kit Carson, and was a guide for explorer John C. Fremont. He became a magistrate in San Luis Rey Mission, California, and then joined the California gold rush in the1850s. In 1866, at the age of 61, he left California in a wagon train for a Montana gold rush and died en route. He is buried in Danner, Oregon, where a monument marks his grave.

Surprising Outcomes: Men of the Corps

William Clark kept track of a number of the men (or they kept track of him) and from 1825 to 1828, he compiled a "List of Men on Lewis and Clark's Trip" listing the whereabouts of as many of the men as he could. About a third of the men of the Corps disappeared from any record, so historians don't know what happened to them. Another third settled on the frontier in Missouri, Illinois, and Indiana; the rest returned to the West to become fur trappers and traders.

Tracing the nine other young men from Kentucky

Clark kept track of most of the men that he personally had chosen for the expedition — the Ten Young Men from around the Louisville, Kentucky, area. In this section, we share what we know about the fate of nine of those early recruits; the tenth is covered in the "Expecting Freedom: York" section.

✔ **William Bratton:** Private William Bratton was a blacksmith and hunter on the expedition and is mentioned in the journals many times: once for shooting but not killing a bear that proceeded to chase him, and once when he was cured from severe back pain by an Indian sweat treatment. Clark named a creek after him — Bratton's Creek — in July of 1806. After the expedition, Bratton moved to Kentucky and fought in the War of 1812. Thirteen years after the expedition, he married. Three years later, he moved to Indiana, where he held several public offices. He died in 1841 at the age of 63.

✔ **John Colter:** Private John Colter left the expedition when it reached the Mandan villages on the return trip in 1806. He joined some fur traders on their way west. Two years later, he and John Potts, another expedition veteran, were trapping on the Jefferson River in Montana when they were attacked by Blackfeet Indians. Colter was stripped of his clothes and shoes and given a running head start in front of the warriors before they tried to kill him. Colter ran for miles through prickly cactus and somehow managed to elude all the warriors but one, whom he killed. He reached the Madison River, where he hid under some driftwood until dark. He hiked 200 miles for the next 11 days (naked and shoeless) to the junction of the Yellowstone and Bighorn rivers and a fur trading post.

While running from the Blackfeet, John Colter stumbled into a land of geysers, boiling mud, and hot water rivers. Later, when he recounted the story and described the geography, people thought he was loopy. They called his tales *Colter's Hell,* although his story was later verified. Congress decided to designate the area as the very first national park in the United States in 1872. They called it Yellowstone National Park (see Figure 18-3).

Figure 18-3:
Colter's Hell, today known as Yellowstone National Park.

05755 Steamboat Geyser.
Photo provided by the National Park Service.

✔ **Joseph and Reuben Field:** The Field brothers (Joseph and Reuben), both privates, were excellent marksmen and hunters and consequently very valuable to the captains and the Corps. There are over 220 references to them in the journals, including the brothers' involvement with Lewis in the skirmish with some Blackfeet Indians, during which two Indians were killed. How Reuben Field died is unknown, but Clark writes that Joseph Field was killed in 1807, a year after the expedition concluded. Reuben, on the other hand, settled in Kentucky, married in 1808, and died in 1823 at the age of 52.

✔ **Charles Floyd:** Charles Floyd was the sergeant who didn't make it home, the only man of the Corps who was lost. He died at age 22, probably from a ruptured appendix, and was buried on a hill near the Missouri River at today's Sioux City, Iowa. A river in Iowa — Floyd River — bears his name.

✔ **George Gibson:** Private George Gibson was an expert marksman and hunter, played the fiddle, and managed one of the *pirogues* (canoe-like boats). Late in the expedition in 1806, Gibson was incapacitated by a tree snag that pierced his thigh two inches deep. Clark named the creek where it happened "Thy [thigh] Snag'd Creek." No one knows how he died two years after returning with the expedition, only that it happened in St. Louis.

✔ **Nathaniel Pryor:** The words of the journals suggest that Sergeant Nathaniel Pryor was "a man of character and ability" — he could do just about anything required of him. After the expedition, in September of 1807, Pryor led an unsuccessful attempt to return Mandan leader Shekeke to his people. Lewis and Clark helped him secure an Army commission as an officer, which he kept until 1810. He became a trader on the Mississippi River in the northern Illinois territory, and then served in the Army again from 1813 to 1815, fighting in the Battle of New Orleans. He settled down with an Osage wife and lived with her people for 16 years as a trader, dying in 1831 at the age of 59. The towns of Pryor, Oklahoma, and Pryor, Montana, are named after him, as are the Pryor Mountains in Montana.

✔ **George Shannon:** Private George Shannon joined the expedition in 1803. He was 18 years old and the youngest man to enlist in the Corps. He was a hunter for the expedition, but he nearly starved to death when he was separated from the expedition in South Dakota in August of 1804 for 16 days. A river near the site where they finally found him was named Shannon's River. While accompanying Nathaniel Pryor on the unsuccessful trip to return leader Sheheke to his Mandan village in 1807, Shannon was injured in an attack by the Arikaras (who were at war with the Mandans), and his leg had to be amputated. Congress awarded him a disability pension.

In 1810, at Clark's request, Shannon helped Nicolas Biddle prepare a history of the expedition, and then Shannon studied law and practiced in Lexington, Kentucky. Shannon became active in politics, first in

Kentucky and then in Missouri, serving as a senator and a U.S. attorney. He died in 1836 at the age of 51 in Palmyra, Missouri.

✔ **John Shields:** Private John Shields was a blacksmith, gunsmith, carpenter, and hunter for the expedition. Shields had so many useful skills that he was a married man allowed to join the expedition, which had a no-married-men rule. Clark's brother, George Rogers Clark, may have helped Mrs. Shields financially while he was gone. Trying to get him some extra money after the expedition, Lewis wrote, "Nothing was more peculiarly useful to us, in various situations, than the skill and ingenuity of this man as an artist, in repairing our guns, accoutrements, etc. . . ." The Shields River in Montana still bears his name. Shields spent time with an apparent relative of his, the renowned Daniel Boone, as a trapper in Missouri in the year after the expedition. Shields settled near Corydon, Indiana, where he died in 1809 at the age of 40.

Discovering more on the Corps

From Clark's notes and other records, historians know a little bit about the post-expedition lives of some of the other explorers on the journey. This section provides the rest of the story on these men, including the less-than-noble Toussaint Charbonneau and the super-competent George Drouillard.

✔ **Toussaint Charbonneau:** At approximately 46 years old, Toussaint Charbonneau was the oldest person on the expedition. He was a French Canadian trader living with the Hidatsa when the expedition arrived at the Mandan and Hidatsa villages in 1804. Lewis didn't think much of him, and Clark also had his doubts about his character. But the Corps needed an interpreter, so he was hired and allowed to bring one of his wives, Sacagawea, a Shoshone teenager.

After the expedition, Charbonneau lived with the Hidatsas until Sacagawea died in 1812, and then worked for Manuel Lisa, the St. Louis trader. He also worked off and on for Clark as an interpreter from 1813 to 1838. He was at Fort Clark in 1833 when the German Prince Maximilian and painter Karl Bodmer arrived to visit the Mandan and Hidatsa tribes. He may have lived until 1843 to the age of 85.

✔ **George Drouillard:** George Drouillard was the expedition's premier hunter and Lewis's favorite among the men. French-Canadian and Shawnee, he was also Lewis's main interpreter. He was highly skilled at sign language and spoke a couple of Indian languages, as well as English and French. He was with Lewis and Reuben Field when they killed two Piegan Blackfeet boys who were trying to take Drouillard's rifle on the return trip. Lewis tried but failed to get Drouillard extra pay for his "ardor which deserves the highest accommodation."

In late 1807, Drouillard was hired by St. Louis merchant Manuel Lisa to retrieve a deserter, dead or alive, from a private fur-trading expedition. Drouillard brought in the deserter dead and was charged with murder, and then acquitted at trial. Working for Lisa, Drouillard returned to the Three Forks region of the Missouri River in 1810 and was killed and scalped by the Blackfeet (some believe in revenge for the killing of their two young men).

✔ **Robert Frazer:** Private Robert Frazer kept a journal on the expedition and found someone to publish it soon after the expedition returned to St. Louis. Frazer published a prospectus and secured Lewis' endorsement but it carried a warning that Frazer was not qualified to talk about the scientific aspects of the expedition. The publication never came out, and Frazer's journal has been lost. Frazer died in Franklin County, Missouri, in 1837.

✔ **Patrick Gass:** Sergeant Patrick Gass remained in the Army and became a career soldier. He lost an eye in the War of 1812, and Congress gave him a pension. He was the first member of the expedition to publish his account of the journey, a book that sold well for several years. He eventually settled down in West Virginia, marrying a 20-year-old when he was 60 and then fathering six children. Of all the Corps, he lived to be the oldest. At 90, he volunteered for the Union in the Civil War, although he was not accepted for service. He died in 1870 at the age of 98.

✔ **Francois Labiche:** Private Francois Labiche joined the expedition as an experienced boatman, trader, and interpreter. After the expedition returned to St. Louis, he and Sergeant Ordway were put in charge of the pack train bound for Washington loaded with plants, seeds, bird skins, animal skeletons, furs, and whatever else had been collected according to Thomas Jefferson's instructions. The entourage also included Lewis and Clark, as well as Mandan and Osage Indian parties. Labiche returned to St. Louis and settled there.

✔ **John Newman:** Private John Newman headed back upstream and became a Missouri River trapper. He was killed by the Yankton Sioux in 1838.

✔ **John Ordway:** Sergeant John Ordway went to Washington D.C. with Lewis and Sheheke in 1806, and then visited his folks in New Hampshire before settling down on his 320 acres in Missouri. Clark noted in 1825 that Ordway was dead by 1817. The journal of Sergeant Ordway, edited by Gary Moulton, was published along with the journal of Charles Floyd in 1996 as Volume 9 of *The Journals of the Lewis and Clark Expedition* (see Chapter 21).

✔ **John Potts:** Private John Potts returned to the West as soon as he could, joining John Colter as a fur trapper. He was killed by the Blackfeet in 1808 at Three Forks. (See the "Tracing the nine young men from Kentucky" section for details.) Colter miraculously escaped death in the same incident.

✔ **Peter M. Weiser:** Private Peter Weiser became a fur trader for St. Louis businessman Manuel Lisa on the Yellowstone and Missouri Rivers. He may have been killed at Three Forks by the Blackfeet in 1810.

✔ **Joseph Whitehouse:** Private Joseph Whitehouse was the expedition tailor. He was arrested in 1807 for unpaid debts, and then rejoined the Army. He fought in the War of 1812 and deserted from the Army in 1817. Part of Joseph Whitehouse's journal was published in 1905.

✔ **Alexander Willard:** Private Alexander Willard was a blacksmith and plied that trade after the expedition, working for the government assigned to the Sauk and Fox Indians, and then later the Delaware and Shawnee tribes. He and his wife and 12 children emigrated to California during the 1852 Gold Rush. Willard died in 1865 near Sacramento at a ripe old age.

Breaking Promises to the American Indians

Lewis and Clark gave designated tribal leaders peace medals depicting the hand of an American Indian shaking the hand of an American, symbolizing "the hand of unalterable friendship, which will never be withdrawn from your nation." (See Chapter 8 for a photo of the medal.) It was the first of many false promises made to tribes by representatives of the federal government.

"Believe us," Lewis told the tribes, "and take our advice and you will have nothing to fear, because the great Spirit will smile upon your nation and in future ages will make you to outnumber the trees of the forest."

"Commerce is the great engine by which we are to coerce [tribes]," Jefferson wrote, "not war."

This section describes what happened to a few of the tribes in the aftermath of the expedition.

✔ **Otoe-Missouria Tribe:** Lewis and Clark had their first Indian council with the Otoe. At the time of the expedition, the Otoe and Missouria occupied much of the territory at the junction of the Missouri and Platte Rivers. Beginning in 1830 (during Clark's tenure as Indian agent), they signed a series of treaties ceding most of their lands.

A treaty signed in 1854 ceded all their land along the Missouri and Platte Rivers and created a ten-square-mile reservation near the Kansas-Nebraska line. In 1881, the Otoe and Missouria were forced to move from their homelands to what was then called Indian Territory and is now known as Oklahoma.

✔ **Great Sioux Nation:** Before and for some time after the expedition, the Teton Sioux dominated the northern Plains. Wholesale slaughter of the buffalo by Euro-Americans eventually destroyed their economy and way of life. The federal government promised to keep whites out of their territory established by treaty in 1868 as the Great Sioux reservation, which encompassed most of South Dakota, including the Black Hills. When prospectors accompanying General George Armstrong Custer and the 7th Cavalry said they had discovered gold in the Black Hills, non-Indians flocked to the area, setting up a conflict including Custer's defeat at Little Big Horn and splitting up of the Great Sioux reservation into six much smaller reservations.

✔ **Mandan, Hidatsa, and Arikara Nations:** The Corps of Discovery spent their first winter with the Mandans and Hidatsas, enjoying their friendship and hospitality. Yet nine out of ten Mandans and Hidatsas were dead by 1837 of smallpox. Smallpox also felled many Arikaras. The Fort Laramie Treaty of 1851 established a reservation for the three tribes of 12 million acres (Fort Berthold in North Dakota), which was gradually reduced by federal policy to one million acres.

In 1954, the U.S. Army Corps of Engineers constructed the Garrison Dam, creating Lake Sakakawea and flooding several hundred thousand acres of the reservation, including farms, ranches, and long-established communities. The project separated families and friends across miles of water. The tribes eventually received $12 million in compensation for losses created by the dam, which amount to less than $5 an acre.

✔ **Shoshone Tribe:** The Shoshones saved the expedition by providing horses, a guide, and women to carry baggage over the Bitterroot Mountains. Under the terms of the Fort Bridger Treaty of 1868, the Shoshones were assigned to the Fort Hall Reservation in Idaho along with the Bannock tribe, their traditional rivals. As the result of a surveying error (a fairly common occurrence in the assessment of Indian land), the reservation was reduced from 1.8 to 1.2 million acres in 1872. The tribes were also forced to cede 420,000 areas in and around the city of Pocatello when the railroad began to stop there and created a large settlement of non-Indians.

✔ **Confederated Tribes of Salish, Kootenai and Pend d'Oreille:** The Salish offered horses and hospitality to the expedition at Ross's Hole. A confederation of tribes led by the Salish signed the 1855 Hellgate Treaty, ceding about 20 million acres and retaining 1.3 million acres for a homeland. They lost over half of the remaining land to non-Indians as a result of federal government policies, but by the 1990s had reversed the trend by buying back the land.

✔ **Nez Perce Tribe:** The Nez Perce Tribe gave the starving Corps of Discovery food and shelter and helped them build canoes for the trip down the Columbia River. The treaty of June 11, 1855, established a Nez Perce reservation of 7.5 million acres. But when gold was discovered on the Nez Perce land in 1863, the United States reduced the size of the reservation to 750,000 acres. Nez Perce bands who refused to sign the treaty, about 700 people (200 warriors) led by their leader, Joseph, were chased by the Army for over three months. The small band fought off 2,000 U.S. soldiers and Indian auxiliaries in four major battles and numerous skirmishes. Surrendering in 1877, Joseph and other Nez Perce (including a red-haired elder said to be the son of William Clark), were exiled to Oklahoma and not allowed to go home until 1885.

✔ **Chinook Tribe:** The playful Chinooks helped and harassed the expedition while the group was in the Columbia River valley in 1805. In the fur trade period after the expedition, the Chinooks were reduced by smallpox and other diseases and were assigned no land by the federal government during the treaty and relocation period. Chinooks are scattered throughout several reservations in the Pacific Northwest and number about 2,000. The tribe has its own government and one acre of land donated by a member. The Chinooks have struggled for years to get federal recognition as a tribe, succeeding in 2001 only to have it taken away again in 2002.

✔ **Blackfeet Nation:** Lewis and a small party that included Drouillard and the Field brothers explored into Blackfeet country and had a tragic skirmish with some Blackfeet youths who tried to take the explorers' rifles and horses. Lewis and Reuben Field killed two of them. The Blackfeet's health and prosperity were diminished along with the buffalo's during the 19th century. Their territory included most of northern Montana east of the Rockies until a series of treaties beginning in 1855 forced them to cede their lands to the United States. The last treaty in 1896 ceded land that later became Glacier National Park.

Altering the Land and Rivers

Since Lewis and Clark opened the road for settlement of the West, the United States has tried to make the West habitable for more people than it can sustain without some intervention; to grow crops that aren't ordinarily compatible with the climate; and to satisfy a desire for cheap electricity, land, water, transportation, food, and other commodities. To meet these demands, people have altered the land and the rivers, sometimes benignly; other times with dire consequences.

Stripping the land and damming the rivers

The fate of the Great Plains was more dependent on the buffalo than people understood when they plowed the land for farming and replaced the 50 million buffalo with 45 million cows.

No other *biome* (ecosystem) on the North American continent has suffered as much loss of diversity, topsoil, and groundwater as the Great Plains. At the time of the expedition, there were over 250 types of grass on the tallgrass prairie, which were oceans of undulating tallgrass. The Great Plains has been reduced to one percent of its former acreage of grass.

In addition, 21 dams have been constructed on the rivers Lewis and Clark depended on to reach the Pacific Ocean. Fourteen dams for power-generation and flood control block the Upper Missouri River. Four dams block the Snake River, and three dams block the Columbia River. Millions of acres of land were inundated when the dams were completed and are now underwater.

One-third of the Missouri River has been transformed into lake environments, due to the six dams built in Montana, North Dakota, South Dakota, and Nebraska. These changes have lowered populations for many river fish and bird species.

Some of the Great Falls of the Missouri River are greatly reduced today because of a hydropower dam. (And the falls are nothing like what Lewis and Clark saw!) Celilo Falls, the location of an ancient tribal fishing and trade center, was similarly diminished by a hydropower dam on the Columbia River.

Salmon in its many variations, the lifeblood of the Columbia River tribes, is endangered primarily as a result of damming of the system rivers. Once 16 million salmon fought their way up the Columbia River system from the ocean to spawn. By 1990, only 257,000 remained to fight their way past the dams. Some subspecies are extinct. Of those that are protected by federal law, 21 are threatened and 5 are endangered.

Threatening plant and animal life

Some of the most charismatic of the animal species that Lewis and Clark recorded as new to science — the buffalo, prairie dog, grizzly bear, whooping crane, gray wolf, sea otter, bighorn sheep, and woodland caribou — were rescued from extinction (or a rescue attempt was begun) in the 20th century.

Three magnificent tree species abundant in Lewis's and Clark's time, the western red cedar, whitebark pine, and Eastern cottonwood, are linchpins in the survival of a number of animal, bird, and fish species. They have been decimated by logging (cedar and pine) and damming rivers (cottonwood).

When the expedition met the Chinookan tribes in the Columbia River valley and on the Pacific coast, the tribes used western red cedar for everything — bowls, bedding, clothing, canoes, and totem poles. Bears made dens in its trunks, and two species of elk depended upon on it for food. A few stands of western red cedar are left and protected in the Pacific Northwest.

Whitebark pine trees have declined 50 percent since 1900 and take 100 years to reach maturity and produce pinecones. Cottonwoods supplied shade, shelter, and transportation to the expedition; they require high springtime water to replenish their roots, so attempts are being made to bring them back on stretches of the rivers where water rises, despite manmade water controls.

In addition, here are a few of the threatened animal species that thrived at the time of the Lewis and Clark expedition:

- **Bison (buffalo):** At their height, around the time Lewis and Clark saw the magnificent herds, 50 million bison roamed the prairies. Annihilated by white settlers and the development of the prairie habitat they depended upon, bison were driven to within 350 animals of extinction by 1883. The population is now back up to over 200,000, buffalo raised on ranches, tribal reservations and federal and state lands, and about 2,500 wild buffalo still roam Yellowstone National Park. Undeveloped prairie, once tens of millions of acres, has shrunk to 550,000 acres.

- **Gray wolves:** The two million wolves that occupied the West during the expedition were deliberately slaughtered from 1850 to 1900, mostly by bounty hunters for the $50 the government paid for each carcass. Nearly wiped out, they came under federal protection as endangered after the U.S. Fish and Wildlife Service worked to reintroduce them in Wyoming and Idaho, where they number about 500. They are also reintroducing themselves over the Canadian border into Montana.

- **Grizzly bears:** In Lewis's and Clark's time, over 100,000 grizzly bears lived west of the Mississippi River. Now about 1,000 live in five isolated groups in Montana, Wyoming, Idaho, and Washington state. They are listed as threatened under the Endangered Species Act.

- **Prairie dogs (called "barking squirrels" in the journals):** Before the West was settled, prairie dogs numbered in the billions, inhabiting over 100 million acres. Today, they inhabit 1 percent of their former habitat.

- **Trumpeter swans:** By the 1930s, trumpeter swans had declined to only 50 individuals in the lower 48 states. Today, thankfully, they are up to 4,000.

- **Whooping cranes:** In 1948, whooping cranes reached a low of 21 birds. Today, they are protected under the Endangered Species Act and are starting to recover.

- **Woodland caribou:** The woodland caribou is the most endangered large mammal in the lower 48 states of the United States, with a population down to 40 animals. They are protected by federal and state endangered species laws.

Proceeding On

Thomas Jefferson believed that the United States would grow from sea to shining sea and its future depended on it, and he was right about that. During his first inaugural address, he said that there was room enough on the American continent for the next 1,000 generations, and there he was wrong. By 1900, only five generations beyond Jefferson's own, 16 million people were living west of the Mississippi River. The West turned out to be a more fragile place than its rugged-looking landscapes suggest, and surging population growth continues to create severe pressures on the environment.

Jefferson believed that peace would reign only if tribes were removed be-yond the frontier, away from settlers, or assimilated into American culture. But he didn't weigh the enormous human cost of that version of peace. Two hundred years of Indian policy later, with all the legally binding treaties broken, tribes continue to assert their right to sovereignty and self-determination, and the United States still finds ways to erode them.

What will the legacy of the Lewis and Clark bicentennial be? The organizers hope that it includes better protected natural and cultural resources and sacred places, the revitalization of native languages, and tribes sharing their side of the Lewis and Clark story. They hope that hearing the stories of courage, determination, and friendship on both sides will provide inspiration for future generations.

Part V
The Part of Tens

LEWIS AND CLARK EXPEDITION: DISCORD AMONG THE MEN

@RICHTENNANT

Captain! Some of the men have started wearin' their fanny packs to the front, whereas we began this expedition all wearing them to the back. I think the front way looks stupid! The Indians are gonna think we're a bunch of DORKS if we walk around with our packs out in front, even though it's easier gettin' stuff out of them that way. So, which way's it gonna be, Captain, to the front or to the rear?

In this part . . .

Get more information about ten places on the Lewis and Clark Trail that are unchanged since Lewis and Clark, along with ten places that have changed completely. You also get a listing of the ten best places to visit on the trail. And if you want to know more about the Lewis and Clark expedition, get acquainted with the ten best resources for more information.

Chapter 19

Twenty Places Lewis and Clark Saw: Ten Changed; Ten Unchanged

In This Chapter

▶ Visiting ten sites beyond recognition

▶ Considering ten pristine places

*I*f you decide to follow Lewis and Clark's path, you'll find that a number of areas they visited have stayed virtually the same, while others have changed dramatically. This chapter shares ten of each.

Ten Places Changed Completely

In this section, you find out about ten landscapes and sites on the trail that would be unrecognizable to Lewis and Clark because of what has either appeared and disappeared since the voyage of discovery. We've put them roughly in order of how Lewis and Clark would have visited them.

✔ **Wood River/Camp Dubois:** Located at the mouth of the Missouri River on the eastern shore of the Mississippi River at Hartford, Illinois. Because floods and erosion have shifted the river's course over the last two centuries, the exact site of Camp Dubois — the winter camp where the expedition recruited and trained the Corps of Discovery (see Chapter 6) — is now thought to be in Missouri. The Wood River/Camp Dubois Lewis and Clark Interpretative Center is on Illinois Route 3, 20 miles north of St. Louis on the banks of the Mississippi River across from the current mouth of the Missouri. For visitor information, call 217-785-1511 or visit www.hartfordillinois.net/lewis_clark.htm.

✔ **Confluence of the Kansas and Missouri Rivers:** The pristine hill where the captains climbed up and agreed that the spot would make be a good place for a fort (see Chapter 17) is now a small park in downtown metropolitan Kansas City, Missouri. For information, call 816-221-5242 or visit.

✔ **Calumet Bluff:** Where the expedition met with the Yankton Sioux tribe for three days and gave out peace medals to three tribal leaders (see Chapter 8). A *calumet* is a smoking pipe, a symbol of peace. Today, instead of looking out over a free-flowing Missouri River, Calumet Bluff looks out over the Gavins Point Dam and Lewis and Clark Lake. On top of the bluff is the Lewis and Clark Visitor Center, managed by the U.S. Army Corps of Engineers. The visitor center interprets the expedition and also the construction of Gavins Point Dam. For information, call 402-667-7873, ext. 3246 or visit www.nwo.usace.army.mil/htm/Lake_Proj/gavinspoint/visit.html.

✔ **Great Falls of the Missouri; Great Falls, Montana:** The Great Falls aren't so great anymore since the Ryan Dam reduced them to a fraction of their glory. These are the falls that Lewis said he could hear roaring from seven miles away and where the famous portage around them continued overland for a month before the party finally rejoined the Missouri River at White Bear Island, west of the present day city of Great Falls. The Lewis and Clark National Historic Trail Interpretive Center, managed by the U.S. Forest Service, is a don't miss attraction on a bluff overlooking the Missouri River. Information, call 406-727-8733 or visit www.fs.fed.us/r1/lewisclark/lcic.htm.

✔ **Travelers' Rest, Travelers' Rest State Park:** The spot where the expedition rested up before and after arduous treks over the Bitterroot Range of the Rocky Mountains, a camping place for thousands of years, Travelers' Rest became surrounded by housing development in the small town of Lolo, Montana in the 20th century. With help from the U.S. Forest Service and The Conservation Fund, the state and community have, in recent years, made the preservation of Travelers' Rest a priority and a Montana state park. For information, call 406-273-4253 or visit www.travelersrest.org.

✔ **Camp Fortunate:** The place where Lewis found the Shoshones and Sacagawea recognized the Shoshone leader Cameahwait as her brother is now under 50 feet of water within the Clark Canyon Reservoir. The Bureau of Reclamation maintains an interpretative overlook and picnic area nearby, 11 miles south of Dillon, Montana. For more information, call 406-683-6472 or visit www.lewisandclark.state.mt.us and click on "On the Trail."

✔ **Confluence of the Snake and Clearwater Rivers:** Traveling down the Clearwater in dugout canoes, the expedition came to its confluence with the Snake River on October 10, 1805 and camped on its banks. Today that campsite, opposite the Clarkston Golf Course, is under the water of the Lower Granite Dam, one of eight dams on the Snake River. Clarkston is across the Snake River from its twin city, Lewiston, Idaho. Lewiston is ten miles west of the Nez Perce Indian Reservation. For information, call 800-473-3543 or go to www.lewistonchamber.org.

↙ **Celilo Falls and The Dalles (eastern end of the Columbia River Gorge):**
Now under 50 feet of water because of the construction of The Dalles
Dam in 1957, Celilo Falls and nearby The Dalles were trading centers
central to the Indian economy in the Pacific Northwest at the time of the
expedition. Tribes used the Columbia River as a highway for at least
11,000 years, and Celilo Falls was one of the best places to catch salmon,
attracting thousands of Indians from many different tribes every spring.
Lewis and Clark had difficult portages at both places on their trip downstream in 1805 and upstream in 1806. For information on the Columbia
River Gorge National Scenic Area, call 360-725-5052.

↙ **Cathlapotle (Ridgefield National Wildlife Refuge):** Cathlapotle was
the Chinook village of about 900 inhabitants at the confluence of the
Columbia, Lake, and Lewis Rivers. The expedition noted the village on
their way downstream in 1805, and then stopped and camped nearby on
their way upstream on March 29, 1806. The Ridgefield National Wildlife
Refuge and the Chinook Tribe are collaborating on a project to build a
traditional plank house at the Cathlapotle site. For information, call
360-887-4106 or visit www.r1.fws.gov/Ridgefield.

↙ **Chinook Point Campsite and Cape Disappointment:** Fort Columbia
State Park (Chinook, Washington) and Fort Canby State Park (Illwaco,
Washington). This is where, on November 15, 1805, the Corps of
Discovery finally viewed the Pacific Ocean, set up camp on a sandy
beach a half mile from Chinook Point, and explored the cape, so named
in 1788 by British sea captain and fur trader John Meares. This is where
the expedition (including Sacagawea and York) voted to leave and
explore a winter camp on the opposite side of the Columbia. From 1896
to 1904, the U.S. built Fort Columbia on Chinook Point and a lighthouse
was built on Cape Disappointment. Then, in the early 20th century, Fort
Canby was built on Cape Disappointment, and its remnants remain. A
U.S. Coast Guard station and National Motor Life Boat School also operate on the Cape. Despite all the changes, you can see the same spectacular views of the Pacific Ocean that Lewis and Clark did and enjoy two
fine Washington state parks. For more information, call 360-902-8844 or
visit www.parks.wa.gov.

Ten Places Unchanged

Many of the landscapes Lewis and Clark saw have been transformed — into
towns, cities, farms, ranches, factories, subdivisions. Yet while all of the landscapes have been altered somewhat, this section shares ten places on the
Lewis and Clark National Historic Trail that are relatively unchanged since
Lewis and Clark's time. Like the preceding section, we've put them in order of
how Lewis and Clark would have visited them.

- ✔ **Missouri River, St. Charles to Boonville, Missouri:** Walk the riverbank the way Lewis often did at Katy Trail State Park, 165 miles of backcountry hiking and biking trails running along the northern shore of the river, with access to places Lewis and Clark camped. Amenities (parking, restrooms, water, food) are located at trailheads every thee to ten miles along the trail. For information, call 800-379-2419 or visit www. mostateparks.katytrail.htm.

- ✔ **Missouri National Recreation River:** Here, you can boat or canoe untamed, unchannelized sections of the river for 59 miles from Ponca State Park in Nebraska to Yankton, South Dakota and 37 miles from Niobrara State Park in Nebraska to Pickstown on the Yankton Sioux Indian Reservation in South Dakota. Views from the bluffs, access to the river, camping, and lodging can be had in the two Nebraska state parks — Ponca State Park and Niobrara State Park. For information, call 402-667-2550 or visit www.nps.gov/mnrr.

- ✔ **The Narrows, Lower Brule Sioux Indian Reservation (30 miles northwest of Chamberlain, South Dakota):** The Narrows is the largest naturally occurring total bend in any river system in the United States. The expedition measured this narrow neck of land at 2,000 yards across, while the distance around the bend in river miles was 30. Nearby is the Buffalo Interpretive Center and Circle of Tipis Information Center. For information, call 605-473-0561 or visit www.lewisandclark200.gov.

- ✔ **Missouri River in North Dakota:** Between two massive lakes formed by equally massive dams built in the mid-20th century, the river flows freely between the Lewis and Clark Interpretive Center at Washburn and the Knife River Indian Villages National Historic Site in North Dakota. Other visitor attractions on this stretch of the Missouri include Fort Clark State Historic Site and Fort Mandan Overlook State Historic Site, including a replica of the fort the expedition built to weather the first winter. For information, call 800-435-5663 or visit www.ndtourism.com.

- ✔ **Missouri National Wild and Scenic River (upper Missouri River Breaks National Monument, Montana):** Where Lewis, awestruck, wrote of "seens of visionary inchantment" without end, you can canoe the river and delight in the same landscapes. There are 149 miles of free-flowing river from Fort Benton, Montana to James Kipp Recreation Area plus 30 free-flowing river miles at the western end of the Charles M. Russell National Wildlife Refuge. For information, call 408-538-7561 or visit www.mt.blm.gov/ldo/um.

- ✔ **Gates of the Mountains:** Seventeen miles north of Helena, Montana in the Helena National Forest, you can take a boat tour through the same spectacular narrow canyon of 1,200-foot sheer cliffs and see bighorn sheep, mountain goats, and osprey just like the Corps of Discovery did. For information, call 406-458-5241 or visit www.gatesofthemountains.com.

✔ **Clark's Lookout:** Clark's Lookout State Park — you can hike up and see the same undeveloped view Clark saw on August 13, 1805, when he climbed a high bluff to look out over the Beaverhead Valley. One mile north on old Highway 91 near Dillon, Montana. For information, call 406-944-4042.

✔ **Lost Trail Pass:** Bitterroot National Forest — unspoiled and remote, Lost Trail Pass can be crossed by car on U.S. 93 near the border between Idaho and Montana a few miles south of Sula, Montana. The Lost Trail is the unknown path the expedition followed on its way from Camp Fortunate over the mountains to Travelers' Rest in 1805. The exact route is unknown because the journals are confused at this point — presumably because of bad weather, high altitude, and hunger. Driving U.S. 93 north toward Lolo, you are roughly paralleling the expedition's path and are surrounded by the rugged beauty of the Bitterroot Valley. For information, call 406-363-7100 or visit www.fs.fed.us/r1/bitterroot/forest.

✔ **Weippe Prairie:** The land that surrounds Weippe Prairie has been changed over the last 200 years, but Weippe Prairie, a National Historic Landmark on Idaho Highway 11 west of Weippe, Idaho, remains undeveloped. It is one of several Lewis and Clark and Nez Perce meeting sites (including Long Camp and Canoe Camp) in the Spaulding Unit of the Nez Perce National Historical Park, managed by the National Park Service. By visiting, you get a good idea of the dramatic change in landscape that the Corps of Discovery found when they staggered out of the Bitterroot Mountains into Nez Perce country.

Weippe Prairie has been a Nez Perce traditional gathering place, an ideal field for growing camas roots, and a great area for camping and socializing for thousands of years. For information, visit www.nps.gov/nepe or call 208-843-2261 ext. 199.

✔ **Fort Clatsop:** Fort Clatsop National Memorial near Astoria, Oregon offers a replica of the fort the expedition built for the winter of 1805–1806. So, it's not the original (and, therefore, not technically "unchanged"), but it's an artful replica, and visiting it, you will understand what the expedition felt as they waited for spring and their return home. For information, call 503-861-2471, ext. 241 or visit www.nps.gov/focl.

Chapter 20

The Ten Best Places to Visit on the Lewis and Clark National Historic Trail

- -

In This Chapter

▶ Visiting historic sites

▶ Biking the trail

▶ Viewing the art

▶ Walking in the footsteps of Lewis and Clark

- -

*W*e could name hundreds of fascinating sites for you to visit on the Lewis and Clark National Historic Trail. Picking the ten best was nearly impossible, but we still tried. Moving from east to west, our list includes historic sites, state parks, bike trails, art museums, replica forts, interpretive centers, and scenic byways. All ten offer fun, recreational, and even academic activities for everyone in your family.

Monticello

Thomas Jefferson's architectural masterpiece, Monticello, sits atop a small mountain, facing west above Charlottesville, Virginia. In its dining rooms and parlors, Jefferson dreamed of a scientific exploration of the West and planned it in detail with his secretary, Meriwether Lewis.

Mr. Jefferson's house and gardens are now a World Heritage site open to the visiting public. Facilities include the Jefferson Library, International Center for Jefferson Studies, the Thomas Jefferson Center for Historic Plants, a public visitor center, and great museum shop.

The house is furnished the way Jefferson left it, and the gardens still grow the fruits and vegetables Jefferson grew. As a working plantation, Monticello housed an entire community of slaves and free workers, and their workplaces are also open to visitors. Monticello is open to the public every day of the year except Christmas, and about 500,000 people visit each year. Visit the Web site, which gives a great overview with photos (www.monticello.org), or call 434-984-9822.

Falls of the Ohio State Park

Beautiful Falls of the Ohio State Park sits on the banks of the Ohio River in Clarksville, Indiana, across the river from Louisville, Kentucky. The park overlooks the Falls in the spring, when the river is high, and the world famous fossil beds in the fall, when the river level is low. In fact, in autumn, you can walk right out onto the 386-million-year-old fossil beds.

The Falls of the Ohio area is where Lewis hooked up with Clark and the whole effort became the Lewis and Clark expedition. Two weeks after Lewis's arrival, Lewis, Clark, and the Ten Young Men from Kentucky recruited by Clark (see Chapter 2) were on their way down the Ohio River to St. Louis.

The lush park is open seven days a week. It offers an interactive interpretive center, special exhibits, fishing, hiking, bird watching, picnicking, guided hikes, and children's storytelling. You can also find summer nature programs, educational programs (archaeological, geological, and environmental), and a young paleontologists' camp. It also has a boat launch, a great gift shop, and an exciting exhibit about Lewis and Clark. For more information, surf to www.fallsoftheohio.org or call 812-280-9970.

Katy Trail State Park

The former route of the Missouri-Kansas-Texas Railroad is now a 200-mile-long bicycle trail and Missouri State Park — part of the national Rails-To-Trails program. The Katy Trail starts in St. Charles, Missouri, and follows the Missouri River and the Lewis and Clark National Historic Trail for most of its route.

If you plan to bike (rentals are available) or hike, you can travel the entire 200 miles, stopping in the picturesque towns along the way for dinner and a good night's sleep. Watch the river birds; go fishing, boating, backpacking, camping, swimming, antique hunting, or sightseeing; and watch the seasons change where Lewis and Clark once paddled upstream. For more information: www.mostateparks.com/katytrail.htm or call 800-334-6946.

If you start your trail ride in St. Charles, be sure to stay a night or two in that charming historic town. Enjoy the perfectly preserved 1800s flavor of historic Main Street and try to catch the replica Lewis and Clark keelboat and pirogues, beautifully and accurately reproduced by the Discovery Expedition of St. Charles. Check out the boats and get more information at `www.lewisandclark.net`.

Joslyn Art Museum

If your purpose in traveling the Lewis and Clark Trail is to view extraordinary art depicting the West as Lewis and Clark saw it, get yourself to Omaha, Nebraska, and the Joslyn Art Museum. The Joslyn is famous for its collections of art about the American West and by American Indian artists.

The museum's greatest renown comes from its collection of 400 works by Swiss artist Karl Bodmer. The 23-year-old Bodmer traveled with German naturalist Prince Maximilian of Wied on his journey up the Missouri River from 1832 to 1834. From St. Louis almost to the Great Falls, Bodmer painted landscapes and everyday life of the frontier, including many tribes and places that Lewis and Clark had met three decades earlier. Bodmer's paintings are sublime, depicting Omaha, Oto, Ponca, Sioux, Mandan, Hidatsa, Arikara, Assiniboine, Cree, Gros Ventre, and Blackfeet people and their lands.

The Joslyn offers tours, children's art classes and camps, music and special exhibitions. For more information check out the great Web site at `www.joslyn.org` or call 402-342-3300.

Native American Scenic Byway

If you plan to drive portions of the Lewis and Clark Trail, the Native American Scenic Byway through South Dakota leads you on the trip of a lifetime. The byway begins just off Interstate 90 near Chamberlain, South Dakota. Follow the signs to delightful explorations through the Lower Brule, Crow Creek, Cheyenne River, and Standing Rock Sioux Reservations. Watch herds of buffalo as they roam freely all across the route.

The Sioux Nations along the Native American Scenic Byway welcome visitors throughout the year and offer many cultural and educational visitor programs and attractions, especially during the Lewis and Clark Bicentennial. Take guided tours through the Cheyenne River Sioux country. Visit the reconstructed 1811 Fort Manuel — where Sacagawea died — on the Standing Rock Sioux Reservation. Stay in authentic tepees along the Missouri River. You'll see plenty of breathtaking scenery and meet friendly natives.

When planning your visit to a tribal community, be sure to contact the tribal offices for visitor information and protocol. For information on the Native American Scenic Byway, visit www.byways.org (which lists nearly 100 scenic byways) and navigate through the site to the Native American Scenic Byway page.

Fort Mandan

Fort Mandan is where where Lewis and Clark met Sacagawea and enjoyed the warmth and generosity of the Mandans. They lived there for 146 days. The authentically reconstructed Fort Mandan, on the banks of the Missouri River, sits quietly in the cottonwoods, and you can almost hear the sounds of the Corps of Discovery in the air.

Located near today's Washburn, North Dakota, Fort Mandan is owned and operated by the private, not-for-profit North Dakota Lewis and Clark Bicentennial Foundation. A stunning nearby interpretive center offers special exhibits, living history, and a terrific gift/book shop.

For more information and a schedule of family activities, visit www.fortmandan.org or call 877-462-8535.

Pompeys Pillar

This is the only place on the Lewis and Clark Trail where physical evidence of the Lewis and Clark expedition still exists. At Pompeys Pillar National Monument, 30 miles east of Billings, Montana, you can see the signature, *Wm. Clark*, and date, *July 25, 1806*, carved into the sandstone wall by William Clark. (See Chapter 16 for a photo of this signature.) You can climb the stairway to the top of the pillar and get the same view that charmed Clark in 1806.

Pompeys Pillar National Monument is managed by the Bureau of Land Management and offers a visitor center, interpretive tours, hiking, picnicking, and beautiful Montana vistas. For more information got to www.mt.blm.gov/pillarmon or call 406-875-2233.

After visiting the monument, take a few days and drive north to Great Falls, Montana, to visit the Lewis and Clark National Historic Trail Interpretive Center. The center sits high on a bluff overlooking the Missouri River and is managed by the U.S. Forest Service. It offers exhibits, a river camp, living history, a lecture series, classes, and a fabulous diorama of the Great Falls portage.

To complement your previous visit to the Joslyn Art Museum, continue north to the Blackfeet Reservation and the Museum of the Plains Indian in Browning, Montana. The beauty and diversity of the museum's historic and contemporary Indian arts is astounding.

Complete your Montana Lewis and Clark odyssey by driving west over Marias Pass through spectacular Glacier National Park. Find your way south to the Peoples Center in Pablo, Montana, on the Flathead Indian Reservation and experience the rich cultural heritage of the Salish, Kootenai and Pend d'Oreille Tribes that Lewis and Clark met in the northern Rocky Mountains.

By all means bring extra cash to spend. Each of these sites has a marvelous gift shop featuring Indian art, books, authentic reproductions, and much more.

Nez Perce National Historical Park

Spanning four states in the Pacific Northwest — Idaho, Montana, Oregon, and Washington — the Nez Perce National Historical Park is a natural and cultural delight. The park has two visitor centers and 38 sites across the four-state area. The park's headquarters are located with the visitor center in Spalding, Idaho, near Lewiston on the Lewis and Clark and Nez Perce National Historic Trails. Enjoy the museum, films, exhibits and gift shop. Take ranger-led tours and go hiking, bicycling, cross-country skiing, fishing, bird-watching, picnicking, and camping. You can also find out about Nez Perce culture, art, and history, including their experiences with the Lewis and Clark expedition. For more information, visit www.1nps.gov/nepe or call 208-843-2261.

Columbia Gorge Discovery Center

The official interpretive center for the Columbia River Gorge National Scenic Area is located at The Dalles, Oregon, in the heart of the spectacular Columbia Gorge. The Columbia Gorge Discovery Center boasts a 26,000-square-foot exhibit wing with interactive displays and 50 acres of riverbank habitat with interpretive trails through cottonwoods, willows, and wildflowers.

The center is home to a large collection of historical objects and Indian baskets from the area. It houses a library and a photo archive that includes images of Celilo Falls before the Columbia was dammed. Discovery Day Camps for kids, family learning activities, gallery talks, classes on ethnobotany (how plants are used in a particular culture), animals of the Gorge, Columbia River salmon, Gorge geology, aboriginal history and, of course, the Lewis and Clark expedition, are some of the center's diverse public programs.

The Discovery Center's executive director is renowned Lewis and Clark archaeologist Ken Karsmizki, whose research provides the basis of a new exhibit on the cargo of the expedition that is open to the public during the Lewis and Clark Bicentennial. To contact the Columbia Gorge Discovery Center, visit www.gorgediscovery.org or call 541-296-8600.

And while you're enjoying the splendor of the Gorge, why not drive across the river to the Washington side and check out the Columbia Gorge Interpretive Center in Stevenson, just a few miles downriver? If you're headed east, plan a trip to Pendleton, Oregon, to the Tamastslikt Cultural Institute, the interpretive center of the Cayuse, Umatilla, and Walla Walla Tribes. You and your family can better understand the tribes that Lewis and Clark met on the Columbia River and the natural beauty of the area. And you can have a lot of fun doing it.

Fort Clatsop National Memorial

As the third winter camp of the Corps of Discovery, Fort Clatsop was situated in the grand, lofty trees of the Pacific Coast, just south of today's Astoria, Oregon. The National Park Service now maintains an exact replica of Fort Clatsop on virtually the same spot as Lewis and Clark's winter quarters of 1805–1806. Park personnel wear buckskins, make candles, carve dugout canoes, smoke meat, and create a living-history experience for the whole family.

The park also includes a modern visitor center with exhibits and public programs, hiking trails, picnic areas, and the Salt Works site in nearby Seaside, Oregon. For more information, visit www.nps.gov/focl or call 503-861-2471.

While visiting Fort Clatsop, make sure you save some time to explore the history, views, and great seafood of nearby coastal towns: Astoria, Warrenton, Seaside, and Cannon Beach, Oregon, and Chinook, Ilwaco, and Long Beach, Washington. Especially make time for a family outing to Ecola State Park, walking the footsteps of Lewis and Clark on the Tillamook Head Trail from Cannon Beach to Seaside and visiting the Lewis and Clark Interpretive Center and Fort Canby State Park at Cape Disappointment.

Chapter 21

Ten Resources for Information about Lewis and Clark

In This Chapter

▶ Reviewing the Lewis and Clark classics

▶ Seeing the National Bicentennial Exhibition

▶ Viewing an excellent video

▶ Logging on to a great Web site

*N*ew books, films, exhibits, Web sites, and TV shows about Lewis and Clark are appearing every day. Nonetheless, we picked our ten (okay, we miscounted: eleven) favorites and recommend them to you as superstars of Lewis and Clark information.

The Journals of the Lewis and Clark Expedition, Volumes 1–13

As *the* definitive resource, the journals give you all of Lewis and Clark's words, plus those of Ordway, Floyd, Gass, and Whitehouse, and a volume on the plant specimens of Lewis and Clark. You also get an atlas and a comprehensive index. The original words are still the best. (Edited by Gary E. Moulton; The University of Nebraska Press 1983–2001.)

Lewis and Clark among the Indians

Definitely the best book ever written about Lewis and Clark, *Lewis and Clark among the Indians* tells the story through the eyes of the Indian Nations who met the explorers. Impeccably researched and wonderfully told. (By James P. Ronda; University of Nebraska Press.)

The Letters of the Lewis and Clark Expedition with Related Documents, 1783–1854

The letters Lewis and Clark wrote during their journey, as well as their pre- and post- expedition correspondence are included in this volume. A revealing and fascinating firsthand look at the adventure — and a great read. (Edited by Donald Jackson; University of Illinois Press.)

Lewis and Clark Pioneering Naturalists

This book details the scientific aspects of the Lewis and Clark expedition. Jefferson instructed Lewis to record scientific data about the West, including the flora, fauna, minerals, astronomy, and weather. Read all about those findings in this amazing account. (By Paul Russell Cutright; University of Nebraska Press.)

Undaunted Courage: Meriwether Lewis, Thomas Jefferson, and the Opening of the American West

The riveting bestseller about Meriwether Lewis as human being and hero reads like a novel. You won't be able to put it down. (By Stephen E. Ambrose; Simon & Schuster.)

Lewis and Clark: The National Bicentennial Exhibition

Just as reading Lewis and Clark's own words is a richer, more emotional experience than reading *about* their words, feasting your eyes on genuine artifacts from the expedition is more satisfying than looking at photos. For the first time since 1806, hundreds of Lewis and Clark's now priceless documents, instruments, and equipment have been borrowed from all their modern resting places and brought together in a once-in-a-lifetime exhibition that travels across the United States during the Lewis and Clark Bicentennial. If you live near one of the following cities, mark your calendar now:

- ✔ **Missouri Historical Museum (St. Louis, MO):** January 14–September 6, 2004
- ✔ **Academy of Natural Sciences (Philadelphia, PA):** November 2004– March 2005
- ✔ **Museum of Nature and Science (Denver, CO):** May–September 2005
- ✔ **Oregon Historical Society (Portland, OR):** November 2005–March 2006
- ✔ **Smithsonian Institution (Washington, D.C.):** May–September 2006

For details about this national touring exhibition, brought to you by the Missouri Historical Society, visit www.lewisandclarkexhibit.org.

In Search of York — The Slave Who Went to the Pacific with Lewis and Clark

An intimate look at the life of York, William Clark's slave. The revised edition has much new material discovered after the original publication and offers one of the most amazing stories of the whole Lewis and Clark saga. (Revised edition, by Robert B. Betts, with a new epilogue by James J. Holmberg; The University Press of Colorado and Lewis and Clark Trail Heritage Foundation.)

Traveling the Lewis and Clark Trail

In planning your own Lewis and Clark exploration, you'll need a good guide to the Lewis and Clark Trail. Several are available, but this one is the best. It is well researched and organized with advice you can rely on. Don't leave home without it. (By Julie Fanselow; Falcon Guide.)

Lewis and Clark — The Journey of the Corps of Discovery

This film by Ken Burns, available on PBS Home Video, offers four hours of breathtaking scenery, great interviews, and the full story of the Corps of Discovery from the comfort of your armchair and VCR.

www.lewis-clark.org

Discovering Lewis and Clark is a flashy and progressive Web site containing over 1,400 pages. It has layers and layers of graphics, photos, maps, animation, and sound files of and about Lewis and Clark. Here you can find the answer to just about any Lewis and Clark question you may have. The information contained in *Discovering Lewis and Clark* has been researched and written by Lewis and Clark scholars and focuses on insights into the significance of the Lewis and Clark expedition in American history and in contemporary American life. Check it out at www.lewis-clark.org.

We Proceeded On

You can find many more details about the Lewis and Clark expedition in the pages of the magazine, *We Proceeded On*. This quarterly publication is a benefit of membership in the Lewis and Clark Trail Heritage Foundation, a not-for-profit member organization that studies and preserves the Lewis and Clark story and works arm and arm with the National Park Service to care for the Lewis and Clark National Historic Trail. Go to www.lewisandclark.org.

Part VI
Appendixes

The 5th Wave   By Rich Tennant

THE CORPS OF DISCOVERY COMES ACROSS
THEIR FIRST FAMILY OF BEARS.

Uh oh. Party's over.

In this part . . .

*I*n this part, find out whose homelands the expedition traveled through and peruse a helpful glossary that highlights 18th-century terminology.

Appendix A

Tribal Homelands Visited by the Expedition

· ·

*O*n their journey from St. Louis to the Pacific Ocean and back, Lewis and Clark traveled through the homelands of over 100 ancient tribal nations. Those original inhabitants of the American West are now represented by the following 57 modern tribal nations. Tribes listed in Oklahoma were living on the route of Lewis and Clark at the time of the expedition but were subsequently removed by the United States Government to Oklahoma to make way for America's Westward expansion.

- ✔ Blackfeet Nation — Browning, Montana
- ✔ Chehalis Tribe — Oakville, Washington
- ✔ Cheyenne River Sioux Tribe — Eagle Butte, South Dakota
- ✔ Cheyenne-Arapahoe Tribes — Concho, Oklahoma
- ✔ Chinook Indian Tribe — Chinook, Washington
- ✔ Chippewa Cree Tribe — Box Elder, Montana
- ✔ Coeur D'Alene Tribe — Plummer, Idaho
- ✔ Comanche Tribe — Lawton, Oklahoma
- ✔ Confederated Salish, Kootenai and Pend d'Oreille Tribes — Pablo, Montana
- ✔ Confederated Tribes of Grand Ronde Community of Oregon — Grande Ronde, Oregon
- ✔ Confederated Tribes of the Colville Reservation — Nespelem, Washington
- ✔ Confederated Tribes of Umatilla Indian Reservation — Pendleton, Oregon
- ✔ Confederated Tribes of Warm Springs Reservation — Warm Springs, Oregon
- ✔ Cowlitz Indian Tribe — Longview, Washington
- ✔ Crow Creek Sioux Tribe — Ft. Thompson, South Dakota

- Crow Tribe — Crow Agency, Montana
- Flandreau Santee Sioux Tribe — Flandreau, South Dakota
- Fort Belknap Indian Community — Harlem, Montana
- Fort Peck Assiniboine Tribe — Wolf Point, Montana
- Fort Peck Tribes — Poplar, Montana
- Gros-Ventre Tribe — Harlem, Montana
- Iowa Tribe of Kansas and Nebraska — White Cloud, Kansas
- Iowa Tribe of Oklahoma — Perkins, Oklahoma
- Kickapoo Tribe of Kansas — Horton, Kansas
- Kiowa Tribe — Carnagie, Oklahoma
- Kootenai Tribe — Bonners Ferry, Idaho
- Little Shell Tribe of Chippewa Indians of Montana — Great Falls, Montana
- Lower Brule Sioux Tribe — Lower Brule, South Dakota
- Nez Perce Tribe — Lapwai, Idaho
- Northern Arapahoe Tribe — Fort Washakie, Wyoming
- Northern Cheyenne Tribe — Lame Deer, Montana
- Northwestern Band of Shoshoni Nation — Blackfoot, Idaho
- Oglala Sioux Tribe of the Pine Ridge Reservation — Pine Ridge, South Dakota
- Omaha Tribe — Macy, Nebraska
- Osage Nation of Oklahoma — Pawhuska, Oklahoma
- Otoe-Missouria Tribe — Red Rock, Oklahoma
- Pawnee Indian Tribe of Oklahoma — Pawnee, Oklahoma
- Ponca Tribe — Ponca City, Oklahoma
- Ponca Tribe of Nebraska — Niobrara, Nebraska
- Prairie Band of Potawatomi of Kansas — Mayetta, Kansas
- Quinault Indian Nation — Taholah, Washington
- Rosebud Sioux Tribe of the Rosebud Indian Reservation — Rosebud, South Dakota
- Sac and Fox Tribe of Iowa — Tama, Iowa
- Sac and Fox Tribe of Missouri — Reserve, Kansas

- Santee Sioux Tribe — Niobrara, Nebraska
- Shoalwater Bay Tribes — Tokeland, Washington
- Shoshone Tribe — Fort Washakie, Wyoming
- Shoshone-Bannock Tribes — Fort Hall, Idaho
- Sisseton-Wahpeton of Lake Traverse Reservation — Sisseton, South Dakota
- Spirit Lake Tribe — Fort Totten, North Dakota
- Spokane Tribe — Wellpinit, Washington
- Standing Rock Sioux Tribe — Ft. Yates, North Dakota
- Three Affiliated Tribes of the Fort Berthold Reservation — New Town, North Dakota
- Turtle Mountain Band of Chippewa — Belcourt, North Dakota
- Yakama Indian Nation — Toppenish, Washington
- Yankton Sioux Tribe of South Dakota — Marty, South Dakota

Appendix B

Glossary

air gun: Lewis's noiseless, smokeless pneumatic rifle that was fired by air pressure, invariably "astonishing" the natives.

battle axe: Short-handled axe used as a weapon by some of the Plains tribes. Lewis thought the design of the Hidatsas' battle axes was "inconvenient," but expedition blacksmith John Shields made them by the dozens to trade for corn during the Mandan winter.

bullboat: Light, round water craft made of twigs and branches woven into a round frame and covered with the hide of a buffalo. The Mandans used bullboats to cross and recross the Missouri and taught Lewis and Clark how to make them. The skill came in handy on several occasions during the expedition.

cache: Place where supplies are hidden to be picked up later. The expedition established caches at several places during the expedition.

camas: Wild onion-like root enjoyed by the Nez Perce as a staple of their diet. Lewis and Clark loved the taste and ate them ravenously upon emerging from their hungry trek over the Bitterroot Mountains into Nez Perce country. Their digestive systems, however, didn't love camas.

capote: Long, woolen, hooded blanket coat, a fashion staple of Canadian fur trappers. George Drouillard's was stolen by Skilloot visitors one day on the Columbia.

carrot: A twisted length of dried tobacco. Lewis and Clark devoted a respectable amount of cargo space to tobacco — mostly as gifts and trade goods for the Indians. They wanted smoking matter to share, enjoy, bless negotiations, and serve as reward for the tobacco-chewing men of the expedition.

celestial navigation: Navigation based on observation of the sun, moon, stars, or planets to determine position and course. Used by Clark to create accurate maps during the journey.

Continental Divide: The spine of the Western Hemisphere from the far Arctic to the tip of South America. If a drop of rain falls on the Continental Divide, half of it would trickle to a stream flowing East to the Atlantic Ocean, and the other half would flow West to the Pacific. Lewis and Clark crossed the Continental Divide over Lolo Pass in today's Idaho.

court martial: A military court to try those accused of violating military law. During the Lewis and Clark expedition, privates John Collins, Hugh Hall, Thomas Howard, John Newman, Moses Reed, William Werner, and Alexander Willard were court martialed — mostly for being drunk, fighting, or stealing, and in one case, for deserting. Each of them was convicted and flogged. *See also* ***flogging.***

dram: ¹⁄₁₂₈th of a pint. Lewis and Clark measured out the expedition's whiskey in drams and gills. *See also* ***gill.***

dugout: A canoe carved out of or burned from a big tree trunk — cottonwood on the Plains; cedar or spruce in the coastal rainforest. Lewis and Clark learned to make dugouts from the Hidatsas, the Nez Perce, and the Chinookan tribes of the Columbia River.

engage: A laborer for the French Canadian fur companies or a boatman hired for a specific trip. Sacagawea's husband, Toussaint Charbonneau, was an *engage* for the North West Company in the Mandan-Hidatsa villages before Lewis and Clark arrived on the Northern Plains.

espontoon: A sort of combination spear-bayonet/walking stick — standard Army issue of the time for infantry officers — that Lewis used to hike 20 to 30 miles a day and fend off grizzly bears.

Federalist party: A political party in the United States from 1789 to 1816 that advocated a strong centralized government and opposed Jefferson before, during, and after his presidency.

flogging: Military punishment of the day administered by a whip, stick, or ramrod. Lewis and Clark flogged several of their men convicted by court martial of drinking, fighting, stealing, or deserting.

gill: Half-cup liquid — a common measurement in Lewis and Clark's day. Also the standard whiskey ration per man per day until the expedition ran out of spirits. On celebratory occasions, the men got two gills. *See also* ***dram.***

Glauber salts: Sodium sulfate — a strong laxative similar to Epsom salt, created originally by German chemist J. R. Glauber. Lewis obtained six pounds of Glauber salts in Philadelphia and prescribed them often to relieve the expedition's chronic constipation.

keelboat: Flat-bottomed boat used in Lewis and Clark's time to haul goods up and down broad, slow rivers like the Ohio and Mississippi. Lewis had a 55-foot keelboat made in Pittsburgh that carried the Corps of Discovery up the Missouri River as far as the Mandan villages.

laudanum: Opium alcohol tincture used frequently in Lewis and Clark's day to ease pain and induce sleep. Lewis included it in his medicine chest for the expedition.

mess: Army term for a group of soldiers who regularly eat their meals together. Lewis and Clark divided the Corps of Discovery into several messes with a cook assigned to each mess.

moccasins: Indian footwear generally made from deerskin or elk skin. The Corps of Discovery had walked through their Army boots by the time they reached North Dakota. After that, they made themselves hundreds of pairs of moccasins to complete the journey. At one point, Clark even made moccasins for his horses.

Northwest Passage: Mythical, easy passage across the continent from eastward-flowing rivers to westward-flowing rivers and the Pacific Ocean — believed in by virtually every 19th-century American. American colonists had hoped and believed from the moment they looked west that there was a reasonable route from one sea to the next. Jefferson sent Lewis and Clark westward primarily to discover that route. It didn't exist.

pine tar or **pitch:** Sticky liquid distilled from pine trees. Lewis counted on using pine tar to seal the elk-skin hull of his experimental iron boat. In one of the expedition's only unlucky episodes, there were no pine trees within hundreds of miles of the spot where the expedition needed the iron boat.

pirogue: French-Canadian term for a canoe-shaped boat. Lewis had two large pirogues — one red, one white — made in Pittsburgh, which carried the Corps of Discovery as far as the Great Falls of the Missouri. Lewis and Clark cached them there in favor of smaller dugouts. They retrieved the white pirogue on the return journey, but the red was destroyed by moisture and they abandoned it.

portage: Act or route of transporting boats and supplies overland between navigable waters. Lewis and Clark had to manage two difficult portages on their voyage — one around the Great Falls of the Missouri, the other around the Great Falls (Celilo Falls) of the Columbia.

poultice: Generally a cloth or leaf wrapped herbal mixture, often hot and moist, applied to heal sore or painful parts of the body. Lewis used many poultices to treat members of the expedition and their Indian hosts.

prickly pear: Pear-shaped cactus with sharp spines that grows across the northern prairies and western desert areas. Prickly pear destroyed many moccasins and ruined the explorers' feet across what is now Montana.

quadrant: Instrument for measuring altitudes.

Rush's pills: "Bilious Pills to order of B. Rush," often called *Rush's thunderbolts,* were pills invented by Dr. Benjamin Rush and made of 10 grains of calomel and 10 grains of jalap (a powdered drug prepared from the root of *Exogonium surga,* a Mexican morning glory). Lewis prescribed Rush's pills freely to his constipated men.

swivel gun: Bronze cannon installed on the keelboat by William Clark. Lewis and Clark bought this large gun in St. Louis and mounted it on a swivel on the keelboat so it could be pointed and fired in any direction. Effectively, it made the Lewis and Clark expedition a gunboat mission.

tab-ba-bone: Shoshone term for "stranger," possibly even "enemy." When Lewis and Clark asked Sacagawea the Shoshone word for "white man," she told them "tab-ba-bone." The Shoshones had never met any white men, so they had no word. Lewis, who proclaimed himself to be "tab-ba-bone," at first frightened the Shoshones.

tepee: Cone-shaped tent structure used by the Plains Indians as a mobile home. Tepees were — and are — constructed of long, straight lodge poles and covered by buffalo hide. The Sioux, Blackfeet, and Salish people used tepees. Lewis and Clark purchased a buffalo hide tepee to house themselves, the Charbonneau family, and George Drouillard after leaving Fort Mandan.

tules: Large reeds like cattails that grow in the wetlands of the Columbia River drainage. Columbia Plateau tribes, such as Wanapum, made homes of mats woven from tules.

volley: Simultaneous discharge of a number of firearms. The men of the Corps of Discovery would fire a volley at sunrise on special days like Christmas, New Year's Day, and Independence Day.

voyageurs: Canoe-men of the French-Canadian wilds. Lewis and Clark hired a few *voyageurs* to help them travel the rivers of the American West.

wappato: Potato-like root that provided dietary staple for the Chinookan tribes of the lower Columbia River. Wappato was also used as a trade item. Lewis and Clark bartered for it whenever they could during the Pacific winter.

Welsh Indians: Popular belief before the Lewis and Clark expedition that a tribe or tribes of blue-eyed, fair-haired, fair-skinned Indians existed in the West.

woolly mammoth: Extinct genus of elephant with hairy skin and long tusks curving upward that Thomas Jefferson thought might still roam the western United States.

Index

• A •

Agency Creek, 206
air gun, 103, 131–132, 138, 153
Aird, James (trader), 302
Ambrose, Stephen E. (*Undaunted Courage:
    Meriwether Lewis, Thomas Jefferson, and
    the Opening of the American West*), 350
American Indians. *See also* gifts; trade
    negotiations; *specific individuals;
    specific tribes*
  assimilation, 15, 334
  bicentennial commemoration of
      expedition, 19–20
  broken promises to, 329–331
  burial mounds, 25
  federal recognition as official tribe, 236
  gifts for tribes, 96–97
  government policies toward, 15–16, 230,
      319
  invitations to visit Washington, 130
  languages, revitalization of, 230
  removal policy, 319, 334
  reservations, 18, 146–147, 292
  role in expedition's survival, 12, 44
  speeches to, by Lewis and Clark, 115, 130
  treaties, 317–319, 329–331
  tribal homelands visited by the
      expedition, 355–357
American Philosophical Society, 66, 75, 94,
    311
American Rivers organization, 17
animals. *See also specific species*
  new to western science, 238
  post-expedition threats to, 332–333
antelope, 121, 170

Anti-Federalist party, 77
Apash Wyakaikt "Flint Necklace" (Nez
    Perce leader), 269
appendicitis, 124
Arapaho (tribe), 144
Arikara (tribe)
  agriculture of, 141–142
  culture, 144–147
  death of leader in Washington, 299, 303
  leaders, 43–44
  Lewis and Clark's return visit to, 298–299
  negotiations with Lewis and Clark,
      143–144
  post-expedition experiences, 330
  Teton Sioux retaliation against, 159
  today, 154
  trade alliance with Teton Sioux, 141–142
Army, life in early 1800s, 76
arrowhead, 237. *See also* wappato
Arrowsmith, Aaron (mapmaker), 63
Ashley Island, 142
Assiniboines (tribe), 158, 188–189
Atsina (tribe), 200–201

• B •

Bad River, 137
Bannock (tribe), 330
Barton, Dr. Benjamin Smith (botanist), 48,
    92–93
Bates, Frederick (acting governor of Upper
    Louisiana Territory), 313, 315
battle axe, 159–160
Battle of Fallen Timbers, 29, 87
beads, blue, 95–96
bears, grizzly, 174–175, 333
beaver, 170, 192

Beaverhead mountains, 200
Beaverhead River, 192–193, 202–203, 205, 280
Beaver's Head Rock, 193
Belt Creek, 180
Betts, Robert B. (*In Search of York-The Slave Who Went to the Pacific with Lewis and Clark*), 351
bicentennial commemoration, 19–21, 350–351
Biddle, Nicholas (editor of *History of the Expedition Under the Command of Captains Lewis and Clark*), 158, 183, 312, 318
Big Blackfoot River, 286
Big Bone Lick, 104
Big Hole River, 192, 280
Big Horse (Missouri leader), 41, 126, 131–134
Big White. *See* Sheheke
Bighorn River, 282
bighorn sheep, 171
billiards, Indian, 156
bird woman. *See* Sacagawea
Bird Woman's River, 171
bison. *See* buffalo
Bitterroot Mountains, crossing of, 59, 215–219, 274
bitterroot (plant), 201–202
Bitterroot River, 207, 209, 213, 280, 286
Black Buffalo. *See* Untongarabar
Black Cat (Mandan leader), 45, 154, 169, 297–298
Black Gun. *See* Cameahwait (Shoshone leader)
Black Hawk (Sauk leader), 318–319
Black Moccasin. *See* Ompsehara
Blackbird (Omaha leader), 132
Blackfeet (tribe)
    European guns, 190
    John Colter and, 325
    killing of George Drouillard, 328
    killing of John Potts, 328
    killing of youths by Lewis's party, 48, 291
    Lewis's meeting with, 289, 290
    post-expedition experiences, 331
    today, 292
Blackfeet River, 287
bloodletting, 91, 161
Bloody Chief. *See* Hohots Ilppilp
blunderbusses, 116, 132, 296
boat. *See also* canoes
    armament, 116, 132
    bull, 284–285
    delay in construction of, 102
    iron, 83–84, 180–183
    keelboat, 84, 102, 110, 132, 168
    leaks, 103
    pirogues, 103, 116, 132
    position of men on, 121
Bob Marshall Wilderness Complex, 186
boils, 123
Bonaparte, Napoleon (French Emperor), 25, 53, 61, 68
books, brought by Lewis on expedition, 93
Boone's Settlement, 120
botany, 81, 92–93, 194
boudin blanc (white pudding), 176
Bozeman Pass, 281
Bratton, Private William (Corps member)
    bear encounter, 174
    biography, 37
    post-expedition life, 324–325
    salt making, 245
    Spirit Mound trek, 125
Broken Arm (Nez Perce leader), 222, 224, 270
buffalo
    Clark's observation of, 300
    expedition's first encounter with, 122
    gentleness of, 170
    Lewis charged by, 179
    post-expedition fate of, 333
    restoration of, 17
    in rut, 284, 288
    slaughter of, 16, 330

buffalo calling ceremony, 164
buffalo hunt, Mandan, 159
Buffalo Medicine (Teton Sioux leader), 43, 138, 301
buffalo robes, 135, 139, 169
bull boats, 284–285
burial mounds, American Indian, 25
Burns, Ken (*Lewis and Clark—The Journey of the Corps of Discovery*), 351
buttons, brass, 96

• *C* •

caching, of supplies, 78, 180, 227
cactus, prickly pear, 163, 173, 333
Calf Looking (Blackfeet youth), 48, 291
Calumet Bluff, 136, 338
camas (root), 222, 224–225, 275
Cameahwait "Black Gun" (Shoshone leader), 12, 45, 201–207
Camp Chopunnish, 271, 274
Camp Disappointment, 290
Camp Dubois, 51, 108–111, 337
Camp Fortunate, 206, 208–209, 338
Canada, MacKenzie's expedition across, 66, 79
candles, eating of, 218
Cann, E. (laborer), 125
cannon, 116, 132, 297
canoes
  Chinook, 235, 247
  construction of, 183, 226, 281
  retrieval of cached, 280
  theft of Clatsop, 262
Canoe Camp, 227
Cape Disappointment, 240, 339
caribou, woodland, 333
Cascades of the Columbia, 264–265
Catherine the Great (Russian Empress), 65
Cathlapotle (Chinook village), 263, 339
cedar, western red, 332–333
Celilo Falls, 56, 223–224, 232–233, 332, 339
certificates, presented to Indians, 133
Charbonneau, Jean Baptiste (son of Sacagawea)

adoption by Clark, 324
biography, 323–324
birth, 31, 157
Clark's request for, 302
death, 324
in flash flood, 181–182
"Pomp" nickname, 31, 157, 241, 282, 323
Charbonneau, Lisette (daughter of Sacagawea), 322, 324
Charbonneau, Touissant (interpreter)
  boat accident, 176
  children given to Clark, 323–324
  cooking skills of, 176
  hiring by Corps of Discovery, 31, 32, 156
  interpreting by, 205, 212
  land warrant, trade of, 323
  payment to, 301
  post-expedition life, 327
  Sacagawea and, 31, 32
Charles M. Russell National Wildlife Refuge, 173
Charlevoix, Pierre (explorer), 64
Cheyenne (tribe), 141, 144, 298–299
Cheyenne River Sioux Reservation, 146–147
Chil-lar-la-wil (Chinook leader), 247
Chinook Point campsite, 339
Chinook (tribe)
  canoes, 235, 247
  customs, misunderstanding of, 236
  expeditions time with, 235–236, 240–244, 260–263
  leaders, 47
  Lewis's treatment of Taucum, 251, 261
  post-expedition experiences, 331
  support of expedition by, 12
Chippewa-Cree (tribe), 189
Chouteau, Auguste (merchant), 49, 114, 303–304
Chouteau, Pierre (merchant), 49, 114, 310, 314
Christmas celebrations, 163, 249
chronometer, 94–95

Clark, George Rogers (brother of William Clark)
  advice from, 105
  financial problems of, 30, 77, 87
  Jefferson's approach to for expedition leadership, 65
  military service, 29, 77, 86
  post-expedition visit to, 310
Clark, William (Corps commander)
  Army rank, 28, 85, 116–117
  biography, 29–30
  childhood, 29, 86
  compensation, 311
  death, 319–320
  discipline of men, 111
  doctoring by, 272–273
  in flash flood, 181–182
  governor of Missouri Territory, 318–319
  Harriet Kennerly Radford (wife), 319
  Jean Baptiste and, 323–324
  Julia "Judith" Hancock (wife), 171, 307, 310, 316–317, 319
  on Lewis's death, 316, 317
  military service, 29–30, 86
  Nez Perce son, 272, 331
  personal traits, 29
  portrait, 30
  qualifications, 87–88
  recruitment by Lewis, 85, 88
  relationship with York, 32–33
  removal policy and, 319
  rheumatism, 151
  Spirit Mound trek, 125
  Superintendent of Indian Affairs, 317–319
Clark's journal
  on the Arikaras, 147
  on Bitterroot crossing, 215, 217
  on buffalo, 300
  on bull boat construction, 284
  Chinook canoe, 235
  on the Clatsops, 144, 242
  drawings, 235, 253–254
  on feet and prickly pears, 190
  at Fort Clatsop, 253–254
  importance of, 14, 35
  on Indians in general, 317
  on lodges of Columbia River tribes, 229
  on Mt. Adams, 230
  on the Nez Perce, 222, 224–226
  on the Otoes and Missouris, 131
  on Pacific Ocean, 238
  on Pompy's Tower, 282
  on the prairie, 121
  on recruits, 109–110
  on return down the Missouri River, 303
  on Rocky Mountains, 274
  on Sacagawea-Cameahwait reunion, 205
  on Sacagawea's guidance, 281
  on Shannon's near starvation, 125
  on tepees, 139
  on the Teton Sioux, 42, 139, 141
  on the Umatillas, 232
  on vote for winter camp, 241
  on whale, 252
  on women of Columbia River tribes, 229
  on York and the Arikaras, 145
Clark's Lookout, 341
Clark's Point (Kansas City, Missouri), 118
Clarksville, 104–105
Clarksville Riverfront Foundation, 105
Clatsops (tribe)
  expedition's time with, 240–244, 246–248, 252–253, 261–263
  games, 244
  leaders, 47, 244, 247, 248
  support of expedition by, 12
  trade with, 246–247
Clearwater River
  expedition's outbound travel on, 223, 227
  expedition's return trip, 269, 271, 275
  today, 338
Clymer, John F. (painter), 175
Coboway "Comowooll" (Clatsop leader), 47, 244, 247, 262
Cokhlarishkit River, 286
Collins, Private John (Corps member)
  biography, 37
  court martial, 111, 126

Colter, Private John (Corps member)
  biography, 37
  meeting Nez Perce, 215
  post-expedition life, 324–325
  recruitment of, 100
  return to the west, 302
  search for Shannon, 124
  Spirit Mound trek, 125
  threat to kill Ordway, 111
  in Yellowstone, 325
Columbia Gorge Discovery Center, 233,
    347–348
Columbia River
  dams, 332
  discovery by Robert Gray, 66
  expedition's outbound travel on, 56,
    228–237
  expedition's return trip on, 262–267
Comcomly (Chinook leader), 47, 247, 248
Comowooll. *See* Coboway
congressional funding of expedition,
    request for, 67, 81–83
conservation efforts, 17
Continental Divide, 58, 161, 196, 207
corn, grown by the Mandans and the
    Hidatsas, 152
Corps of Discovery. *See also specific
    individuals*
  disbanding of, 307, 310
  land grants and payments to, 311
  members of, 26–27, 84
  organization of men, 113, 121
  painting of, 26
  recruitment of, 100–101, 109–113
cost, of expedition, 81, 100
cottonwood, 332–333
Council Bluff, 57, 129
court martial
  of Corps members, 111, 126, 133
  of Lewis, 77
  of recruits, 111
cows, 304
Coyote. *See* Sheheke
crane, whooping, 333

Crooked Falls, 178
Crow At Rest. *See* Kakawissassa
Crow Creek Indian Reservation, 146
Crow (tribe), 281, 285, 321
Cruzatte, Private Pierre (Corps member)
  biography, 37
  boatman skills of, 176
  fiddling of, 163
  recruitment of, 118
  search for Indians, 128
  shooting of Lewis, 293
Cuscalar (Clatsop leader), 47, 244, 248
Custer, George Armstrong (General), 330
Cut Bank Creek, 289
Cutnose (Nez Perce leader), 269–270
Cutright, Paul Russell (*Lewis and Clark
    Pioneering Naturalists*), 350
Cutssahnem (Wanapum leader), 47,
    228–230, 230

• D •

Dakota Rendezvous, 141
The Dalles, 232,265-267,339
dams, 16, 332
de Urujo, Carlos Martinez (Spanish
    minister), 67
Dearborn, Henry (Secretary of War), 116,
    187, 311, 314
Dearborn River, 187, 287
Delassus, Colonel (Spanish governor of
    Upper Louisiana), 108
Democratic-Republican party, 77
Deschutes River, 228, 233
desertion, penalty for, 76, 126
diet. *See also specific foods*
  dinner, 130
  at Fort Clatsop, 255
  meat, 122–123, 175–176
  Sacagawea's contributions to, 176
diplomacy, with the Mandans and the
    Hidatsas, 158–160
discipline, 110–111, 126

Discovering Lewis and Clark (Web site), 352
Dixson, Joseph (trapper), 286, 299
dog
    eating of, 34, 227, 265
    Seaman, 34, 101, 125, 170, 265
Dorion, Sr., Pierre (trader), 120, 135, 303
drinking. *See also* whiskey
    by Lewis, 28–29, 313, 315
    by recruits, 104, 107, 110–111
Drouillard, George (Corps member)
    bears, 174, 175
    biography, 33
    capture of Reed, 126, 132–133
    death, 328
    hunting by, 203
    post-expedition life, 327–328
    recruitment of, 112
    sale of land warrants by, 307
    search for Indians, 128, 129
    search for Shannon, 124, 193
    Spirit Mound trek, 125
Dubois (river), 51
dysentery, 123

• E •

Eagle's Feather. *See* Piahito
Ellicott, Andrew (tutor of Meriwether
    Lewis), 49, 94
Eneeshur (tribe), 266
environmental organizations, 17
Eustis, William (Secretary of War), 314
Evans, John (explorer), 114, 213
extinctions, 16

• F •

Fairfong, Mr. (trader), 129–130
Falls of the Ohio, 51, 105, 344
Falls of the Ohio State Park, 344
Fanselow, Julie (*Traveling the Lewis and
    Clark Trail*), 351
Federalist party, 77, 78, 97

Field, Private Joseph (Corps member)
    biography, 37–38
    post-expedition life, 326
    salt making, 245
    Spirit Mound trek, 125
    Yellowstone River exploration, 170
Field, Private Reuben (Corps member)
    biography, 37–38
    killing of Calf Looking (Blackfeet youth),
        48, 291
    post-expedition life, 326
Five Big Hearts. *See* Yoomparkkartim
flash flood, 181–182
Flathead. *See* Salish
Flathead Indian Reservation, 212
fleas, 232, 239, 243, 249
Flint Necklace. *See* Apash Wyakaikt
Floyd Monument, 124
Floyd River, 124, 326
Floyd, Sergeant Charles (Corps member)
    biography, 36
    death of, 119, 123–124, 326
    grave visitation, 302
    monument to, 124
food. *See* diet; supplies
Fort Belknap Reservation, 189
Fort Bellefontaine, 304
Fort Berthold Reservation, 154
Fort Bridger Treaty of 1868, 330
Fort Canby, 339
Fort Clatsop
    building, 242–244
    departure from, 260–263
    restriction of Indian visits, 250–251
    today, 242, 341
Fort Clatsop National Memorial, 341, 348
Fort Columbia, 339
Fort Hall Reservation, 330
Fort Mandan
    building of, 58, 154–155
    replica, 155, 346
Fort Manuel, 147, 322, 324
Fort Mountain, 186
Fort Peck reservation, 189

Fort Pickering, 315
Fort Randall Dam, 146
Fort Rock Camp, 233
fossils
  plesiosaur, 128
  study by Meriwether Lewis, 93–94
Fox (tribe), 314
France, 68–69
Frazer, Private Robert (Corps member)
  biography, 38
  loss of journals, 312, 328
  post-expedition life, 328
  replacement of Reed in permanent party,
    126
  Spirit Mound trek, 125
frostbite, 161
fur trade
  British, taking over of, 13, 285–286, 289
  Jefferson's goals for expedition and, 13,
    15, 99
  sea otter, 235
  Three Forks and, 192

• *G* •

Gallatin, Albert (Secretary of the
    Treasury), 63, 82, 97, 191
Gallatin River, 191, 280–281
games
  Clatsop, 244
  Mandan, 156
  Nez Perce, 273
garden, plants available for, 184
Garreau, Joseph (trader), 298
Garrison dam, 330
Gass, Sergeant Patrick (Corps member)
  biography, 36
  post-expedition life, 328
  promotion, 124
Gass's journal
  on the Arikaras, 145
  on Bitterroot Mountains, 215, 218
  publication, 312, 328
  on the Salish, 213
  on the Teton Sioux, 115

Gates of the Mountains, 59, 186–187, 340
gauntlet, running of the, 76, 126
geography, of the expedition
  eastern stage, 50–53
  Great Plains, 57–58
  Pacific Northwest, 59–60
  Rocky Mountains, 58–59
  waterways, 53–57
Gibbon's pass, 280
Gibson, Private George (Corps member)
  biography, 38
  injury to, 281
  post-expedition life, 326
  salt making, 245
gifts, for tribes
  to the Arikaras, 143
  to the Cheyenne, 299
  at Grand Council at Portages des Sioux,
    318
  to the Nez Perce, 225
  to the Otoes and Missouris, 129–131,
    133–134
  selection of, 96–97
  to the Teton Sioux, 138
  to the Walla Wallas, 268
  to the Wanapums, 228
  to the Yankton Sioux, 136
gnats, 123, 173
Goforth, William (doctor), 104
Goodrich, Private Silas (Corps member), 38
Grand Pass Wildlife Area, 118
Grand River, 142
grasshoppers, 284
Gratiot, Charles (trader), 49, 114
Gravelines, Joseph (trader), 49, 142–143,
    303
graveyards, 227
Gray, Captain Robert (explorer), 66, 235
Great Falls, Montana, 179
Great Falls of the Missouri, 161, 178–179,
    279, 332, 338
Great Plains
  important expedition sites in, 57–58
  post-expedition alteration of, 331–332

Grey Eyes (Arikara leader), 298
Grinder's Stand, 315–316
grizzly bears, 174–175, 333
guns
  air, 103, 131–132, 138, 153
  blunderbusses, 116, 132, 296
  given to the Walla Wallas, 268
  requisitioning of, 83
  supply of, 95
  traded to the Shoshones, 210
  tribes desire for, 96

• *H* •

hail, 181, 182
Half Man (Yankton Sioux leader), 136, 4142
Hall, Private Hugh (Corps member)
  biography, 38
  court martial, 111, 126
Hancock, Forrest (trapper), 286, 299
Hancock, Julia "Judith" (wife of Clark), 171,
    307, 310, 316–317, 319
Harpers Ferry, West Virginia, 51, 82, 83
Hassler, Ferdinand, 312
Hawk's Feather. *See* Piahito
Hay. *See* Pocasse
Helena, Montana, 186
Hellgate Treaty (1855), 330
Heney, Hugh (agent), 285
Hennepin, Louis (explorer), 63
herbal medicine, 90
heroic therapy, 91
Hidatsa (tribe)
  agriculture, 152
  fascination with York, 145
  language, 162
  leaders, 43–45, 145
  Lewis and Clark's return visit to, 296–297
  lodges, 152
  maps, 161
  post-expedition experiences, 330
  raids on the Shoshones and the Blackfeet,
    158, 160, 200, 297
  Sacagawea's capture, 30–31
  support of expedition, 12

today, 154
  trade negotiations with, 150–154
  villages, 151, 152–153
*History of the Expedition Under the
    Command of Captains Lewis and Clark*
    (Nicholas Biddle, editor), 318
Hohots llppilp "Bloody Chief" (Nez Perce
    leader), 270
Hooke, Lieutenant Moses, 86
horses
  of Columbia River tribes, 265–267
  eating of, 217–218, 273
  moccasins for, 281
  Nez Perce, 269–270
  Salish, 212
  Shoshone, 157, 188–189, 205–206, 210
  theft by Indian tribes, 138, 281, 285, 288
  Walla Walla, 268
Howard, Private Thomas P. (Corps
    member), 38–39
Hudson's Bay Company, 150

• *I* •

*In Search of York—The Slave Who Went to
    the Pacific with Lewis and Clark*
    (Robert B. Betts), 351
Independence Creek, 121
Indian Creek Recreation Area, 147
Indian Territory, 329
Indians. *See also* gifts; trade negotiations;
    specific individuals; specific tribes
information resources, 21, 349–352. *See
    also* Web sites
iron boat, 83–84, 180–183
Israel, Lost Tribes of, 62

• *J* •

Jackson, Donald (*The Letters of the Lewis
    and Clark Expedition with Related
    Documents, 1783-1854*), 350
Jackson, William H. (photographer), 272
James River, 135, 141

Jarrot (fur trader), 108
Jefferson Peace Medal, 130–131
Jefferson River, 191, 280
Jefferson, Thomas (President)
  Andre Michaux expedition and, 66
  biography, 23–25
  choice of Lewis to lead expedition, 79–80
  Clark's rank and, 116–117
  congressional funding of expedition,
    request for, 67, 81–83
  contradictions of, 24–25
  exploration of the West, fascination with,
    23, 25, 52, 61, 64–66
  Indian vocabularies, 162
  instructions to Lewis, 97–100
  John Ledyard expedition and, 65
  Lewis's letter to (September 1806),
    304–306
  Lewis's return and, 310
  Louisiana Purchase, 25, 53, 68–70
  Monticello, 50, 81, 343–344
  portrait, 24
  prairie dog sent to, 122, 163
  relationship with Meriwether Lewis, 73
Jeffersonville, Indiana, 105
Jessaume, Rene (fur trader), 31, 156–157,
    162, 297–298, 310
Joliet, Louis (explorer), 62, 63
Joseph (Nez Perce leader), 272, 331
Joslyn Art Museum, 345
journals, expedition. *See also specific*
    individuals
  Jefferson's instructions concerning, 35, 98
  publication of, 311–312, 318
  by sergeants, 35
  value of, 14–15, 35
The Journals of the Lewis and Clark
    Expedition (Gary E. Moulton), 1, 328,
    349
Judith River, 171
Jumping Fish (Shoshone woman), 205

• *K* •

Kagohhami "Little Raven" (Mandan
    leader), 45, 152, 298

Kakawissassa "Crow At Rest" (Arikara
    leader), 43, 143, 144
Kakawita "Man Crow" (Arikara leader), 43,
    143
Kansas City, Missouri, 118
Kansas River, 126, 337
Kathlamet (tribe), 263
Katy Trail State Park, 340, 344–345
keelboat, 84, 102, 110, 132, 168
King, Nicholas (mapmaker), 63
Klickitat (tribe), 267
Knife River, 151–153
Knife River Indian Villages, 152
Kooskooskee River, 217, 268
Kootenai (tribe), 212, 330

• *L* •

La Charette (settlement), 304
La Liberte (laborer), 129
Labiche, Private Francois (Corps member)
  biography, 39
  post-expedition life, 328
  recruitment of, 118
Lake Francis Case, 146
Lake Sharpe, 146
Lakota. *See* Teton Sioux
land awards, to expedition members,
    307, 311
languages
  Lewis and Clark's recording of, 162
  of Nez Perce, 225
  revitalization of Indian, 230
  Sahaptian, 225–226
Larocque, Francois-Antoine (trader), 160
lashing, as punishment, 111, 126
La't'cap (Clatsop village), 244
laudanum, 91, 272
Le Borgne "One Eye" (Hidatsa leader), 45,
    145, 152, 297
Ledyard, John (English adventurer), 65
Lemhi Pass, 196–197, 199–200, 202, 207–209
Lemhi River, 206–207, 208, 210
Leonard, Zenas (trapper), 321
LePage, Private Jean Baptiste (Corps
    member), 39

The Letters of the Lewis and Clark Expedition with Related Documents, 1783-1854 (Jackson, Donald), 350

Lewis and Clark among the Indians (James P. Ronda), 349

Lewis and Clark Lake, 118

Lewis and Clark National Historic Trail
best places to visit on, 343–348
establishment of, 18–19

Lewis and Clark Pass, 286, 287

Lewis and Clark Pioneering Naturalists (Paul Russell Cutright), 350

Lewis and Clark River, 243

Lewis and Clark State Park, 118

Lewis and Clark—The Journey of the Corps of Discovery (film by Ken Burns), 351

Lewis and Clark: The National Bicentennial Exhibition, 350–351

Lewis, Lucy (mother of Meriwether Lewis), 27, 74

Lewis, Meriwether (Corps commander)
American Philosophical Society, election to, 311
biography, 27–29
childhood, 27–28, 74–75
choice by Jefferson to lead expedition, 79–80
compensation, 311
credit given to Clark by, 305
debts, 315
depression, bouts of, 29, 74, 80
derangement, 315–316
doctoring by, 157, 160–161
dog (Seaman), 34, 101, 125, 170, 265
drinking by, 28–29, 313, 315
education, 75
family history, 73–74
father, 27, 74
governor of Upper Louisiana Territory, 313–315
grizzly bear encounters, 174–175, 178
Indian vocabularies, 162
iron boat and, 182–183

Jefferson's instructions to, 97–100
killing of Blackfeet youth, 48, 291
letter to Clark's brother, 306
letter to Jefferson (September 1806), 304–306
medical treatment of Sacagawea, 180
midlife crisis, 208
military service, 28, 76–77
mother, 27, 74
personal traits, 29, 74
portrait, 27
preparation for expedition, 28, 48–49, 80–84
publication of journals, 311–312
rambling, love of, 75
recruitment of Clark, 85, 88
relationship with Jefferson, 73
return to Washington D.C., 310
as secretary to Jefferson, 28, 50, 77–79
shot in buttocks by Cruzatte, 293
speech to American Indians, 130, 133, 136
Spirit Mound trek, 125
suicide, 316
tutors, 48–49, 75, 89–95

Lewis, Nicholas (guardian of Meriwether Lewis), 74

Lewis, William (father of Meriwether Lewis), 27, 74

Lewis's journal
on air gun incident, 103
on Bitterroot crossing, 218–219
on the Blackfeet, 289
on blowing sand, 172
on boudin blanc (white pudding), 176
on buffalo rut, 288
on the Chinookan women, 247
on the Chinooks, 251, 261
on cooking sturgeon, 255
drawings, 253–254
on fork in the Missouri River, 177
at Fort Clatsop, 253–254
Fort Mountain, 186
on the Gates of the Mountains, 187

on the Great Falls of the Missouri, 178–179
on grizzly bears, 174
importance of, 14, 35
lapses in writing, 249–250
on leaving Fort Mandan, 169
on Missouri River head, 190, 196
on the Nez Perce, 270, 271
on pin cherry, 294
on prickly pear cactus, 186
on the Rocky Mountains, 272
on Sacagawea, 176, 252
on the Shoshones, 191, 194, 201–204
on splitting the expedition, 280
sunflower seed bread recipe, 196
on the Walla Wallas, 269
on White Cliffs, 171
on wildlife, 170
on yellow currents, 194
Lewis's River, 208
Lincoln, Levi (Attorney General), 80, 97
Lisa, Manuel (trader), 49, 114, 192, 283, 328
Little Big Horn, 330
Little Raven (Mandan leader), 45, 152, 298
Little Thief (Otoe leader), 41, 126, 131–134
Livingston, Robert (U.S. Ambassador to France), 69–70
Lochsa River, 217, 275
Locust Hill (Lewis plantation), 27, 74, 75, 310, 313
lodges
  Columbia River tribe, 228–229
  Mandan and Hidatsa, 152
  Nez Perce, 226
Lolo Creek, 213, 215, 278
Lolo Hot Springs, 214, 275
Lolo, Montana, 214
Lolo Pass, 209, 214, 216
Lolo Trail, 214, 215
Lost Trail Pass, 211, 341
Louisiana Purchase, 25, 53, 68–70
Louisville, 105
L'Ouverture, Touissaint (leader of Santo Domingo insurrection), 69
Lower Brule Reservation, 146
Loyal Land Company, 65
Lukens, Isaiah (gunsmith), 132

• *M* •

Mackay, James (trader/explorer), 50, 114
MacKenzie, Alexander (explorer), 66, 79
MacKenzie, Charles (trader), 160
Madison, James (President), 191, 314, 318
Madison River, 191
Madoc (Welsh prince), 213
Mahawha (Hidatsa village), 152, 296
mammoth skeleton, observation by Lewis, 104
Man Crow. See Kakawita
Mandan (tribe)
  agriculture, 152
  buffalo calling ceremony, 164
  buffalo hunt, 159
  expedition's winter encampment with, 154–157, 160–164
  leaders, 43–45
  Lewis and Clark's return visit to, 297–298
  lodges, 152
  post-expedition experiences, 330
  support of expedition, 12
  Teton Sioux attack on, 159
  today, 154
  trade negotiations with, 150–154
  villages, 151–152
Manifest Destiny doctrine, 15
maps
  available to Lewis and Clark, 63, 114
  Bitterroot Mountains crossings, 216
  Clark's, 254
  from Columbia River tribes, 230
  expedition, 11
  Lewis and Clark Pass, 287
  Louisiana Purchase, 68
  made at Fort Mandan, 161, 162
  Mandan and Hidatsa villages, 151
  from the Nez Perce, 223–224
  Oregon and Washington coasts, 60

maps *(continued)*
  rivers traveled by Lewis and Clark
    expedition, 54–55
  Rocky Mountains, 58
  United States in 1800, 52
Marias River, 57, 178, 278–279, 286, 288–294
Marks, John (stepfather of Meriwether
    Lewis), 27, 74, 75
Marks, Lucy Lewis (mother of Meriwether
    Lewis), 27, 74
Marquette, Jacques (explorer), 62, 63
McClallen, John (friend of Lewis), 303
McNeal, Private Hugh (Corps member)
  biography, 39
  threat to life, 253
meat diet, 122–123, 175–176
medicine
  doctoring by Clark, 272–273
  doctoring by Lewis, 157, 160–161
  herbal, 90
  study by Meriwether Lewis, 90–92
Medicine River, 178, 179, 287, 288
Menetarra (Hidatsa village), 152
merchants, 49–50
mercurous chloride, 91
mercury, 91, 161
Metaharta (Hidatsa village), 152, 296
Michaux, Andre (botanist), 66, 75
Milk River, 171
Mission Canyon, 189
missions, of the expedition, 12–14, 81, 97,
    127, 296
Mississippi River, 53, 108–109
Missoula, Montana, 214
Missouri Breaks, 171
Missouri River
  condition today, 337–338, 340
  dams, 332
  early explorations of, 62–64
  fork with Marias River, 177–178
  Gates of the Mountains, 186–187
  Great Falls of the Missouri, 161, 178–179,
    332, 338
  headwaters, 191, 196

Lewis and Clark return on, 292–293,
    296–304
  Missouri Breaks, 171
  obstacles, 56, 120, 137
  Three Forks of the Missouri, 191, 280
  tribes along, 56
  White Cliffs, 171–172, 173
Missouri (tribe), 41, 57, 129–134, 329
Mitutanka (Mandan village), 151, 163, 297
moccasins, for horses, 281
Monroe, James (President), 69–70
Monticello (Jefferson's home), 50, 81,
    343–344
mosquitoes
  at Camp Dubois, 111
  on expedition's outbound trip, 123, 131,
    137, 172–173, 181
  on expedition's return trip, 284, 289
Moulton, Gary E. (*The Journals of the Lewis
    and Clark Expedition*), 1, 328, 349
Multnomah River, 264
Museum at Warm Springs, 231
Museum of the Plains Indians, 292
music, early American, 164
Musselshell River, 171

• *N* •

The Narrows, 340
Native American Graves and Repatriation
    Act (1990), 25
Native American Scenic Byway, 345–346
natural history. *See also specific plants and
    animals*
  animals and plants new to western
    science, 238
  collections and observations by Lewis,
    14, 114, 192, 194, 294
  post-expedition threats to plant and
    animal life, 332–333
  prairie, 121–123
  study by Meriwether Lewis, 92–93

navigation, study by Meriwether Lewis, 94–95

Neahkeluk (Clatsop village), 244

Necanicum River, 253

Neely, James (Indian agent), 315–316

Neerchekioo (tribe), 264

Neeshneparkkeook "Cutnose" (Nez Perce leader), 269–270

Netul River, 243

New Orleans, 68–69, 115

Newman, Private John (Corps member), 328

newspaper, accounts of expedition, 305–306

Nez Perce (tribe)
  annual crossing of Rocky Mountains, 207
  guides, 286
  leaders, 46
  Lewis and Clark's return to, 269–275
  Lewis and Clark's time with, 222–227
  meeting Lewis and Clark, 215, 219, 222–227
  post-expedition experiences, 330–331

Nez Perce National Historical Park, 347

Nez Perce Trail, 209, 215

Nimiipuu. *See* Nez Perce

Nixluidix (Wishram village), 232

North West Company, 150, 160, 285

Northwest Passage, 12, 14, 25, 61–62

• 0 •

Ohio River, 52, 80, 101–106

Old Toby (Shoshone man)
  departure of, 227
  guidance of, 12, 45, 207–210, 213–218

Omaha (tribe), 131–134, 135, 139

Ompsehara "Black Moccasin" (Hidatsa leader), 45, 296

One Arm (Arikara leader), 299

One Eye. *See* Le Borgne

opium, 91

Orderly Book, 110

Ordway, Sergeant John (Corps member)
  biography, 35
  discipline of recruits under, 110
  life threatened by Shields and Colter, 111
  post-expedition life, 328
  search for Indians, 132
  Spirit Mound trek, 125

Ordway's journal
  on the Arikaras, 144–145
  on Mandan game, 156
  on the Nez Perce, 226
  purchase by Lewis, 312
  on the Salish, 213
  on Teton village, 139

Osage (tribe), 314, 317, 318

Otoe (tribe), 41, 57, 129–134, 329

otters, 192, 235

• P •

Pacific Northwest, 59–60

Pacific Ocean, 57, 238, 240–241

Partisan, The. *See* Tortohongar

Passage to India, 61–62, 64–65. *See also* Northwest Passage

passenger pigeons, 284, 288, 289

Patterson, Robert (tutor of Meriwether Lewis), 49, 94–95

Paul Wilhelm of Wuerttemberg (duke), 324

Pawnee (tribe), 134

Peale, Charles (portraitist), 312

pelicans, 122

Pend d'Oreille (tribe), 212, 330

Pernia, John (servant to Lewis), 315

Philadelphia, Pennsylvania, 51, 94

Philosophy River, 192

Piahito "Hawk's Feather" or "Eagle's Feather" (Arikara leader), 44, 143, 144

Piegan Blackfeet. *See* Blackfeet

Pierced Nose Indians. *See* Nez Perce

pigeons, passenger, 284, 288, 289

pin cherry, 294

pine, whitebark, 332–333

pirogues, 103, 116, 132

Pishquitpah (tribe), 267

Pittsburgh, Pennsylvania, 51, 80, 83–84, 102

plants. *See also specific species*
  for home garden, 184
  new to western science, 238
  post-expedition threats to, 332–333
Platte River, 127–128, 130
plesiosaur fossil, 128
Pocasse "Hay" (Arikara leader), 43, 143, 144
Pompeys Pillar National Monument, 283, 346
Pompy's Tower, 57, 282–283
Porcupine River, 171
portage, around Great Falls, 178–181
Portage Creek, 180
Portages des Sioux, 318
Portland, Oregon, 237
Posecopsahe "Black Cat" (Mandan leader), 45, 152, 154, 169, 297–298
Potts, Private John (Corps member)
  biography, 39
  post-expedition life, 328
powwows, 18, 154, 189, 212
prairie, 121–123
prairie dogs, 122, 163, 333
prickly pear cactus, 173, 181, 186
primogeniture, law of, 75
pronghorn antelope, 121, 170
Pryor, Sergeant Nathaniel (Corps member)
  biography, 35–36
  mission to the Mandans, 281–282
  post-expedition life, 326
  Yankton Sioux and, 135
purging, 91, 123, 161, 225
Pursh, Frederick (botanist), 312

• *Q* •

quinine, 91

• *R* •

Radford, Harriet Kennerly (wife of Clark), 319
rattlesnake rings, 157

Raven Man Chief (Mandan leader), 152
Reed, Private Moses (Corps member), 126, 133
reservations, 18, 146–147, 154, 189, 212, 292, 322, 330. *See also specific reservations*
Rhtarahe (village), 143, 144
Ridgefield National Wildlife Refuge, 339
River of No Return, 208. *See also* Salmon River
rivers, traveled by expedition, 53–57. *See also specific rivers*
Rivet, Francois, 163
Rochejhone River, 170. *See also* Yellowstone River
Rock Fort Camp, 265
Rocky Boy Reservation, 189
Rocky Mountains
  crossing of, 215–219, 274
  Lewis's view from Lemhi Pass, 200
  map, 58
  noteworthy sites, 59
Ronda, James P. (*Lewis and Clark among the Indians*), 349
Rooptahee (Mandan village), 152, 169, 297
Ross's Hole, 211, 280
Ruby River, 192
Rush, Dr. Benjamin (tutor of Meriwether Lewis), 49, 90–92

• *S* •

Sacagawea (Shoshone woman)
  boating accident, 176
  capture by Hidatsa tribe, 30–31, 156
  daughter (Lisette), 322, 324
  death, 322, 324
  diet, contributions to, 176
  in flash flood, 181–182
  illness, 180
  "Janey" nickname, 157, 241, 322
  Jean Baptiste (son), birth of, 157
  legend in three cultures, 321

marriage, 31
parting from expedition, 301–302
reunion with Shoshones, 205–206
role of, 157, 281
selection for Corps of Discovery, 31
in Shoshone territory, 190, 193
spelling of name, 1–2, 158
statues, 322–323
vote on winter camp location, 241
whale, trip to see, 252
Sacagawea Dollar, 322
Sacagawea Spring, 180
Sahaptian language, 225–226
Saint-Memin (painter), 312
Salish (tribe)
leaders, 46
meeting Lewis and Clark, 211–213
post-expedition experiences, 330
support of expedition, 12
today, 212
salmon, 16–17, 228–229, 234, 260, 332
Salmon River, 206–207, 208, 210
salt
making, 245
mountain of, 13, 62
sand, blowing, 172
Santo Domingo, 69
Sauk (tribe), 314
Sawa-haini (village), 142–143
scientific knowledge, expedition's addition
to, 14
Seaman (dog of Meriwether Lewis)
antelope kill, 170
deer retrieval, 186
purchase of, 34, 101
Spirit Mound trek, 125
theft of, 34, 265
value to expedition, 34, 101
sextant, 94–95
sexual relations
with the Arikaras, 147
with the Mandans, 161, 164
with the Nez Perce, 271
with the Teton Sioux, 139–140

Shannon, Private George (Corps member)
biography, 39
disappearances of, 119, 124–125, 193
post-expedition life, 326
recruitment of, 100
Shannon's River, 326
Shawnee (tribe), 86–87
Sheheke "Big White" or "Coyote" (Mandan
leader)
aid to expedition, 12, 44, 154
meeting Lewis and Clark, 151
return from Washington, 314–315
trip to visit Washington, 298, 299, 304,
305, 310
Shields, Private John (Corps member)
battle axe construction, 159–160
biography, 39
post-expedition life, 327
recruitment, 100
Spirit Mound trek, 125
threat to kill Ordway, 111
Watlala confrontation, 265
Shields River, 327
Shoshone Cove, 194, 279–280
Shoshone (tribe)
aid to Lewis and Clark crossing
Continental Divide, 209–210
horses of, 157, 188–189, 205–206, 210
leaders, 45
meeting Lewis and Clark, 194–195,
201–205
post-expedition experiences, 330
raids on by the Hidatsas and the Atsinas,
200–201, 297
search for, 189–191, 193–194, 200
Sierra Club, 17
Sioux. *See also* Teton Sioux; Yankton Sioux
nation today, 146–147
post-expedition experiences, 330
reservations, 146–147, 330
spelling and meaning of term, 116
Skilloot (tribe), 263, 265–266

smallpox
  Arikara, 142, 154, 330
  Chinook, 331
  Mandan, 151
  Omaha, 132
  vaccine, 99
Smith River, 187
Smith, Robert (Secretary of the Navy), 187
Snake Butte, 189
Snake Indians. *See* Shoshone
Snake River, 223, 227–228, 332, 338
Soulard, Antoine (surveyor general for
    Spain), 114
Spain, 67–68, 120
Spirit Mound, 57, 125
Square Butte, 186, 286
St. Charles, 53, 111, 117–119, 304, 344–345
St. Louis, Missouri
  Clark in, 317–320
  expedition's preparations in, 51, 113–114
  Lewis and Clark's return to, 304
  Lewis in, 313–315
  transfer to the United States, 112
St. Louis Missouri River Fur Company, 314
Standing Rock Sioux Reservation, 146–147
Stoddard, Amos (governor of Upper
    Louisiana), 112, 118
Struck By the Ree (Yankon Sioux leader),
    146
Stump Island Park, 118
sturgeon, 255
sulfur water, 180
Sun River, 178, 287, 288
sunflower seed bread, recipe for, 196
supplies
  caching of, 78, 180, 227
  Clark's list for 40 days of provisions, 113
  gifts for tribes, 96–97
  purchase of initial, 95–97
  St. Louis purchases, 113–114
surveying, study by Meriwether Lewis, 94
swan, trumpeter, 333
sweating, 91
sweetgrass, 284

syphilis
  mercury treatment of, 91
  of Meriwether Lewis, 311, 313, 315, 316

• *T* •

Tabeau, Pierre-Antoine (trader), 50, 142
Tallyrand, Charles-Maurice de (French
    foreign minister), 69
Tamastslikt Cultural Institute, 231
Taucum (Chinook leader), 248, 251, 261
Tedesco, Guy, 105
tepee, 139, 141, 182
Tetoharsky (Nez Perce leader), 46, 226–228,
    234, 269
Teton Sioux
  Clark's journal entries on, 42, 139, 141
  expedition's worries concerning, 115–116,
    134–135
  Hidatsas and, 297
  leaders, 43
  meeting Lewis and Clark, 137–141
  name derivation, 116
  plan to neutralize influence of, 285
  post-expedition experiences, 330
  return meeting of, 300–301
theft
  by the Chinooks and the Clatsops,
    236–237, 242, 251, 261–262
  of Clatsop canoe, 262
  by the Crows, 281, 285
  of guns by the Blackfeet, 291
  of horses by Indians, 138, 281, 285, 288
  of Seaman, 265
  by the Skilloots, 266
  by the Teton Sioux, 138
theodolite, 95
Thompson, Private John B. (Corps
    member), 40
Three Eagles (Salish leader), 46, 212
Three Forks of the Missouri, 191, 280
thunderclappers, 91, 123, 225
Tillamook (tribe), 244, 252
Timber Lake Area Museum, 146

tobacco
  as gift, 133.96, 136–137, 140
  grown by the Mandans and the
    Hidatsas, 152
Tonwantonga (Omaha village), 132
Tortohongar "The Partisan" (Teton Sioux
    leader), 43, 137–140
Tower Creek, 210
trade negotiations, with Indian tribes
  Arikaras, 142–144
  Chinooks and Clatsops, 246, 260–263
  Columbia River tribes, 264–266
  as expedition mission, 127
  Mandans and Hidatsas, 150–154
  Nez Perce, 226, 270–271
  Otoes and Missouris, 130–131
  Teton Sioux, 137
  Yankton Sioux, 136
traders, 49–50. *See also specific individuals*
trail. *See* Lewis and Clark National Historic
    Trail
Travelers' Rest, 213–215, 278, 285, 338
Traveling the Lewis and Clark Trail (Julie
    Fanselow), 351
treaty
  Black Hawk (Sauk) signing, 319
  Blackfeet, 331
  Confederated Tribes of Salish, Kootenai,
    and Pend d'Oreille, 330
  at Grand Council at Portages des Sioux,
    318
  of Greenville, 87
  Mandan, Hidatsa, and Arikara, 330
  Nez Perce, 330–331
  with Osage, 317
  Otoe-Missouri tribe, 329
  Shoshone, 330
  Sioux, 330
Treaty of 1858 Monument, 146
tutors, of Meriwether Lewis, 48–49, 75,
    89–95
Twisted Hair (Nez Perce leader)
  argument with Cutnose, 269–270
  canoe construction, help with, 226

meeting Lewis and Clark, 46, 223–224
travel with the expedition, 46, 226–228, 234
Two Medicine River, 59, 288, 289

• *U* •

Umatilla (tribe), 231–232, 267
*Undaunted Courage: Meriwether Lewis,
    Thomas Jefferson, and the Opening of
    the American West* (Stephen E.
    Ambrose), 350
Untongarabar "Black Buffalo" (Teton Sioux
    leader), 12, 43, 137–141, 300
Upper Missouri River Breaks National
    Monument, 173

• *V* •

vaccine, 99
venereal disease, 161
Vermillion River, 125
vote, on winter camp location, 241

• *W* •

Wahkiakum (tribe), 237, 244
Waho-erha (village), 143, 144
Walammottinin "Twisted Hair" (Nez Perce
    leader), 46, 223–224, 226–228, 234,
    269–270
Walla Walla (tribe), 12, 47, 230–231, 267–269
Wanapum (tribe), 47, 228–230, 231
Wanapum Dam Heritage Center, 231
wappato, 237, 246–248, 264
War of 1812, 318
Warfington, Corporal Richard (expedition
    member), 113, 125, 168
Wasco (tribe), 232
Washington, D.C., 50, 79
watermelons, 129
Watkuweis (Nez Perce woman), 12, 46, 223
Watlala (tribe), 263–264, 265

Wayne, General "Mad Anthony," 28–29, 76–77, 87

We Proceed On (magazine), 352

Web sites
   bicentennial commemoration, 21
   Discovering Lewis and Clark, 352
   environmental organizations, 17
   Lewis and Clark National Historic Trail, 19
   tribal, 18

Weippe Prairie, 219, 222, 273–274, 341

Weiser, Private Peter (Corps member)
   biography, 40
   post-expedition life, 329

Welsh Indians myth, 213

Werner, Private William (Corps member)
   biography, 40
   court martial, 111

West Whitlock Recreation Area, 146

Weuche (Yankton Sioux leader), 41, 136

whale, 252

Whelan, Israel (purveyor of supplies), 95

whiskey
   final ration, 183–184
   as gift, 96, 133–134, 138, 143
   ration of, 110, 126
   stealing, 126
   supply of, 126

Whiskey Rebellion, 76

White Bear Islands, 181, 188, 279

White Buffalo Robe Unfolded (Hidatsa leader), 296

White Catfish Camp, 128

White Cliffs, 171–172, 173

White Crane (Yankton Sioux leader), 136

White, Germaine (Confederated Salish and Kootenai Tribes), 42

White House (Washington D.C.), 28, 78, 79

white pudding (boudin blanc), 176

White Stone River, 125

Whitehouse, Private Joseph (Corps member)
   biography, 40
   post-expedition life, 329
   writings of, 213, 214

whooping crane, 333

wildlife, tameness of, 170. *See also specific animals*

Willard, Private Alexander Hamilton (Corps member)
   biography, 40
   court martial, 126
   post-expedition life, 329

Willamette River, 264

Wind River Indian Reservation, 322

Windsor, Private Richard (Corps member)
   accident, 177
   biography, 40

Wisdom River, 192, 193, 280

Wishram (tribe), 232

Wistar, Dr. Caspar (tutor of Meriwether Lewis), 49, 93–94

wolf, 170, 288, 333

wolverine, 196

women. *See also specific individuals*
   Arikara, 147
   Chinookan, 247
   Clatsop, 244
   Columbia River tribes, 229
   Mandan and Hidatsa, 152, 161, 164
   Nez Perce, 222
   offered to Lewis and Clark by Teton Sioux, 139–140
   Salish, 212
   Shoshone, 210

Wood River, 51, 108, 337

woolly mammoth, 13, 62, 93

• *Y* •

Yakama (tribe), 228, 231, 268

Yakama Nation Cultural Center, 231

Yankton Sioux, 42, 135–137, 146, 301

Yankton Sioux Reservation, 146

Yelleppit (Walla Walla leader), 47, 230, 267–268

Yellowstone National Park, 325

Yellowstone River, 57, 170, 279–286, 314

Yoomparkkartim "Five Big Hearts"
    (Nez Perce leader), 270
York (slave)
  Arikaras and, 145, 147
  "Big Medison," 33, 147
  biography, 32–33
  death, 321
  expedition experiences, 33
  freedom, 320–321
  Le Borge and, 145
  marriage, 320
  vote on winter camp location, 241

FOR DUMMIES®

The easy way to get more done and have more fun

PERSONAL FINANCE

0-7645-5231-7

0-7645-2431-3

0-7645-5331-3

Also available:

Estate Planning For Dummies
(0-7645-5501-4)

401(k)s For Dummies
(0-7645-5468-9)

Frugal Living For Dummies
(0-7645-5403-4)

Microsoft Money "X" For
Dummies
(0-7645-1689-2)

Mutual Funds For Dummies
(0-7645-5329-1)

Personal Bankruptcy For
Dummies
(0-7645-5498-0)

Quicken "X" For Dummies
(0-7645-1666-3)

Stock Investing For Dummies
(0-7645-5411-5)

Taxes For Dummies 2003
(0-7645-5475-1)

BUSINESS & CAREERS

0-7645-5314-3

0-7645-5307-0

0-7645-5471-9

Also available:

Business Plans Kit For
Dummies
(0-7645-5365-8)

Consulting For Dummies
(0-7645-5034-9)

Cool Careers For Dummies
(0-7645-5345-3)

Human Resources Kit For
Dummies
(0-7645-5131-0)

Managing For Dummies
(1-5688-4858-7)

QuickBooks All-in-One Desk
Reference For Dummies
(0-7645-1963-8)

Selling For Dummies
(0-7645-5363-1)

Small Business Kit For
Dummies
(0-7645-5093-4)

Starting an eBay Business For
Dummies
(0-7645-1547-0)

HEALTH, SPORTS & FITNESS

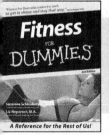

0-7645-5167-1

0-7645-5146-9

0-7645-5154-X

Also available:

Controlling Cholesterol For
Dummies
(0-7645-5440-9)

Dieting For Dummies
(0-7645-5126-4)

High Blood Pressure For
Dummies
(0-7645-5424-7)

Martial Arts For Dummies
(0-7645-5358-5)

Menopause For Dummies
(0-7645-5458-1)

Nutrition For Dummies
(0-7645-5180-9)

Power Yoga For Dummies
(0-7645-5342-9)

Thyroid For Dummies
(0-7645-5385-2)

Weight Training For Dummies
(0-7645-5168-X)

Yoga For Dummies
(0-7645-5117-5)

Available wherever books are sold.
Go to www.dummies.com or call 1-877-762-2974 to order direct.

A world of resources to help you grow

HOME, GARDEN & HOBBIES

Feng Shui FOR DUMMIES — 0-7645-5295-3

Gardening FOR DUMMIES — 0-7645-5130-2

Guitar FOR DUMMIES — 0-7645-5106-X

Also available:

Auto Repair For Dummies
(0-7645-5089-6)

Chess For Dummies
(0-7645-5003-9)

Home Maintenance For
Dummies
(0-7645-5215-5)

Organizing For Dummies
(0-7645-5300-3)

Piano For Dummies
(0-7645-5105-1)

Poker For Dummies
(0-7645-5232-5)

Quilting For Dummies
(0-7645-5118-3)

Rock Guitar For Dummies
(0-7645-5356-9)

Roses For Dummies
(0-7645-5202-3)

Sewing For Dummies
(0-7645-5137-X)

FOOD & WINE

Cooking FOR DUMMIES — 0-7645-5250-3

Cookies FOR DUMMIES — 0-7645-5390-9

Wine FOR DUMMIES — 0-7645-5114-0

Also available:

Bartending For Dummies
(0-7645-5051-9)

Chinese Cooking For
Dummies
(0-7645-5247-3)

Christmas Cooking For
Dummies
(0-7645-5407-7)

Diabetes Cookbook For
Dummies
(0-7645-5230-9)

Grilling For Dummies
(0-7645-5076-4)

Low-Fat Cooking For
Dummies
(0-7645-5035-7)

Slow Cookers For Dummies
(0-7645-5240-6)

TRAVEL

Italy FOR DUMMIES — 0-7645-5453-0

Hawaii FOR DUMMIES — 0-7645-5438-7

Las Vegas FOR DUMMIES — 0-7645-5448-4

Also available:

America's National Parks For
Dummies
(0-7645-6204-5)

Caribbean For Dummies
(0-7645-5445-X)

Cruise Vacations For
Dummies 2003
(0-7645-5459-X)

Europe For Dummies
(0-7645-5456-5)

Ireland For Dummies
(0-7645-6199-5)

France For Dummies
(0-7645-6292-4)

London For Dummies
(0-7645-5416-6)

Mexico's Beach Resorts For
Dummies
(0-7645-6262-2)

Paris For Dummies
(0-7645-5494-8)

RV Vacations For Dummies
(0-7645-5443-3)

Walt Disney World & Orlando
For Dummies
(0-7645-5444-1)

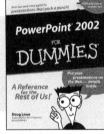

FOR DUMMIES®

The advice and explanations you need to succeed

SELF-HELP, SPIRITUALITY & RELIGION

Sex
0-7645-5302-X

Parenting
0-7645-5418-2

Religion
0-7645-5264-3

Also available:

The Bible For Dummies
(0-7645-5296-1)

Buddhism For Dummies
(0-7645-5359-3)

Christian Prayer For Dummies
(0-7645-5500-6)

Dating For Dummies
(0-7645-5072-1)

Judaism For Dummies
(0-7645-5299-6)

Potty Training For Dummies
(0-7645-5417-4)

Pregnancy For Dummies
(0-7645-5074-8)

Rekindling Romance For Dummies
(0-7645-5303-8)

Spirituality For Dummies
(0-7645-5298-8)

Weddings For Dummies
(0-7645-5055-1)

PETS

Puppies
0-7645-5255-4

Dog Training
0-7645-5286-4

Cats
0-7645-5275-9

Also available:

Labrador Retrievers For Dummies
(0-7645-5281-3)

Aquariums For Dummies
(0-7645-5156-6)

Birds For Dummies
(0-7645-5139-6)

Dogs For Dummies
(0-7645-5274-0)

Ferrets For Dummies
(0-7645-5259-7)

German Shepherds For Dummies
(0-7645-5280-5)

Golden Retrievers For Dummies
(0-7645-5267-8)

Horses For Dummies
(0-7645-5138-8)

Jack Russell Terriers For Dummies
(0-7645-5268-6)

Puppies Raising & Training Diary For Dummies
(0-7645-0876-8)

EDUCATION & TEST PREPARATION

Spanish
0-7645-5194-9

Algebra
0-7645-5325-9

The ACT
0-7645-5210-4

Also available:

Chemistry For Dummies
(0-7645-5430-1)

English Grammar For Dummies
(0-7645-5322-4)

French For Dummies
(0-7645-5193-0)

The GMAT For Dummies
(0-7645-5251-1)

Inglés Para Dummies
(0-7645-5427-1)

Italian For Dummies
(0-7645-5196-5)

Research Papers For Dummies
(0-7645-5426-3)

The SAT I For Dummies
(0-7645-5472-7)

U.S. History For Dummies
(0-7645-5249-X)

World History For Dummies
(0-7645-5242-2)

Available wherever books are sold. Go to www.dummies.com or call 1-877-762-2974 to order direct.

CPSIA information can be obtained
at www.ICGtesting.com
Printed in the USA
BVOW11s0445261017
498650BV00003B/4/P